ATTACKING
TERRORISM

ATTACKING TERRORISM

TERRORISM

Elements of a Grand Strategy

Audrey Kurth Cronin and
James M. Ludes, Editors

In cooperation with the
Center for Peace and Security Studies
Edmund A. Walsh School of Foreign Service
Georgetown University

Georgetown University Press
Washington, D.C.

Georgetown University Press, Washington, D.C.
© 2004 by Georgetown University Press. All rights reserved.
Printed in the United States of America

10 9 8 7 6 5 4 3 2 1   2004

This book is printed on acid-free paper meeting the requirements of the American National Standard for Permanence in
Paper for Printed Library Materials.

Audrey Kurth Cronin is the author of the introduction, chapter
1, and the conclusion. The views expressed therein are hers
and do not represent those of the Library of Congress or any
other public or private organization.

Library of Congress Cataloging-in-Publication Data

Attacking terrorism : elements of a grand strategy / Audrey
Kurth Cronin and James M. Ludes, editors.
        p. cm.
"In cooperation with the Center for Peace and Security Studies,
Edmund A. Walsh School of Foreign Service, Georgetown Uni-
versity."
Includes bibliographical references and index.
    ISBN 0-87840-347-7 (pbk. : alk. paper)
    1. Terrorism—United States—Prevention. 2. Terrorism—
Government policy—United States. 3. United States—Foreign
relations—2001– I. Cronin, Audrey Kurth, 1958– II. Ludes,
James M. III. Georgetown University. Center for Peace and
Security Studies.
    HV6432.A88 2004
    363.32′0973—dc22

                                2003019462

contents

Preface   vii

Introduction: Meeting and Managing the Threat   1
Audrey Kurth Cronin

PART I: THE NATURE OF TERRORISM

one   Sources of Contemporary Terrorism   19
Audrey Kurth Cronin

two   The Four Waves of Modern Terrorism   46
David C. Rapoport

three   Terrorism, Strategies, and Grand Strategies   74
Martha Crenshaw

PART II: POLICY INSTRUMENTS IN THE CAMPAIGN AGAINST INTERNATIONAL TERRORISM

four   Diplomacy   97
Michael A. Sheehan

five   Intelligence   115
Paul R. Pillar

six   Law Enforcement   140
Lindsay Clutterbuck

seven   Military Force   162
Timothy D. Hoyt

eight   The Laws of War   186
Adam Roberts

nine   Psychological-Political Instruments   220
             Carnes Lord

ten   Foreign Aid   238
             Patrick M. Cronin

eleven   Homeland Security   261
             Daniel Gouré

             Conclusion: Toward an Effective Grand Strategy   285
             Audrey Kurth Cronin

             Contributors   301
             Index   305

preface

Since the end of the cold war, a growing chorus of scholars and observers have warned that the next challenge facing the western world would not be another state driven by a messianic vision, but the growing threat of terrorists with access to increasingly destructive weapons. The specific attacks of September 11, 2001, may not have been foretold, but the threat was understood by many who, although they reported their concerns, had their warnings lost in the noise of the 1990s. That noise dissipated on September 11, 2001. In its place emerged a high-fidelity clarity of the stakes and a near-global consensus to bring down the terrorist organization responsible for the attacks.

This book was initially conceived as a series of articles in the *National Security Studies Quarterly*. The original intent was to survey how the attacks would affect the U.S. national security community in everything from budgeting to planning. As discussions progressed over the course of several months, however, our attention began to focus on the conduct of U.S. counterterrorist operations and the need for an integrated, multifaceted approach to the campaign mounted and led by the United States to root out terrorist organizations of global reach. Instead of a series of articles, we determined that a book providing a comprehensive examination of the challenges facing the United States and its allies in the war on terror would be of greater value to audiences in academia and government, and to the general public.

The enormity of the campaign against international terrorism cannot be overstated. As a society, we are confronted by a reflexive, adaptive adversary with great patience. We face daunting military, political, economic, financial, and diplomatic challenges. And we have been saddled with false assumptions about our adversaries and the environment in which they act. In this book, we provide a more accurate view of the challenges we face, the tools at our disposal, and the boundaries of a path which, though long and arduous, offers the greatest promise of success in the campaign against international terrorism.

This project is the result of the tireless devotion and support of countless individuals. We are particularly indebted to Michael E. Brown, director of the Center for Peace and Security Studies at Georgetown University, whose support for this project was unflagging. Thanks to the Center's generous financial support, we were able to bring together a group of outstanding scholars to contribute the chapters to this book. Lindsay Clutterbuck, Martha Crenshaw, Patrick Cronin, Daniel Gouré, Timothy Hoyt, Carnes Lord, Paul Pillar, David Rapoport, Adam Roberts, and Michael Sheehan not only wrote chapters but contributed to a very collegial process that benefited the entire project. It should be noted that each of the contributors may not necessarily agree with everything that is written here.

We would also like to take special note of Richard E. Brown, director, and the staff of Georgetown University Press. Through workshops, questions, delays, and despite two scattered editors, their diligence, patience, professionalism, and dedication to this project brought the final product to fruition. The Press is a pleasure to work with and we are grateful to them.

In addition, several other individuals provided critical support to this project at various stages, including Christina Zechman Brown, Bernard Finel, Kristen MacDonald, and Erin Roussin. Crucial to the research support for the book were Christopher Connell, Sara Skahill, and William Josiger. We are grateful to them all.

Any faults in the book rest solely with the two of us.

The effort that produced this book was filled with numerous reminders of the September 11, 2001, attacks. We hope that as that day grows more distant, our response to the challenge of international terrorism will be guided by an appreciation of the complexity of the task before us and a long-term vision of success.

Audrey Kurth Cronin
James M. Ludes

INTRODUCTION: MEETING AND MANAGING THE THREAT

Audrey Kurth Cronin

This volume came together as a result of measured thinking about what the long-term trajectory of American policy should be in a campaign that will stretch well into the twenty-first century. It is not a naïve or ahistorical tome about short-term tactics for victory against al-Qaeda; international terrorism is an enduring challenge that will not be "defeated" as in a "war." Terrorism is not (as it once may have been) a peripheral issue, like piracy or criminal behavior, destined to remain on the perimeter of global concerns, actually and figuratively. Terrorism has been evolving for at least a decade into a core threat to international security, and anachronistic mindsets and paradigms must adapt if we are to respond effectively.

Americans are not naturally well prepared to respond to this type of threat. Public discourse about terrorism is infused with received wisdom that is not based on an understanding of the sources, history, patterns, strategies, and range of effective policy tools for dealing with terrorism. We are by nature an impatient people, litigious and intolerant of risk, accustomed to "fixing" problems, using superior technologies to defeat enemies, defining threats in Manichean terms, and responding with military force. We like to think that our challenges are unprecedented, our solutions novel and unique. The threat of terrorism, on the other hand, requires not only a focus on a relatively small group of extremists who seek to kill Americans but also a toleration of nuance, a phlegmatic attitude, a long-term perspective, an under-

standing of past mistakes, and an acceptance of higher risk. This is not de-
featist thinking or "appeasement"; it is the recognition that the world evolves
and that the United States must adapt to manage and minimize the threat.

The feeling of well-being that the United States enjoyed in the years immediately after the collapse of the Soviet Union, the complacency that went
with being the primary power with unprecedented strength, has been undermined by an unexpected threat that thrives on asymmetrical expressions
of power. As a result, the national strategy debate must turn from issues such
as effecting a "revolution" in military affairs, discussing the theoretical effects of globalization on security, determining the criteria for humanitarian
intervention, studying the growing influence of benign transnational actors,
or evaluating the likelihood of being eclipsed in future decades by other rising powers. Although these things remain important, they are lower on the
priority list than they were prior to September 11. The U.S. government faces
a more immediate yet long-term threat to which it must respond effectively
if it is to maintain the implicit contract with its own people.[1] Terrorism has
become an unprecedented threat not only because it is associated with a radical religiously inspired ideology but also because it has access to unprecedented technologies and avenues through which to deliver them. It also is
dangerous because international terrorism is not well understood, and, if we
respond unwisely, the dynamic interaction of terrorism and counterterrorism may make another catastrophic attack or even a major, systemic conventional war more likely.

The United States and its allies have made considerable progress already
in this campaign; yet the knowledge we have gained with the capture of terrorist operatives and information from Afghanistan leads to the certain conclusion that there will be additional, serious terrorist attacks. The threat has
evolved since Operation Anaconda sought to choke out al-Qaeda from its
mountainous hideouts, but it has not gone away. It is more diffuse, yet still
menacing. At this writing, there have been terrorist attacks in Indonesia,
Kenya, Kuwait, Pakistan, Saudi Arabia, Morocco, and elsewhere. Numerous other attempts have been thwarted. It is obvious from the pattern of terrorist behavior that there will be more actual and attempted attacks, including attacks on the U.S. homeland. There is evidence that al-Qaeda has
evolved into a more decentralized, franchised organization, with less direct
control over its cells but more connections with other groups and an increasing convergence of formerly distinct causes. Especially in light of the
clear indications of growing anti-Americanism and popular support in Islamic countries for al-Qaeda, this problem will not die away in the near future.[2] Simplistic ahistorical, acultural, and astrategic treatment of the terrorist
threat will only lead to its enhancement and further undermining of Western
security.

This book is directed to a broad audience grappling with the security challenge that threatens innocent civilians in the United States, Europe, and throughout the world. Its purpose is to broaden and deepen the debate about the American and allied response to the terrorist threat well into the twenty-first century. The contributors to this collection are virtually all experienced scholars of international terrorism or practitioners of counterterrorism. These writers are not newly minted "experts" who have emerged following September 11 or generalists who suddenly have discovered terrorism as a security threat. The chapters in this collection represent decades of scholarly and practical experience in the field and the wisdom of thousands of pages of books, articles, and analyses of the evolving threat of globalized terrorism.

Defining Terrorism

No book about terrorism for the general reader can avoid beginning with a clarification of the concept. Terrorism is notoriously difficult to define, in part because the term has evolved and in part because it is associated with an activity that is designed to be subjective. Generally speaking, the targets of a terrorist episode are not simply the victims who are killed or maimed in an attack but governments, publics, or constituents among whom the terrorists hope to engender a reaction—such as fear, repulsion, intimidation, over-reaction, or radicalization. Eminent specialists in the area of terrorism studies have devoted dozens of pages to the effort to develop an unassailable standard definition of terrorism—only to conclude that the effort is fruitless: Terrorism is intended to be a matter of perception and therefore is regarded differently by different observers.[3]

Although individuals can disagree about whether particular actions constitute terrorism, some aspects of the concept are fundamental. First, terrorism has a political nature. It involves the commission of outrageous, violent acts to precipitate political change.[4] At its root, terrorism is about justice—or, at least, someone's perception of justice, whether its source is human or divine. Second, although many other uses of violence are inherently political, including conventional war among states, terrorism is distinguished by its nonstate character—even when terrorists receive military, political, economic, and other means of support from states. This is not to excuse states that provide support to groups who employ terror tactics. One can usefully distinguish, however, between a supporting and a leading role. Obviously states employ many types of force for political ends. When state force is used internationally, it is considered an act of war; when it is used domestically, it is called various things, including law enforcement, state terror, oppression, or civil war. Although states can terrorize, by definition they cannot be terrorists. Third, terrorism deliberately targets innocent persons—which also distinguishes it from state uses of force that inadvertently kill innocent bystanders. In any given example, the latter may or may not be regarded as justified; again, however, this use of force is different from terrorism. Hence, precision-guided missiles that sometimes go astray and kill innocent civilians represent a tragic use of force, but not terrorism. Finally, state use of force is subject to international norms and conventions that may be invoked or at least consulted. Terrorists do not abide by international laws or norms and, to maximize the psychological effect of an attack, their activities have a deliberately unpredictable quality.[5]

Thus, at a minimum, instances of terrorism contain the following elements: a political nature, the surprise use of violence against seemingly random targets, and attacks on innocent persons carried out by nonstate actors.[6] All of these attributes are illustrated by recent examples of terrorism—from the numerous incidents committed by al-Qaeda, including the 1998 bombings of the U.S. embassies in Kenya and Tanzania and the September 11 attacks, to the kidnapping of tourists by the Abu Sayyef group in the Philippines. For the purposes of this book, the shorthand (and admittedly imperfect) definition of terrorism used is as follows: *The surprise threat or use of seemingly random violence against innocents for political ends by a nonstate actor.*

Organization of the Book

This book is organized in two major sections. Part I, "The Nature of Terrorism," provides an overview and foundation for the current counterterrorism campaign, placing it within the political and historical context of previous threats and responses. Familiarity with the causes and history of terrorism, as well as strategies of counterterrorism, is an important intellectual starting point. Part II, "Policy Instruments in the Campaign against International Terrorism," looks at the range of policy instruments required in an effective strategy against terrorism. Included are analyses of how these instruments—including diplomacy, intelligence, psycho-political instruments, international law, criminal law enforcement, military force, foreign aid, and homeland security—are currently being employed. The contributors also offer recommendations for how these measures can be used more effectively. Together these two sections provide a comprehensive picture of the challenges and opportunities of the campaign against international terrorism. The concluding chapter draws the lessons of theory and practice together for guidance as we move ahead.

The Nature of Terrorism

Effective counterterrorism is not possible without an accurate analysis of the sources of terrorism, so the book begins there. The first chapter provides insight into the issues surrounding terrorism's origins, examining the range of explanations and revealing the analytical biases that hamper the search for answers. It uses the familiar device of dividing the field into four levels of analysis—the individual, the organization, the state, and the international system—explaining prominent areas of terrorism research and important conclusions at each level. The purpose of the exercise is to review our knowledge of the sources, but also to demonstrate the degree to which there is poor coordination among different disciplines and across perspectives.

Intellectual frameworks fractionate the field. Common popular and scholarly explanations draw mainly from one analytical framework and slight the other three. The question of terrorism's origins is hard enough to analyze, but in the absence of a comprehensive framework the result can be myth, misperception, and politicization. Chapter 1 explains that becoming aware of the full range of ideas and perspectives in the literature on the sources of terrorism would enrich the thinking of academics and policymakers alike. It also would highlight the oversights or oversimplifications that are distorting their choices. The chapter aims to lay an intellectual foundation for the cross-disciplinary academic and policy chapters in the remainder of the book.

Chapter 2 places the current campaign within its broader historical context. David Rapoport provides an original typology of modern international terrorism, placing the events of September 11 and the threat of al-Qaeda in perspective. His examination of the relationships among ideas, cultures, raised expectations, and dramatic political change casts new light on the terrorist violence that seems so exceptional in the wake of tragic events. In discerning four "waves" of international terrorism, Rapoport gives the reader insight into the larger patterns of terrorism in the recent past. Terrorism is meant to shock, but that shock too often results in amnesia, encouraging observers to see individual terrorist events as exceptional. Rapoport shows that the history of modern terrorism reveals connections between groups not just in logistical or resource terms but also in terms of inspiration.

According to Rapoport, waves of modern terrorism were generated first by the anarchist movement in the late nineteenth century; second by the anticolonial movement in the 1920s; and finally by the radical ideas of the "New Left" in the 1960s. Rapoport posits that we are now witnessing a new, gathering movement: the "Fourth Wave," which began with the Iranian revolution of 1979. If this analysis is accurate, any strategy designed to engage this menace will be more effectively crafted with an awareness of the life cycles, vulnerabilities, and challenges of its modern predecessors—the subject of chapter 2.

Is a consistent, comprehensive strategy against terrorism even a realistic aim, however? Martha Crenshaw grapples with this question in chapter 3. The history of the U.S. approach to countering terrorism has been characterized by piecemeal, reactive policies, often made in the absence of a comprehensive intellectual analysis. Although terrorism has been a serious threat to the United States since at least the early 1990s, Crenshaw points out that specialists in security studies, international relations, and foreign policy—those engaged in the debate over "grand strategy" during the past decade—have shown little interest. When the September 11 attacks occurred, most writers regarded the tragedies as confirmation of their preconceived arguments about grand strategy. Terrorism was not important as a threat, did not lend itself to abstract theory or modeling, and was too policy-oriented to be of interest to general security studies experts, Crenshaw writes.

On the other hand, terrorism specialists from their varied disciplinary backgrounds did not regard terrorism as a strategic issue, either. With the exception of those who focused on the threat of chemical, biological, nuclear, or radiological weapons (none of which was involved in the September 11 attacks), most saw the unique aspects of individual cases as obstacles to generalization about terrorism strategy. This perspective was not a promising intellectual foundation for the much-needed substantive debate in the United States regarding strategies, grand strategies, or even policies against terrorism following September 11.

Crenshaw evaluates the current campaign against international terrorism as an American strategy and finds it wanting. The relationship between ends and means in a campaign to eradicate "terrorism with a global reach" is unclear. Crenshaw points out that measuring success may not be possible; the goal may be too ambitious for any strategy. Moreover, the traditional realist focus on a state-centric world of rival powers, though comfortable and familiar, is not really a forward-looking approach for dealing with nonstate actors. With academics and policymakers alike falling back on comfortable preconceptions, Crenshaw urges a creative reevaluation of U.S. grand strategy, strategy, and policy against international terrorism.

The Response to Terrorism

Crenshaw's argument for crafting a more effective American grand strategy leads naturally to an examination of the crucial policy tools with which to carry out the campaign against international terrorism—the purpose of the second part of this book. The first chapter in part II is Michael Sheehan's examination of diplomatic measures against terrorism—the leading instrument considered in this book but almost never the first priority in the aftermath of major attacks. As Sheehan argues, diplomacy is the use of all available foreign policy instruments to influence critical countries—friends and enemies—to deny terrorists the physical and political space in which to operate. These important measures include bilateral, regional, and international efforts to cooperate in the areas of intelligence, law enforcement, military force, and others.

The United States cannot defeat al-Qaeda's international network on its own without ensuring that other states maintain the political will and practical resources to fight terrorism, Sheehan argues. Terrorism is an opportunistic threat that operates in the unexpected "spaces"—geographical, political, tactical, even chronological. The United States cannot be everywhere, all the time. Sheehan presents specific policy recommendations for a comprehensive, long-term diplomatic counterterrorism strategy to meet the threat, including (among other things) increased funding for assistance in law enforcement, targeted use of economic aid in areas of potential terrorist activity, and much broader cooperation with our international allies—which Sheehan terms "a necessity, not a luxury."

Intelligence—often a crucial element of bilateral counterterrorist diplomacy—is one of the most-mentioned policy instruments in the campaign against international terrorism. In chapter 4 Paul Pillar provides an incisive discussion of the role of the U.S. intelligence community in the past and the future. Above all, Pillar argues for realism in understanding what intelligence can and cannot do. For example, intelligence can provide information about groups, disrupt specific cells, or give warning of general threats; even the best intelligence, however, is only rarely able to provide specific, tactical information about imminent attacks that may be known only to a few people. Just as its capabilities are overstated in some areas, however, counterterrorist intelligence is underappreciated in others, Pillar writes. The intelligence community's role is vital in aiding diplomacy, determining responsibility for specific attacks after the fact, aiding military targeting, and underpinning law enforcement, for example. Ignorance about what can appropriately be expected of intelligence may lead to tragic misuse of this vital tool.

At times, intelligence analysis is a matter of helping the consumer of information understand what is knowable and what is unknowable. This image is not glamorous, but it sometimes is the reality. Plots that are still evolving in the heads of terrorist operatives, in the absence of communication with others, cannot be uncovered by intelligence alone. Pillar makes a plea for recognizing the degree to which intelligence can truly be a "first line of defense" against terrorism, as well as the degree to which it must be considered within the context of other crucial and complementary policy instruments.

Like other such instruments, U.S. intelligence must rely on domestic support from a democratic public, including political and financial backing that has faltered in the post–cold war years. Moreover, public support is vital to enabling the intelligence community to be effective at home and abroad. Pillar concludes by arguing forcefully for shifting the U.S. focus from a peripatetic obsession with the next terrorist plot toward sustaining a more mature, longer-term commitment to strengthening counterterrorist intelligence.

The debate over whether terrorism is a crime or an act of war is an old argument that is fundamentally artificial: Terrorism is both, of course, and the response must include law enforcement and military means, depending on the situation. Still, it often is difficult to find forums where specialists in law enforcement (usually police officers or academics who study criminology, sociology, or law) discuss counterterrorism with specialists in the use of military force (usually military officers or academics in security studies, international relations, political science, or military history). It is equally challenging to bring together the disparate approaches, cultures, networks, biases, and bodies of research involved. Thus, productive dialogue (much less a synthesis) is rarely accomplished. Most studies of terrorism stress either law enforcement or military force, with adherents on one side or the other sometimes turning the debate into virtually a theological contest. (No wonder that policymakers often are no more successful in integrating these approaches.)

This book includes contributions by counterterrorism experts from both backgrounds who understand the interconnectivity between policy tools oriented toward law enforcement and military force. Lindsay Clutterbuck's chapter on law enforcement tools first reviews the two conceptual models— the "criminal justice model" and the "war model"—critiquing the arguments put forth in support of each. Clutterbuck concludes that no comprehensive counterterrorist response can be based entirely on one or the other approach. The two are situated at opposite ends of a continuum of potential responses, with many possible combinations between the poles. As long as the rule of law underpins the strategy, he argues, the state should use the widest and most flexible possible combination of tools, encouraging organizations such as police, military, and intelligence agencies to find ways to cooperate with each other in pursuit of a common goal.

To provide specific evidence of how this approach works, Clutterbuck explains the evolution of the United Kingdom's counterterrorism policy since the 1970s. The criminal justice system is at the heart of British counterterrorism strategy, and the work of the police, intelligence agencies, and the military is closely integrated. The experience of the British in Northern Ireland has demonstrated that relying on the military alone can be only a temporary short-term fix, he argues. Overuse of the military leads to resentment and alienation within the population that in turn give rise to the next generation of terrorists. Above all, Clutterbuck writes, over the long term the rule of law can be the only successful underpinning for all counterterrorism efforts.

Clutterbuck's conclusions are relevant to debates in the United States about the organization of homeland security, postconflict reconstruction of Iraq, and the priorities of counterterrorism. In particular, Clutterbuck describes police-to-police cooperation that has evolved in the past thirty years among member states in the European Union. This cooperation offers ample lessons that are useful for developing regional and international law enforcement cooperation in the wake of September 11—one of the major recommendations put forth in Michael Sheehan's chapter on diplomacy, as well.

As a counterpart to Clutterbuck's contribution, Timothy Hoyt's chapter on the use of military force stridently argues for the existence of a new paradigm in the era since September 11, especially with respect to American use of military force against terrorists. Hoyt deliberately emphasizes the concept of a "war on terrorism" in his analysis, arguing that the post–September 11 removal of many of the traditional constraints on the use of force against terrorism leaves no doubt that the United States is in a war. Reviewing the history of American use of force against terrorism, Hoyt describes three incidents—the 1986 El Dorado Canyon strikes against Libya, the 1993 cruise missile strikes on Iraq following the attempted assassination of President George Herbert Walker Bush, and the 1998 cruise missile strikes against Afghanistan and Sudan—and explains the legal and political constraints that typically have proscribed such attacks. These precedents, often cited by terrorism experts as examples of the (at best) limited effectiveness of military force, are of questionable relevance now, Hoyt contends. In the current American political climate, the new paradigm carries increased legitimacy for the use of military retaliation, preemptive action, and regime overthrow, on one hand, as well as decreased concern over the proportionality of response and high-risk operations, on the other. This is a new era.

According to Hoyt, however, that new paradigm does not mean that combating terrorism with military force is easy. Most important, military forces configured for conventional war generally are ill-suited for fighting terrorism. Drawing on the classical strategic concepts of Carl von Clausewitz and Sun Tzu, Hoyt presents a theoretical argument about the strengths and weaknesses of fighting this type of "war." Above all, terrorists target the enemy's political will. Their military means may be quite limited, but they assert control over the theoretical dimensions of time and space—that is, they maintain the initiative and usually do not present fixed targets. They operate primarily on the technical and tactical levels, avoiding the operational level of war, which is the focal point of the modern military. Therefore they are, in Hoyt's words, "difficult to find, difficult to fix, and difficult to destroy and lack a military center of gravity."

Thus, the obstacles to using even the highly sophisticated modern U.S. military are considerable, regardless of the strong political mandate present in the wake of the September 11 attacks. The apparently successful operation against the Taliban—essentially a fixed target—may not be typical of future counterterrorist operations. Ultimately, like Clutterbuck on law enforcement tools, Hoyt concludes that the U.S. military must cooperate not just among joint military components (which has been challenge enough at times) but also with all the other American agencies and international allies that deal with counterterrorism. Only in this way can the U.S. fashion a truly strategic response to al-Qaeda.

The state use of military force in the modern world carries with it an obligation to abide by international legal and moral conventions. This can be extremely difficult when the targets are terrorists. In his chapter on terrorism and international law, Adam Roberts examines the conduct of the parties involved in the current counterterrorist campaign, as well as the degree to which the laws themselves are adequate for this atypical use of violence. Terrorist attacks frequently occur in times of peace. As Roberts points out, such attacks also must be evaluated with reference to the national laws of states and international treaties. The particular relevance of the laws of war, especially in considering the most appropriate way to retain legitimacy in any response, is crucial to the current campaign.

Roberts briefly describes the laws of war, including their historical foundation, application, elements, and principles. He then discusses the history of their use in counterterrorist operations and particular problems in abiding by them. For example, because terrorist attacks target innocent civilians, and terrorist groups rarely take the form of defined military forces that are easily distinguishable from civilians, it can be extremely difficult to target noncombatants in response. There also is a concern that having one side abide by the laws of war but not the other unfairly handicaps the targeted civilians and their state governments. Moreover, some analysts worry that international law might be misused to provide a degree of recognition to terrorists, placing them on the same legal plane with the states involved.

Laws of war are problematic with regard to dealing with terrorism, in no small part because they were initially written in response to traditional war but also because terrorist attacks virtually always violate them and thus inspire little eagerness to abide by them in retaliating. The emotional aftermath of a shocking attack is powerful. Overwhelming punitive responses are an understandable reaction, but over time they can undermine the strategic goals being sought by eroding the legitimacy of the state that is responding and encouraging moral equivalence in examining both sides. Terrorist attacks are oriented toward an audience, and audiences should be considered in retaliating to them as well.

If terrorism is a struggle grounded in a sense of injustice, then the last thing the targeted states want to do is offer examples of apparently unjust behavior in response. This is not a theoretical academic argument but a practical strategic policy. Roberts admits that modest evolutionary changes in the law may be necessary—for example, regarding targeting, the threat of suicide bombers, and the treatment and classification of detainees. While directly confronting the issues that make interstate military operations against terrorists legally challenging, Roberts demonstrates the advantages of operating within the context of the laws of war to the maximal extent possible, in the interests of the long-term success of the campaign.

Terrorism, arguably, is as much or more about perceptions than objective reality. A central purpose of terrorist attacks is to have an impact on an audience, and it is only logical for counterterrorist campaigns to target perceptions as well. Carnes Lord's chapter on the subject begins with an explanation of the many tools that are oriented toward the psychological element of international terrorism, including public diplomacy, political action, psychological operations, and covert political action. Lord's argument is that to counter the current wave of international terrorism effectively, the United States and its allies must isolate militant Islam (the relatively few radical Muslims who want to kill those they hate) from the broader sea of moderate Islamic population. Without attacking the shared objectives of al-Qaeda and its associates, he asserts, no amount of military action can defeat this type of terrorism. Twisted ideas will inspire more adherents and more attacks.

Unfortunately, Lord observes, as things currently stand the United States and its allies start from a serious position of weakness in the Arab world. This weakness is partly a result of policies that are perceived to be directed against the Palestinian people and oriented toward domination of the Middle East. Also contributing to this impression are the expanded presence of the U.S. military in the Arabian Gulf and the war in Iraq. At a minimum, American policies are not being well explained, Lord writes, and the weak use of psychological-political methods is at least partly to blame.

The capacity for the United States to project a positive image abroad was consciously dismantled in the wake of the cold war, leaving the interpretation of American policy largely in the hands of others. Having won a long-term war of ideas in the cold war, the United States has been first slow and then quick to sense a new clash, not between civilizations but within one—the Muslim world. The George W. Bush administration's faltering efforts to change this situation have not succeeded and are too little, too late. This situation is not helped by U.S. domestic antipathy toward anything perceived to be "propaganda" or misinformation, which extends even to the dissemination of information abroad to serve the strategic goals of a war—a very naïve attitude. No campaign can succeed in the long haul in the absence of more effective measures to shape public opinion, at home and abroad.

The American effort to project a positive image in the Muslim world in general and the Arab world in particular is not going well. Ultimately, Lord argues, the remedy is to reformulate our strategy in this area, moving toward developing closer ties with moderate Islamic spokesmen, directly addressing substantive religious issues, and countering misconceptions of American society. The U.S. government also must do a much better job of explaining the rationale for American policies and work harder to understand and be aware of their effects. Lord concludes by providing specific recommendations to counter radical ideas, oppose organizations that disseminate extreme ideas, and purge violent "Islamist" elements from public education.

Having a long-term effect on the environment in which terrorism thrives also is a goal of U.S. development policy, writes Patrick Cronin in his chapter on foreign aid. The role of foreign assistance in fighting terrorism is complex and controversial; it cannot be understood without appreciating the tradeoffs that must be made in devoting what are always insufficient resources for dealing with the manifold problems in the world. In the United States there has been a tendency after the cold war to avoid setting priorities in foreign aid. U.S. spending on foreign aid declined in the 1990s, even as worthy causes multiplied—long before the "war on terrorism" was declared. The policy has careened from theme to theme (the AIDS pandemic, democracy advocacy, gender discrimination, etc.), adding missions without adding resources. Cronin argues forcefully for setting clear priorities to avoid the inevitable disappointment that results from trying to continue all the other missions even as we embark on a new and compelling focus on counterterrorism.

This approach is nothing new. Foreign aid has a long tradition of use as a security tool by the United States—from the Marshall Plan to increased assistance to Latin America under the Reagan administration. The role of foreign aid has evolved dramatically, however, and the trajectory of that evolution continues to influence the effectiveness of all foreign aid. Since the mid-twentieth century, the United States has moved from supporting local leadership and stimulating economic growth to, in some cases, merely shoring up regimes that were willing to back U.S. policies. Furthermore, writes Cronin, state-controlled assistance to the developing world has dramatically declined in overall importance compared to resources flowing from the private sector. This trend has reduced the leverage of state policies in comparison to other measures of economic globalization. Easy bromides about the role of foreign aid in fighting terrorism are undercut by the realization that there has been little focus and virtually no domestic political constituency for long-term foreign aid programs in the United States.

What can U.S. and allied foreign aid programs do to fight terrorism? In the short term, they can do little more than agenda-setting and signaling a deeper commitment to development in the Arab and Muslim worlds. Comprehensive strategies for counterterrorism must have tools that are oriented toward the long term as well, however. Cronin points out that foreign assistance can shore up moderate institutions and strengthen communities that provide alternatives to violent expressions of frustration and anger. Although investments in foreign aid are unlikely to have any effect on established terrorist groups, they can decrease support for terrorist organizations in areas where they recruit members or gather resources. Such programs also can strengthen the counterterrorist capabilities of governments that otherwise might lack the resources to police their borders and gather local intelligence. The relationship between terrorism, on one hand, and variables such as poverty, demography, education, and gender equity, on the other, is extremely complex. Over the long run, however, an effective strategy against terrorism must confront not only the proximate causes of terrorism but also some of the contributing root sources of political alienation and rage that fuel the frustrations of terrorist groups. Providing specific countries and communities with knowledge, a sense of justice, and economic opportunity can shape perceptions of the United States, strengthen moderate institutions and leaders within a context of improving governance, and deny terrorist groups the easy recruiting grounds of a failed radicalized state.

Unfortunately, strategies for using foreign aid in the campaign against terrorism are plagued with contradictions. Arguing that counterterrorism should be a crucial priority in foreign assistance is easy to do in a vacuum, but there are many other laudable, competing priorities. How should the U.S. government choose among them? More to the point, who will display the necessary political courage to stop spending in some areas to concentrate our resources in others? These are thorny issues. For example, how much money should be devoted to disaster relief and humanitarian assistance versus support of potential failed states on whose territory terrorists might thrive? What happens when a regime whose support is needed for counterterrorism violates the basic human rights of its own people? At what point should the international community cut its losses in a state that is deliberately mismanaging its assistance and devote the resources to other worthy recipients? Does counterterrorism trump all other concerns in foreign aid? What is the appropriate balance between democratic reform and economic growth in major Islamic countries? The truth of the matter is that these kinds of choices rarely have been made, and the disappointing record of postwar American aid is the result. In analyzing the role of foreign aid in the campaign against terrorism, Cronin urges greater realism in recognizing the tradeoffs to maximize the effect that this tool can have over the long term.

The last chapter in the section on policy responses to terrorism deals with the equally complex challenge of homeland security. Dan Gouré's discussion of the strategic issues surrounding defense against terrorist attacks on U.S. soil penetrates the platitudes about keeping Americans safe at home. The harsh reality is that there is no way to protect the entire United States against the threat of terrorist attacks, particularly in an age of globalization when the means of penetrating a state are countless and multiplying. That is not to suggest abandoning the effort to make wise choices and to improve readiness. The U.S. government (both the executive and legislative branches) must resist the temptation, however, to craft policies primarily on the basis of emotions and myopic politics, rather than hard-headed decisions about costs and benefits. Perhaps even more than in other areas of counterterrorism, there are difficult domestic political, financial, and ethical tradeoffs to make in strengthening homeland security. Homeland security measures themselves have the dangerous potential to change the nature of the assets they are trying to protect.

Gouré highlights the difficulties of applying traditional analytical techniques to the development of a homeland security strategy. It is not just a matter of directing particular means toward a known threat in the pursuit of predetermined ends. Fundamental assumptions must be explored first. How, exactly, do we define the threat? Experts disagree about major issues—for example, the relative importance of the threat of catastrophic terrorism versus other types of terrorism. Should we rank threats in terms of likelihood or potential effects? Should a homeland security strategy address all threats? Are the investments involved worth the marginal gains in "security"? Definition of the threat and analysis of the level of risk are typical starting points, yet they are absent or debated with respect to terrorist attacks on U.S. soil. Without a more focused, informed approach to evaluating the threat, planners are tempted to squander resources everywhere, simultaneously, on the basis of worst-case scenarios. There are no obvious, measurable strategic objectives with regard to homeland security, Gouré writes. Phrases such as "reduce vulnerability" and "minimize damage and recovery," though politically palatable, ultimately are subjective and virtually meaningless. Reduce or minimize them compared to what? Without a clear identifiable "end state" for homeland security, the traditional Clausewitzian matching of ends and means is impossible. Bankrupting the national treasury will not increase security, Gouré observes.

Likewise, traditional concepts such as deterrence are of limited relevance to the protection of the homeland. A strategy of imposing unacceptable costs on an opponent does not apply in this context; the goal instead is to deny terrorist objectives that may be countless and unknowable in advance. In theory individual terrorist leaders and organizations may be deterrable because their personal survival and the survival of the group are typical vulnerabilities. In a broader sense, however, when the goal of some terrorists is to wreak destruction purely for the sake of its shock effect, the dynamic, reciprocal nature of most cold war–era strategic theory does not apply. Gouré finds existing models of strategy-making inadequate for guiding homeland security efforts.

As U.S. homeland security plans currently are devised, they place means and methods ahead of strategic objectives. Gouré reviews the priorities placed on strategies such as barrier systems and transportation security, intrusion detection, and consequence management and concludes that it is impossible to rationalize and coordinate the different initiatives. There is no way to make optimal decisions about where to put resources in domestic programs without an understanding of the broader picture, he writes. Ultimately, Gouré asserts that plans for homeland security can make sense only as part of a grand strategy for counterterrorism that reduces the threat in a broad-based way, coordinated with the many other policy tools discussed in this book. In counterterrorism, defensive measures at home are best judged in relation to offensive measures abroad, including covert action, preemptive measures against weapons of mass destruction, and long-term political strategies to gain allies and delegitimize international terrorism.

This assessment logically brings us back to where we started in the second half of the book—emphasizing the wide range of coordinated policy tools that are critical to a global strategy against international terrorism in the twenty-first century. International terrorism did not begin to be a serious threat to the United States and its allies on September 11, 2001, although the widespread awareness of it and the amassing of political capital with which to build a long-term response did. The United States has a long tradition of adjusting its broad strategic goals in reaction to major, shocking events. In a democracy, the most brilliant minds, the most prescient predictions, and the most forward-looking projections by themselves cannot result in effective long-term strategy because the political will to implement it soon dissipates in the absence of a widespread perception of threat. Thus, it is a waste of time to engage in recriminations and look for scapegoats to blame for failing to prevent the tragedies that occurred on September 11, 2001. Changes in the American approach to terrorism have been needed for some time; tragically, now the capacity to make them exists. As the campaign against international terrorism unfolds, a crucial, forward-looking process of strategic reassessment is under way in the United States, and this book is intended to be a part of it.

Notes

1. See Audrey Kurth Cronin, "Rethinking Sovereignty: American Strategy in the Age of Terrorism," *Survival* 44, no. 2 (summer 2002): 119–39.

2. See the Gallup survey of nine Muslim countries, "The 2002 Gallup Poll of the Islamic World," available at www.gallup.com/poll/summits/islam.asp (accessed December 20, 2002).

3. On the difficulty of defining terrorism see, for example, Omar Malik, *Enough of the Definition of Terrorism!* (London: Royal Institute of International Affairs, 2001), and Alex P. Schmid, *Political Terrorism: A Research Guide* (New Brunswick, N.J.: Transaction Books, 1984); Schmid spends more than 100 pages grappling with the question of a definition, only to conclude that none is universally accepted.

4. Saying that terrorism is political in nature is not the same as arguing that the political ends toward which it is directed are necessarily negotiable. If violent acts do not have a political aim, then by definition they are criminal acts.

5. The diabolical nature of terrorism has given resonance to Robert Kaplan's view that the world is a "grim landscape" littered with "evildoers" and requiring Western leaders to adapt a "pagan ethos." Such conclusions deserve more scrutiny than space allows here. See Steven Mufson, "The Way Bush Sees the World," *Washington Post*, Outlook section, 17 February 2002.

6. R. G. Frey and Christopher W. Morris, "Violence, Terrorism and Justice," in *Violence, Terrorism, and Justice* (Cambridge: Cambridge University Press, 1991), 3.

PART I

THE NATURE OF TERRORISM

one

SOURCES OF CONTEMPORARY TERRORISM

Audrey Kurth Cronin

In the aftermath of September 11, 2001, academics, policymakers, commentators, and pundits have speculated on the origins of the terrorist attacks against the United States. Common themes in these appraisals are bewilderment at the motivations of the terrorists, speculation about the conditions that would produce or permit such acts, and loose assertions regarding prescriptions for correcting the causes.[1] This groping for an answer is understandable in the context of the attacks, particularly as the United States and its allies attempt to calibrate responses for the long term. Yet although the extent of the destruction caused by al-Qaeda is unprecedented,[2] these questions are not new; attempts to understand the sources of terrorism are many and have yielded important lessons regarding the nature of the current threat.[3]

In this chapter I focus on understanding the sources of contemporary transnational terrorism by examining the phenomenon from four levels of analysis: the individual, the organization, the state, and the international system. These four analytical "lenses" provide clarity and intellectual coherence to what is in reality a complex and intricately intertwined series of factors. Many popular and scholarly explanations draw mainly from one of these analytical frameworks and slight the other three. Understanding the causes of terrorism actually requires simultaneous consideration of all of them. Still, human beings think in structures and sequences (sometimes without even realizing it), so I use this heuristic device in this chapter to highlight implicit assumptions, demonstrate the limitations of some explanations, and encourage a more comprehensive approach.

Most people understand that the causes of terrorism are complex and that there is no single variable that leads inexorably to terrorist acts. Few realize, however, the degree to which consistent intellectual frameworks influence most analyses. Terrorism is a multidisciplinary challenge: The study of sources of terrorism requires the ability to translate between the fields of criminology, comparative politics, economics, history, international relations, psychology, sociology, theology, and arguably others. Moreover, it is not just a matter of interdisciplinary differences. There also is an important intellectual bias related to levels of analyses on which causes are evaluated. Revealing those analytical frameworks illuminates areas in which the policy community and academia are failing to communicate effectively, to the disadvantage of both and to the detriment of the long-term campaign against twenty-first–century international terrorism.

I use the four levels of analysis to draw from insights gained in the scholarly literature to shed light on the threat facing the United States and its allies today, as well as to suggest lessons that are relevant to effectively employing the counterterrorism policy instruments examined in the second part of this book. Although I do not offer an inclusive survey of all the research that has been done, I strive to explain how the range of perspectives in existing literature on sources of terrorism can enrich policymakers' thinking and highlight oversights or oversimplifications that in some cases may be distorting their choices. I also demonstrate that a set of inaccurate or incomplete assumptions about the causes of terrorism often provides the impetus for policy prescriptions. These assumptions should be reexamined to improve the likelihood of success. Effective counterterrorism is not possible if we do not start with an accurate and comprehensive analysis of the sources of terrorism.

Background: Dissecting the Sources of Terrorism

It would be a mistake to underestimate the challenges of this undertaking. Although much has been written about political violence, for example, there is no definitive study of the causes of terrorism.[4] There are many reasons for this research gap.

First, it is virtually impossible to control enough of the potential variables involved to isolate and study only a few. Hypothesized causes of terrorism are legion and have differed across time: Terrorism is at least partly a reaction to the particular political, economic, and historical context within which potential terrorists exist.[5] Although an examination of these separate situations can be extremely informative, and much insight has been gained through the use of case studies, specific domestic or international contexts are virtually impossible to duplicate and may or may not be relevant in other contexts. Some writers have even argued that the causes of terrorism are impossible to generalize,[6] although this claim is a minority viewpoint in the field. There are numerous benefits to be gained in studying the various contexts of terrorism, as long as the lessons learned in each case study are not oversimplified and applied unthinkingly across contexts.

Second, looking at the conditions under which terrorism can arise is examining only part of the equation. Terrorism is not exclusively a response to external conditions; it also is a result of the strategic decisions of political actors.[7] Human beings are not laboratory rats that react reliably and repeatedly to the same external environmental stimuli in the same way. The actions of regimes, which also respond to terrorism in a broad variety of ways, likewise elicit a reaction from individuals and groups. The action/reaction relationship between counterterrorism and terrorism is very important but often slighted in devising state policy. It is crucial to realize that policy decisions and actions may affect the nature, severity, and form of the threat, which in turn may affect future policy decisions, and so on. Sorting out the cause and effect in this relationship can be a conundrum in examining a historical case study—much more so when the dynamic relationship is in the process of unfolding.

Third, different types of terrorism may be caused (or enabled) by different factors; right-wing terrorism, for example, may have different roots than does left-wing terrorism, or ethnonationalist/separatist terrorism or religious terrorism. Much more work needs to be done in this area. Many observers have argued—especially with respect to religiously inspired terrorism, for example—that it is dangerous to an unprecedented degree and will manifest different preferences and behaviors over time.[8] In any case, there is reason to doubt the similarity of the origins. Comparative case studies of terrorism provide many interesting insights; finding consistent explanations for terrorism across cultures, time, geography, ideologies, however, while also accounting for individual personalities and preferences, is challenging indeed.

The preferences of the analyst are a fourth factor. Explanations of the causes of terrorism often have reflected the subjective views of the observer, projecting political, sociological, or economic explanations on phenomena that are similarly related to the politics of the observer. Neither policymakers nor academic researchers are immune to this problem (although the latter may be more aware of it). This phenomenon is most evident in the op-ed pages of every major newspaper since September 11: Ideologically biased tracts typically amplify the preexisting opinions of the authors. This tendency also is evident in the writings of some academics. Objective analysis about a phenomenon that is so deliberately designed to elicit an emotional response is hard to achieve and is a standard that only a few experienced and long-established experts have reached.

Another reason the causes of terrorism are difficult to isolate is that in some cases they may be as simple and as complex as the persuasive power of the political or ideological passion behind the movement, as well as the receptiveness of a given population to the "message." Terrorism is a fundamentally political phenomenon, driven by political motives and oriented toward political ends. Sometimes, in an attempt to be objective or scientific, the power of passionate ideas can be slighted. Few thinkers predicted, for example, that fascism and communism would achieve such a dramatic following in the twentieth century. Explaining the variances in human passions, the power of ideas, and the resulting and often surprising actions taken by human beings in response is a daunting task that is not confined to the study of terrorism.

The sources of terrorism are many, complex, and often unpredictable. The phenomenon seems to be almost developmental in nature, with elements of innate and environmental factors.[9] Efforts to draw direct correlations between single variables and terrorism are virtually certain to fail. In any given case there is a complex causal chain from societal conditions to the formation (usually) of a group, to the carrying out of an act. Along the way, some of the steps in that process may be accidental or opportunistic. Analysts often seem to be talking past each other, focusing on or ignoring certain stages; generally, in any given case study no single stage is definitive. The best that can be achieved is to search for patterns among cases, environments where terrorism is more or less likely to be enabled, political movements or leaders that are more or less likely to inspire use of the tactic, and—most important for our purposes—policy instruments that are more or less likely to discourage that use.

There is no more compelling or important question today than the sources of transnational terrorism. The coalition of states that are now arrayed in a long-term campaign against "terrorism with a global reach" must carefully calibrate its response to the threat to be effective in reducing that threat over time. As difficult as the task is, examining and analyzing terrorism's causes is a crucial starting point toward developing sound responses. Faulty premises can lead to tragically flawed policy. Without a clear understanding of the sources of contemporary terrorism, or at least recognition of the assumptions that are being made, the United States and its allies run the risk of failing in their effort to respond to the attacks and may even exacerbate the causes.

Level One: The Role of the Individual

As one would expect, a study of the causes of terrorism that focuses on the role of the individual considers the factors that affect individual human beings and their behavior. Individual terrorist behavior has been studied in some depth since the mid-twentieth century, in direct correlation with the growth of behavioral science and its methods in the United States. The questions raised by an individual-level analysis of the sources of terrorism are at the intersection of the fields of psychology, sociology, criminology, and political science. The issues include, on one hand, external factors that lead a person to choose to engage in terrorist activities, as well as, on the other hand, innate characteristics that give some people more or less proclivity to become terrorists. For practical purposes, four major areas of terrorism research are of broad interest at this first level: studies of the psychologies of individual terrorists, studies of the "profiles" of terrorists (and future terrorists), studies of the conditions that encourage or enable individuals to resort to terrorism, and examinations of the distinctive characteristics of terrorist leaders and their followers.

There is a popular tendency to believe that terrorism results from the psychological pathology or aberrant behavior of individuals. Some of our most eminent policymakers have perpetuated this perception—sometimes deliberately, sometimes not.[10] Although there is wide agreement that killing innocent noncombatants is against the teachings of virtually all long-established legal and religious traditions, this view considers the source of such behavior to be the inability of potential terrorists to reason normally. Their decision to carry out abhorrent acts is assumed to be the result of personality disorders (such as narcissism or paranoia), mental deficiencies, or impulsive behavior. Others regard terrorism as arising from the self-aggrandizement and glorification of leaders or the arrested psychological development of followers. Implicit in this view is the argument that if the West can neutralize delusional individuals—either leaders or followers—then the most important sources of contemporary transnational terrorism will diminish sharply. The policy prescription is to apprehend or kill perpetrators and capture or kill their leaders—not only to bring the criminals to justice but also to wipe out the sources of deviant behavior.

Academics have done a great deal of research in this area in the past, although much work remains to be done.[11] Particularly interesting questions have included discussion of the degree to which terrorist behavior is a result of rational choice—where decisions to use terrorism reflect the careful cost/benefit analysis of the perpetrator—or a reflection of psychological forces over which the terrorist may have little control. The latter would include emotional scarring in childhood, an inordinate desire for action, frustration over issues of identity, personal feelings of inadequacy, and so on.[12]

With regard to the question of psychological abnormality, the popular perception of inherent psychological deviance is wrong. Although the data set of terrorists available to study admittedly is quite small, there is predominant agreement among specialists in the field: Psychological pathology does not seem to be present in higher rates among terrorism perpetrators than it is among members of the general public. It is understandable to want to separate the terrorist from the rest of "normal" humanity, but despite the widespread temptation to speak of "senseless" violence engaged in by "crazy" terrorists, there is strong evidence that they are surprisingly "normal" in their psychological characteristics and behaviors prior to engaging in violent acts. Even suicide bombers, about whom there has been considerable research, apparently exhibit normal psychologies overall.[13]

What seems to be aberrant is the channeling of the frustrations or talents of psychologically normal people into violent or desperate behavior, often as a result of peer pressure or loyalty to the group or a need to belong, but not individual psychological abnormality. Certain childhood events or personality traits may lead individuals to be more or less inclined to identify strongly with a group (the second-level analysis addresses this issue), although it is difficult to determine whether inherent personality traits existed before an individual joined a group or whether these traits were accentuated as a result of membership in a terrorist organization. In any case, the individual's psychological make-up alone rarely is sufficient explanation for involvement in terrorist activities.[14] On average, terrorists are no more "crazy" than the rest of humanity.

Related to the issue of terrorist psychology is the question of whether potential terrorists can be identified in advance by certain traits that would make them more or less likely to be attracted to terrorist behavior.[15] If there is a particular psychological "profile" for most terrorists or particular characteristics or experiences that lead to terrorism, those characteristics should be identified and the attacks preempted. Profiling of potential terrorists has been an important area of research in classified and unclassified settings, not only for academic reasons but for the promised benefit of identifying potential future threats before they materialize. Vigorous efforts have been made to identify the demographic characteristics of most terrorists; in the past they generally were thought to be male, young, unmarried, reasonably educated but of limited connections and prospects.[16]

Specifically with respect to al-Qaeda and its associated groups, for example, there has been a widespread attempt to understand what made the nineteen hijackers who carried out the attacks of September 11, 2001, "different"—not only because of academic interest in the issue but more urgently to serve the need to identify other potential perpetrators who may be preparing future attacks. Considerable attention has been focused on the extent to which our past understanding of the "profile" of terrorists must be revised.[17] Although such profiles naturally are popular with the people who are responsible for defending against terrorism, in the present context the broader benefit and relevance of such profiles must be questioned. Most profiles have been developed as a result of studies of a limited number of groups associated with Arab-Israeli violence, which may or may not be representative of the larger pool of potential transnational terrorists.[18] The relevance of profiling becomes even more questionable when applied specifically to al-Qaeda members, who are distinct from members of longstanding and more-studied groups such as Hezbollah and Hamas and may exhibit different characteristics.[19] Profiles of terrorists may differ from group to group, but this question needs more research. In any case, in the current situation the evidence indicates that the United States and its allies should take care not to rely too heavily on incorrect assumptions in identifying potential al-Qaeda activists. Across all types of groups, the field is far too immature and the research too spotty to rely on broad conclusions about terrorist profiles.

Another concern that begins at this level is the question of whether certain environmental conditions cause or enable individuals to turn to violent terrorist behavior. There has been much discussion and writing about the connection between objective conditions such as poverty, lack of education (or access to inappropriate and substandard education), and political disenfranchisement, on one hand, and resort to terrorist violence, on the other.[20] The socialization of young males in *madrassas* in Pakistan and Afghanistan, for example, apparently has led to the development of a devoted pool of potential terrorists with few alternative outlets for their livelihoods, passions, or energies.[21] The policy prescription is to offer other sources of aid, education, and employment to channel such energies in more productive directions and provide alternate avenues of hope.

Studies of terrorism in other contexts, however, teach that people may respond to conditions of deprivation in different ways. For example, one important study argues that the extent to which societal conditions lead to a sense of "indignation" might be the crucial factor for the decision about whether to turn to terrorist violence. In other words, the objective conditions that face an individual are not as important as the perceived difference between what one has and what one deserves (in either material or political terms).[22] Another work interprets this sense of anger as an outgrowth of frustrated ambition, whereby upwardly mobile individuals are blocked in their attempts to translate their capabilities or assets into political power.[23] If either of these theories is correct, the provision of aid, which may not provide avenues of personal advancement quickly enough, could have the potential to destabilize a society further. Arguably, it might enhance the frustrations and anger that can lead to violent behavior. Unfortunately, the available academic research is suggestive but not conclusive, and from the policymaker's point of view there are many gaps.

Regarding the response to al-Qaeda and its associated groups, these differing views of the sources of terrorism lead to different policy prescriptions. If the cause of terrorist events is the unjust and oppressive societal conditions under which people live, the aid programs that the United States and its allies have initiated may go a long way toward reducing the environment that leads to such acts of desperation. If the source is "indignation" or "blocked ambition," however, the question of how to deal with the upward mobility of a portion of the population becomes more complex. The fundamentally political nature of the threat must be emphasized, as well as other important foreign policy priorities in addition to counterterrorism. Although reducing the analysis to only one level—the focus on the individual—may be intellectually convenient, it also may be misguided because the audience for the policy prescriptions of the United States and its allies is not just the potential individual terrorist but also the broader community of nations that, over time, may become more or less radicalized by actions taken. (See discussion of level four, below.) Terrorism is a psychological weapon whose target may not be immediately apparent. In this day of globalized communications, "indignation" is not just an individual phenomenon and may be much more broadly contagious than in the past.

Also at the level of the focus on the individual is the important question of psychological and sociological differences between individuals who are recruited to participate in political violence and their leaders. Generalizing about the characteristics of leaders, who represent an extremely small set of potential subjects, is even more difficult and problematic than drawing conclusions about followers, who represent a small enough data set already.[24] Much more research needs to be done in this area. It seems clear by empirical observation that the psychology, motivations, and behavior of the potential pool of "recruits" to al-Qaeda, for example, must be distinguished from the individual characteristics of the leaders, such as Osama bin Laden. Bin Laden's enormous wealth, advanced education, connections to the Saudi royal family, and personal charisma certainly mark him as atypical. In any case, policies that are indiscriminately directed at leaders and followers may not succeed.

Whatever the sincerity of bin Laden's personal commitment to a radical religious ideology, he and his organization are extremely adept at the politics of mass mobilization. By all accounts bin Laden is a genius of corporate management and organization—which goes a long way toward explaining the resilience and autonomy of the al-Qaeda enterprise, regardless of whether bin Laden is still alive.[25] Moreover, there are many other leaders, present and past, whose characteristics belie the stereotype of the downtrodden, desperate, or crazy individual who turns to terrorism. In any case, different forces may be driving individual leaders and their recruits, which points to different prescriptions for affecting those forces and identifying which ones they are—an important factor to keep in mind as the campaign against the current transnational terrorism continues to unfold. This conclusion leads naturally to the second level of analysis: the terrorist group or organization.

Level Two: The Group or Organization

Any understanding of the causes of terrorism must devote considerable attention to the dynamics of the group or organization. Much of the research conducted in the past several decades has led to the conclusion that terrorism is fundamentally a group activity that cannot be understood without reference to concepts such as shared ideological commitment and group identity.[26] This is not just a matter of the enabling conditions for terrorist activity within a group but also the perpetuation of violence as a result of the internal dynamics or belief system of the organization. Likewise, understanding the structure and functioning of a group (or associated groups) becomes crucial in evaluating the impact of counterterrorist methods aimed at dismantling terrorist operations. Thus, level two is an extremely important lens through which to analyze a developing terrorist threat, as well as the potential effectiveness of measures taken to offset it.

Because most individual terrorists are apparently psychologically normal, group identity provides the crucial link in justifying violence against innocent civilians, spreading blame across many group members, and devaluing the humanity of the enemy (especially prospective victims).[27] The belief system within a terrorist organization or group may bear little relationship to a more broadly perceived reality; nonetheless it may be reinforced and perpetuated among the members through the dynamics of peer pressure, indoctrination, mutual reinforcement, and group identification. Individual members see themselves as part of a larger cause, which provides rationalization of acts that they might not otherwise be likely to commit. The relationship of the individual to the group often is crucial to understanding the genesis of individual terrorist plots as well as the longer-term perpetuation of the threat. Thus, we must crack the code of that belief structure to understand the sources of terrorism.

The practical policy implication of this element in the genesis of terrorist behavior is that as governments formulate counterterrorism policy they must consider that their actions may feed into that belief structure in ways that may be contrary to their interests and the defeat of a terrorist organization over time. This is not to argue that the belief structure is in any way legitimate but only to recognize that it exists and that it may affect the evolution of the threat in ways that are important to bear in mind. For example, the 1998 launching of cruise missiles against al-Qaeda training camps in Afghanistan and against the El Shifa pharmaceutical plant in Sudan, though a justifiable response to the 1998 African embassy bombings, also unfortunately fed a perception that the United States was opposed to all Muslims and lionized bin Laden in the eyes of his followers and potential followers.[28] There are numerous other factors to consider, including the perceptions of allies and domestic populations; but a *strategy* against terrorism must be mindful of the broad longer-term effects of tactical actions on the enemy's group identity and organizational strength—a lens that often is slighted in the urgency of policymaking after an event.

Another important level two analytical consideration is the structure and functioning of the group itself. In the past, terrorist organizations generally were closed, clandestine cells with a hierarchical leadership structure and regular contact among members.[29] Much of the research about terrorist organizations therefore has focused on understanding the dynamics of the relationships among members, as a way to evaluate the motivations behind terrorist attacks, the vulnerability of the hierarchy, weaknesses in the organizational structure, and so on. Sometimes attacks are undertaken to perpetuate the organization itself—cementing the links among members, preventing a challenge to the leadership by bored or disgruntled members, or projecting the group ahead of its competitors, for example. The organizational process approach, which analyzes the behavior of organizations from the perspective of the needs of the organization itself, has been very important in analyzing the behavior of terrorist organizations.[30] It was particularly influential in studying the behavior of leftist and ethnonationalist/separatist groups of the 1970s and 1980s.

Many researchers who study terrorism argue, however, that terrorist organizations are evolving into a different model. Newer terrorist organizations such as al-Qaeda increasingly are adopting a decentralized, nonhierarchical cell structure, connected by technology such as the Internet and satellite telephones and inspired by a common ideology or religion. The new structures are less dependent on internal organizational dynamics to perpetuate themselves and their activities and more characterized by decentralized designs with stand-alone groups that are only loosely transnationally connected.[31]

This type of terrorist organization essentially reflects the management theories that were introduced into business during the early- to mid-1990s. These models are characterized by information sharing and an emphasis on individual initiative, resulting in mission-driven organizations, flat organizational structures, emphasis on computer network connections, employee empowerment, and bottom-up management. Facilitated and catalyzed by the growth of information technology, all of these techniques began to be introduced in the private sector more than ten years ago. To some degree, at least, terrorists are reflective of and influenced by the societies within which they function. It is not surprising to see the translation of these methods into terrorist organizations led by experienced businessmen such as Osama bin Laden.

In practical terms, the implications of an apparent shift in the structure of new terrorist organizations are several. First, component cells that operate independently are much more difficult to eliminate; destroying the leadership has limited effect on the health of the overall organization. Second, and related, there is no proverbial "center of gravity," so it is virtually impossible to target the most vulnerable point in the organization. Instead of aiming an attack at one point whose annihilation leads a group to self-destruct in the wake of an attack, for example, destroying a terrorist organization that has multiple independently operable cells requires targeting each and every one of the cells. Third, the ideologies motivating these "terror networks" are broadly conceived—the relationship between terrorism and religion is particularly worrisome because as an organization matures the "inspiration" behind a terrorist act is provided by a tract, belief, or even a deity, not necessarily a human interpreter or leader. In business, "mission-driven" organizations are designed to be much stronger than leader-driven organizations, and this concept translates directly into twenty-first–century terrorism. Likewise, the technological connections between members of the organization (and even, potentially, members of other organizations driven by the same mission) are the *modus operandi,* in place of regular personal interaction that might be observed or disrupted. Finally, in the international arena, networked organizations can be more autonomous actors than are those that rely on the sponsorship of a state.

As a result of the changes facilitated by globalization and the information revolution, the new terrorist organization is more difficult to counter with traditional policy instruments. Just to name a few examples, inserting human intelligence operatives is more complex than ever: If there is no clear hierarchy, it can be tricky to ensure that intelligence assets are even in the right place—if they are successfully placed at all. The use of military force becomes complicated by the enhanced challenge of identifying the most effective target—if a target is identified at all. And homeland security against terrorists who have little traceable interaction with other terrorists and are empowered to act independently has the potential to become an exercise in paranoia. Especially against a networked organization, no single policy instrument trumps the others; they must be used in coordination with each other to maximize the potential for success.

These and other considerations are suggested by an examination of changes at the level of substate terrorist organizations. Sometimes, however, the dynamics of the organization are controlled, influenced, or facilitated by the clandestine involvement of a state. Particularly in the 1980s, terrorism became a mechanism whereby states violently pursued their foreign policy aims (usually secretly) without taking the risks of overt military action and the ensuing retaliation. The state continues to be the most powerful actor in international affairs, and in any terrorist activity the actual or potential role of a state must be suspected. A study of the causes of terrorism would be incomplete without an examination of the role of state actors—the third lens through which a conscientious analyst must peer.

Level Three: The Role of the State

Level three is the predominant level of analysis in foreign policy circles. Many observers and policymakers focus on the role of the state in perpetuating or supporting acts of transnational terrorism. The general assumption is that whether it is immediately apparent or not, the support of a sponsoring state usually is essential to the execution of major and devastating international terrorist attacks. In the international system, states are the most dangerous perpetrators of terrorism, many analysts argue, because states have amassed the most resources—including weapons, money, and people—as well as the most powerful sustained motivations to use terrorism as a means to attack stronger states. Understanding the role of the state is extremely important to understanding the sources of international terrorism. Although numerous terrorist attacks occur without the direct support of any state, many observers continue to believe that state-supported terrorism is the most dangerous current threat to the interests and safety of the United States and its allies in the coalition against international terrorism.

The policy prescriptions that flow from this argument are obvious: The most effective response to transnational terrorism is to target states that are proven to have sponsored international terrorism in the past, to reduce the threat of global terrorism overall. Most important, the policy should be to prevent proven state sponsors of terrorism from developing, or continuing to develop, arsenals of weapons of mass destruction such as nuclear, chemical, biological, and radiological weapons. The devastating attacks by al-Qaeda may be regarded as proof that transnational terrorist organizations are willing to use existential weapons to attack the West. It is only a matter of time before state sponsors of terrorism that have such weapons likewise use them—or enable transnational organizations to do so. In short, according to this view, the best way to respond to twenty-first–century international terrorism, including al-Qaeda and its associated groups, is to target U.S. national policy toward these states.

The role of the state in interacting with and spawning terrorism has been very well examined, and there are many interesting case studies and revelations in the terrorism literature. Particularly with respect to responding to the threat of indigenous terrorism, regime behavior has been carefully studied, with historical examples of terrorism on one hand being catalyzed in reaction to the use by the state of unexpected or unusual force and on the other hand arising in situations where there are weak central state mechanisms to prevent or respond forcefully to it.[32] Unfortunately, however, broad generalizations about the most effective state responses to domestic terrorism are problematic and easily disproven with historical examples; thus, they usually fail to be a direct guide to contemporary state policy.

The rise of state sponsorship was one of the most important developments in international terrorism in the late twentieth century. Although there was significant state sponsorship of terrorism before then, most notably by the Soviet Union and its clients, the Iranian revolution of 1979 embodied a dramatic increase in the use of terrorism as an instrument of foreign policy.[33] At a time of increasing American dominance, terrorism was a mechanism through which a relatively weak state could promote its interests through covert terrorist activity against the property and citizens of a stronger state. In 1983 and 1984, for example, more U.S. lives were lost to international terrorism than in the previous fifteen years combined; with very few exceptions, the attacks were carried out by state-sponsored groups.[34] This development was the source of considerable alarm because states were able to provide far more resources to support terrorist activity than had previously been the case. Through the 1980s, acts of terrorism carried out by groups supported by states were much more lethal than those carried out in previous decades by groups without state assistance had been.[35]

The United States has tried to respond to the state as a source of international terrorism in a variety of ways—most notably including establishing the formal designation of state sponsors of terrorism under the Export Administration Act of 1979. This designation carries with it automatic sanctions against states on the list, including prohibitions on exports of weaponry from the United States, prohibition of any assistance under the Foreign Assistance Act, and numerous other tax and income disadvantages.[36] Unfortunately, the list is an extremely inflexible instrument from which it is nearly impossible to remove a state once it has appeared—a fact that seriously undermines any potential leverage in affecting the behavior of listed states. Some states are on the list for important foreign policy and security reasons other than sponsorship of terrorism, which in the case of states such as North Korea, Libya, and Cuba, for example, has radically declined in recent years. This approach feeds into the popular tendency to conflate state sponsorship of terrorism with other dangerous and abhorrent behavior, including weapons proliferation, human rights abuses, breach of treaties, and slaughter or mistreatment of citizens. The result is an undermining of the effort to get directly at the sources of terrorism and influence state support for terrorist groups, as well as an ineffectual response to the other behaviors that the United States hopes to change or condemn.

State-sponsored terrorism was and continues to be a deadly and serious challenge; there is reason to believe, however, that in the new millennium it is evolving into something even more worrisome. The end of the twentieth century saw a gradual transition away from direct state sponsorship and toward more amorphous groups, often having access to state resources but less and less likely to be under the control of the state.[37] Many observers have worried about the increased availability of nuclear weapons and fissile material following the breakup of the Soviet Union, the movement of former Soviet scientists into potentially profitable terrorist enterprises, and the increasing accessibility of information about massively destructive weapons on the Internet. Whereas in the past the development of advanced technologies required the resources of a state, this no longer seems to be the case; the state monopoly on advanced technical information apparently is being undermined. The danger has proved to have substance: The 1995 use of the nerve agent sarin in the Tokyo subway system by the Japanese cult Aum Shinrikyo has been regarded as an important watershed, both by those concerned with counterterrorism and arguably by terrorists themselves. Although more familiar threats, especially ethnonationalist/separatist terrorism, continue to predominate, an increase in religiously motivated nonstate terrorism—with open-ended goals and a Manichean tendency to separate "believers" from others—has led to serious concern about their potential lack of constraint in carrying out terrorist attacks unbridled by the longer-term interests of a state.[38]

Yet American policy in the campaign against international terrorism reflects a firm focus on the model of state sponsorship and control over international terrorism. In that respect, it may be anachronistic and destined to be overtaken by events. Al-Qaeda was not sponsored by a state; it was virtually a state in itself.[39] First in Sudan and then in Afghanistan, al-Qaeda took over the traditional elements of state sovereignty, including control of population and territory and an effective monopoly over the use of force. They were more than just honored guests. Yet Afghanistan never appeared on the U.S. State Department's list of state sponsors of terrorism,[40] and al-Qaeda was not even listed as a foreign terrorist organization until 1999.[41] The well-established habit of focusing on war between organized states and the elaborate and inflexible bureaucratic structures that have been erected to support that activity may be blinding policymakers to an untraditional and unprecedentedly dangerous threat. Transnational terrorism, as represented by al-Qaeda and its associated groups, has the potential to undermine the integrity and value of the state itself, destroying the domestic contract of the state by undermining its ability to protect its citizens from direct attack. This form of terrorism is a threat to the sovereignty and the legitimacy of the state itself.[42] It is much easier to accept the familiar myth that states are behind existential terrorist threats because policymakers have long experience in dealing with states, as well as many (and growing) traditional state-oriented military resources to rely upon. Besides, states can more easily be deterred. With respect to evolving transnational terrorism, however, this focus might be misguided and trapped in a single, limited level of analysis.

Also at this level of analysis is the argument that an important source of terrorism is the internal collapse of some states—that is, that the problem is not "rogue states" but "failed states." This viewpoint reflects especially the fact that al-Qaeda training camps, business enterprises, and headquarters have been located on the territories of states such as Sudan and Afghanistan. The implication is that functioning states should be held accountable for violent acts that occur as a result of terrorist organizations being "hosted" on their territory. This perspective is difficult to locate, however, in an argument about sources of terrorism: Failed states themselves generally are more likely to be *enablers* of terrorism than causes. They provide desirable autonomy to terrorists and are attractive targets of opportunity; by definition, however, they usually are unable to control the territory on which the groups operate. The closest thing to a cause is the fact that a sea of potential recruits often exists among destitute populations, tempted by relatively wealthy terrorist entities. We must go back to level one to give any real substance to this factor, however.

A related concern at the third level of analysis is the question of the relationship between terrorism and a democratic state government. Enthusiasm for the United States' system of government, as well as an idealistic belief that the American model can and should be developed elsewhere, has led to an assertion in the United States that the injustices of authoritarian governments are the source of terrorism. The view is that lack of freedoms such as the right to vote, a free press, equality between genders, and equal access to employment opportunities has led to frustration that erupts in terrorism. Likewise, within the Arab world the foundation of past American policy—in essence considered to be supporting corrupt or unjust regimes in exchange for regional stability and access to oil resources—is regarded as the root of anti-American terrorism. For this interpretation as well, the spreading of democratic institutions and greater freedoms among the peoples of the Middle East and South Asia are regarded as the solutions to the problem of extremist-driven international terrorism.

Thus, the relationship between democracy and terrorism is important in understanding the sources of twenty-first–century terrorism for several reasons. First, many analysts have argued that the terrorism threat emanating from the Middle East and Persian Gulf region is a response to funneling political dissent into religious channels, which in turn have focused peoples' frustrations about the nature of their own regimes into violence directed against the United States. The argument is that if these regimes—for example, in Egypt and Saudi Arabia—were to permit greater mass political participation, dissent would have an outlet and the threat to the United States would diminish. American policies in the region, particularly those that help to perpetuate antidemocratic regimes, are blamed for the terrorist violence that erupts against the United States. Because helping to prop up corrupt Arab regimes, not to mention enabling the actions of the Israeli government against the Palestinians, is regarded as hypocritical by some, the United States becomes the target of rage. If American policy were aimed toward promoting democracies in the Arab world, including Palestinian democracy, the reasoning goes, the dual benefits would be a more just society for many Arab and Persian Muslims and an opportunity for dissent to vent itself in less destructive ways. This view is not confined to American observers; it is shared by many respected thinkers in the Arab world.[43]

The nature of the state has been an area of considerable recent research and controversy, particularly the question of correlations between democracy and terrorism. This issue has been a particular focus during the past decade, when interest in a democratic peace predominated in American security studies. Unfortunately, the weight of the available evidence, as presented in descriptive historical reviews and quantitative studies, leads to the disappointing and unexpected conclusion that terrorism has been more predominant in democratic states than in states with other types of regimes.[44] There are various mitigating factors, such as the extent to which information about terrorist attacks in authoritarian states may be less accessible to researchers.[45] It also is possible that the studies are skewed by episodes of left-wing and right-wing violence in Europe and the United States during the middle of the twentieth century. Nonetheless, the weight of the available evidence to date does not bear out the idealistic hopes of many people in the West that democracy leads to a reduction in terrorism.

An important distinction may be emerging between the location of attacks and the origins of the group. In twentieth-century case studies, groups responsible for terrorist attacks usually (with some exceptions) came from areas close to the location of the attack; that does not seem to be the trend today. Changes in the evolution of terrorism in the twenty-first century may lead to the conclusion that incidents of terrorism and sources of terrorism are diverging. Researchers do not know yet whether the existence of a democratic government will decrease or increase the incidence of attack against *other* territories. Much more research needs to be done on the relationship (if there is one) between terrorism and democracy. There certainly is no foundation in existing research for the belief that democracy and terrorism are incompatible or that encouraging the growth of democracy will necessarily reduce the terrorist threat.

The academic literature shows that the assumption that democratic regimes necessarily bring with them decreasing levels of terrorism is unsupported. Policy that flows simply from this assumption likewise may be flawed and may result in an exacerbation of the situation, at least from the perspective of counterterrorism.[46] As in many other issues, there may be other compelling and overriding concerns that rightfully should take precedence over counterterrorism. On this issue, unfortunately, what seems just and what serves the arguably narrow interests of counterterrorism may be completely at odds.

Level Four: The International System

Perhaps the most difficult level of analysis—but also the one at which the most sweeping recent hypotheses have been produced by international relations specialists and political scientists—is the role of the international system in the causes of twenty-first–century terrorism. There are many arguments put forth, and I do not present a comprehensive survey of all of them here; I consider three of the most notable, influential, and serious interpretations of the sources of terrorism at the fourth level of analysis.

No study of international systemic causes can avoid beginning with the influential argument put forth by Samuel Huntington in his 1993 *Foreign Affairs* article "The Clash of Civilizations" (and the later book by the same name).[47] Huntington's thesis is that there is a growing and fundamental cultural and ideological incompatibility between the Islamic world and the West and that the next great contest after the cold war will be a global confrontation between the forces of militant Islam and the model of modernity presented by the West. Especially after September 11, this perspective leads to the conclusion that the sources of threats such as that posed by al-Qaeda and its associated groups (sometimes referred to as the "international jihad") are fundamentally religious, cultural, and systemic. They reach beyond the nation-state and are better understood as an international ideological movement like twentieth-century Communism.

The relationship between terrorism and ideas is firmly established in modern international history. Indeed, arguably a distinguishing feature of modern terrorism has been the connection between sweeping political or ideological concepts and increasing levels of terrorist activity internationally. David Rapoport describes these broad "waves" in chapter 2 of this book. According to Rapoport, in the early modern era of terrorism—which dates to the French Revolution—broad international waves of terrorism were directed first against the power of monarchies; second against the power of colonial empires; and third in an international backlash against the American involvement in the Vietnam War. The question is whether the current era, characterized by what Rapoport calls "Fourth Wave" terrorism, is driven by a comparably sweeping international force and if so whether, as Huntington argues, that force is a radical internationalized form of Islam—or something else.

If the source of the current threat from international terrorism is primarily an international movement or ideology, the threat grows in its overall implications for the international community and the likelihood of successfully meeting the threat, especially in the short run, becomes significantly reduced. If Huntington's thesis is correct, that there is a clash of civilizations drawing to a culminating point, the prescription for meeting that challenge in the guise of terrorism is more likely to be use of traditional national and international tools of power to attack the source of the problem.

That "if" is extremely important, however. Some actions taken in response to this interpretation of the causes of international terrorism could seriously exacerbate other sources of the phenomenon, potentially bringing about the very clash that Huntington describes. It also is important to note, of course, that despite the natural tendency to focus on a certain type of terrorism in the wake of a major event, international terrorism that is completely unrelated to Islam continues to threaten thousands of innocent people in many parts of the world. Terrorism is a very long-established phenomenon. As Huntington probably would be the first to point out, many sources of international terrorism have nothing to do with a "clash of civilizations." The understandable ethnocentric bias of most American commentators in the wake of September 11 should not be allowed to skew the analytical integrity of efforts to understand sources of global terrorist behavior overall.

At the fourth level of analysis, the international system produces many familiar political motivations that defy state boundaries, such as extreme ideologies (e.g., Marxism, which has inspired left-wing groups such as the Red Army Faction and Sendero Luminoso), alternative viewpoints about state authority and make-up (e.g., fascism, which has inspired right-wing neo-Nazi groups, Aryan Nations, and followers of the Christian Identity movement), and clashes over control of territory (e.g., nationalism, which has driven ethnonationalist/separatist groups such as the Palestine Liberation Organization, the Tamil Tigers, or the Irish Republican Army). Although the number of right-wing and left-wing groups has declined somewhat in recent years, these political motivations have not gone away—especially not the fractionating compulsions of ethnonationalist/separatist groups, many of which reached new levels of activity after the cold war ended.

Like most forms of political violence in the international system, terrorism may arise from shifts in the broader organizing principles of humankind, including both the evolution and the devolution of modern secular states, not to mention the theoretical attractions of alternative models of governance. The sources of international terrorism are more diverse and complex than any one culture or religion. In any case, if there is a clash of civilizations—or if one is in the process of developing, in part as a result of the widely cited hypothesis—it potentially gives us insight into only one level of analysis and is, of course, not the exclusive cause of international terrorism even in the Arab world.

Martha Crenshaw has argued that recent acts of terrorism are the result of the expansion of civil war to the international system. She considers the increasing susceptibility of the United States to international terrorism to be a result of its engagement abroad and the attacks on U.S. interests to be efforts to achieve radical political change within other states. Crenshaw regards terrorism such as that which occurred on September 11, 2001, as a "strategic reaction to American power in the context of globalized civil war."[48]

If Crenshaw is correct, the projection of domestic civil conflict through international terrorism is not just an American problem; it may be a systemic challenge for the international community. Particularly in an age of increasing global links, the far-flung projection of localized conflicts has serious implications. It raises the specter of a broad and destabilizing generalization of grievances that previously were contained within the affected territories or regions and directed toward the governance of indigenous or contiguous states. International links among terrorist groups are not new, and projections of attacks to distant places (especially Europe) also have a long history; a growing preponderance of a tendency to "internationalize" local grievances through the use of terrorism may be an emerging pattern, however.

This hypothesis has interesting implications for counterterrorism responses. If localized grievances within states are erupting into systemic challenges, the system itself must devise a means to respond to the broader implications of terrorist threats that in the past were within the purview of the state. In a sense, then, the lenses of analysis here must be employed in reverse, with threats to the system being met with systemic responses that cross over into the sovereign province of the state. Threats that cross state boundaries may be newly threatening, requiring unprecedented coordination within the international community to meet them.[49]

Another, related interpretation of sources of terrorism through the fourth analytical lens is the view that it is a reaction to the international forces of globalization. "Globalization" is an overly popularized, vague, and often sloppily used term; for the present purpose, it means a gradually expanding process of international interpenetration in the economic, political, social, and security realms, uncontrolled by (or apart from) traditional notions of state sovereignty.[50] In this perspective, globalization in forms including Westernization, secularization, democratization, consumerism, and the growth of market capitalism is a challenge to conservative cultures that resist the changes these forces entail—or at least the distortions and inequalities that they inevitably bring. The current phenomenon of anti-American terrorism therefore is explained mainly as an international response to American-led globalization.[51]

According to this hypothesis, contemporary international terrorism is both a reaction to globalization—with new objectives defined as a result—and facilitated by globalization, with new avenues of coordinating and carrying out attacks. In other words, both the ends and the means of modern international terrorism arguably are affected by this systemic phenomenon. The *means* include the use of new technologies, the unprecedented movement of terrorist groups across international boundaries, and changes in sources of support from mostly indigenous populations to more broadly diverse international backers. According to this view, anti-Americanism is closely related to antiglobalization because (intentionally or not) the primary driver of the powerful forces resulting in globalization is the United States. The *ends* mainly include attacks on the United States, leader of the unipolar system, as well as other symbols of Western-style modernization.

This hypothesis focuses on the currency of traditional realist interpretations of international relations—power—but sees its gradual devolution from the control of the state as portending more acts of violence like terrorism, a clear challenge to the state's monopoly on the use of force. Terrorism is a byproduct of broader historical shifts in the international distribution of power in all of its forms—political, economic, military, ideological, and cultural—the same forms of power characterizing the forces of western-led globalization. At times of dramatic international change, human beings (especially those not benefiting from the change—or not benefiting as much or as rapidly from the change) grasp for alternative means to control and understand their environments. If current trends continue, widening global disparities, coupled with burgeoning information and connectivity, are likely to accelerate well into the twenty-first century—unless the terrorist backlash, increasingly taking its inspiration from radical misoneistic religious or pseudoreligious concepts, successfully counters these trends.

Like the civil wars hypothesis, this theory requires international, coordinated responses aimed at preventing the mutation of threats through new territorial or technological means. Globalization of terrorism also must be met with a systemic response, using the avenues of globalization against the terrorist exploiters of those channels.

Many scholars recently have pointed to a connection between globalization and terrorism in a changing international system, but the relationship is still very imperfectly understood. A tremendous amount of analytical research remains to be done on the fourth level of analysis to substantiate or disprove the many hypotheses that have been put forth. It is a particularly underdeveloped body of research in part because—as Martha Crenshaw points out in chapter 3—there has been a general lack of overlap between the fields of terrorism studies and international relations. The distinctive perspectives and modes of research engaged in by scholars in each of those disciplines have led most to rely on the familiar perspectives and long-established arguments that are prevalent in each field. Overreliance on fourth-level analyses, to the exclusion of detailed understanding of the other analytical frameworks, is one of the results.

Conclusion

Studying the levels of analyses employed in evaluating sources of international terrorism leads to the obvious conclusion that it is crucial to be aware of all four. In trying to determine the causes of terrorism, it is best to be as comprehensive as possible to avoid skewing the conclusions reached about policy options to use in counterterrorism. That conclusion is logical in any such intellectual exercise because complexity is virtually always more reflective of the world as it exists than is oversimplification. The observation is more compelling than ever in the very complicated, untidy, interdisciplinary realm of international terrorism.

There is more to consider, however. There is clear evidence that past dependence on limited analytical frameworks regarding the sources of terrorism has had and will continue to have real-world effects on the debates over policy choices in the current campaign against international terrorism. I cite many examples in this chapter, but a few leap to mind. Within the first level of analysis, for example, overreliance on the belief that the goal must be to capture Osama bin Laden to neutralize the threat slights other factors such as the strength of the organization and the potential for adverse reactions by potential recruits (level two). The best policy recognizes that even such an apparent success would have its disadvantages and prepares to offset them. On the second level of analysis, counterterrorism policy sometimes fails to take into account the belief structure that may prevail in a terrorist group—a worldview that may be fed, for example, by military operations that reinforce the perception that the group is in a fight for survival. Planning military operations in conjunction with other policy tools, such as public diplomacy and foreign aid, that may be more effective at undermining group cohesion therefore is essential. These nonmilitary tools should not be afterthoughts. On the third level of analysis, the focus on the role of the state in sponsoring terrorism may blind policymakers to the dispersed nature of the al-Qaeda organization and its relative autonomy with respect to the traditional territorial, financial, and logistical resources of the state. There is a danger that directing attacks against actual or potential state sponsors in an effort to undermine international terrorism may be driven by a narrow, anachronistic image that is not relevant to new twenty-first–century terrorist organizations. On the fourth level of analysis, some sweeping assertions about factors such as international globalization and culture clashes may obscure more than they clarify with respect to the sources of contemporary terrorism. Policymaking on the basis of unproven assertions about the global causes of international terrorism is particularly unwise and risks being more ideological than analytical. Terrorism research at this level is still at an embryonic stage and sometimes is ignorant of conclusions reached at other levels of analysis where longstanding terrorism experts traditionally have focused more attention.

Terrorism is an extremely complex phenomenon whose causes seem almost uniquely subject to oversimplified passionate interpretation, especially after a tragic event. Although much more work remains to be done, it is important to take advantage of the important and helpful research that has been carried out on all four levels of analysis described here. Knowledge derived from this research can make the responses of the United States and its allies much more likely to succeed over time. It is crucial not to sample selectively from the conclusions reached regarding terrorism but to examine and help build the whole body of research to determine which lessons are applicable across case studies and which are not. The best approach is consciously to reach across conceptual, disciplinary, cultural, and sometimes even ideological divisions to base policy choices in counterterrorism on the optimal objective analysis of the sources of international terrorism.

Notes

1. See, for example, Elaine Sciolino, "Who Hates the U.S.? Who Loves It?" *New York Times*, 23 September 2001; Anthony Lewis, "Abroad at Home: The Inescapable World," *New York Times*, 20 October 2001; Gordon Brown, "Marshall Plan for the Next 50 Years," *Washington Post*, 17 December 2001; "Getting the Brains Behind Bin Ladin," *Washington Post*, 14 November 2001; Eric Holder, Jr., "Keeping Guns Away from Terrorists," *Washington Post*, 25 October 2001; "Poverty and Terror," *Washington Post*, 5 October 2001; "Broaden the War

Plan," *Washington Post*, 3 October 2001; William Raspberry, "Terrorism's Fertile Fields," *Washington Post*, 1 October 2001; Charles Krauthammer, "The War: A Road Map," *Washington Post*, 28 September 2001; Ron K. Noble, "Invest in Global Policing," *New York Times*, 15 September 2001; and David M. Kennedy, "Fighting an Elusive Enemy," *New York Times*, 16 September 2001. See also Daniel Goleman, "The Roots of Terrorism Are Found in Brutality of Shattered Childhood," *New York Times*, 2 September 1986; Daniel Pipes, "God and Mammon: Does Poverty Cause Militant Islam?" *National Interest* no. 66 (winter 2001/2002): 14–21; and Gary T. Dempsey, "Old Folly in a New Disguise: Nation Building to Combat Terrorism," *Policy Analysis* no. 429, 21 March 2002.

2. Before September 11, 2001, the deadliest terrorist attack against Americans had been the truck bombing of the Marine barracks in Beirut, Lebanon, in 1983 (241 killed). The casualties of September 11 also far outstrip what had been the costliest terrorist attack ever recorded: On August 20, 1978, Islamic extremists set fire to a cinema in Abadan, Iran, killing 477 people. See Richard A. Falkenrath, "Analytic Models and Policy Prescription: Understanding Recent Innovation in U.S. Counterterrorism," *BCSIA Discussion Paper 2000-31, ESDP Discussion Paper ESDP-2000-03*, John F. Kennedy School of Government, Harvard University, October 2000. In fact, the September 11 attacks killed almost three times more Americans than the combined total of terrorist casualties since 1968.

3. The definition of terrorism I use here is "the sudden use or threat of use of violence by a nonstate actor against innocents for political ends." For further explanation, see Audrey Kurth Cronin, "Rethinking Sovereignty: American Strategy in the Age of Terrorism," *Survival* 44, no. 2 (summer 2002): 121–22. On the causes of terrorism, some of the best sources are Martha Crenshaw, "The Causes of Terrorism," *Comparative Politics* (July 1981): 379–400, and Walter Reich (ed.), *Origins of Terrorism: Psychologies, Ideologies, Theologies, States of Mind* (Washington, D.C.: Woodrow Wilson Center Press, 1998); in the latter, see particularly Martha Crenshaw, "The Logic of Terrorism: Terrorist Behavior as a Product of Strategic Choice," Jerrold M. Post, "Terrorist Psycho-Logic: Terrorist Behavior as a Product of Psychological Forces," and Ehud Sprinzak, "The Psychological Formation of Extreme Left Terrorism in a Democracy: The Case of the Weathermen."

4. Crenshaw, "The Causes of Terrorism," 379.

5. Martha Crenshaw, "Introduction: Thoughts on Relating Terrorism to Historical Contexts," *Terrorism in Context* (University Park: Pennsylvania State University Press, 1995), 3–7.

6. For example, see Walter Laqueur, "Interpretations of Terrorism: Fact, Fiction and Political Science," *Journal of Contemporary History* 12 (1977): 1–42, and Walter Laqueur, *The New Terrorism: Fanaticism and the Arms of Mass Destruction* (New York: Oxford University Press, 2000), 79–80.

7. Crenshaw, *Terrorism in Context*, 4–5.

8. For example, see Mark Juergensmeyer, *Terror in the Mind of God: The Global Rise of Religious Violence* (Berkeley: University of California Press, 2001), on the causes of terrorism motivated by religion; Daniel Byman, "The Logic of Ethnic Terrorism," *Studies in Conflict and Terrorism* 21, no. 2 (April–June 1998): 149–70, on ethnonationalist terrorism; Konrad Kellen, "Ideology and Rebellion: Terrorism in West Germany," in Reich, *Origins of Terrorism*, for one look at left-wing terrorism; and Leonard Weinberg, "On Responding to Right-Wing Terrorism," *Terrorism and Political Violence* 8, no. 1 (spring 1996): 80–92, on right-wing terrorism. For good overviews of the typologies of terrorism, see Bruce Hoffman, *Inside Terrorism* (New York: Columbia University Press, 1998); Paul Wilkinson, *Terrorism vs. Democracy: The Liberal State Response* (Portland, Ore.: Frank Cass, 2000); and Laqueur, *The New Terrorism*.

9. I am indebted to Martha Crenshaw for this observation.

10. President George W. Bush said of al-Qaeda, "We have no intention of ignoring or appeasing history's latest gang of fanatics trying to murder their way to power." George W. Bush, "President's Address to the Nation," U.S. Department of State International Information Pro-

grams, 11 September 2002; available at http://usinfo.state.gov/911/02091151.htm. Bush also said, "I'm particularly sad today because of American families who cry today and weep at the loss of a loved one, because there's some fanatic who believes that killing innocent life is positive." George W. Bush, "Remarks by the President and His Majesty King Abdullah of the Hashemite Kingdom of Jordan in Photo Opportunity The Oval Office," White House Office of the Press Secretary, 1 August, 2002; available at www.whitehouse.gov/news/releases/2002/08/20020801-2.html. Reagan said of the terrorists responsible for the 1983 bombing of the Marine Barracks in Beirut, Lebanon, "They are possessed by a fanatical intensity that individuals of a democratic society can only barely comprehend." Ronald Reagan, "Remarks and a Question-and-Answer Session with Reporters on the Pentagon Report on the Security of the United States Marines in Lebanon," *Public Papers of the President,* 27 December 1983, 1748. Reagan characterized terrorists as "the strangest collection of misfits, looney tunes, and squalid criminals since the advent of the Third Reich." Ronald Reagan, "American Bar Association," *Weekly Compilation of Presidential Documents*, 8 July 1985, 881. Reagan also said terrorists were "irrational" and "flaky" "zealots" who exhibited "fanatical hatred." Ronald Reagan, "President's News Conference of January 7, 1986," *Weekly Compilation of Presidential Documents*, 7 January 1986, 26.

Furthermore, here is a statement by a respected Arab academic in this vein: "'Terrorists don't know the methods of rational, calm debate . . . terrorists impose darkness on the climate of the intellect because they try to force their backward ideas on public opinion under the veil of religious correctness,' [Nabil Luka] Bibawi wrote. 'They construe religious thought to suit their political objectives to reach power. He accused such extremists of disfiguring religious tolerance with insane acts. It seems that bin Laden has become a revolutionary in a world of his own imagination. He would not hesitate to break any taboo. How did he come to create this fantasyland of terror?'" See Nora Boustany, "Bin Laden Now a Target in Arab Media; Criticism Emerges as Scholars Emphasize Distance from 'Distortion of Religion,'" *Washington Post*, 23 November 2001, A31. See also the following: "We must now fight a war against terrorists who are crazy and evil but who, it grieves me to say, reflect the mood in their home countries more than we might think"; Thomas L. Friedman, "Hama Rules," *New York Times*, 21 September 2001, 35.

11. For an extremely helpful explanation of much of the literature and the areas of needed future research, see Martha Crenshaw, "The Psychology of Terrorism: An Agenda for the Twenty-first Century," *Political Psychology* 21, no. 2 (June 2000): 405–20.

12. The classic source on this is the debate between Martha Crenshaw and Jerrold Post in *Origins of Terrorism*, edited by Walter Reich. See Crenshaw, "The Logic of Terrorism," and Post, "Terrorist Psycho-Logic," chapters 1 and 2 in Reich, *Origins of Terrorism*, 7–40. Also see Goleman, "Roots of Terrorism."

13. For more on the phenomenon of suicide terrorism, see Ehud Sprinzak, "Rational Fanatics," *Foreign Policy* (September–October 2000), 66–73; Harvey W. Kushner, "Suicide Bombers: Business as Usual," *Studies in Conflict and Terrorism* 19 (1996): 329–37; Ariel Merari, "The Readiness to Kill and Die," in Reich, *Origins of Terrorism*; Raphael Israeli, "Islamikaze and Their Significance," *Terrorism and Political Violence* 9, no. 3 (autumn 1997): 96–121; and Tovah Lazaroff, "Experts: Suicide Bombers Not Crazy," *Jerusalem Post*, 27 May 2002, 3.

14. Crenshaw, "Psychology of Terrorism," 407–11.

15. See Post, "Terrorist Psycho-Logic;" Kellen, "Ideology and Rebellion," and Merari, "The Readiness to Kill and Die," as well as other chapters in Reich, *Origins of Terrorism*.

16. Charles A. Russell and Bowman H. Miller, "Profile of a Terrorist," in *Perspectives on Terrorism*, ed. by Lawrence Zelic Freedman and Yonah Alexander (Wilmington, Del.: Scholarly Resources, Inc., 1993) (revised version of their article in *Terrorism: An International Journal* 1, no. 1 [1977]: 17–34); cited by Robin Morgan, *The Demon Lover: The Roots of Terrorism* (New York: Pocket Books, 1989, 2d ed., 2001), 63–65.

17. Jerrold Post, "Killing in the Name of God: Bin Laden and Radical Islam," *Foreign Service Journal* (December 2001), 31–33. Also see Pipes, "God and Mammon."

18. See, for example, Merari, "The Readiness to Kill and Die"; and Kushner, "Suicide Bombers: Business as Usual."

19. See the interesting study by Alan Krueger and Jitka Maleckova, "Education, Poverty, Political Violence and Terrorism: Is There a Causal Connection?" unpublished paper, May 2002. It looks at Hezbollah in the late 1980s and early 1990s and Jewish settlers who engaged in violence against Palestinians on the West Bank in the early 1980s.

20. Krueger and Maleckova, "Education, Poverty, Political Violence and Terrorism," 2; Pipes, "God and Mamon," 14; and Gary T. Dempsey, "Old Folly in a New Disguise: Nation Building to Combat Terrorism," *Policy Analysis* no. 429 (21 March 2002).

21. Jessica Stern, "Pakistan's Jihad Culture," *Foreign Affairs* (November/December 2000); Peter Bergen, *Holy War, Inc.: Inside the Secret World of Osama Bin Laden* (New York: Free Press, 2001).

22. Peter A. Lupsha, "Explanation of Political Violence: Some Psychological Theories Versus Indignation," *Politics and Society* 2, no. 1 (fall 1971): 89–104.

23. Luigi Bonanate, "Some Unanticipated Consequences of Terrorism," *Journal of Peace Research* 16, no. 3 (1979): 197–211; and Pipes, "God and Mamon." Pipes refers to an argument by Martin Kramer (no formal citation is provided).

24. See, for example, Magnus Ranstorp, "Hizbollah's Command Leadership [in Lebanon]: Its Structure, Decision-Making and Relationship with Iranian Clergy and Institutions," *Terrorism and Political Violence* 6, no. 3 (autumn 1994): 303–99; Leonard Weinberg and William Lee Eubank, "Leaders and Followers in Italian Terrorist Groups," *Terrorism and Political Violence* 1, no. 2 (April 1989): 156–76; John Horgan and Max Taylor, "The Provisional Irish Republican Army: Command and Functional Structure," *Terrorism and Political Violence* 9, no. 3 (autumn 1997): 1–32; and Joel Garreau, "Disconnecting the Dots," *Washington Post*, 17 September 2001.

25. See, for example, Bergen, *Holy War, Inc.*; and Simon Reeve, *The New Jackals: Ramzi Yousef, Osama bin Laden, and the Future of Terrorism* (Boston: Northeastern University Press, 1999).

26. Crenshaw, "The Psychology of Terrorism," 409.

27. Albert Bandura, "Mechanisms of Moral Disengagement," in *Origins of Terrorism*, 161–91.

28. According to Peter Bergen, *Holy War, Inc.*, 125–26, "The attacks . . . had a major unintended consequence: They turned bin Laden from a marginal figure in the Muslim world into a global celebrity. When I visited Pakistan a couple of weeks after the U.S. strikes, two instant biographies about bin Laden were already on sale in the bookshops of Islamabad. Osama is now a common name for newly born sons in Pakistan. Maulana Sami ul-Haq, a corpulent cleric who runs what is probably Pakistan's largest religious academy, explained that the strikes had made bin Laden 'a symbol for the whole Islamic world. Against all those outside powers who were trying to crush Muslims. He is the courageous one who raised his voice against them. He's a hero to us, but it is America that first made him a hero.'"

29. Crenshaw, "The Psychology of Terrorism," 413–14.

30. Martha Crenshaw, "Theories of Terrorism: Instrumental and Organizational Approaches," in *Inside Terrorist Organizations*, 2d ed., ed. David C. Rapoport (London: Frank Cass, 2001), 19–27.

31. Ian Lesser et al., *Countering the New Terrorism* (Santa Monica, Calif.: RAND, 1999); John Arquilla and David Ronfeldt (eds.), *Networks and Netwars* (Santa Monica, Calif.: RAND, 2001); and Rapoport, *Inside Terrorist Organizations*.

32. Crenshaw, "Causes of Terrorism," 382–85.

33. Clandestine state use of foreign terrorist organizations dates from at least the 1920s, when the Mussolini government in Italy aided the Croat Ustasha, for example.

34. Hoffman, *Inside Terrorism*, 186.

35. Ibid., 189. See also Neil C. Livingston and Terrell E. Arnold (eds.), *Fighting Back: Winning the War against Terrorism* (Lexington, Mass.: Lexington Books, 1986), 12.

36. For an excellent and more lengthy explanation of the role of states and the implications of being on the list, see Paul Pillar, *Terrorism and U.S. Foreign Policy* (Washington, D.C.: Brookings Institution, 2001), chap. 6.

37. This argument is made in more detail in Audrey Kurth Cronin, "Rethinking Sovereignty: American Strategy in the Age of Terrorism," *Survival* 44, no. 2 (summer 2002): 119–39.

38. There are many books and articles published on this issue. Among the best are Juergensmeyer, *Terror in the Mind of God*; Jessica Stern, *The Ultimate Terrorist* (Cambridge, Mass.: Harvard University Press, 1999); and Richard Falkenrath, Robert D. Newman, and Bradley A. Thayer, *America's Achilles' Heel: Nuclear, Biological, and Chemical Terrorism and Covert Attack* (Cambridge, Mass.: MIT Press, 1998).

39. Steve Simon and Daniel Benjamin, "The Terror," *Survival* 43, no. 4 (winter 2001–2002): 10.

40. Afghanistan was the subject of Executive Order 13129, which imposed sanctions on the Taliban, but it was never on the state sponsors list because the United States did not recognize the Taliban as a government. See Pillar, *Terrorism and U.S. Foreign Policy*, 158–59. Of course, this fact underlines the very problem that we are grappling with: how to respond to dangerous nonstate actors using traditionally state-oriented tools.

41. Mary Pat Flaherty, David B. Ottaway, and James V. Grimaldi, "How Afghanistan Went Unlisted as Terrorist Sponsor," *Washington Post*, 5 November 2001, A1. The list has never been very logical or complete and has always reflected other foreign policy priorities. For example, in 1986 the list did not include Nicaragua—despite its sponsorship of antigovernment rebels in El Salvador, Honduras, and Costa Rica—or the Eastern European Soviet satellites Bulgaria, East Germany, and Czechoslovakia, which were actively transferring weapons and training terrorists, nor even the Soviet Union, whose support for international terrorism was well-established. See Neil C. Livingstone and Terrell E. Arnold, "The Rise of State-Sponsored Terrorism," in *Fighting Back*, 20–21.

42. This argument is more developed in Cronin, "Rethinking Sovereignty."

43. See David Kibble, "Monarchs, Mosques, and Military Hardware: A Pragmatic Approach to the Promotion of Human Rights and Democracy in the Middle East," *Comparative Strategy* 17 no. 4 (1998): 381–91; Richard Murphy and Gregory Gause III, "Democracy and U.S. Policy in the Muslim Middle East," *Middle East Policy* 5, no. 1 (January 1997): 58–67; Gawdat Bahgat, "Democracy in the Middle East: The American Connection," *Studies in Conflict and Terrorism* 17, no. 1 (January–March 1994): 87–96.

44. Simon and Benjamin, "The Terror," 13; William Lee Eubank and Leonard Weinberg, "Does Democracy Encourage Terrorism?" *Terrorism and Political Violence* 6, no. 4 (winter 1994): 417–35; and responses to Eubank and Weinberg's article by Abraham H. Miller, Christopher Hewitt, and the authors themselves, pp. 435–43.

45. Alex Schmid, "Terrorism and Democracy," *Terrorism and Political Violence* 4, no. 4 (winter 1992): 14–25.

46. Moreover, the assumption that democracies would emerge in Egypt and Saudi Arabia if there were regime changes is highly dubious. If the authoritarian regimes lost power, it is just as likely that they would be replaced by religious fundamentalist governments. See Simon and Benjamin, "The Terror," 13.

47. See Samuel Huntington, "The Clash of Civilizations?" *Foreign Affairs* 72, no. 3 (summer 1993): 22–49; and idem, *The Clash of Civilizations and the Remaking of World Order* (New York: Simon and Schuster, 1996).

48. Martha Crenshaw, "Why America? The Globalization of Civil War," *Current History* (December 2001): 425–32.

49. Some might even argue that this threat emerging from globalized civil wars requires an unprecedentedly conscious organization of the international community in response. Historically, however, mention of "global governments" has engendered its own violent political backlash in response—for example, on the part of right-wing groups in the United States such as the National Alliance.

50. Victor D. Cha, "Globalization and the Study of International Security," *Journal of Peace Research* 37, no. 3 (2000): 391–93. I am indebted to him for this definition.

51. For more on this argument, see Audrey Kurth Cronin, "Behind the Curve: Globalization and International Terrorism," *International Security* 27, no. 3 (winter 2002/2003): 30–58.

two

THE FOUR WAVES OF MODERN TERRORISM

David C. Rapoport

September 11, 2001, is the most destructive day in the long, bloody history of terrorism. The casualties, economic damage, and outrage were unprecedented. It could turn out to be the most important day too, because it led President Bush to declare a "war (that) would not end until every terrorist group of global reach has been found, stopped, and defeated."[1]

However unprecedented September 11 was, President Bush's declaration was not altogether unique. Exactly 100 years ago, when an anarchist assassinated President William McKinley in September 1901, his successor Theodore Roosevelt called for a crusade to exterminate terrorism everywhere.[2]

No one knows if the current campaign will be more successful than its predecessors, but we can more fully appreciate the difficulties ahead by examining features of the history of rebel (nonstate) terror. That history shows how deeply implanted terrorism is in our culture, provides parallels worth pondering, and offers a perspective for understanding the uniqueness of September 11 and its aftermath.[3] To this end, in this chapter I examine the course of modern terror from its initial appearance 125 years ago; I emphasize continuities and change, particularly with respect to international ingredients.[4]

The Wave Phenomena

Modern terror began in Russia in the 1880s and within a decade appeared in Western Europe, the Balkans, and Asia. A generation later the wave was completed. Anarchists initiated the wave, and their primary strategy—assassination campaigns against prominent officials—was adopted by virtually all the other groups of the time, even those with nationalist aims in the Balkans and India.

Significant examples of secular rebel terror existed earlier, but they were specific to a particular time and country. The Ku Klux Klan (KKK), for example, made a striking contribution to the decision of the federal government to end Reconstruction, but the KKK had no contemporary parallels or emulators.[5]

The "Anarchist wave" was the first global or truly international terrorist experience in history;[6] three similar, consecutive, and overlapping expressions followed. The "anticolonial wave" began in the 1920s and lasted about forty years. Then came the "New Left wave," which diminished greatly as the twentieth century closed, leaving only a few groups still active today in Nepal, Spain, the United Kingdom, Peru, and Colombia. In 1979 a "religious wave" emerged; if the pattern of its three predecessors is relevant it could disappear by 2025, at which time a new wave might emerge.[7] The uniqueness and persistence of the wave experience indicates that terror is deeply rooted in modern culture.

The wave concept—an unfamiliar notion—is worth more attention. Academics focus on organizations, and there are good reasons for this orientation. Organizations launch terror campaigns, and governments are always primarily concerned to disable those organizations.[8] Students of terrorism also focus unduly on contemporary events, which makes us less sensitive to waves because the life cycle of a wave lasts at least a generation.[9]

What is a wave? It is a cycle of activity in a given time period—a cycle characterized by expansion and contraction phases. A crucial feature is its international character; similar activities occur in several countries, driven by a common predominant energy that shapes the participating groups' characteristics and mutual relationships. As their names—"Anarchist," "anticolonial," "New Left," and "Religious"—suggest, a different energy drives each.

Each wave's name reflects its dominant but not its only feature. Nationalist organizations in various numbers appear in all waves, for example, and each wave shaped its national elements differently. The Anarchists gave them tactics and often training. Third-wave nationalist groups displayed profoundly left-wing aspirations, and nationalism serves or reacts to religious purposes in the fourth wave. All groups in the second wave had nationalist aspirations, but the wave is termed anticolonial because the resisting states were powers that had become ambivalent about retaining their colonial status. That ambivalence explains why the wave produced the first terrorist successes. In other waves, that ambivalence is absent or very weak, and no nationalist struggle has succeeded.

A wave is composed of organizations, but waves and organizations have very different life rhythms. Normally, organizations disappear before the initial wave associated with them does. New Left organizations were particularly striking in this respect—typically lasting two years. Nonetheless, the wave retained sufficient energy to create a generation of successor or new groups. When a wave's energy cannot inspire new organizations, the wave disappears. Resistance, political concessions, and changes in the perceptions of generations are critical factors in explaining the disappearance.

Occasionally an organization survives its original wave. The Irish Republican Army (IRA), for example, is the oldest modern terrorist organization—emerging first in 1916, though not as a terror organization.[10] It then fought five campaigns in two successive waves (the fourth struggle, in the 1950s, used guerrilla tactics).[11] At least two offshoots—the Real IRA and Continuity IRA—are still active. The Palestine Liberation Organization (PLO), founded in 1964, became active in 1967. When the Viet Cong faded into history, the international connections and activity of the PLO made it the preeminent body of the New Left wave, although the PLO pursued largely nationalist ends. More recently, elements of the PLO (e.g., Fatah) have become active in the fourth wave, even though the organization initially was wholly secular. When an organization transcends a wave, it reflects the new wave's influence—a change that may pose special problems for the group and its constituencies, as we shall see.

The first three waves lasted about a generation each—a suggestive time frame closest in duration to that of a human life cycle, in which dreams inspiring parents lose their attractiveness for children.[12] Although the resistance of those attacked is crucial in explaining why terror organizations rarely succeed, the time span of the wave also suggests that the wave has its own momentum. Over time there are fewer organizations because the enterprise's problematic nature becomes more visible. The pattern is familiar to students of revolutionary states such as France, the Soviet Union, and Iran. The inheritors of the revolution do not value it in the same way its creators did. In the anticolonial wave, the process also seems relevant to the colonial powers. A new generation found it much easier to discard the colonial idea. The wave pattern calls one's attention to crucial political themes in the general culture—themes that distinguish the ethos of one generation from another.

There are many reasons the first wave occurred when it did, but two critical factors are conspicuous and facilitated successive waves. The first was the transformation in communication and transportation patterns. The tele-graph, daily mass newspapers, and railroads flourished during the last quar-ter of the nineteenth century. Events in one country were known elsewhere in a day or so. Prominent Russian anarchists traveled extensively, helping to inspire sympathies and groups elsewhere; sometimes, as the journeys of Peter Prodhoun indicate, they had more influence abroad than at home. Mass transportation made large-scale emigrations possible and created diaspora communities, which then became significant in the politics of both their "new" and "old" countries. Subsequent innovations continued to shrink time and space.

A second factor contributing to the emergence of the first wave was doc-trine or culture. Russian writers created a strategy for terror, which became an inheritance for successors to use, improve, and transmit. Sergei Nechaev was the leading figure in this effort; Nicholas Mozorov, Peter Kropotkin, Serge Stepniak, and others also made contributions.[13] Their efforts perpetu-ated the wave. The KKK had no emulators partly because it made no effort to explain its tactics. The Russian achievement becomes even more striking when we compare it to the practices of the ancient religious terrorists who always stayed within their own religious tradition—the source of their jus-tifications and binding precedents. Each religious tradition produced its own kind of terrorist, and sometimes the tactics within a tradition were so uni-form that they appear to be a form of religious ritual.[14]

A comparison of Nechaev's *Revolutionary Catechism* with Osama bin Laden's training manual, *Military Studies in the Jihad Against the Tyrants,* shows that they share one very significant feature: a paramount desire to be-come more *efficient* by learning from the experiences of friends and enemies alike.[15] The major difference in this respect is the role of women. Nechaev considers them "priceless assets," and indeed they were crucial leaders and participants in the first wave. Bin Laden dedicates his book to protecting the Muslim woman, but he ignores what experience can tell us about female ter-rorists.[16] Women do not participate in his forces and are virtually excluded in the fourth wave, except in Sri Lanka.

Each wave produces major technical works that reflect the special prop-erties of that wave and contribute to a common modern effort to formulate a "science" of terror. Between Nechaev and bin Laden there were Georges Grivas, *Guerrilla War,* and Carlos Marighella, *Mini-Manual of the Urban Guerrilla,* in the second and third waves, respectively.

"Revolution" is the overriding aim in every wave, but revolution is un-derstood in different ways.[17] Revolutionaries create a new source of political legitimacy, and more often than not that meant national self-determination. The anticolonial wave was dominated by this quest. The principle that a people should govern itself was bequeathed by the American and French revolutions. (The French Revolution also introduced the term *terror* to our vocabulary.)[18] Because the definition of "the people" has never been (and perhaps never can be) clear and fixed, however, it is a source of recurring conflict even when the sanctity of the principle is accepted everywhere. Revolution also can mean a radical reconstruction of authority to eliminate all forms of equality—a cardinal theme in the first wave and a significant one in the third wave. Fourth-wave groups use a variety of sacred texts or revelations for legitimacy.

This chapter treats the great events precipitating each wave and the aims and tactics of participating groups. The focus, however, is the international scene. I examine the interactions of the five principal actors: terrorist organizations; diaspora populations; states; sympathetic foreign publics; and, beginning with the second wave, supranational organizations.[19]

First Wave: Creation of a Doctrine

The creators of modern terrorism inherited a world in which traditional revolutionaries, who depended on pamphlets and leaflets to generate an uprising, suddenly seemed obsolete. The masses, Nechaev said, regarded them as "idle word-spillers."[20] A new form of communication (Peter Kropotkin named it "Propaganda by the Deed") was needed—one that would be heard and would command respect because the rebel took action that involved serious personal risks that signified deep commitment.

The anarchist analysis of modern society contained four major points. It noted that society had huge reservoirs of latent ambivalence and hostility and that the conventions society devised to muffle and diffuse antagonisms generated guilt and provided channels for settling grievances and securing personal amenities. By demonstrating that these conventions were simple historical creations, however, acts once declared immoral would be hailed by later generations as noble efforts to liberate humanity. In this view, terror was thought to be the quickest and most effective means to destroy conventions. By this reasoning, the perpetrators freed themselves from the paralyzing grip of guilt to become different kinds of people. They forced those who defended the government to respond in ways that undermined the rules the latter claimed to respect.[21] Dramatic action repeated again and again invariably would polarize the society, and the revolution inevitably would follow—or so the anarchists reasoned.

An incident that inspired the turbulent decades to follow illustrates the process. On January 24, 1878, Vera Zasulich wounded a Russian police commander who abused political prisoners. Throwing her weapon to the floor, she proclaimed that she was a "terrorist, *not* a killer."[22] The ensuing trial quickly became that of the police chief. When the court freed her, crowds greeted the verdict with thunderous applause.[23]

A successful campaign entailed learning how to fight and how to die, and the most admirable death occurred as a result of a court trial in which one accepted responsibility and used the occasion to indict the regime. Stepniak, a major figure in the history of Russian terrorism, described the Russian terrorist as "noble, terrible, irresistibly fascinating, uniting the two sublimities of human grandeur, the martyr and the hero."[24] Dynamite—a recent invention—was the weapon of choice because the assailant usually was killed too, so it was not a weapon a criminal would use.[25]

Terror was violence beyond the moral conventions used to regulate violence: the rules of war and punishment. The former distinguishes combatants from noncombatants, and the latter separates the guilty from the innocent. Invariably, most onlookers would label acts of terror atrocities or outrages. The rebels described themselves as terrorists, not guerrillas, tracing their lineage to the French Revolution. They sought political targets or those that could affect public attitudes.[26] Terrorism was a strategy, not an end. The tactics used depended upon the group's political objective and on the specific context faced. Judging a context constantly in flux was both an art and a science.

The creators of this strategy took confidence from contemporary events. In the Russian case, as well as in all subsequent ones, major unexpected political events dramatized new government vulnerabilities. Hope was excited, and hope is always an indispensable lubricant of rebel activity.[27] The turn of events that suggested Russian vulnerability was the dazzling effort of the young Czar Alexander II to transform the system virtually overnight. In one stroke of the pen (1861) he freed the serfs (one-third of the population) and promised them funds to buy their land. Three years later he established limited local self-government, "westernized" the judicial system, abolished capital punishment, and relaxed censorship powers and control over education. Hopes were aroused but could not be fulfilled quickly enough, as indicated by the fact that the funds available for the serfs to buy land were insufficient. In the wake of inevitable disappointments, systematic assassination strikes against prominent officials began—culminating in the death of Alexander himself.

Russian rebels encouraged and trained other groups, even those with different political aims. Their efforts bore fruit quickly. Armenian and Polish nationalist groups committed to assassination emerged in Russia and used bank robbery to finance their activities. Then the Balkans exploded, as many groups found the boundaries of states recently torn out of the Ottoman Empire unsatisfactory.[28] In the West, where Russian anarchists fled and found refuge in Russian diaspora colonies and among other elements hostile to the czarist regime, a campaign of anarchist terror developed that influenced activities in India too.[29] The diaspora produced some surprising results for groups still struggling in Russia. The Terrorist Brigade in 1905 had its headquarters in Switzerland, launched strikes from Finland (an autonomous part of the Russian empire), got arms from an Armenian terrorist group Russians helped train, and were offered funds by the Japanese to be laundered through American millionaires.[30]

The high point of the first wave of international terrorist activity occurred in the 1890s, sometimes called the "Golden Age of Assassination"—when monarchs, prime ministers, and presidents were struck down, one after another, usually by assassins who moved easily across international borders.[31] The most immediately affected governments clamored for international police cooperation and for better border control, a situation President Theodore Roosevelt thought ideal for launching the first international effort to eliminate terrorism:

> Anarchy is a crime against the whole human race, and all mankind should
> band together against the Anarchist. His crimes should be made a crime
> against the law of nations . . . declared by treaties among all civilized powers.[32]

The consensus lasted only three years, however. The United States refused to send a delegation to a St. Petersburg conference to consider a German/Russian-sponsored protocol to meet these objectives. It feared that extensive involvement in European politics might be required, and it had no federal police force. Italy refused too, for a very different and revealing concern: If anarchists were returned to their original countries, Italy's domestic troubles might be worse than its international ones.

The first great effort to deal with international terrorism failed because the interests of states pulled them in different directions, and the divisions developed new expressions as the century developed. Bulgaria gave Macedonian nationalists sanctuaries and bases to aid operations in the Ottoman Empire. The suspicion that Serbia helped Archduke Franz Ferdinand's assassin precipitated World War I. An unintended consequence of the four terrible years that followed was a dampened enthusiasm for the strategy of assassination.

Second Wave: Mostly Successful, and a New Language

A wave by definition is an international event; oddly, however, the first one was sparked by a domestic political situation. A monumental international event, the Versailles Peace Treaty that concluded World War I, precipitated the second wave. The victors applied the principle of national self-determination to break up the empires of the defeated states (mostly in Europe). The non-European portions of those defeated empires, which were deemed not yet ready for independence, became League of Nations "mandates" administered directly by individual victorious powers until the territories were ready for independence.

Whether the victors fully understood the implications of their decisions or not, they undermined the legitimacy of their own empires. The IRA achieved limited success in the 1920s,[33] and terrorist groups developed in all empires except the Soviet Union (which did not recognize itself as a colonial power) after World War II. Terrorist activity was crucial in establishing the new states of Ireland, Israel, Cyprus, and Algeria, among others. As empires dissolved, the wave receded.

Most terrorist successes occurred twenty-five years after Versailles, and the time lag requires explanation. World War II reinforced and enlarged the implications of Versailles. Once more the victors compelled the defeated to abandon empires; this time the colonial territories were overseas (Manchuria, Korea, Ethiopia, Libya, and so forth) and were not made mandates. The victors began liquidating their own empires as well, and in doing so they generally were not responding to terrorist activity, as in India, Pakistan, Burma, Ceylon, Tunisia, Egypt, Morocco, the Philippines, Ghana, and Nigeria—which indicated how firmly committed the Western world had become to the principle of self-determination. The United States had become the major Western power, and it pressed hardest for eliminating empires. As the cold war developed, the process was accelerated because the Soviets were always poised to help would-be rebels.[34]

The terror campaigns of the second wave were fought in territories where special political problems made withdrawal a less attractive option. Jews and Arabs in Palestine, for example, had dramatically conflicting versions of what the termination of British rule was supposed to mean. The considerable European population in Algeria did not want Paris to abandon its authority, and in Northern Ireland the majority wanted to remain British. In Cyprus, the Turkish community did not want to be put under Greek rule—the aim of Ethniki Organosis Kyprion Agoniston (EOKA)—and Britain wanted to retain Cyprus as a base for Middle East operations.

The problem of conflicting aspirations was reflected in the way the struggles were or were not settled. The terrorists did get the imperial powers to withdraw, but that was not the only purpose of the struggle. Menachem Begin's *Irgun* fought to gain the entire Palestine mandate but settled for partition.[35] IRA elements have never accepted the fact that Britain will not leave Northern Ireland without the consent of the territory's population. EOKA fought to unify Cyprus with Greece (*enosis*) but accepted an independent state that EOKA tried to subvert for the sake of an ever-elusive *enosis*. Algeria seems to be the chief exception because the Europeans all fled. The initial manifesto of the Front de Liberation Nationale, Algeria (FLN) proclaimed, however, that it wanted to retain that population and establish a democratic state; neither objective was achieved.[36]

Second-wave organizations understood that they needed a new language to describe themselves because the term *terrorist* had accumulated so many negative connotations that those who identified themselves as terrorists incurred enormous political liabilities. The Israeli group *Lehi* was the last self-identified terrorist group. Begin, leader of the *Irgun* (*Lehi*'s Zionist rival)—which concentrated on purpose rather than means—described his people as "freedom fighters" struggling against "government terror."[37] This self-description was so appealing that all subsequent terrorist groups followed suit; because the anticolonial struggle seemed more legitimate than the purposes served in the first wave, the "new" language became attractive to potential political supporters as well. Governments also appreciated the political value of "appropriate" language and began to describe all violent rebels as terrorists. The media, hoping to avoid being seen as blatantly partisan, corrupted language further. Major American newspapers, for example, often described the same individuals alternatively as terrorists, guerrillas, and soldiers in the same account.[38]

Terrorist tactics also changed in the second wave. Because diaspora sources contributed more money, bank robberies were less common. The first wave demonstrated that assassinating prominent political figures could be very counterproductive, and few assassinations occurred in the second wave. The Balkans was an exception—an odd place especially when one considers where World War I started.[39] Elsewhere only *Lehi* (the British renamed it the Stern Gang) remained committed to a strategy of assassination. *Lehi* was much less effective than its two competitors, however, which may have been an important lesson for subsequent anticolonial movements. Martyrdom, often linked to assassination, seemed less significant as well.

The new strategy was more complicated than the old because there were more kinds of targets chosen, and it was important to strike them in proper sequence. Second-wave strategy sought to eliminate the police—a government's eyes and ears—first, through systematic assassinations of officers and/or their families. The military units replacing them, second-wave proponents reasoned, would prove too clumsy to cope without producing counter-atrocities that would increase social support for the cause. If the process of atrocities and counter-atrocities were well planned, it could favor those perceived to be weak and without alternatives.[40]

Major energies went into guerrilla-like (hit-and-run) actions against troops—attacks that still went beyond the rules of war because weapons were concealed and the assailants had no identifying insignia.[41] Some groups, such as the Irgun, made efforts to give warnings in order to limit civilian casualties. In some cases, such as Algeria, terror was one aspect of a more comprehensive rebellion that included extensive guerrilla forces.

Compared to terrorists in the first wave, those in the second wave used the four international ingredients in different and much more productive ways. Leaders of different national groups still acknowledged the common bonds and heritage of an international revolutionary tradition, but the heroes invoked in the literature of specific groups were overwhelmingly national heroes.[42] The underlying assumption seemed to be that if one strengthened ties with foreign terrorists, other international assets would become less useful.

Diaspora groups regularly displayed abilities not seen earlier. Nineteenth-century Irish rebels received money, weapons, and volunteers from the Irish-American community, but in the 1920s the exertions of the latter went further and induced the U.S. government to exert significant political influence on Britain to accept an Irish state.[43] Jewish diaspora communities, especially in the United States, exerted similar leverage as the horror of the Holocaust was finally revealed.

Foreign states with kindred populations also were active. Arab states gave the Algerian FLN crucial political support, and those adjacent to Algeria offered sanctuaries from which the group could stage attacks. Greece sponsored the Cypriot uprising against the British and against Cyprus when it became a state. Frightened Turkish Cypriots, in turn, looked to Turkey for aid. Turkish troops then invaded the island (1974) and are still there.

Outside influences obviously change when the purpose of the terrorist activity and the local context are perceived differently. The different Irish experiences illustrate the point well. The early effort in the 1920s was seen simply as an anticolonial movement, and the Irish-American community had its greatest or most productive impact.[44] The diaspora was less interested in the IRA's brief campaigns to bring Northern Ireland into the Republic during World War II or, later, during the cold war. Conflicting concerns weakened overseas enthusiasms and influences.

As the second wave progressed, a new, fifth ingredient—supranational organization—came into play. When Alexander I of Serbia was assassinated in Marseilles (1934), the League of Nations tried to contain international terror by drafting two conventions, including one for an international court (1937). Neither came into effect. Two League members (Hungary and Italy) apparently encouraged the assassination and blocked the antiterror efforts.[45] After World War II, the United Nations inherited the League's ultimate authority over the colonial mandates—territories that were now scenes of extensive terrorist activity. When Britain decided to withdraw from Palestine, the UN was crucial in legitimizing the partition; subsequently all anticolonial terrorists sought to interest the UN in their struggles. The new states admitted to the UN were nearly always former colonial territories, and they gave the anticolonial sentiment in that body more structure, focus, and opportunities. More and more participants in UN debates regularly used Begin's language to describe anticolonial terrorists as "freedom fighters."[46]

Third Wave: Excessive Internationalism?

The major political event stimulating the third, or "New Left," wave was the agonizing Vietnam War. The effectiveness of the Viet Cong's "primitive weapons" against the American goliath's modern technology rekindled radical hopes that the contemporary system was vulnerable. Groups developed in the Third World and in the Western heartland itself, where the war stimulated enormous ambivalence among the youth about the value of the existing system. Many Western groups—such as American Weather Underground, the West German Red Army Faction (RAF), the Italian Red Brigades, the Japanese Red Army, and the French Action Directe—saw themselves as vanguards for the Third World masses. The Soviet world encouraged the outbreaks and offered moral support, training, and weapons.

As in the first wave, radicalism and nationalism often were combined, as evidenced by the struggles of the Basques, Armenians, Corsicans, Kurds, and Irish.[47] Every first-wave nationalist movement had failed, but the linkage was renewed because ethnic concerns always have larger constituencies than radical aspirations have. Although self-determination ultimately obscured the radical programs and nationalist groups were much more durable than other groups in the third wave, none succeeded, and their survivors will fail too. The countries concerned—Spain, France, the United Kingdom, and Turkey—simply do not consider themselves to be colonial powers, and the ambivalence necessary for nationalist success is absent.

When the Vietnam War ended in 1975, the PLO replaced the Viet Cong as the heroic model. The PLO originated after the extraordinary collapse of three Arab armies in the six days of the 1967 Middle East war; its existence and persistence gave credibility to supporters who argued that only terror could remove Israel. Its centrality for other groups was strengthened because it got strong support from Arab states and the Soviet Union and made training facilities in Lebanon available to the other groups.

The first and third waves had some striking resemblances. Women in the second wave had been restricted to the role of messengers and scouts; now they became leaders and fighters once more.[48] "Theatrical targets," comparable to those of the first wave, replaced the second wave's military targets. International hijacking is one example. Terrorists understood that some foreign landing fields were accessible. Seven hundred hijackings occurred during the first three decades of the third wave.[49]

Planes were hijacked to secure hostages. There were other ways to generate hostage crises, however, and the hostage crisis became a third-wave characteristic. The most memorable episode was the 1979 kidnapping of former Italian Prime Minister Aldo Moro by the Red Brigades. When the government refused to negotiate, Moro was brutally murdered and his body dumped in the streets. The Sandinistas took Nicaragua's Congress hostage in 1978—an act so audacious that it sparked the popular insurrection that brought the Somoza regime down a year later. In Colombia the M-19 tried to duplicate the feat by seizing the Supreme Court on April 19, 1985, but the government refused to yield and in the struggle nearly 100 people were killed; the terrorists killed eleven justices.

Kidnappings occurred in seventy-three countries—especially in Italy, Spain, and Latin America. From 1968 to 1982 there were 409 international kidnapping incidents yielding 951 hostages.[50] Initially hostages gave their captors political leverage, but soon another concern became more dominant. Companies insured their executives, and kidnapping became lucrative. When money was the principal issue, kidnappers found that hostage negotiations were easier to consummate on their terms. Informed observers estimate the practice "earned" $350 million.[51]

The abandoned practice of assassinating prominent figures was revived. The IRA and its various splinter organizations, for example, assassinated the British ambassador to Ireland (1976) and Lord Mountbatten (1979) and attempted to kill prime ministers Thatcher (1984) and Major (1991).[52] The Palestinian Black September assassinated the Jordanian prime minister (1971) and attempted to assassinate Jordan's King Hussein (1974). Black September killed the American ambassador when it took the Saudi embassy in Khartoum (1973). Euskadi ta Askatasuna (Basque Nation and Liberty; ETA) killed the Spanish prime minister in the same year.

First- and third-wave assassinations had a different logic, however. A first-wave victim was assassinated because he or she held a public office. New Left–wave assassinations more often were "punishments." Jordan's prime minister and king had forced the PLO out of their country in a savage battle. Similarly, the attempt against British Prime Minister Margaret Thatcher occurred because she was "responsible" for the death of the nine IRA hunger strikers who refused to be treated as ordinary criminals.[53] Aldo Moro was assassinated because the Italian government refused to enter hostage negotiations. The German Red Army Faction provided a second typical pattern:

15 percent of its strikes involved assassination. Although the RAF did not seek the most prominent public figures, it did kill the head of the Berlin Supreme Court and a well-known industrialist.[54]

For good reason, the abandoned term "international terrorism" was revived. Again the revolutionary ethos created significant bonds between separate national groups—bonds that intensified when first Cuban and then PLO training facilities were made available. The targets chosen reflected international dimensions as well. Some groups conducted more assaults abroad than on their home territories; the PLO, for example, was more active in Europe than on the West Bank, and sometimes more active in Europe than many European groups themselves were. Different national groups cooperated in attacks such as the Munich Olympics massacre (1972) and the kidnapping of OPEC ministers (1975), among others.

On their own soil, groups often chose targets with international significance. Strikes on foreign embassies began when the PLO attacked the Saudi embassy in Khartoum (1973). The Peruvian group *Tupac Amaru*—partly to gain political advantage over its rival *Sendero Luminoso* (The Shining Path)—held seventy-two hostages in the Japanese Embassy for more than four months (1996–97) until a rescue operation killed every terrorist in the complex.

One people became a favorite target of most groups. One-third of the international attacks in the third wave involved American targets—a pattern reflecting the United States' new importance. American targets were visible in Latin America, Europe, and the Middle East, where the United States supported most governments under terrorist siege.[55]

Despite its preeminent status as a target, cold war concerns sometimes led the United States to ignore its stated distaste for terror. In Nicaragua, Angola, and elsewhere the United States supported terrorist activity—an indication of how difficult it was to forgo a purpose deemed worthwhile even when deplorable tactics had to be used.

Third-wave organizations discovered that they paid a large price for not being able to negotiate between the conflicting demands imposed by various international elements.[56] The commitment to a revolutionary ethos alienated domestic and foreign liberal elements, particularly during the cold war. The IRA forfeited significant Irish American diaspora support during the third wave. Its initial goal during the third wave was a united socialist Ireland, and its willingness to accept support from Libya and the PLO created problems. Most of all, however, the cold war had to end before the Irish diaspora and an American government showed sustained interest in the Irish issue again and assisted moves to resolve the conflict.

Involvement with foreign groups made some terrorist organizations neglect domestic constituencies. A leader of the 2nd of June, a German anarchist body, suggested that its obsession with the Palestinian cause induced it to attack a Jewish synagogue on the anniversary of *Kristall Nacht*—a date often considered the beginning of the Holocaust. Such "stupidity," he said, alienated potential German constituencies.[57] When the power of the cooperating terrorist entities was very unequal, the weaker found that its interest did not count. Thus, the German Revolutionary Cells, hijacking partners of the Popular Front for the Liberation of Palestine (PFLP), could not get help from their partners to release German prisoners. "(D)ependent on the will of Wadi Haddad and his group," whose agenda was very different from theirs after all, the Revolutionary Cells terminated the relationship and soon collapsed.[58]

The PLO, always a loose confederation, often found international ties expensive because they complicated serious existing divisions within the organization. In the 1970s Abu Iyad, PLO founding member and intelligence chief, wrote that the Palestinian cause was so important in Syrian and Iraqi domestic politics that those states felt it necessary to capture organizations within the PLO to serve their own ends. That made it even more difficult to settle for a limited goal, as the Irgun and EOKA had done earlier.

Entanglements with Arab states created problems for both parties. Raids from Egyptian-occupied Gaza helped precipitate a disastrous war with Israel (1956), and the *fidayeen* were prohibited from launching raids from that territory ever again. A Palestinian raid from Syria brought Syria into the Six-Day War, and ever afterward Syria kept a tight control on those operating from its territories. When a PLO faction hijacked British and American planes to Jordan (1970) in the first effort to target non-Israelis, the Jordanian army devastated the PLO, which then lost its home. Finally, an attempted assassination of an Israeli diplomat in Britain sparked the 1982 invasion of Lebanon and forced the PLO to leave a home that had given it so much significance among foreign terrorist groups. (Ironically, the assassination attempt was organized by Abu Nidal's renegade faction associated with Iraq— a group that had made two previous attempts to assassinate the PLO's leader Yasser Arafat.) Subsequently, Tunisia—the PLO's new host—prohibited the PLO from training foreign groups, and to a large extent the PLO's career as an effective terrorist organization seemed to be over. Paradoxically, the Oslo Accords demonstrated that the PLO could achieve more of its objectives when it was less dangerous.[59]

To maintain control over their own destiny, states again began to "sponsor" groups (a practice abandoned in the second wave), and once more the sponsors found the practice costly. In the 1980s Britain severed diplomatic relations with Libya and Syria for sponsoring terrorism on British soil, and France broke with Iran when it refused to let the French interrogate its embassy staff about assassinations of Iranian émigrés. Iraq's surprising restraint during the 1991 Gulf War highlighted the weakness of state-sponsored terror. Iraq did threaten to use terror—a threat that induced Western authorities to predict that terrorists would flood Europe.[60] If terror had materialized, however, it would have made bringing Saddam Hussein to trial for crimes a war aim, and the desire to avoid that result is the most plausible explanation for the Iraqi dictator's uncharacteristic restraint.

The third wave began to ebb in the 1980s. Revolutionary terrorists were defeated in one country after another. Israel's invasion of Lebanon (1982) eliminated PLO facilities to train terrorist groups, and international counterterrorist cooperation became increasingly effective.

As in the first wave, states cooperated openly and formally in counter-terror efforts. The United States, with British aid, bombed Libya (1986) because of its role as a state sponsor, and the European Community imposed an arms embargo. The international cooperation of national police forces sought at St. Petersburg (1904) became more significant as Trevi—established in the mid-1970s—was joined in this mission by Europol in 1994. Differences between states remained, however; even close allies could not always cooperate. France refused to extradite PLO, Red Brigade, and ETA suspects to West Germany, Italy, and Spain, respectively. Italy spurned American requests to extradite a Palestinian suspect in the seizure of the *Achille Lauro* cruise ship (1984), and Italy refused to extradite a Kurd (1988) because Italian law forbids capital punishment whereas Turkish law does not. The United States has refused to extradite some IRA suspects. Events of this sort will not stop until that improbable day when the laws and interests of separate states are identical.

The UN's role changed dramatically in the third wave. Now "new states"—former colonial territories—found that terrorism threatened their interests, and they particularly shunned nationalist movements. Major UN conventions from 1970 through 1999 made hijacking, hostage taking, attacks on senior government officials, "terrorist bombing" of a foreign state's facilities, and financing of international activities crimes. A change of language is some indication of the changed attitude. "Freedom fighter" was no longer a popular term in UN debates, and the term *terrorism* actually was used for the title of a document: "International Convention for the Suppression of Terrorist Bombing" (1997).[61] Evidence that Libya's agents were involved in the Pan Am Lockerbie crash produced a unanimous Security Council decision obliging Libya to extradite the suspects (1988), and a decade later when collective sanctions had their full effects Libya complied; this episode will continue to shape UN responses to Libya's terrorist activities.

Yet very serious ambiguities and conflicts within the UN remained, reflecting the ever-present fact that terror serves different ends—and some of those ends are prized. Ironically, the most important ambiguity concerned the third wave's major organization: the PLO. It received official UN status and was recognized by more than 100 states as a state that is entitled to receive a share of the Palestine Mandate.

Fourth Wave: How Unique and How Long?

As its predecessor began to ebb, the "religious wave" gathered force. Religious elements have always been important in modern terror because religious and ethnic identities often overlap. The Armenian, Macedonian, Irish, Cypriot, French Canadian, Israeli, and Palestinian struggles illustrate the point.[62] In these cases, however, the aim was to create secular states.

Today religion has a vastly different significance, supplying justifications and organizing principles for a state. The religious wave has produced an occasional secular group—a reaction to excessive religious zeal. Buddhists in Sri Lanka tried to transform the country, and a terrorist response among the largely Hindu Tamils aims at creating a separate secular state.

Islam is at the heart of the wave. Islamic groups have conducted the most significant, deadly, and profoundly international attacks. Equally significant, the political events providing the hope for the fourth wave originated in Islam, and the successes achieved apparently influenced religious terror groups elsewhere.[63]

Although there is no direct evidence for the latter connection, the chronology is suggestive. After Islam erupted, Sikhs sought a religious state in the Punjab. Jewish terrorists attempted to blow up Islam's most sacred shrine in Jerusalem and waged an assassination campaign against Palestinian mayors. One Jew murdered twenty-nine Muslim worshippers in Abraham's tomb (Hebron, 1994), and another assassinated Israeli Prime Minister Rabin (1995). Aum Shinrikyo—a group that combined Buddhist, Hindu, and Christian themes—released nerve gas on the Tokyo subway (1995), killing 12 people and injuring 3,000 and creating worldwide anxiety that various groups would soon use weapons of mass destruction.

Christian terrorism, based on racist interpretations of the Bible, emerged in the amorphous American "Christian Identity" movement. In true medieval millenarian fashion, armed rural communes composed of families withdrew from the state to wait for the Second Coming and the great racial war. Although some observers have associated Christian Identity with the Oklahoma City bombing (1995), the Christian level of violence has been minimal—so far.

Three events in the Islamic world provided the hope or dramatic political turning point that was vital to launch the fourth wave. In 1979 the Iranian Revolution occurred, a new Islamic century began, and the Soviets made an unprovoked invasion of Afghanistan.

Iranian street demonstrations disintegrated the Shah's secular state. The event also was clear evidence to believers that religion now had more political appeal than did the prevailing third-wave ethos because Iranian Marxists could only muster meager support against the Shah. "There are no frontiers in Islam," Ayatollah Khomeini proclaimed, and "his" revolution altered relationships among all Muslims as well as between Islam and the rest of the world. Most immediately, the Iranians inspired and assisted Shiite terror movements outside of Iran, particularly in Iraq, Saudi Arabia, Kuwait, and Lebanon. In Lebanon, Shiites—influenced by the self-martyrdom tactic of the medieval Assassins—introduced suicide bombing, with surprising results, ousting American and other foreign troops that had entered the country on a peace mission after the 1982 Israeli invasion.

The monumental Iranian revolution was unexpected, but some Muslims had always believed that the year would be very significant because it marked the beginning of a new Islamic century. One venerable Islamic tradition holds that a redeemer will come with the start of a new century—an expectation that regularly sparked uprisings at the turn of earlier Muslim centuries.[64] Muslims stormed the Grand Mosque in Mecca in the first minutes of the new century in 1979, and 10,000 casualties resulted. Whatever the specific local causes, it is striking that so many examples of Sunni terrorism appeared at the same time in Egypt, Syria, Tunisia, Morocco, Algeria, the Philippines, and Indonesia.

The Soviet Union invaded Afghanistan in 1979. Resistance strengthened by volunteers from all over the Sunni world and subsidized by U.S aid forced the Soviets out by 1989—a crucial step in the stunning and unimaginable disintegration of the Soviet Union itself. Religion had eliminated a secular superpower, an astonishing event with important consequences for terrorist activity[65] in that the third wave received a decisive blow. Lands with large Muslim populations that formerly were part of the Soviet Union—such as Chechnya, Uzbekistan, Kyrgyzstan, Tajikistan, and Azerbaijan—became important new fields for Islamic rebels. Islamic forces ignited Bosnia. Kashmir again became a critical issue, and the death toll since 1990 has been more than 50,000.[66] Trained and confident Afghan veterans were major participants in the new and ongoing conflicts.

"Suicide bombing," reminiscent of anarchist bomb-throwing efforts, was the most deadly tactical innovation. Despite the conventional wisdom that only a vision of rewards in paradise could inspire such acts, the secular Tamil Tigers were so impressed by the achievement in Lebanon that they used the tactic in Sri Lanka to give their movement new life. From 1983 to 2000 they used suicide bombers more than all Islamic groups combined, and Tamil suicide bombers often were women—a very unusual event in the fourth wave.[67] Partly to enhance their political leverage at home, Palestinian religious groups began to use suicide bombers, compelling secular PLO elements to emulate them.

The fourth wave has displayed other distinctive international features. The number of terrorist groups declined dramatically. About 200 were active in the 1980s, but in the next decade the number fell to 40.[68] The trend appears to be related to the size of the primary audiences (nation versus religion). A major religious community such as Islam is much larger than any national group. Different cultural traditions also may be relevant. The huge number of secular terrorist groups came largely from Christian countries, and the Christian tradition has always generated many more religious divisions than the Islamic tradition has.[69] Islamic groups are more durable than their third-wave predecessors; the major groups in Lebanon, Egypt, and Algeria have persisted for two decades and are still functioning.[70] These groups are large organizations, and bin Laden's al-Qaeda was the largest, containing perhaps 5,000 members with cells operating in seventy-two countries.[71] Larger terrorist groups earlier usually had nationalist aims—with a few hundred active members and a few thousand available for recruitment. The PLO was a special case at least in Lebanon, where it had about 25,000 members and was trying to transform itself into a regular army. Likewise, most al-Qaeda recruits served with the Taliban in the Afghan civil war.

The American role too changed. Iran called the United States the "Great Satan." Al-Qaeda regarded America as its chief antagonist immediately after the Soviet Union was defeated—a fact not widely appreciated until September 11.[72] From the beginning, Islamic religious groups sought to *destroy* their American targets, usually military or civilian installations, an unknown pattern in the third wave. The aim was U.S. military withdrawal from the Middle East. U.S. troops were driven out of Lebanon and forced to abandon a humanitarian mission in Somalia. Attacks on military posts in Yemen and Saudi Arabia occurred. The destroyer USS *Cole* experienced the first terrorist strike against a military vessel ever (2000). All of the attacks on the U.S. military in the Arabian Peninsula and Africa drew military responses; moreover, Americans did not withdraw after those incidents. The strikes against American embassies in Kenya and Tanzania (1998) inflicted heavy casualties, and futile cruise missile attacks were made against al-Qaeda targets—the first time missiles were used against a group rather than a state. As Peter Bergen has noted, "The attacks, however, had a major unintended consequence: They turned bin Laden from a marginal figure in the Muslim world to a global celebrity."[73] Strikes on American soil began in 1993 with a partially successful effort on the World Trade Center. A mission to strike on the millennial celebration night seven years later was aborted.[74] Then there was September 11.

Al-Qaeda was responsible for attacks in the Arabian Peninsula, Africa, and the American homeland. Its initial object was to force U.S. evacuation of military bases in Saudi Arabia, the land containing Islam's two holiest sites. The Prophet Muhammed had said that only one religion should be in the land, and Saudi Arabia became a land where Christians and Jews could reside only for temporary periods.[75] Al-Qaeda's aim resonates in the Sunni world and is reflected in its unique recruiting pattern. Most volunteers come from Arab states—especially Egypt, Saudi Arabia, and Algeria—and the Afghan training camps received Sunnis from at least sixty Muslim and non-Muslim countries. Every previous terrorist organization, including Islamic groups, drew its recruits from a single national base. The contrast between PLO and al-Qaeda training facilities reflects this fact; the former trained units from other organizations and the latter received individuals only.

Beyond the evacuation of bases in Islam's Holy Land, al-Qaeda later developed another objective—a single Islamic state under the Sharia. Bin Laden gave vigorous support to Islamic groups that were active in various states of the Sunni world—states that many Muslims understand to be residues of collapsed colonial influence. Just as the United States refused to leave Saudi Arabia, it helped to frustrate this second effort by aiding the attacked states. The United States avoided direct intervention that could inflame the Islamic world, however. The support given to states attacked had some success, and perhaps September 11 should be understood as a desperate attempt to rejuvenate a failing cause by triggering indiscriminate reactions.[76]

The response to September 11 was as unprecedented as the attack itself. Under UN auspices, more than 100 states (including Iran) joined the attack on Afghanistan in various ways. Yet no one involved expected the intervention to be so quick and decisive. Afghanistan had always been difficult for invaders. Moreover, terrorist history demonstrates that even when antiterrorist forces were very familiar with territories containing terrorists (this time they were not), entrenched terrorists still had considerable staying power.

There are many reasons why al-Qaeda collapsed so quickly in Afghanistan. It violated a cardinal rule for terrorist organizations, which is to stay underground always. Al-Qaeda remained visible to operate its extensive training operations,[77] and as the Israelis demonstrated in ousting the PLO from Lebanon, visible groups are vulnerable. Moreover, al-Qaeda and the PLO were foreign elements in lands uncomfortable with their presence. Finally, al-Qaeda did not plan for an invasion possibility. The reason is not clear, but there is evidence that its contempt for previous American reactions convinced it that the United States would avoid difficult targets and not go to Afghanistan.[78]

The PLO regrouped in Tunisia, on condition that it would abandon its extensive training mission. Could al-Qaeda accept such limits, and if it did, would any state risk playing Tunisia's role? Pakistan's revolving-door policy suggests a much more likely reaction. Once al-Qaeda's principal supporter, Pakistan switched under U.S. pressure to give the coalition indispensable aid.

As of this writing, the world does not know what happened to al-Qaeda's leadership, but even if the portion left can be reassembled, how can the organization function without a protected sanctuary? Al Zawahiri, bin Laden's likely successor, warned his comrades before the Afghan training grounds were lost that "the victory . . . against the international alliance will not be accomplished without acquiring a . . . base in the heart of the Islamic world."[79] Peter Bergen's admirable study of al-Qaeda makes the same point.[80]

The disruption of al-Qaeda in Afghanistan has altered the organization's previous routine. Typically, al-Qaeda sleeper cells remained inactive until the moment to strike materialized, often designated by the organization's senior leadership. It was an unusual pattern in terrorist history. Normally cells are active and, therefore, need more autonomy so that police penetration in one cell does not go beyond that unit. Cells of this sort have more freedom to strike. They generally will do so more quickly and frequently, but the numbers and resources available to a cell constantly in motion limit them to softer or less protected targets. If direction from the top can no longer be a feature of al-Qaeda, the striking patterns will necessarily become more "normal."[81] Since the Afghan rout, strikes have been against "softer," largely unprotected civilian targets. As the destruction of tourist sites—such as the ancient synagogue in Tunisia and the nightclubs in Bali, Indonesia—suggests, however, the organization displays its trademark by maximizing casualties.

Concluding Thoughts and Questions

Unlike crime or poverty, international terrorism is a recent phenomenon. Its continuing presence for 125 years means, however, that it is rooted in important features of our world. Technology and doctrine have played vital roles. The latter reflects a modern inclination to rationalize activity or make it efficient, which Max Weber declared a distinctive feature of modern life. A third briefly noted factor is the spread of democratic ideas, which shapes terrorist activity in different ways—as suggested by the fact that nationalism or separatism is the most frequently espoused cause.[82]

The failure of a democratic reform program inspired the first wave, and the main theme of the second was national self-determination. A dominant, however confused, third-wave theme was that existing systems were not truly democratic. The spirit of the fourth wave appears explicitly antidemocratic because the democratic idea is inconceivable without a significant measure of secularism.

For many reasons, terrorist organizations often have short lives; sometimes their future is determined by devastating tactical mistakes. A decision to become visible is rare in the history of terror, and the quick success of the coalition's Afghan military campaign demonstrates why. If al-Qaeda successfully reconstructs itself, it may discover that it must become an "ordinary" terrorist group living underground among a friendly local population. That also suggests but, alas, does not demonstrate that its strikes will become more "ordinary" too.

No matter what happens to al-Qaeda, this wave will continue, but for how long is uncertain. The life cycle of its predecessors may mislead us. Each was inspired by a secular cause, and a striking characteristic of religious communities is how durable some are. Thus, the fourth wave may last longer than its predecessors, but the course of the Iranian revolution suggests something else. If history repeats itself, the fourth wave will be over in two decades. That history also demonstrates, however, that the world of politics always produces large issues to stimulate terrorists who regularly invent new ways to deal with them. What makes the pattern so interesting and frightening is that the issues emerge unexpectedly—or, at least, no one has been able to anticipate their tragic course.

The coalition assembled after September 11 was extraordinary for several reasons. September 11 was not only an American catastrophe: The World Trade Center housed numerous large foreign groups, and there were many foreign casualties. The UN involvement climaxed a transformation; it is hard to see it as the same organization that regularly referred to terrorists as freedom fighters forty years ago.

The only other coalition against terrorism was initiated a century ago. It aimed to make waves impossible by disrupting vital communication and migration conditions. Much less was expected from its participants, but it still fell apart in three years (1904). Will the current coalition last longer? September 11 will not be forgotten easily,[83] and the effort is focused now on an organization—a much easier focus to sustain.

When the present campaign against al-Qaeda and the small groups in Asia loosely associated with it concludes, what happens next? No organization has been identified as the next target, and until that happens one suspects that the perennial inclination for different states to distinguish groups according to the ends sought rather than the means used may reappear. Kashmir and Palestine are the two most important active scenes for terrorist activity. In Kashmir, Islamic insurgents are seriously dividing two important members of the coalition. India considers them terrorists, but Pakistan does not. War between those states, both possessing nuclear weapons, will push the coalition's war against terror aside. Successful outside mediation may produce a similar result because that would require some acceptance of the insurgents' legitimacy. The Israeli-Palestinian conflict has a similar meaning; so many important states understand the issue of terror there differently.

Islam fuels terrorist activity in Kashmir, but the issue—as in Palestine, where religious elements are less significant—is a local one. To what extent are other organizations in the fourth wave local too? How deeply can the coalition afford to get involved in situations where it will be serving the interests of local governments? Our experience supporting governments dealing with "local" terrorists has not always served our interests well, especially in the Islamic world.

The efforts of Aum Shinrikyo to use weapons of mass destruction has made American officials feel that the most important lesson of this wave is that those weapons will be used by terrorists against us.[84] September 11 intensified this anxiety even though suicide bombers armed with box cutters produced that catastrophe, and the history of terrorism demonstrates that cheap, easy to produce, portable, and simple to use weapons have always been the most attractive.

The fourth wave's cheap and distinctive weapon is suicide bombing. The victory in Lebanon was impressive, and suicide bombers have been enormously destructive in Sri Lanka and Israel. Driving foreign troops out of a country is one thing, however; compelling a people to give up a portion of its own country (Sri Lanka) or leave its own land (Israel) is another. In the latter case, the bombers' supporters seem to be suffering a lot more than their enemies are.

How does September 11 affect our understanding of foreign threats? This is a serious question that needs more discussion than it has received. Nechaev emphasized that the fear and rage rebel terror produced undermined a society's traditional moral conventions and ways of thinking. He was thinking of the domestic context, and indeed the history of modern terrors shows that domestic responses frequently are indiscriminate and self-destructive.[85] Can the same pattern be observed on the international scene?

The 2003 invasion of Iraq suggests that Nechaev's observation is apt for the international scene as well. The justifications for the war were that Iraq might give terrorists weapons of mass destruction or use them itself against the West—considerations that are applicable to a variety of states, as the "axis of evil" language suggests. After September 11 the United States scrapped the deterrence doctrine, which we developed to help us cope with states possessing weapons of mass destruction and served us well for more than fifty years. Preemption seemed to fit the new age better. Deterrence worked because states knew that they were visible and could be destroyed if they used the dreaded weapons. Underground terrorist groups do not have this vulnerability, which is why preemption has been an important part of police counterterrorist strategy since the first wave. Deterrence is linked to actions, whereas preemption is more suitable when intentions have to be assessed—a task always shrouded in grave ambiguities. Is there any reason to think the crucial distinction between states and terrorist groups has disappeared, however, and that we should put decisions of war and peace largely in the hands of very imperfect intelligence agencies?

The significance of the Iraqi war for the war against terrorism remains unclear. The coalition's cohesion has been weakened, and the flagging fortunes of Islamic groups could be revived. Both possibilities are more likely if preemption is employed against another state or if the victory in Iraq ultimately is understood as an occupation.

Notes

An earlier version of this essay was published in *Current History* (December 2001): 419–25. Another version was delivered at the annual John Barlow Lecture, University of Indiana, Indianapolis. I am indebted to Jim Ludes, Lindsay Clutterbuck, Laura Donohue, Clark McCauley, Barbara Rapoport, and Sara Grdan for useful comments, even those I did not take. The problems in the essay are my responsibility.

1. On September 20, 2001, the president told Congress that "any nation that continues to harbor or support terrorism will be regarded as a hostile regime. [T]he war would not end until every terrorist group of global reach has been found, stopped, and defeated."

2. See Richard B. Jensen, "The United States, International Policing, and the War against Anarchist Terrorism," *Terrorism and Political Violence* (hereafter *TPV*) 13, no. 1 (spring 2001): 5–46.

3. No good history of terrorism exists. Schmid and Jongman's monumental study of the terrorism literature does not even list a history of the subject. See *Political Terrorism: A New Guide to Actors, Authors, Concepts, Theories, DataBases, and Literature*, rev. ed. (New Brunswick, N.J.: Transaction Books, 1988).

4. I lack space to discuss the domestic sphere, which offers important parallels as well. The unusual character of terrorist activity made an enormous impact on national life in many countries beginning in the latter part of the nineteenth century. Every state affected in the first wave radically transformed its police organizations as tools to penetrate underground groups. The Russian *Okhrana*, the British Special Branch, and the FBI are conspicuous examples. The new organizational form remains a permanent, perhaps indispensable, feature of modern life. Terrorist tactics, *inter alia*, aim at producing rage and frustration, often driving governments to respond in unanticipated, extraordinary, illegal, socially destructive, and shameful ways. Because a significant Jewish element, for example, was present in the several Russian terrorist movements, the *Okhrana* organized pogroms to intimidate Russian Jews, compelling many to flee to the West and to the Holy Land. *Okhrana* fabricated *The Protocols of Zion*, a book that helped stimulate a virulent anti-Semitism that went well beyond Russia. The influence of that fabrication continued for decades and still influences Christian and Islamic terrorist movements today.

Democratic states "overreacted" too. President Theodore Roosevelt proposed sending all anarchists back to Europe. Congress did not act, but more than a decade later President Wilson's Attorney General Palmer implemented a similar proposal and rounded up all anarchists to ship them back "home," regardless of whether they had committed crimes. That event produced the 1920 Wall Street bombing, which in turn became the justification for an immigration quota law that for decades made it much more difficult for persons from southern and eastern European states (the original home of most anarchists) to immigrate—a law Adolph Hitler praised highly. It is still too early to know what the domestic consequences of September 11 will be. The very first reactions suggested that we had learned from past mistakes. The federal government made special efforts to show that we were not at war with Islam, and it curbed the first expressions of vigilante passions. The significance of subsequent measures seems more problematic, however. Our first experience with terror led us to create important new policing arrangements. Now Congress has established a Department of Homeland Security with 170,000 employees—clearly the largest change in security policy in our history. No one knows what that seismic change means. One casualty could be the Posse Comitatus law, which prohibits the military forces from administering civil affairs—a law that ironically was passed because we were unhappy with military responses to KKK terrorist activity after the Civil War! A policy of secret detentions, a common reaction to serious terrorist activities in many countries, has been implemented. Extensive revisions of immigration regulations are being instituted. Prisoners taken in Afghanistan are not being prosecuted under the criminal law, reversing a long-standing policy in virtually all states including our own. Previous experiences suggest that it will take time for the changes to have their effect because so much depends on the scope, frequency, and duration of future terrorist activity.

5. David M. Chalmers, *Hooded Americanism: The History of the Ku Klux Klan,* 3d ed. (Durham, N.C.: Duke University Press, 1987), 19.

6. The activities of the Thugs and Assassins had international dimensions but were confined to specific regions; more important, there were no comparable groups operating at the same time in this region or elsewhere. See David C. Rapoport, "Fear and Trembling: Terror in Three Religious Traditions," *American Political Science Review* 78, no. 3 (1984): 658–77.

7. The lineage of rebel terror is very ancient, going back at least to the first century. Hinduism, Judaism, and Islam produced the Thugs, Zealots, and Assassins, respectively; these names still are used to designate terrorists. Religion determined every purpose and each tactic of this ancient form. See Rapoport, "Fear and Trembling."

8. By far most published academic articles on terrorism deal with counterterrorism and with organizations. Judging by my experience as an editor of *TPV,* the proportions increase further in this direction if we also consider articles that are rejected.

9. See note 1.

10. The rebels fought in uniform and against soldiers. George Bernard Shaw said, "My own view is that the men who were shot in cold blood . . . after their capture were prisoners of war." Prime Minister Asquith said that by Britain's own standards, the rebels were honorable, that "they conducted themselves with great humanity . . . fought very bravely and did not resort to outrage." The *Manchester Guardian* declared that the executions were "atrocities." See my introduction to part III of David C. Rapoport and Yonah Alexander, eds., *The Morality of Terrorism: Religious Origins and Ethnic Implications,* 2d ed. (New York: Columbia University Press, 1989), 219–27.

11. Guerrillas carry weapons openly and wear an identifying emblem—circumstances that oblige a state to treat them as soldiers.

12. Anyone who has tried to explain the intensity of the 1960s experience to contemporary students knows how difficult it is to transmit a generation's experience.

13. Nechaev's "Revolutionary Catechism" is reprinted in David C. Rapoport, *Assassination and Terrorism* (Toronto: CBC, 1971). See Michael Bakunin and Peter Kropotkin, *Revolutionary Pamphlets* (New York: Benjamin Bloom, 1927); Nicholas Mozorov, *Terroristic Struggle* (London, 1880); Serge Stepniak, *Underground Russia: Revolutionary Profiles and Sketches from Life* (New York, 1892).

14. See Rapoport, "Fear and Trembling."

15. It took time for this attitude to develop in Islam. If one compares bin Laden's work with Faraj's *Neglected Duty*—a work primarily written at the beginning of the fourth wave to justify the assassination of Egyptian President Sadat (1981)—the two authors seem to be in dif-

ferent worlds. Faraj cites no experience outside the Islamic tradition, and his most recent historical reference is to Napoleon's invasion of Europe. See David C. Rapoport, "Sacred Terror:
A Case from Contemporary Islam," in *Origins of Terrorism,* ed. Walter Reich (Cambridge: Cambridge University Press, 1990), 103–30. I am grateful to Jerry Post for sharing his copy of the
bin Laden treatise. An edited version appears on the Department of Justice website
www.usdoj.gov/ag/trainingmanual.htm.

16. Bin Laden's dedication reads as follows:

Pledge, O Sister

To the sister believer whose clothes the criminals have stripped off:

To the sister believer whose hair the oppressors have shaved.

To the sister believer whose body has been abused by the human dogs.

. . .

Covenant, O Sister . . . to make their women widows and their children orphans. . . .

17. I ignore right-wing groups because more often than not they are associated with government reactions. I also ignore "single issue" groups such as the contemporary antiabortion
and Green movements.

18. The term *terror* originally referred to actions of the Revolutionary government that went
beyond the rules regulating punishment in order to "educate" a people to govern itself.

19. Vera Figner, the architect of Narodnaya Volya's foreign policy, identifies the first four
ingredients. The fifth was created later. For a more extensive discussion of Figner, see David C.
Rapoport, "The International World as Some Terrorists Have Seen It: A Look at a Century of
Memoirs," in *Inside Terrorist Organizations*, 2d ed. (London: Frank Cass, 2001), 125*ff.*

20. Nechaev, "Revolutionary Catechism."

21. An equivalent for this argument in religious millennial thought is that the world must
become impossibly bad before it could become unimaginably good.

22. Adam B. Ulam, *In the Name of the People* (New York: Viking Press, 1977), 269 (emphasis added).

23. Newspaper reports in Germany the next day interpreted the demonstrations to mean
that a revolution was coming. See *New York Times,* 4 April 1878.

24. Stepniak, *Underground Russia,* 39–40.

25. The bomb was most significant in Russia. Women were crucial in Russian groups but
sometimes were precluded from throwing the bomb, presumably because bombers rarely escaped. Other terrorists used the bomb extensively but chose other weapons as well.

26. A guerrilla force has political objectives, as any army does, but it aims to weaken or destroy the enemy's military forces first. The terrorist, on the other hand, strikes directly at the political sentiments that sustain the enemy.

27. Thomas Hobbes may have been the first to emphasize hope as a necessary ingredient of
revolutionary efforts. The first chapter of Menachem Begin's account of his experience in the
Irgun contains the most moving description of the necessity of hope in terrorist literature. Menachem Begin, *The Revolt: Story of the Irgun* (Jerusalem: Steinmatzky's Agency, 1997).

28. There were many organizations: the Internal Macedonian Revolutionary Organization,
Young Bosnia, and the Serbian Black Hand.

29. See Peter Heehs, *Nationalism, Terrorism, and Communalism: Essays in Modern Indian
History* (Delhi: Oxford University Press, 1998), chap. 2.

30. The Japanese offer to finance Russian terrorists during the Russo-Japanese War (1905)
encouraged Indian terrorists to believe that the Japanese would help them too. Heehs, *Nationalism, Terrorism, and Communalism,* 4. The Russians turned the Japanese offer down, fearing
that knowledge of the transaction during a time of war would destroy their political credibility.

31. Italians were particularly active as international assassins, crossing borders to kill French
President Carnot (1894), Spanish Premier Casnovas (1896), and Austrian Empress Elizabeth
(1898). In 1900 an agent of an anarchist group in Patterson, New Jersey, returned to Italy to
assassinate King Umberto.

32. Jensen, "The United States, International Policing, and the War against Anarchist Terrorism," 19.

33. The IRA's success in 1921 occurred when the British recognized the Irish state. Northern Ireland remained British, however, and the civil war between Irish factions over the peace settlement ended in defeat for those who wanted to continue until Northern Ireland joined the Irish state.

34. For an interesting and useful account of the decolonialization process, see Robert Hager, Jr., and David A. Lake, "Balancing Empires: Competitive Decolonization in International Politics," *Security Studies* 9, no. 3 (spring 2000): 108–48. Hager and Lake emphasize that the literature on decolonization "has ignored how events and politics within the core (metropolitan area) shaped the process" (145).

35. Begin said that his decision was determined by the fact that if he pursued it, a civil war among Jews would occur, indicating that most Jews favored partition. Begin, *The Revolt*, chapters 9 and 10.

36. Alistair Horne, *A Savage War of Peace* (London: Macmillan, 1977), 94–96.

37. Begin, *The Revolt*.

38. For a more detailed discussion of the definition problem, see David C. Rapoport, "Politics of Atrocity," in *Terrorism: Interdisciplinary Perspectives*, ed. Yonah Alexander and Seymour Finger (New York: John Jay Press, 1987), 46.

39. Alexander I of Yugoslavia (1934) was the most prominent victim, and historians believe that Hungary and Italy were involved in providing help for Balkan terrorists. Begin points out in *The Revolt* that it was too costly to assassinate prominent figures.

40. The strategy is superbly described in the film "Battle of Algiers," based on the memoirs of Yaacev Saadi, who organized the battle. Attacks occur against the police, whose responses are limited by rules governing criminal procedure. In desperation, the police set a bomb off in the Casbah, inadvertently exploding an ammunition dump and killing Algerian women and children. A mob emerges screaming for revenge, and at this point the FLN has the moral warrant to attack civilians. There is another underlying element that often gives rebel terrorism in a democratic world special weight. The atrocities of the strong always seem worse than those of the weak because people believe that the latter have no alternatives.

41. See note 11.

42. See Rapoport, "The International World as Some Terrorists Have Seen It."

43. Irish Americans have always given Irish rebels extensive support. In fact, the Fenian movement was born in the American Civil War. Members attempted to invade Canada from the United States and then went to Ireland to spark rebellion there.

44. World War I, of course, increased the influence of the United States, and Wilson justified the war with the self-determination principle.

45. Martin David Dubin, "Great Britain and the Anti-Terrorist Conventions of 1937," *TPV* 5, no. 1 (spring 1993): 1.

46. See John Dugard, "International Terrorism and the Just War," in Rapoport and Alexander, *Morality of Terrorism*, 77–78.

47. Basque Nation and Liberty (ETA), the Armenian Secret Army for the Liberation of Armenia (ASALA), the Corsican National Liberation Front (FNLC), and the IRA.

48. The periods of the first and third waves were times when the rights of women were asserted more strenuously in the general society.

49. Sean Anderson and Stephen Sloan, *Historical Dictionary of Terrorism* (Metuchen, N.J.: Transaction Press, 1995), 136.

50. Although bank robbing was not as significant as in the first wave, some striking examples materialized. In January 1976 the PLO, together with its bitter enemies the Christian Phalange, hired safe breakers to help loot the vaults of the major banks in Beirut. Estimates of the amount stolen range between $50 and a $100 million. "Whatever the truth the robbery was large enough to earn a place in the *Guinness Book of Records* as the biggest bank robbery of all time"; James Adams, *The Financing of Terror* (New York: Simon and Schuster, 1986), 192.

51. Adams, *Financing of Terror,* 94.

52. The attack on Major actually was an attack on the cabinet, so it is not clear whether the prime minister was the principal target (Lindsay Clutterbuck, personal communication to author).

53. The status of political prisoner was revoked in March 1976. William Whitelaw, who granted it in the first place, ranked it as one of his "most regrettable decisions."

54. Anderson and Sloan, *Historical Dictionary of Terrorism,* 303.

55. Sometimes there was American support for terrorist activity (e.g., the Contras in Nicaragua).

56. When a disappointed office-seeker assassinated President Garfield, Figner's sympathy letter to the American people said that there was no place for terror in democratic states. The statement alienated elements of her radical constituency in other countries.

57. Michael Baumann, *Terror or Love* (New York: Grove Press, 1977), 61.

58. Interview with Hans J. Klein in Jean M. Bourguereau, *German Guerrilla: Terror, Rebel Reaction and Resistance* (Sanday, U.K.: Cienfuegos Press, 1981), 31.

59. Abu Nidal himself was on a PLO list of persons to be assassinated.

60. W. Andrew Terrill, "Saddam's Failed Counterstrike: Terrorism and the Gulf War," *Studies in Conflict and Terrorism* 16 (1993): 219–32.

61. In addition to four UN conventions there are eight other major multilateral terrorism conventions, starting with The Tokyo Convention of 1963, dealing with the aircraft safety. See http://usinfo.state.gov/topical/pol/terror/conven.htm and http://untreaty.un.org/English/Terrorism.asp.

62. Khachig Tololyan, "Cultural Narrative and the Motivation of the Terrorist," in Rapoport, *Inside Terrorist Organizations,* 217–33.

63. See David C. Rapoport, "Comparing Militant Fundamentalist Movements and Groups," in *Fundamentalisms and the State,* ed. Martin Marty and Scott Appleby (Chicago: University of Chicago Press, 1993), 429–61.

64. To those in the West the most familiar was the nineteenth-century uprising in the Sudan, which resulted in the murder of legendary British General "Chinese" Gordon.

65. This was not the first time secular forces would help launch the careers of those who would become religious terrorists. Israel helped Hamas to get started, thinking it would compete to weaken the PLO. To check left-wing opposition, President Sadat released religious elements from prison that later assassinated him.

66. Peter Bergen, *Holy War Inc.: Inside the Secret World of Osama Bin Ladin* (New York: Free Press, 2001), 208.

67. In the period specified, Tamil suicide bombers struck 171 times; the combined total for all thirteen Islamic groups using the tactic was 117. Ehud Sprinzak cites the figures compiled by Yoram Schweitzer in "Rational Fanatics," *Foreign Policy* (October 2001): 69. The most spectacular Tamil act was the assassination of Indian Prime Minister Rajiv Gandhi. (Religion did not motivate the notorious Kamikaze attacks during World War II either.) The example of the Tamils has other unusual characteristics. Efforts to make Sri Lanka a Buddhist state stimulated the revolt. Although Tamils largely come from India, there are several religious traditions represented in the population, and religion does not define the terrorists' purpose.

68. See Ami Pedahzur, William Eubank, and Leonard Weinberg, "The War on Terrorism and the Decline of Terrorist Group Formation," *TPV* 14, no. 3 (fall 2002): 141–47.

69. The relationship between different religious terror groups is unusual. Groups from different mainstream traditions (Christianity, Islam, etc.) do not cooperate. Even traditional cleavages within a religion—as in Shiite and Sunni Islam, for example—sometimes are intensified. Shiite terror groups generally take their lead from Iran regarding aid to Sunnis. Iran has helped the Palestinians and is hostile to al-Qaeda and the Saudi religious state.

70. I have no statistical evidence on this point.

71. Rohan Gunaratna, *Inside Al Qaeda: Global Network of Terror* (New York: Columbia University Press, 2002), 97.

72. The stated object of al-Qaeda is to recreate a single Muslim state, and one could argue that if the United States had withdrawn military units from the Muslim world, the attacks would have ceased. What if the issue really was the impact of American secular culture on the world?

73. Bergen, *Holy War Inc.*, 225.

74. Those attacks, as well as the expected attacks that did not materialize, are discussed in a special volume of *TPV* 14, no.1 (spring 2002) edited by Jeffrey Kaplan, titled *Millennial Violence*. The issue also was published as a book: *Millennial Violence: Past, Present, and Future* (London: Frank Cass, 2002).

75. Bernard Lewis, "License to Kill," *Foreign Affairs* (November/December 1998).

76. For a very interesting discussion of the circumstances that provoke American military responses to terrorist attacks, see Michelle Mavesti, "Explaining the United States' Decision to Strike Back at Terrorists," *TPV* 13, no. 2 (summer 2001): 85–106.

77. If the organization understood its vulnerability, it might have thought that an attack on the sovereignty of the state protecting it was unlikely. One reason the Taliban government refused a repeated UN demand to expel al-Qaeda was because without al-Qaeda support it could not survive local domestic opposition. Because most al-Qaeda recruits served in the Taliban forces in the ongoing civil war, the Taliban must have felt that it had no choice. Clearly, however, there must have been a failure to plan for an invasion possibility; the failure to resist is astonishing otherwise.

78. Gunaratna, *Inside Al Qaeda*.

79. Quoted by Nimrod Raphaeli, "Ayman Muhammad Rabi Al-Zawahri: The Making of an Arch-Terrorist," *TPV* 14, no. 4 (winter 2002): 1–22.

80. Bergen, *Holy War Inc.*, 234.

81. The Spaniards conquered the Aztecs and Incas easily, but the United States had more difficulty with the less powerful but highly decentralized native Americans. Steven Simon and Daniel Benjamin make a different argument, contending that bin Laden's group is uniquely decentralized and therefore less likely to be disturbed by destroying the center. See "America and the New Terrorism," *Survival* 42, no. 2 (2000): 156–57.

82. We lack a systematic comparison of the aims sought by organizations in the history of modern terror.

83. September 11 has had an impact on at least one terrorist group: The Tamils found diaspora financial support suddenly disappearing for suicide bombing—an opportunity the Norwegians seized to bring them to the bargaining table again.

84. See David C. Rapoport, "Terrorism and Weapons of the Apocalypse," *National Security Studies Quarterly* 5, no. 3 (summer 1999): 49–69, reprinted in Henry Sokolski and James Ludes, *Twenty-First Century Weapons Proliferation* (London: Frank Cass, 2001), 14–33.

85. See note 3.

three

TERRORISM, STRATEGIES, AND GRAND STRATEGIES

Martha Crenshaw

After September 11, 2001, terrorism took center stage in the debate among security studies, international relations, and foreign policy specialists over a grand strategy for the United States in the post–cold war era. Stephen Walt, for example, asserted that the September 11 attack had triggered the most rapid and dramatic change ever in the history of U.S. foreign policy.[1] The transition commonly was termed a "watershed."

The threat of terrorism was not prefigured, however, by the debate over grand strategy. Prevailing theories of international relations did not predict the outcome of developments that had begun much earlier, much as they failed to foresee the end of the cold war. Terrorism was not generally considered an important national security threat unless it combined two dangers: a threat to the U.S. homeland *and* the use of "weapons of mass destruction"—defined as nuclear, chemical, biological, or radiological weapons. Even then, the idea that terrorism was critically important to national security was not widely accepted by foreign policy specialists inside and outside of government.

Nor did analysts in the "terrorism studies" community—a group distinct from national security specialists—offer much substantive input to the debate over grand strategy. They tended to focus on explaining terrorism rather than prescribing solutions, and they rarely considered terrorism in the context of other foreign policy issues. In fact, these specialists often doubted that a consistent approach to terrorism was possible.

The September 11 attacks call for a rethinking of terrorism and the response to it. This task requires the combined efforts of foreign policy and terrorism specialists in government and in academia. Whether the response to terrorism is a set of individual counterterrorist operations, designed for specific circumstances, or a general strategy applied to a variety of cases, it must be shaped in terms of a larger conception of American security and interests. Such an integrated conception must be based on new ideas of both power and security. Strategic thinking in the post–cold war world must account for the unconventional power of nonstate actors: risk-takers who are willing to violate norms and who may be immune to military threats. A new conception of security also must consider the harmful consequences of the lack of power, as well as the damage that can be inflicted by power.

In this chapter I first establish the requirements for the development of a coherent response that would link means and ends. Next I analyze the period before the shock of September 11 in terms of the debate over grand strategy, the arguments of the "terrorism studies" specialists about responding to terrorism, and the government's actions. I then evaluate the impact of September 11 on grand strategy proposals and on the government's response to terrorism. Last, I ask whether the current American stance on terrorism meets the requirements for effective strategy, grand strategy, and policy.

Defining Strategy, Grand Strategy, and Policy

A necessary preliminary to analyzing the response to terrorism is a definition of the respective conceptual requirements for strategies, grand strategies, and policy in the abstract. It is worth noting, however, that in practice many accounts use the terms interchangeably.

A strategy—which typically refers to military operations—requires a precisely specified political objective. Strategy is a scheme for making the means produce the desired ends.[2] It is concerned with the relationship between means and ends—that is, with how the government's actions are designed to produce desired outcomes. The means must be sufficient to accomplish the ends, but a good design does not have goals that are so ambitious that resources cannot support them or so ambiguous that purposive actions cannot be crafted to reach them. The costs of any strategy must be acceptable in terms of the expected benefits, and the risks must be sensible. Yet however necessary strategy may be, it is not always possible. The constraints may be prohibitive.

"Grand strategy" represents a more inclusive conception that explains how a state's full range of resources can be adapted to achieve national security. It determines what the state's vital security interests are, identifies critical threats to them, and specifies the means of dealing with them. Thus, a "grand strategy" is complex, multifaceted, and directed toward a distant time horizon. It establishes a comprehensive framework that coordinates the objectives of individual strategies. It would explain how defending the nation against terrorism can and should relate to other foreign policy objectives—such as, for example, preventing the emergence of great power challengers, spreading democracy, and controlling the proliferation of weapons of mass destruction (WMD).

Policy defines the goals of strategy and "grand" or higher strategy. It is a statement of purpose. The central purpose of counterterrorist strategy is to prevent attacks on U.S. territory that cause large numbers of civilian casualties. Terrorism does not pose the threat of annihilation that the Soviet Union's nuclear capabilities did during the cold war. What was and is at stake is not national survival, material power, or the integrity of our armed forces and national defense system but the individual security of American civilians at home. This objective, however, must be coordinated with other policy purposes. Policy must determine priorities among competing values.

The Grand Strategy Debate before September 11

Scholars engaged in the debate over the future of American foreign policy in the 1990s agreed about the purpose of grand strategy—it should define and rank American interests, identify the major threats to them, and establish policy guidelines for protecting those interests—while they disagreed with regard to its content. They shared, however, a lack of concern about terrorism. The policy recommendations of scholars in the security studies and international relations fields typically did not cite terrorism as a major threat to American security.[3] Advocates of American primacy or preponderance focused on potential great power challengers, not terrorism. Advocates of "selective engagement" urged the United States to concentrate its efforts only on the most powerful states. Proponents of "offshore balancing," who thought that the United States should play the role of balancer in the international system and avoid foreign commitments, were more likely to cite the risk of terrorism as a reason for decreased international involvement, but only as a peripheral argument. For instance, Layne supported the case for disengagement with the general claim that "the risk of conflict, and the possible exposure of the American homeland to attack, derive directly from the overseas commitments mandated by preponderance's expansive definition of U.S. interests."[4] A similar argument for "restraint" mentioned terrorism in a footnote as an exception to "the great news is that America faces almost no discernible security threats."[5] One paragraph subsequently was devoted to explaining that the United States should continue to try to prevent and respond to terrorism but that restraint in world affairs would reduce the incentives to attack U.S. targets.[6]

One reason for this neglect may be that studies of grand strategy usually proceeded from realist assumptions,[7] despite some attempts to include domestic variables.[8] In such a framework, threats emanate from states, not non-states, and the most powerful states are the most important for American interests. Weak or failed states and shadowy underground conspiracies do not constitute challenges to the American position in the world. From this perspective, threats are simple to interpret. They stem from rival states that can challenge one's power now or in the future. The dominant mode of thought is worst-case analysis, by which one necessarily associates hostile intent with rising power.

Furthermore, the security studies and international relations fields were not especially hospitable to scholars interested in terrorism precisely because it was not considered an important problem for the discipline or for the development of grand strategy. As an intellectual approach, it did not lend itself to abstract theory or modeling.[9] The study of terrorism was too policy oriented to be of serious academic significance.

There were some exceptions to this general rule. Robert J. Art, defending a grand strategy of selective engagement, argued that a key American interest was preventing a WMD attack on the American homeland and that such an attack might come from "fanatical terrorists" using nuclear, biological, or chemical weapons.[10] In this framework, however, terrorism became a danger only when combined with WMD proliferation, and states continued to pose a greater threat than transnational actors. The most prescient analysts were Ashton B. Carter and William J. Perry, who defined "catastrophic" terrorism as a key threat and called for the response to terrorism to be incorporated into a general strategy of "preventive defense."[11] Their contribution had little impact on the overall "grand strategy" debate, however, perhaps because both authors were former high government officials rather than scholars.

"Terrorism Studies" before September 11

In their turn, terrorism specialists tended to neglect the strategic dimensions of the issue. The study of terrorism was divorced from the study of foreign policy and national security, as well as from theories of international relations. As Ian Lesser, an analyst for the Rand Corporation, concluded, "Most contemporary analyses of terrorism focus on terrorist political violence as a stand-alone phenomenon, without reference to its geopolitical and strategic context. Similarly, counterterrorism policy is rarely discussed in terms of its place in broader national security planning."[12] Lesser implied that this over-sight was due to the perception that terrorism was not an existential threat unless it used WMD.

In contrast, Richard Falkenrath argued that scholars focusing on terror-ism were skeptical of the WMD threat.[13] In his view, the specialists were criti-cal of the Clinton administration's domestic preparedness program because they regarded the threat of WMD terrorism as highly unlikely and distract-ing—a judgment they based on observations of the past. Falkenrath sug-gested that the study of terrorism was useful for a variety of things, such as understanding motivation, but that it could not provide tactical warning, as-sess threats, or set priorities. Its predictions tended to be linear: a straight projection of the future from the past.

A possible explanation for the neglect of international relations was that specialists on terrorism usually represented interdisciplinary interests. Con-tributors came from backgrounds in sociology, psychology, anthropology, history, law, criminal justice, and communications, as well as political sci-ence. Within political science, scholars focusing on terrorism did not often work in the field of international relations. They were equally or more likely to be specialists in civil conflict. Multidisciplinarity made it hard to build a unifying set of theoretical assumptions that could coordinate different ap-proaches to understanding the threat of terrorism or analyzing responses.

Nevertheless, before September 11 most specialists on terrorism, inside and outside of government, had concluded that an undifferentiated response to terrorism was either inappropriate or politically impossible. The reasons for this conclusion were based on the character of the threat and on the na-ture of domestic policies.

Character of the Threat

In 2000, Paul Pillar warned against inflexibility: "The terrorist threat is not really 'a threat' but rather a method used by an assortment of actors who threaten U.S. interests in varying ways and degrees."[14] Critical differences among contexts should "form the basis for tailoring what is, in effect, a dif-ferent counterterrorist policy for each group or state."[15] Because the response should be shaped to individual circumstances, it is complicated and difficult and does not lend itself to generalization or rhetorical flourish. In Pillar's view, "Much attention has been paid to making counterterrorist measures stronger, broader, or more numerous. . . . More needs to be paid to gauging how effective or applicable such measures are to individual cases."[16]

Earlier analyses had made similar points. In 1986 Livingstone and Arnold observed that "the task of designing and implementing effective national policies to deal with terrorism is overwhelming in its scope and permutations and argues less for a general all-embracing strategy to address the problem than a multitude of less-ambitious component strategies, which in sum provide an overall framework for controlling and suppressing terrorism on a global scale."[17] Likewise, Marc Celmer—also analyzing the response of the Reagan administration—agreed that the issue did not lend itself to strategy.[18] Grant Wardlaw, an Australian defense specialist and terrorism analyst, also cautioned that "the idea of a general policy against terrorism is inherently faulty—terrorism has to be countered in a discriminating, case-by-case way."[19] Wardlaw warned that policy should remain at a general level to retain flexibility and imagination in dealing with what he regarded as a "literally infinite range of possible terrorist scenarios." Similar observations continued in the 1990s. Jeffrey D. Simon, for example, concluded that one of the key lessons learned from the experience of countering terrorism was "do not declare any official 'policy' on terrorism."[20]

In fact, critics considered public statements of general policy not only ineffectual but also counterproductive in that they undermined domestic political support. Wardlaw argued that strident policy rhetoric was likely to embarrass the government when principles had to be compromised, as they inevitably would. He also noted that when the government announced to the public that it had a strategy for managing terrorism, each subsequent terrorist incident made that policy look ineffective. Similarly, as Simon pointed out, the no-concessions principle—an ostensible cornerstone of U.S. policy since 1974—often was violated.[21] The Iran–Contra affair was only the most conspicuous of such public contradictions. Consistency in policy is necessary only if the government has promised it.

An additional aspect of the conceptual difficulty of dealing with terrorism was the tension between criminal justice and national security approaches to the issue, which was reflected in institutional rivalries within the government. Since the early 1980s specialists had debated whether terrorism should be defined as crime or as warfare. Each type of problem calls for a different set of policy responses. If it is a crime, a law enforcement strategy is appropriate. If it is warfare, a military response is warranted.

Domestic Politics

An alternative position within the "terrorism studies" school aspired to the development of a more systematic and overarching policy structure but considered it unlikely for reasons of domestic politics rather than the inherent intractability of the problem. Yehezkel Dror, an Israeli scholar specializing in policy analysis, argued that "terrorism is an unusual, though not extraordinary, phenomenon with some features of an extreme case"—which makes it difficult to understand and almost impossible to predict.[22] He concluded, however, that "grand policies" or "grand strategies" were unlikely because democratic governments were not disposed to construct them, not because the phenomenon was indeterminate. He observed that as long as "disjointed incrementalism" and normal decision making seemed to work, governments had no incentive for more ambitious strategies. Thus, "when a problem is handled in what is perceived to be a satisfying way, there will be little propensity to engage in policy innovation."[23] Because governments confront so many pressing problems, they are tempted to keep an issue in the "realm of the ordinary" as long as possible. At the same time, democracies lack the requirements for preparing grand policies. They learn poorly and handle complexity badly. Furthermore, Dror suspected that democracies, characterized by dispersed authority and ad hoc reactions, would not implement grand policies even if they were available. He predicted that a catastrophic shock might jolt a democratic government into action, if the shock revealed decisively that incremental policies had failed.

Over the years analysts emphasized the same domestic obstacles to effective strategy.[24] One barrier was the ever-expanding number of government agencies tasked with a counterterrorism mission. In many ways bureaucratic proliferation was the result of the complexity of the threat, but the expansion of responsibilities also was the result of inertia and incrementalism, as new functions were layered on old ones. The policymaking process also required coordinating the activities of agencies with both domestic and foreign policy jurisdictions. In this context, critics noted the absence of strong leadership from the top. The process was highly decentralized, permitting and encouraging rivalries among different executive branch agencies. The result of intermittent attention from the White House and the president was uncoordinated policy. With each terrorist crisis, terrorism rose to the top of the presidential agenda. In between crises, it sank to the bottom, as other critical issues competed for attention. Presidential advisers tended to regard terrorism as a no-win issue. Sequential attention also was encouraged by the news media, especially television. During the 1980s more interest groups became involved in the policy process, including victims' families (for example, the families of the victims of Pan Am 103). Largely as a result of public awareness, Congress also came to play a stronger role in pressing the executive to be more proactive and forward-looking. With such widely dispersed and autonomous centers of authority, all sensitive to public constituencies, any American government would find planning and implementing a consistent strategy a formidable task.

Government Response before September 11

The Clinton and elder Bush administrations tended to interpret terrorism in light of their preconceptions about American policy in a post–cold war world. As scholars did, policymakers defined the threat of terrorism and formulated counterterrorist strategies in a way that supported worldviews that were established in other contexts. Terrorism was fitted into a preexisting framework.

Although terrorism became an increasingly serious threat in the post–cold war world, the Clinton administration was not initially inclined to regard terrorism as a major national security issue. For example, David Tucker, a former Foreign Service officer writing a history of American policy toward terrorism, concluded that a "strategic vacuum" followed the Reagan administration strategy, which linked terrorism to the Soviet Union and the cold war.[25] Terrorism was not part of general foreign policy planning, as Paul Pillar confirmed.[26]

The Clinton administration entered office holding to the principle that terrorism best fit into a category of "modern" problems such as global organized crime, epidemics of disease, and environmental disasters. These dangers were not represented as threats directed specifically against American interests but common perils all states face. This framing of the issue was consistent with the administration's preferences for a multilateral approach. Thus, the Clinton administration took a modest position. Its policy was based on four simple principles: no concessions or rewards for terrorists, sanctions against state sponsors, international cooperation, and implementation of the rule of law.

Events quickly commanded the government's attention, however. The 1993 bombing of the World Trade Center and then the 1995 Aum Shinrikyo sarin gas attack on the Tokyo subway system and the Oklahoma City bombing brought terrorism onto the domestic policy agenda. Pressure from Congress and from local law enforcement agencies and "first responders" created a sense of urgency about the prospect of terrorist use of WMD—particularly chemical and biological weapons. "Homeland defense" against chemical and biological threats preoccupied policymakers, even though terrorism specialists remained dubious about the prospect of WMD terrorism.[27] Even the simultaneous bombings of American embassies in Kenya and Tanzania in 1998, the "millennium" plots of 1999, and the October 2000 attack on the USS *Cole* in Yemen did not make terrorism a national security priority or an essential element of foreign policy planning. A series of congressionally mandated reports and studies warned that terrorism should rank higher on the national agenda, but other international issues competed for attention: for example, crises in Somalia, Haiti, Bosnia, Kosovo, and South Asia and managing relations with Russia, North Korea, and China. The president also focused on mediating a settlement of the Israeli–Palestinian conflict.

The Clinton administration was not passive. The government responded to the East Africa bombings with cruise missile attacks on a pharmaceuticals plant in the Sudan suspected of links to al-Qaeda and on training camps in Afghanistan, some run by Pakistani intelligence services. Covert operations by the Central Intelligence Agency (CIA) to disrupt bin Laden's operations expanded steadily from 1996 to 2001. These operations focused on apprehending bin Laden and bringing him to trial—or possibly killing him, should these efforts fail. Arrests of suspected al-Qaeda militants led to more than thirty successful prosecutions in U.S. courts. These convictions included the persons responsible for the first World Trade Center bombing as well as some of the perpetrators of the 1998 East African bombings. Economic and diplomatic sanctions against the Taliban regime in Afghanistan were gradually tightened, with the support of the United Nations. The administration believed, however, that the public would not support an escalation of military counterterrorist efforts—especially not the use of ground troops. The government also declined to put strong pressure on Pakistan to cease its support for the Taliban.

In the period between the resolution of the drawn-out contest over the 2000 presidential election and September 2001, the second Bush administration also had other concerns, most domestic. There appears to have been no great sense of urgency about dealing with terrorism.[28] In the last months of the Clinton administration, the National Security Council (NSC) staff had developed a plan for a more active counterterrorist strategy, including arming the Northern Alliance against the Taliban. The new NSC decided to put the proposal through a policy review process that did not conclude until the following September.

Impact of September 11 on the Grand Strategy Debate

The attacks of September 11 propelled terrorism from obscurity to prominence in the wider field of international relations and foreign and security policy. It now took center stage in the grand strategy debate. Scholars who had previously ignored terrorism now acknowledged it as a major national security concern; in fact, some saw the threat of terrorism as occasion for a complete reorientation of post–cold war foreign policy. Barry Posen, for example, called for an end to treating terrorism as "administered policy" and the inauguration of a genuine strategy—the prior absence of which he blamed on domestic politics, bureaucratic inertia, and a weak intelligence effort.[29] Similarly, Stephen Walt cited faults associated with the domestic political process: the lack of serious public interest in foreign policy, the failure of leaders to see the risks inherent in foreign engagements, their partisanship, the influence of special interests, and congressional irresponsibility. He proposed that the United States take the role of being a great power more seriously.[30]

As Barry Posen observed, however, after September 11 the advocates of alternative grand strategies generally superimposed them on their interpretation of terrorism rather than using the case to reexamine their prior assumptions.[31] Each proponent of a foreign policy vision saw the "new" threat of terrorism as justification for the opinions or theories he proposed before September 11.[32] Several analysts thought that American policy was unlikely to change course. Walt, for example, did not think that the United States needed a new grand strategy, merely a reordering of priorities to include managing the antiterrorism coalition, controlling weapons of mass destruction, reconstructing Afghanistan, and improving relations with the Arab and Muslim worlds. Although not necessarily favoring the status quo, Steven Miller agreed that the September 11 attacks would not alter the basic policy of unilateralism that the Bush administration had originally pursued.[33] Although in the short run the issue captured the public and presidential agendas, grand strategy was not likely to change. Miller predicted that the impact of the attacks would be transitory.

On the other hand, Ashton Carter regarded the events of September 11 as confirmation of his prior view that the United States was pursuing the wrong grand strategy and urgently needed a new one, along the lines of the one he proposed before September 11.[34] In his view, catastrophic terrorism, not great-power rivalry, was likely to be the centerpiece of international security studies for the foreseeable future.

Proponents of a restrained American foreign policy predictably cited the U.S. pursuit of preponderance as a partial cause of the September 11 attacks, which they interpreted as a wake-up call for a new and radically different grand strategy of reduced international involvement.[35] In their view, American hegemony was the cause; reorientation of American foreign policy toward a less prominent world role would be the solution. Responsibility for maintaining order and stability should be devolved onto other states, so as to encourage multipolarity rather than primacy. The United States should become a fatalistic bystander in international affairs.

American Response after September 11

The history of American foreign policy exhibits a pattern of reaction to shock, and it may have been inevitable that only a devastating blow from terrorism, causing thousands of civilian casualties on American soil, could bring about fundamental policy change.[36] The United States was slow in responding to emerging threats in the past, and comparisons to the galvanizing effects of the 1941 attack on Pearl Harbor and the 1950 North Korean invasion of South Korea became commonplace after September 11.

After the shock of the multiple hijackings, the Bush administration declared a war on terrorism. The purpose of a war on terrorism is to destroy the enemy's capacity to act, not influence his decision making to deter or compel. Using the metaphor of war defined the problem as a threat to national security, prescribed the solution as military engagement, and predicted eventual victory over the adversary, although officials cautioned the public that the war would be long. In this framework, the alternative to an offensive strategy was defeat, which was unacceptable. The war metaphor also was compatible with American political culture and discourse, which also endorsed wars on drugs, poverty, crime, and other social problems.

The extraordinarily high number of casualties caused by the September 11 surprise attacks, as well as the nature of the targets (actual and intended), raised the stakes considerably. The United States was now willing to use means previously considered politically unacceptable: intervention with ground forces to overthrow a regime that actively supported a terrorist organization and destruction of that organization's territorial base. Both the Clinton and Bush administrations previously had considered and employed alternative options to end the Taliban's support for bin Laden. The military campaign in Afghanistan in October 2001 followed a series of unsuccessful demands that the Taliban surrender bin Laden, accompanied by the imposition of multilateral sanctions endorsed by the UN. In fact, Secretary of State Colin Powell suggested after bombing began that "moderate elements" of the Taliban might have a place in a future government.

Regional and international alliances were cemented to support the campaign. Pakistan—formerly an ally of the Taliban—was induced to support the American war effort, as were Uzbekistan and Tajikistan. The war effort went beyond direct military operations to defeat the Taliban regime in Afghanistan and destroy the infrastructure of the al-Qaeda organization; it also incorporated military assistance, including training, to regimes confronting local insurgencies with links to al-Qaeda—principally Yemen, the Philippines, and Georgia. The United States also organized an international coalition to legitimize the war on terrorism, provide operational assistance in Afghanistan, and disrupt al-Qaeda operations. National police and intelligence services from Europe to Asia were mobilized to apprehend al-Qaeda suspects and cut off their financial resources. The CIA's covert operations against terrorism were intensified. Hundreds of suspects were seized—some kept as "unlawful combatants" at Guantanamo Bay in Cuba, others left in the hands of governments willing to hold and interrogate them. The American government also emphasized public diplomacy to reduce the popular support bases of Islamic militancy in Muslim countries, especially in the Middle East.

The State Department's annual report for 2001 described American policy as (1) make no concessions to terrorists and no "deals" if hostages are seized; (2) bring terrorists to justice (i.e., to trial in the United States); (3) isolate and apply pressure to states that support terrorism to induce them to change their behavior; and (4) bolster the counterterrorist efforts of countries that help the United States.[37] The statement summarized efforts in the fields of diplomacy, intelligence, law enforcement, and finance. Military instruments, principally Operation Enduring Freedom, were mentioned last. The document emphasized international cooperation on all fronts.

After the Taliban regime was overthrown and al-Qaeda's territorial base in Afghanistan eliminated, the Bush administration began to expand its foreign policy conceptions. The formal statement of a new set of principles came in September 2002 with the release of *The National Security Strategy of the United States of America*.[38] Many elements of this plan predated the war on terrorism.[39] According to National Security Adviser Condoleeza Rice, however, September 11 was an "earthquake" or tectonic plate shift, analogous to the events that precipitated the cold war in 1945–47. This jolt clarified and sharpened the American conception of its role in the world.[40] Opposing terrorism and preventing irresponsible states from acquiring WMD, in her view, now defined the national interest.

The 2002 national security strategy recognized that nonstates are important enemies and that weak states are dangerous. It called for a response to threats before they are fully formed and justified preemption as anticipatory self-defense. To this end, the United States would seek international support but would act alone if American interests and "unique" responsibilities required. The strategy required a more global military presence. At the same time, it included public diplomacy or a "war of ideas" to delegitimize terrorism and alter the conditions and ideologies that permit it to flourish. The Bush administration explained this strong response as a moral necessity in dealing with "evil." The designated "rogue state" enemies—Iran, Iraq, and North Korea—were states that demonstrated generally hostile intent, oppressed their own citizens, threatened their neighbors, and possessed or were in the process of acquiring WMD as well as the means of delivery.[41]

A first requirement of the national security strategy was regime replacement in Iraq.[42] Replacing Saddam Hussein was considered to be a solution not only to the threat of a rogue state with the potential to use highly lethal weapons but also to a range of problems in the Middle East, including the Palestinian–Israeli conflict and lack of democracy. The expectation was that a new, democratic Iraq could serve as a model for other Arab states and a new source of regional stability. The administration also claimed that Iraq was linked to al-Qaeda and was likely to supply the organization with WMD. Thus, Saddam Hussein's removal also would serve the purposes of the war on terrorism.

In February 2003 the administration published a complementary *National Strategy for Combating Terrorism*. The strategy is based on the assumption that the September 11 attacks were acts of war, that terrorism, rather than a named adversary, is the enemy, and that defeating terrorism is the primary and immediate priority of the U.S. government. The strategy's purpose is to identify and defuse threats before they materialize into attacks on U.S. territory and interests. It stipulates that the United States will act unilaterally if need be and that it will act preemptively in self-defense. The United States will not wait for terrorists to act; instead it will employ an aggressive offensive strategy that is based on law enforcement and intelligence, military power, and international cooperation to block terrorist financing. All aspects of U.S. power will be employed in the struggle, and the United States will assist states that lack the resources to combat terrorism. Preventing terrorists from acquiring and using WMD is a central goal of the strategy; this threat is regarded as real and immediate. The "4D" strategy is summarized as "defeat, deny, diminish, and defend": The United States will destroy terrorist organizations; deny them the support of states; address the underlying conditions that permit and encourage terrorism (including finding a solution to the Israeli–Palestinian conflict); and defend the country, its citizens, and its interests abroad against attack. Victory is defined as the achievement of a world in which terrorism does not define the daily lives of Americans and their friends and allies. The goal, attainable only after long and sustained effort, is to eliminate terrorism as a threat to the American way of life.

Shortly after the announcement of the counterterrorist strategy, the Bush administration demonstrated the new reality of its preemptive and unilateralist strategy by launching the war against Iraq. The military campaign was justified as necessary to remove a regime that did and was likely to continue to support terrorism and had acquired and intended to keep acquiring WMD. The United States was successful in quickly ending Saddam Hussein's reign in Iraq and in doing so with a minimum of U.S. and allied casualties. The cost, however, was the alienation of many of the United States' closest allies. Furthermore, the postwar occupation proved arduous and vexed, in part because of the emergence of violent opposition groups and individuals using guerrilla tactics. The prospect that Saddam Hussein survived the assault to lead a war of attrition against the occupying forces seemed increasingly likely. The failure to discover WMD also undermined U.S. credibility in the eyes of its critics—although not in the view of the American public, whose support for the war and the occupation remained strong in the war's immediate aftermath.

Critical Evaluation

How well did the American response fulfill the requirements of strategy? Can the response to terrorism—whether a comprehensive general approach or a set of case-by-case reactions tailored to circumstances—be fitted into a grand strategy for the United States? What is the relationship between defeating terrorism and intervening to overthrow the Iraqi regime or other "rogue states"?

Consider first counterterrorist strategy. The September 11 attacks broke what appeared to be a pattern of incrementalism in the American response to terrorism. The ambitiousness of the war on terrorism is not in doubt, although there was more continuity between the Clinton and Bush administrations' responses than the latter preferred to recognize. The definition of the objective and the logic of the relationship between ends and means in the war on terrorism, however, are not entirely clear. Are the ends so ambitious that no means could reach them? What is victory over terrorism? How can the removal of terrorism as a threat to the American way of life be measured?

The war in Afghanistan had two objectives. As a war against the Taliban regime, the strategy apparently succeeded in the short run because the Taliban regime was overthrown. Mullah Omar, however, remained unaccounted for. The outcome of the military campaign against al-Qaeda was problematic. Elements of the organization remained in areas of Afghanistan and Pakistan and continued to use terrorism against Western interests. Significant attacks occurred in Tunisia, Morocco, Saudi Arabia, Kenya, and Indonesia. Furthermore, such an adversary—a nonstate actor structured as a global network or conglomeration of franchise operations, with considerable local autonomy and flexibility—seemed to be able to reconstitute itself even after a physical defeat in a specific location. Al-Qaeda appeared to be independent of state support; conceivably, the organization could exist without a fixed territorial base, relying on multiple decentralized operational centers. Thus, preemptive strikes against states might have little effect.

The United States initiated the war not just against the Taliban and al-Qaeda but in principle against "terrorism of global reach." This war was waged not against al-Qaeda as a distinct nonstate entity but against the means the organization—or, for that matter, any other organization—chose to employ. This goal was so open-ended that accomplishing it might never be possible.

Moreover, an unintended and potentially costly consequence of counterterrorist strategy specifically as well as the new national security strategies could be the encouragement of future incarnations of the threat, as a reaction to extended U.S. military involvement around the world, outside Iraq. Encouraging states to crush terrorism could lead to the suppression of all opposition, provoking the establishment of new underground conspiracies with radical objectives and hatred for the United States. The strategy did not define limits to American assistance to regimes battling various violent challenges linked to terrorism "with global reach"—a phrase also left undefined. For example, how strong should the link be between a local conflict and al-Qaeda for the United States to intervene?

The strategy of preemption announced in 2002 applied to all threats, not just terrorism. It aimed to destroy the enemy's capacity to attack in advance, not influence its "will" or calculus of decision. The strategy's advocates perceived it as an attempt to alter a threatening status quo to defend American interests. Reliance on preemption also is a way of escaping the dilemma created by lack of tactical warning of terrorist attack or absence of a "smoking gun" of proven state complicity.[43] At the same time, fear of a preemptive attack can lead adversaries to strike first. North Korea, Syria, and Iran could be cases in point.

Thus, the war on terrorism was the centerpiece of a grand strategy of preponderance and unilateralism that the administration favored well before the September 11 attacks.[44] However, the use of military force to preempt state adversaries, particularly Iraq, could be costly in terms of defeating terrorism. If the new national security strategy can be defined as a grand strategy, it may not be compatible with an effective counterterrorist strategy. One consequence was that the war against Iraq alienated members of the antiterrorist coalition, which are essential to American law enforcement and intelligence efforts. NATO was painfully divided over the issue.

American strategic planners seemed not to have thought deeply about what happens after a preemptive war is fought and won. The United States appeared unprepared to cope with the level of insecurity and disorder that followed the collapse of the Iraqi regime. The consequences for the war on terrorism could be extremely negative. For example, the postwar occupation of Iraq could inspire terrorism from al-Qaeda or other extremist groups if it is perceived as evidence that the United States is hostile to Islam. Ironically, American actions might produce a surge of Iraqi nationalism that would unite and motivate violent opposition, including terrorism. Similarly, Afghanistan remained unstable and volatile after a military victory was declared. Neither Saddam Hussein nor Osama bin Laden was conclusively killed or taken into custody.

If in the long term the removal of Saddam Hussein's regime results not in the democratization of Iraq and neighboring regimes but in heightened instability and repressiveness, the prospect of continued terrorism is further heightened.[45] If one conceives of terrorism directed against U.S. interests as a form of internationalized civil conflict—a spillover of local grievances onto the international scene, facilitated by the processes of globalization[46]—then violence that initially is limited and localized could be transformed into "terrorism of global reach" in areas beyond Iraq. It is worth noting that past demonstrations of U.S. power did not dissuade terrorists. The raid on Libya in 1986 was followed by the bombing of Pan Am 103 in 1988. The 1998 strikes against the Sudan and Afghanistan did not halt al-Qaeda.

American efforts to "diminish" the conditions that are presumed to give rise to terrorism included resolving the Israeli–Palestinian conflict as well as establishing democratic stability in Iraq. After the war in Iraq, the Bush administration took on a much more active role than it had initially anticipated. The risks of failure remained high, however. The consequences could extend far beyond the scope of the conflict itself. If the United States—by virtue of its involvement, its power, and its alliance with Israel—is held responsible for continued Israeli violence against Palestinians, its attractiveness as a target of terrorism will grow.

Conclusions

This review of the American response to terrorism raises several critical questions. What sort of American foreign policy or grand strategy would be compatible with controlling terrorism? How might the material and the ideological or normative environment be shaped to discourage and prevent resort to such means? How can all the resources of the United States be coordinated? In particular, how should military means relate to economic and political instruments?

A first conclusion is that policymakers should avoid decontextualizing terrorism. For this reason, counterterrorist strategy must be linked to grand strategy and grand strategy to policy goals. These distinctions are not always clear in the American response to terrorism. It is tempting to attach the response to terrorism to an overarching conceptual structure that dictates top-down reasoning. However, the local political context within which terrorism emerges shapes its trajectory, and threat assessments should not overgeneralize or assume that terrorism is a monolithic force. Strategy must be flexible. Policymakers must learn to deal with complexity and ambiguity.

For example, al-Qaeda evolved under specific and perhaps unique historical circumstances. The Soviet invasion of Afghanistan, the American support for the moudjahidin, and the allied victory in the 1991 Gulf War were key precipitating events that will not be duplicated. Thus, the assumption that al-Qaeda will be a model for future terrorism may be incorrect. A successful strategy for defeating al-Qaeda might not be effective against other threats. In fact, responding uniformly can be dangerous if adversaries thereby are enabled to design around the threats they know.

Moreover, wars are waged against adversaries, not methods. Whether or not one can outlaw a practice by waging war against those who use it is an open question. Eradicating all "terrorism of global reach" establishes an open-ended policy goal. It may be too ambitious for any strategy. Measuring success may not be possible, especially if one considers the number and variety of actors that could practice terrorism.[47]

Although in the past states may have been the only adversaries who counted, the United States can no longer afford to act under this assumption. Yet efforts to justify a strategy of preemption toward Iraq in terms of a war on terrorism demonstrated just such a reliance on old thinking. The threat was no longer the autonomous nonstate actor al-Qaeda but a familiar adversary: Iraq. Reference to the possibility that Iraq might provide chemical, biological, nuclear, or radiological weapons to al-Qaeda was a way of shifting the focus of policy back to a state-centric world and its power balances. In this framework, nonstate actors acquire significance only if they are proxies of states; they are not regarded as independent actors.

Encouraging the liberalization of regimes that are intolerant of dissent, opening space for the expression of moderate opposition, and promoting democracy also form part of a grand strategy that shapes the international environment to make it less conducive to terrorism. The United States must work toward providing an attractive alternative future to persons dissatisfied with the status quo.[48] Otherwise many of the aggrieved are likely to be attracted to radical and anti-American causes. It is not clear that a grand strategy of preemption furthers this purpose.

It is equally critical that U.S. counterterrorist efforts be legitimate in the eyes of the international community. The support of other nations is indispensable to the disruption of terrorist operations and controlling the spread of weapons of mass destruction, but the war against Iraq ignored the dissent of allies. U.S. grand strategy should not ignore interdependence in the domain of international security.

Notes

I want to thank Audrey Kurth Cronin and Douglas Foyle for their helpful comments on earlier drafts.

1. Stephen M. Walt, "Beyond bin Laden: Reshaping U.S. Foreign Policy," *International Security* 26, no. 3 (winter 2001–2002): 56.

2. See Richard K. Betts, "Is Strategy an Illusion?" *International Security* 25, no. 2 (fall 2000): 5–50.

3. See Michael Mastanduno, "Preserving the Unipolar Moment: Realist Theories and U.S. Grand Strategy after the Cold War," *International Security* 21, no. 4 (spring 1997): 49–88, and Barry R. Posen and Andrew L. Ross, "Competing Visions for U.S. Grand Strategy," *International Security* 21, no. 3 (winter 1996–97): 5–53.

4. Christopher Layne, "From Preponderance to Offshore Balancing: America's Future Grand Strategy," *International Security* 22, no. 1 (summer 1997): 116. This brief mention occurs in a lengthy article (pp. 86–124).

5. Eugene Gholz, Daryl G. Press, and Harvey M. Sapolsky, "Come Home, America: The Strategy of Restraint in the Face of Temptation," *International Security* 21, no. 4 (spring 1997): 8.

6. Ibid., 30. The article runs from pp. 5–48.

7. Mastanduno, "Preserving the Unipolar Moment."

8. According to Richard Rosecrance and Arthur Stein, grand strategy is not just an optimal response to international pressures, threats, and power configurations but the outcome of domestic orientations, resources, constraints, and conditions. See Richard Rosecrance and Arthur A. Stein (eds.), *The Domestic Bases of Grand Strategy* (Ithaca, N.Y.: Cornell University Press, 1993).

9. Bruce W. Jentleson, "The Need for Praxis: Bringing Policy Relevance Back In," *International Security* 26, no. 4 (spring 2002): 169–83. See also Peter Katzenstein, "September 11th in Comparative Perspective," paper presented to the American Political Science Association 98th Annual Meeting, Boston, August–September 2002; available at http://apsaproceedings.cup.org.

10. Robert J. Art, "Geopolitics Updated: The Strategy of Selective Engagement," *International Security* 23, no. 3 (winter 1998–99): 85.

11. Ashton B. Carter and William J. Perry, *Preventive Defense: A New Security Strategy for America* (Washington, D.C.: Brookings Institution Press, 1999). The concept of preventive defense goes beyond terrorism to target the full range of threats to national security. Furthermore, the authors define "catastrophic terrorism" as acts that are an order of magnitude more severe than "ordinary" terrorism and are unprecedented outside of warfare (p. 150). Catastrophic terrorism need not involve the use of WMD.

12. Ian O. Lesser, "Countering the New Terrorism: Implications for Strategy," in Ian O. Lesser, Bruce Hoffman, John Arquilla, David Ronfeldt, and Michele Zanini, *Countering the New Terrorism* (Santa Monica, Calif.: Rand, 1999), 140. Lesser advocated a "core" strategy and "multidimensional" approach that would include not just direct responses to terrorism but shaping of the international environment (ibid., 140–42).

13. Richard Falkenrath, "Analytic Models and Policy Prescription: Understanding Recent Innovation in U.S. Counterterrorism," *Studies in Conflict and Terrorism* 24, no. 3 (May–June 2001): 159–82.

14. Paul R. Pillar, *Terrorism and U.S. Foreign Policy* (Washington, D.C.: Brookings Institution Press, 2001), 223.

15. Ibid.

16. Ibid., 229.

17. Neil C. Livingstone and Terrell E. Arnold, *Fighting Back: Winning the War against Terrorism* (Lexington, Mass.: D. C. Heath and Co., 1986), 229.

18. Marc A. Celmer, *Terrorism, U.S. Strategy, and Reagan Policies* (Westport, Conn.: Greenwood Press, 1987).

19. Grant Wardlaw, "State Response to International Terrorism: Some Cautionary Comments," in *Current Perspectives on International Terrorism*, ed. Robert A. Slater and Michael Stohl (London: Macmillan, 1988), 214.

20. Jeffrey D. Simon, *The Terrorist Trap: America's Experience with Terrorism* (Bloomington: Indiana University Press, 1994), 376.

21. The principle of no concessions to terrorist demands in cases of hostage seizures was developed under the Nixon administration, primarily by Henry Kissinger. It was first applied in 1973, when American diplomats were held hostage and subsequently murdered by members of the Black September Organization in Khartoum. Its application has been inconsistent.

22. Yehezkel Dror, "Terrorism as a Challenge to the Democratic Capacity to Govern," in *Terrorism, Legitimacy, and Power: The Consequences of Political Violence*, ed. Martha Cren-

shaw (Middletown, Conn.: Wesleyan University Press, 1983), 65. Dror also blamed social science: "This ignorance [of terrorism] principally stems from the state of the social sciences, which lack the frames of appreciation, cognitive maps, concept packages, and methodology to comprehend complex phenomena that cannot be understood through decomposition into easier-to-analyze subelements. Our generation, like earlier generations, is overwhelmed by events we cannot adequately comprehend with contemporary modes of thinking and tacit models" (ibid., 67).

23. Ibid., 81.

24. See, for example, William R. Farrell, *The U.S. Government Response to Terrorism: In Search of an Effective Strategy* (Boulder, Colo.: Westview Press, 1982); Martha Crenshaw, "Counterterrorism Policy and the Political Process," *Studies in Conflict and Terrorism* 24, no. 5 (2001): 329–38; Laura K. Donohue, "In the Name of National Security: U.S. Counterterrorist Measures, 1960–2000," *Terrorism and Political Violence* 13, no. 3 (autumn 2001): 47; Laura K. Donohue and Juliette N. Kayyem, "Federalism and the Battle over Counterterrorist Law: State Sovereignty, Criminal Law Enforcement, and National Security," *Studies in Conflict and Terrorism* 25, no. 1 (2002): 1–18; and Richard A. Falkenrath, "Problems of Preparedness: U.S. Readiness for a Domestic Terrorist Attack," *International Security* 25, no. 4 (spring 2001): 147–86.

25. David Tucker, *Skirmishes at the Edge of Empire: The United States and International Terrorism* (Westport, Conn.: Praeger, 1997), 134. Marc Celmer disagreed, however, and argued that even the Reagan administration lacked a strategy (Marc A. Celmer, *Terrorism, U.S. Strategy, and Reagan Policies* [Westport, Conn.: Greenwood Press, 1987]).

26. Pillar, *Terrorism and U.S. Foreign Policy*, 220–21.

27. See Falkenrath, "Analytic Models and Policy Prescription."

28. For example, Condoleezza Rice, then foreign policy adviser to the Bush campaign, wrote an article on "Promoting the National Interest" for the January–February 2000, issue of *Foreign Affairs*. Among the five key priorities the United States should focus on, she cited dealing with rogue regimes, whose threat increasingly was taking the form of potential for terrorism and the development of WMD. She devoted the most attention to China and Russia. The only specific reference to terrorism was in the context of rogue regimes, particularly Iraq, and their capacity to use chemical and biological weapons. Here she called for expanding intelligence capabilities rather than an active response.

29. Barry R. Posen, "The Struggle against Terrorism: Grand Strategy, Strategy, and Tactics," *International Security* 26, no. 3 (winter 2001–2002): 39–55. No mention is made of the fact that security specialists also had ignored the absence of strategy before September 11.

30. Walt, "Beyond bin Laden," especially 77–78.

31. Posen, "The Struggle against Terrorism," 53, 55.

32. In this respect, the debate over the failure to predict a major terrorist attack recalls the debate over the end of the cold war.

33. Steven E. Miller, "The End of Unilateralism or Unilateralism Redux?" *Washington Quarterly* 25, no. 1 (winter 2002): 15–29.

34. Ashton B. Carter, "The Architecture of Government in the Face of Terrorism," *International Security* 26, no. 3 (winter 2001–2002): 5–23. Carter, however, continued to dismiss the threat of "ordinary" terrorism, failing to see the causal links between terrorism that does not cause mass casualties and terrorism that does.

35. See Benjamin Schwarz and Christopher Layne, "A New Grand Strategy," *The Atlantic Monthly* 289, no. 1 (January 2002): 36–42. Available at www.theatlantic.com.

36. See Audrey Kurth Cronin, "Rethinking Sovereignty: American Strategy in the Age of Terrorism," *Survival* 44, no. 2 (summer 2002): 119–39. This outcome is what Dror also expected.

37. *Patterns of Global Terrorism 2001*. U.S. Department of State publication 10940, May 2002.

38. White House, 17 September 2002. The report is mandated by Congress.

39. See Nicholas Lemann, "Letter from Washington: The Next World Order," *The New Yorker*, April 1, 2002. Lemann suggested that the ideas behind the plan stemmed from officials in the first Bush administration. See also Rice, "Promoting the National Interest."

40. Lemann, "Letter from Washington."

41. The Clinton administration had abandoned the term "rogue states" in favor of "states of concern."

42. See the president's address to the United Nations General Assembly, New York, 12 September 2002; available at www.whitehouse.gov.

43. Whether this new idea should be called preemptive or preventive war is open to question. Preemption assumes that the defender has almost certain knowledge of an impending attack within a short time frame.

44. See Frances FitzGerald, "George Bush and the World," *New York Review of Books*, 26 September 2002.

45. See Marina Ottaway, Thomas Carothers, Amy Hawthorne, and Daniel Brumberg, *Democratic Mirage in the Middle East*, Carnegie Endowment for International Peace Policy Brief 20, October 2002.

46. Martha Crenshaw, "Why America? The Globalization of Civil War," *Current History* 100 (December 2001): 425–32.

47. One need only look at the Department of State's annual reports on international terrorism to see that hundreds of different groups have used terrorism fitting the definition of "international," which means involving the citizens or territory of more than one country. It is not clear how "terrorism of global reach" is distinguished from international terrorism.

48. This is not to argue that underlying grievances are a direct cause of terrorism, but they motivate audiences whose support is anticipated and sought by organized radical groups. Terrorism can be regarded as a way of soliciting and mobilizing support. Al-Qaeda is by no means a mass movement.

PART II

POLICY INSTRUMENTS IN THE CAMPAIGN AGAINST INTERNATIONAL TERRORISM

four

DIPLOMACY

Michael A. Sheehan

The United States cannot defeat international terrorism on its own. The elimination of al-Qaeda's sanctuary in Afghanistan by the United States and its allies will increase the relative importance of alternate al-Qaeda bases from the southern Philippines to northern Africa. For this reason, the role of foreign governments is more important now than ever. Most of the future work of identifying and arresting terrorists will be done by foreign law enforcement agencies. Each country, however, has a different perspective of the threat, varying degrees of commitment, and a range of capabilities to sustain the counterterrorism effort. Few countries fully share the American level of commitment. Some may regard the problem as a low priority in a litany of other, more pressing, national issues and are passive or apathetic as a result. Others may care but simply do not have the means to take on the terrorists. Others may fear direct retribution or the risk of alienating local radical groups in their own societies if they crack down on al-Qaeda and its supporters.

The challenge of American leadership is to build and sustain an effective counterterrorism coalition—and effective diplomacy will be the foundation of the effort. The terrorists are determined, patient, and sure to sustain their attacks against the United States and other targets. They will not be defeated in the short term. It will take an equally sustained and focused endeavor on the part of American leadership to accomplish the task. An effective strategy will not eliminate occasional attacks by dedicated fanatics, and we will learn to live with these in the years ahead. However, a successful strategy is required to marginalize these groups and at a minimum prevent them from organizing catastrophic attacks, acquiring weapons of mass destruction, or destabilizing the Islamic world, particularly Pakistan and Indonesia. The administration of President George W. Bush and its successors will need to remain focused, with counterterrorism at the top of its foreign policy agenda. This focus is necessary not only to sustain U.S. efforts; it also is crucial in maintaining the commitment of key partners.

In the context of the campaign against international terrorism, American diplomacy is management of our relations with key partners to convince, cajole, or compel them to defeat the principal international terrorist threat: al-Qaeda and its associated groups. In other words, American diplomacy seeks to ensure that key nations maintain the *political will* to take on the terrorists, especially those residing in their own countries. If political will is established, subsequent programs to provide training and equipment or to share intelligence will bear fruit. Without genuine political will, these efforts will fail. Of course, resources help muster and sustain will, and American diplomats will need to pursue parallel approaches—cajoling countries to do more, providing intelligence and resources to support specific programs, and, ultimately, holding key partners accountable for results.

As such, diplomacy is the cornerstone of a comprehensive, long-term, international counterterrorism strategy that seeks to politically discredit, operationally disrupt, and eventually defeat the most violent groups. Diplomacy is more than dialogue; it is the leveraging of all available foreign policy instruments to influence countries—allies and enemies alike—to deny terrorists the physical and political space they need to operate. Diplomatic interactions include cooperation within the intelligence, law enforcement, and military communities at the bilateral, regional, and international level. Sustained diplomatic activities seek not only to provide the American counterterrorism strategy with the commensurate commitment of political and financial capital but also to harmonize it with our other national interests: promotion of human rights; strengthening of democracy; and defense of American global economic, political, and security interests.

In this chapter I discuss the role of American diplomacy in the campaign to defeat the threat of international terrorism. Although the focus is on al-Qaeda and its associated radical groups, the principles of international diplomatic engagement to deny terrorists the space to assemble, move, communicate, train, raise money, broadcast their message, and eventually strike are applicable to any terrorist organization.

The al-Qaeda Threat Transformed

The threat posed by al Qaeda has changed significantly since the September 11 attacks, placing greater emphasis on the role of diplomacy in defeating the reconstituted and dispersed organization that has emerged from their destroyed camps in Afghanistan. The al-Qaeda network, although severely damaged, remains the primary terrorist threat to American interests around the world. Unlike hierarchical and highly structured groups (such as the Peruvian Shining Path or Turkey's Kurdistan Workers' Party), in which the capture of revered leaders has resulted in the organization's near collapse, the loosely structured al-Qaeda has a diffused central command apparatus. Al-Qaeda is best characterized as a network of networks. The group's central leadership provides funds, guidance, and expertise to its subsidiary cells, as operational concepts develop from the bottom up as well as top down. Small, local cells have considerable independence and initiative in planning and executing terrorist attacks, only loosely coordinated from the central leadership. The simultaneous attacks on the U.S. embassies in East Africa and the attacks of September 11 demonstrate this lethal dual capability for local action and centralized planning and support.

The U.S. military campaign has disrupted the ease with which al-Qaeda may operate in Afghanistan and probably will force al-Qaeda to adapt and evolve in several ways. First, because of U.S. military action, Afghanistan has ceased to be a sanctuary of impunity for al-Qaeda's senior leadership.[1] Al-Qaeda has "gone to ground"—hiding from the assault of superior training and weaponry. It now seeks alternative physical and political space to regroup and to reconstitute the infrastructure it lost in Afghanistan, which included training camps as well as its command, control, and communications. This task is difficult but not impossible. Hundreds and perhaps thousands of al-Qaeda personnel have escaped across the porous Afghan borders, most of them to the tribal areas in western Pakistan and some via Iran to the Middle East and other destinations.[2] Further evidence of this "going to ground" is that by late March 2002, despite the extensive U.S. military operations (*Operation Anaconda*) in Afghanistan, half of the known senior al-Qaeda leaders were still at large,[3] with bin Laden himself reportedly moving along the Afghanistan and Pakistan border.[4] *Operation Alamo Sweep*, the October 2002 U.S. mop-up operation by the 82nd Airborne Division inside Afghanistan along the Afghan-Pakistani border, uncovered little more than abandoned arms caches but confirmed that remnant al-Qaeda forces are festering across the border in Pakistan near the town of Mirim Shah.[5] Also in October 2002, counterterrorism officials assessed that senior al-Qaeda are not only still at large but also have resumed their terrorist activities.[6] These officials cite the audiotape released by Ayman al-Zahwahri calling for attacks on the American economy, as well as the renewed activities of other mid-level leaders, as evidence of the persistent al-Qaeda threat. Moreover, some senior al-Qaeda leaders have moved farther away from the reach of U.S. conventional forces to Iran, along with dozens of other al-Qaeda fighters. According to the *Washington Post* two senior al-Qaeda leaders, Saif al-Adel and Mahfouzm Ould Walid, found sanctuary at guesthouses in the Iranian border cities of Mashhad and Zabol.[7]

The resilience of the al-Qaeda network and its shift to smaller-scale terrorist operations were demonstrated with deadly effect when, in October 2002 alone, al-Qaeda associates launched small arms attacks on U.S. forces on a training exercise on a small island near Kuwait City; detonated bombs in a crowded karaoke bar in Zamboanga City in the southern Philippines; rammed an explosives-laden boat into the French oil tanker *Limburg* off the coast of Al Mukalla, Yemen; and devastated the idyllic beach resort of Bali with high-explosive car bombs killing more than 180 people, in addition to other smaller bombings in Karachi and Manila.

Second, to protect its existing operating space al-Qaeda will employ clandestine tradecraft to elude authorities. This effort includes the use of cells to protect the identity of the broader organization; widespread use of multiple aliases, particularly when moving; and limiting most forms of conventional communications between cells, especially prior to an operation. It has been widely reported that al-Qaeda maintains semiautonomous cells in sixty countries around the world. Past experiences have shown that these cells can operate anywhere from Florida to Faisalabad, from Hamburg to Hebron, from New Jersey to Jakarta. In early 2002 counterterrorism experts in London asserted that there were 100 al-Qaeda supporters in the United Kingdom alone.[8] In July 2002 *Time* magazine reported that as many as 3,000 members of the organization's inner core dispersed throughout the Arab and Muslim world with the aim of replenishing and extending the network globally.[9]

Third, and perhaps most important, al-Qaeda will seek to create symbiotic relationships with local radical Islamic organizations and terrorist groups that are sympathetic with al-Qaeda's international goals. Concurrently, it will align itself with local themes to gain additional "political space" to maneuver in countries with weak governments afraid to antagonize their local Islamists. The foundations for such alliances were already established more than two decades ago when an Islamic *Internationale* took shape. Its roots lie in the Afghani jihad against the Soviet Union and subsequent civil war, in which thousands of *mujahideen* from Saudi Arabia, Algeria, Egypt, Yemen, Pakistan, Sudan, and many other Muslim countries received training and combat practice.[10] The shared experience of the war and the personal contacts established during this period laid the groundwork for an international network that survives today.

Afghanistan and its immediate border areas in Pakistan and central Asia most likely will remain the "primary swamp" for al-Qaeda and its associated organizations. They already are building on previous links in other parts of the world, however, to make up for this lost sanctuary. These areas are mainly in countries that face a domestic situation in which Islamic militants have a foothold of support, primarily against local authorities, but may also share with al-Qaeda an anti-American or broader anti-Western, anti-Israeli sentiment.

In Europe, a significant threat for terrorist operations is posed by al-Qaeda proxy groups from North Africa. Algerians, Moroccans, and others have been apprehended in significant numbers while engaged in preoperational terrorist planning in Britain, Italy, and France. These arrested individuals, some associated with a group called the North African Front, presumably were acting on behalf of either the Armed Islamic Group or the Salafist Group for Preaching Call and Combat. Their plans apparently included mass casualty-producing attacks and the use of biological and possibly chemical agents to create fear. Despite their preoperational planning activities, these groups have been under great pressure by counterterrorist agencies and have failed to achieve a single tactical success in Europe in the recent past. If the pressure from European government security forces increases, extremist operators may seek refuge in Canada or South America—thus bringing their beliefs and operations to the western hemisphere.

In the Caucasus and central Asia, these groups include the Islamic militants fighting for an independent Chechnya from the Russian Federation in the Pankisi Gorge and the Islamic Movement of Uzbekistan (IMU) operating in the Ferghana Valley, which seeks the creation of a single Islamic state in all of central Asia. In southeast Asia, the Jemaah Islamiyah (JI) aims to establish an independent Islamic state encompassing Indonesia, Malaysia, and the Muslim islands of the southern Philippines;[11] in the Philippines the Abu Sayyaf, the Moro Islamic Liberation Front (MILF), and the Moro National Liberation Front (MNLF) all have the potential to strengthen their links with al-Qaeda. The extent to which the al-Qaeda network has penetrated southeast Asia was revealed in a *New York Times* article that argued that the organization in southeast Asia is more deadly and more virulently anti-America today than it was a year ago. It also noted that Riudan Isamuddin, one of bin Laden's most trusted lieutenants, is known to be in the region and is now the subject of an intensive manhunt by Indonesian authorities for his involvement in the October 2002 Bali bombing.[12] In the Middle East, recent evidence suggests that some Palestinian groups may have ties with al-Qaeda. In Germany, for instance, authorities broke up a terrorist cell in the spring of 2002 belonging to al Tawhid, a group that is controlled by top al-Qaeda leader Musaab Zarqawi. Four of those arrested in the German operation were Palestinian.[13]

U.S. intelligence analysts believe that as many as 800 terrorists from various groups, up to 100 linked to al-Qaeda, have taken refuge in the region of the lawless Pankisi Gorge in northeastern Georgia—a cross-border transit base for militants fighting in the breakaway republics of Chechnya (Russia) and Abkhazia (Georgia). Yemen, bin Laden's ancestral homeland, is another location where al-Qaeda followers have found refuge.[14] Yemen's place in the lineup of terrorist havens was illustrated again when Pakistani authorities captured ten alleged members of al-Qaeda, at least eight of them Yemenis, including suspected September 11 operative Ramzi Binalshibh.[15]

Al-Qaeda also may seek to rebuild its infrastructure in Iran, Sudan, or Syria. These states are unlikely to provide a future operational base for al-Qaeda, however, for several reasons. They would be foolish to attract the wrath of the United States by inviting its most sought-after enemies onto their soil. Moreover, a closer look at these individual regimes indicates that although they may be opposed to U.S. policy and have supported or used terrorism, they are not natural allies of al-Qaeda.

Al-Qaeda will survive the first phase of the U.S. counterterrorism campaign. It will dig in and adapt to survive the longer-term effort to root its members out of their current hiding places. Nevertheless, al-Qaeda still will require and employ rural and urban centers. Remote rural locations—whether in Afghanistan, central Asia, the Caucasus, Indonesia, or the Philippines—are required for training camps; combat, weapons, and demolition training; indoctrination; and radicalizing of terrorist cadres. In addition, these camps provide critically important venues for terrorists to establish trust and confidence—and the essential bona fides required to operate clandestine cells in the future. Urban centers in densely populated cities such as Karachi, Jakarta, London, or even Detroit are key to al-Qaeda's access to modern communications, command, and control while eluding law enforcement. Therefore, although the U.S. military campaign must continue to root out al-Qaeda from Afghanistan and its environs, a longer-term diplomatic effort with local law enforcement and intelligence operatives to crack down on the smaller terrorist swamps will be increasingly important.

The Role of Diplomacy

The centrality of diplomacy in a counterterrorism strategy derives from the fact that international terrorism by definition is a political act. With regard to al-Qaeda, although its political agenda has evolved over the past five years the group's consistent themes are focused on opposition to U.S. policy—in particular, the U.S. military presence in Saudi Arabia, its attacks against Iraq, and U.S. support for Israel. Al-Qaeda seeks a war with the West and secular Arab regimes and the establishment of a pan-Islamic fundamentalist regime in those same Islamic lands. Mixed with this political agenda is pure rage against the West, especially the United States and its way of life.

An effective U.S. counterterrorism strategy must seek to establish political will—to seek "zero tolerance" of terrorism by all nations. To achieve this goal, diplomats must establish several parallel tracks of effort that are mutually reinforcing. The first challenge for the United States is to strip away terrorists' political agenda and focus on their criminal deeds. Diplomacy seeks to assemble a consensus on the nature of the terrorist threat that underscores a zero-tolerance policy on all forms of terrorism—even "just causes." This is not easy, and it will take persistent work in diplomatic channels and through international public diplomacy. Some diplomats unwittingly diffuse the focus of the counterterrorism effort by calling for lengthy analysis of "root causes." Indeed there is a need to understand the environment where some terrorists seem to thrive, especially those associated with local insurgencies, but this inquiry should not be permitted to divert attention from the focus on breaking up al-Qaeda cells and their associates. An exclusive focus on "root causes"—such as poverty—may be counterproductive anyway. Al-Qaeda's ideology, funding, and leadership come from one of the richest parts of the world (Saudi Arabia and the Persian Gulf), and its leadership, as well as many key operatives, come from the upper and middle classes.

Effective diplomacy will be essential to developing the international consensus that regards terrorism as a criminal act and transforms that consensus into concrete actions that are high on the priority lists of all states. Diplomats then need to set in motion a series of separate but mutually reinforcing tracks that will defeat local terrorist organizations. These tracks include measures to strengthen international and national counterterrorism laws; increased funding for training, equipment, intelligence exploitation, and other programs; and application of coercive measures such as sanctions and the rare but important option of military force. Finally, diplomats must carefully orchestrate these programs, each in their own regional and national context, to manage competing priorities and sustain the efforts of key partners to denounce terrorism unequivocally and to build effective police and intelligence apparati that arrest terrorists or, at a minimum, deter, disrupt, or diminish their activities.

These traditional instruments of counterterrorism have been used with mixed results against previous terrorist threats. Each of these tools must be adapted to the current threat and, more important, sustained with an unrelenting determination.

Zero Tolerance for Terrorism: International and National Laws

International and national laws provide the legal framework for cooperation and action against terrorism. The twelve United Nations Conventions on Terrorism focus comprehensively on a wide range of commonly agreed and specific terrorist activities (such as hijacking aircraft, manufacturing unmarked plastic explosives, taking hostages); these Conventions form the basis of an international counterterrorism legal regime. Such an approach underpins the argument that law enforcement should be the primary response to terrorism, eliminating the moral ambiguity that often muddles counterterrorism discussion and, more important, action. In the immediate aftermath of the September 11 attacks, the UN Security Council adopted resolution 1373 (September 28, 2001), under Chapter VII (use of force) of the UN Charter. This resolution obliges all member states to prevent and suppress the financing of terrorist acts, criminalizes the provision or collection of funds by their nationals for terrorist actions, and calls on member states to freeze funds and other financial assets that may be used for terrorism. With an acute focus on crushing the financial lifeline of terrorists, this resolution establishes a network of information-sharing and cooperative executive action among key international institutions such as Interpol and the Finance Action Task Force. A standing Counter Terrorism Committee (CTC) also was set up to track member state implementation, as well as to provide technical and other assistance.[16] The United States can play a key role in encouraging member states to sign, ratify, and implement these conventions and resolutions by reinforcing the UN's basic premise that counterterrorism should be based on international law.[17]

The importance of this effort may not be as immediately apparent as the arrest of an al-Qaeda operative, but in the long term it is very important. These laws and the Security Council resolution have a political and legal dimension. Legally, they confirm the specific criminality of the act, stripping away the political motive of the terrorist. Politically, they provide a framework for subsequent national laws that, if properly implemented, will result in signatories establishing domestic laws that prohibit fundraising and other acts of conspiracy with terrorist organizations, giving law enforcement authorities new instruments that are within the rule of law. For countries that want to enact these laws but may not know how—or may be reluctant to do so—it provides expertise and political cover. For those that are slow to implement these laws, it gives American diplomats pressure points consistent with international law and points of departure for subsequent assistance programs. For example, if a country is lax in its banking laws, allowing terrorists to move money through its banks, this expanding body of law enables

American diplomats to put pressure on these countries to comply with international law, not just American fancy.

On the national level in the United States, the designation of Foreign Terrorist Organizations (FTOs) by the Department of State is an important instrument in garnering international support against terrorists. This FTO process—which identifies terrorist groups, outlaws them, and seizes their assets—also serves an important signaling effect for other countries. For instance, the inclusion of the Harkat-ul-Mujahiddin (HUM) on the list of foreign terrorist groups in 1997 prompted Pakistan security agencies to distance themselves from the organization. Outlawing a group has an immediate and discernible impact: It automatically becomes illegal to be a member of the group or to raise money or be otherwise associated with it. The current FTO process is carefully prepared, reviewed legally, credible, and implemented in cooperation with the Department of State, the Department of Justice, and the intelligence community. This process should be kept apolitical, and other governments must follow the U.S. lead in outlawing terrorist groups.

After years of describing the benefits of such laws and friendly pressure among counterparts in the counterterrorism business, the United Kingdom has joined the United States in instituting a similar set of laws that criminalizes certain terrorist groups—giving authorities new legal instruments to disrupt the activities of individuals that clearly constitute a terrorist threat. A similar sustained effort should be expanded to other countries as well, demonstrating the value of FTO processes and pressuring for an FTO or similar process to be implemented in as many nations as possible.

International consensus must transcend the writing of new laws and the designation of terrorist organizations. It also requires a real commitment to tackling the terrorist threat. International efforts can only succeed on a quid pro quo approach: "I will pursue the terrorists that threaten you if you go after those that threaten me." In this regard, a state's own internal initiatives remain the most crucial factor. This factor also applies to the United States. For instance, in the 1990s the government of Sri Lanka complained of the considerable funding the Liberation Tigers of Tamil Elam (Tamil Tigers) received from the Detroit area. Although U.S. officials were aware of this flow of support, this activity was a low priority because it was not a direct threat to U.S. nationals. To their credit, U.S. federal counterterrorist officials responded to the appeals of the Sri Lankan government and cracked down on the Detroit-based organizations providing the funding to the Tamil Tigers, thereby bolstering U.S. credibility with foreign partners to do more against other terrorist groups within their jurisdiction.

Building Counterterrorism Capacity: U.S. Assistance Programs

Direct counterterrorism, economic, and military assistance from the United States represents one of the most effective tools to help states improve their counterterrorist efforts. Part of this effort includes the Department of State's Anti-Terrorism Assistance (ATA) program. Many governments have a vital interest in receiving U.S. assistance that allows them to improve the work of their civilian and military security services. By 2000, 20,000 foreign law enforcement officers and airport security personnel from 100 countries had been trained within the framework of the ATA training program.[18] The Bush administration in its fiscal year 2003 budget submission requested $121 million for counterterrorism engagement programs, training, and equipment to help other countries fight global terror. As part of this commitment, $52 million is to be used to establish a Center for Anti-Terrorism and Security Training (CAST), which, once operational, will train 7,500 partner law enforcement personnel annually in advanced antiterrorism and security measures.[19] This amount is a significant increase over previous budget allocations to the ATA program, which received $23 million and $38 million in 1997 and 2001, respectively.[20] Apart from the Department of State, the Central Intelligence Agency (CIA), the Federal Bureau of Investigation (FBI), and the Pentagon also may play useful cooperative roles in the bilateral and multilateral arena. In fact, today these other agencies have increasingly large "foreign aid" budgets that eclipse that of the Department of State. Although these programs are helpful, the diffuse nature of the separate U.S. programs misses a key opportunity to leverage the host country. Again, the key is political will; to ensure political will and to reap real results from the investment the United States should package its aid to insist on a coherent and integrated strategy that gets results. Virtually all countries (except those with political problems of a too-close association with Washington) are more than happy to receive training and assistance for their military, intelligence, or law enforcement agencies. However, assuring that these investments are directed effectively at the threats that interest the United States is much more difficult. The Department of State should take the lead in pressuring the host country for results. Because they depend on smooth relations to develop certain legal cases or intelligence leads, FBI and CIA operatives often are reluctant to put pressure on host governments. The State Department, however—given the right leadership—often is in a better position to bring leverage to bear on the country's political leadership to deliver results.

Thus, to maximize effectiveness and the ability to coordinate the locals, to the extent possible counterterrorism budgets should be managed by the Department of State and implemented by the appropriate expert agency. This approach is not new. The multibillion-dollar cold war security assistance programs—which included foreign military financing (military equipment), international military training (for training of foreign officers in U.S schools), and economic support funds (for economic aid)—were managed by the Department of State. Consolidating the programs in one budget line also would give the Congress better leverage. Congress can evaluate the results of aid provided and increase pressure or make adjustments accordingly. Departments and agencies will resist such measures; they prefer to have their own programs, as do their congressional committees. However, the effort to consolidate is a worthy one.

Military assistance and cooperation also may be used successfully against terrorists. Foreign security forces acting decisively, in close coordination with U.S. intelligence or operational support, can be critically effective in the pursuit of terrorist networks. This approach is particularly pertinent to the new environment in which al-Qaeda will seek sanctuaries where government control is weak. Local security capabilities must be strengthened and supplemented to provide the main effort against terrorism. Wendy Chamberlain, the former U.S. Ambassador to Pakistan, notes, "You don't beat terrorism only by building better fences around our homeland. You beat terrorism by cooperating with Pakistani police to bash down doors of Abu Zubaydah's al-Qaeda safe house."[21] Since February 2002 the United States has embarked on widespread training and equipping for counterterrorist warfare.[22] For example, apart from a considerable U.S. military presence in Uzbekistan and Kyrgyzstan, the Pentagon has sent 1,200 troops and $100 million in aid to the Philippines,[23] 100 troops to Yemen,[24] and 150 military trainers to Georgia, where U.S. Special Forces have provided training and equipment to the Georgian military fighting militants in the Pankisi Gorge.[25] In return, the United States has received significant support in its counterterrorist campaign. To date, 136 nations have offered some form of military assistance in the war on terrorism, and 46 multilateral organizations have issued declarations of support. The North Atlantic Treaty Organization (NATO); the Organization of American States (OAS); and Australia, New Zealand, and U.S. Treaty states (ANZUS) have invoked their collective defense treaty obligations with the United States.[26]

Given the transnational nature of terrorism, the United States also must assist countries by coordinating collective efforts to combat terrorism on a regional level. Toward this end, American diplomats can support the creation of regional and international mechanisms that foster closer cooperation, discussion of policy choices, and development of new means to diminish the terrorist threat. This strategy is particularly important in regions such as the Caucasus, as well as central and southeast Asia, where terrorist groups take advantage of porous borders and the dearth of cooperation among intelligence and law enforcement authorities. American diplomats can help broker common work among states that sometimes have difficulty working together because of other bilateral strains. Regional counterterrorism fora, sponsored by U.S. diplomats, often can pull together these groups and get them talking—the first step that hopefully leads to intelligence sharing and combined training and operations.

Three aspects of these bilateral and regional programs require fine-tuning, however. First, the United States must provide more financial resources to assist foreign governments to intensify the war against terror. The U.S. government's counterterrorism budget increased from $6 billion in 1998 to $9.7 billion in 2001. This is a first step in the right direction,[27] but much of this increase is absorbed by the U.S. bureaucracy building defensive measures against terrorism itself. More resources need to be accorded to assistance programs to train and equip countries such as Georgia, Yemen, the Philippines, and Indonesia that will take the fight closer to its source. Before the attacks of September 11, during the transition from the Clinton administration to the current Bush administration the Office of the Coordinator for Counter-Terrorism in the Department of State had already designed a draft program for ATA funding to be raised to $200 million. In this post–September 11 milieu, the ATA program for foreign training and security assistance must be expanded to at least $250 to $300 million, with an aggressive program of training and assistance to military, intelligence, and law enforcement organizations in a range of states.

Second, the Department of State must coordinate all U.S. overseas counterterrorism programs, regardless of executing agency, to make more efficient use of limited resources and maximize the political leverage on a country. When necessary, the National Security Council staff can help arbitrate differences between agencies, but implementation should remain coordinated by the State Department. If the United States cannot coordinate its own approaches, it will only exacerbate the difficulties of interdepartmental coordination in the country it seeks to assist. One way of overcoming this hurdle is to significantly increase the Department of State budget for counterterrorism, which will enable it to fund interagency programs. One good example of such interagency cooperation funded and coordinated by the Department of State was the training of the Philippines Special Forces by the Department of Defense (DoD) in early 2001 from a $2 million allocation out of the ATA budget.

Third, in granting the ATA and other forms of security and military aid, the United States must ensure that recipient states do not eventually turn their security apparatus, developed with American assistance, against legitimate local opposition. Most of the recipients of U.S. aid have weak justice systems and weak democratic institutions, particularly in south Asia, central Asia, and the Caucasus. There will be a temptation to unleash the newly trained and equipped personnel against the opponents of the regime in the name of fighting terrorism. The United States also risks being associated with undemocratic or otherwise authoritarian regimes—further validating the charges from radical Islamic terrorist organizations that target it.

Sanctions and the Use of Force

The campaign against terrorism also relies on disincentives to compel states and institutions to action. Sanctions have proven effective in reducing state sponsorship of terrorism in the past. Most notably, the combination of unilateral U.S. sanctions and UN Security Council–mandated sanctions regime clearly contributed to Muammar Qaddafi's decision to back away from terror. However, the changing nature of international terrorism may limit the value of sanctions against rogue states because few states would want to be caught supporting international terrorists such as bin Laden and suffer the collective wrath of the international community.

Sanctions will be a more difficult instrument to apply in the case of al-Qaeda. Since the Taliban has been eliminated, al-Qaeda has no direct governmental sponsor—nor is it likely to gain one. The United States should not eliminate the instrument of sanctions from its arsenal, however. This tool must be revised to deal with underperforming countries in the war against terrorism when positive incentives prove to be less than convincing. In these cases, sanctions should be targeted against specific institutions within a state rather than against the state as a whole. This category may include security organizations that have ties to terrorist organizations, banks that are lax in enforcing antilaundering laws, airlines, airports, or seaports that fail to implement effective security procedures.

In addition, the United States may consider revising its report card on key states involved in the fight against terrorism. Currently, the Department of State has only two categories: state sponsors of terrorism—which require a wide range of sanctions to be immediately applied—and states "not fully cooperating," which have a limited set of sanctions tied primarily to the sale of defense articles. The first category, state sponsorship, has worked fairly well in reducing or at least limiting the support of these states to terrorism. The second has not been used extensively because it would have been aimed at important allies. For instance, the Congressional Panel on Terrorism recommended that Pakistan and Greece (the latter for its weak response to the November 17 organization) should be listed as countries not fully supporting efforts to combat terrorism.[28] This has proven politically difficult. As in the case of previous counterterrorism instruments, including the FTO process and state sponsorship, Congress probably will have to require the executive branch to prepare a more realistic report card on performance that will enable the legislative branch to review its subsequent assistance funding. A system, if developed, should be careful not to impose too harsh a penalty initially, or the executive branch will not take the measure seriously.

The use of force should be the last resort in the counterterrorism campaign, but it is an important instrument. For the most part, military operations should be conducted by the national forces of the country in which the operation is to be taken. At times, the United States might consider participation if the host country would benefit from particular U.S. expertise. There are times, however, when the United States should consider direct action against foreign terrorists. The U.S. campaign in Afghanistan in October 2001 is a good example of how effective military action was achieved by a small group of Special Forces and CIA operatives assisting the Northern Alliance in the north and forces loyal to Hamid Karzai in the south to rout the Taliban and al-Qaeda. However, future military operations are more likely to involve small, special operations strikes against terrorist cells or camps. The record of U.S. operatives in this area is weak but should be improving with experience in the latter stages of the Afghan campaign that is directed against smaller targets. Intelligence—especially human intelligence from sources inside terrorist organizations—is critical to provide operational planners with sufficient detail to attack terrorist cells and minimize the risk of collateral damage to innocent civilians.

The Case of Pakistan

Pakistan is a key ally in the war against terrorism. Pakistan straddles the center of gravity for the international jihadist movement in south Asia and central Asia. It is a nuclear power and a leader in the Islamic world. American diplomats need to "get it right" in Pakistan and forge a more comprehensive U.S.-Pakistan relationship that delivers results in the struggle against terrorism, while strengthening Pakistan's democratic institutions.

The first step for diplomats is to gain a consensus between the United States and Pakistan on the nature of the threat in Pakistan and in neighboring Afghanistan, where they have enduring political and security interests. The remnants of al-Qaeda already are finding refuge within Pakistan, linking up with the local groups that sympathize with their goals. They also find supporters from the ranks of the radical Islamic schools (or *madrassas*) that train many would-be terrorists with a violent aberration of Islamic theology. It is insufficient only to identify radicalized madrassas in Pakistan as the source of terrorism; we must help the Pakistani authorities provide alternative schools that produce engineers and computer programmers instead of radicalized extremists. In addition, the United States must assist Pakistan's efforts to take on the violent Islamic groups within its political spectrum, while allowing others legitimate political space. Washington should condemn any links of the Pakistan Army to Kashmiri groups that indulge in terrorism. The policy of zero tolerance must be kept uniform. National laws should be strengthened—perhaps with a form of the United States' FTO process that will enable the law enforcement community to break up groups that support terrorist activity—while protecting the political expression of all groups, including the nonviolent Islamic parties.

Another key component of the relationship is assistance programs with security institutions in military, police, and intelligence organizations. Both the Pakistani army's intelligence service (ISI) and the national police (IB) play important roles in counterterrorism. The army, however, has troubling relationships with certain Kashmiri groups—some of them on the U.S. State Department's list of terrorist organizations. In addition, the army's previous relationship with the Taliban was very troubling to the United States. U.S. assistance programs with the ISI must be carefully calibrated to ensure that its overall policies and programs are consistent with U.S. goals and principles. The United States also has training programs with the IB, an institution with historically fewer links to troubling groups. The United States should consider targeting its assistance to institutions with the best track record, thereby providing a positive incentive. This method, of course, risks unhealthy bureaucratic competition; ideally, both institutions can be robustly supported. However, some tough decisions may be required to ensure that U.S. objectives are met with training assistance funds. As suggested above, aid should be coordinated by the State Department to maximize coordination and leverage. The diplomatic action should follow the steps outlined above: establish mutual understanding of the threat, improve local laws, and strengthen security institutions with expanded programs. Monitoring by the State Department ensures human rights standards are adhered to as well—and results are measured.

In short, an effective U.S. counterterrorist strategy in south Asia comprises a set of coherent and mutually reinforcing long-term policies that promote a Pakistan that is at peace with its neighbors, educates its youth for productive work, and is capable of tackling domestic and cross-border terrorists while respecting the rule of law. Such a strategy requires a serious commitment of U.S. economic, military, and counterterrorism aid to Pakistan. Pakistan currently receives $50 million in military aid and $200 million in economic aid annually. These amounts are modest in contrast to the $2.1 billion in military aid and $600 million in economic aid given annually to Israel or the $1.3 billion in military aid and $615 million for social programs spent annually in Egypt.[29] Simply to assist in the training and reform of the Pakistan security agencies would require a program in the magnitude of about $100 million annually, at least. Compared to cold war funding levels of key countries such as El Salvador, this is still a small sum.

As in the cold war, the United States may find itself supporting regimes that are undemocratic or—perhaps more generously—in various stages of democratic transition. In some cases the United States will have to deal with these regimes in the short term. Democratic transition should remain a high priority, however—not only because of its intrinsic foreign policy benefits for the United States but also for its long-term counterterrorism objectives. Strong democratic societies, with respect for the rule of law, ultimately are the best counterterrorism partners as well.

Conclusion

Since September 11, 2001, the United States has undergone a transformation of epic proportions. The images of passenger-filled airplanes crashing into the icons of our nation's pride and prestige and the memories of the people lost are forever seared into the world's memory. The notion of an impregnable continental United States has been shattered, and U.S. vulnerabilities are now being reassessed. Our response must be commensurate with the scale of the attacks and the evolved terrorist threat to U.S security and interests at home and abroad.

The United States needs a comprehensive, long-term, diplomatic counterterrorism strategy. Such a strategy must first seek to address the diverse localities where terrorist operate: in remote and often lawless rural conflict zones in the Caucasus, central Asia, and southeast Asia, as well as modern and densely populated cities around the world. Our policy instruments must be as diverse, nuanced, and effective as the preferred localities and diversity of the terrorist networks.

International cooperation in combating this global menace is a necessity, not a luxury. The twelve United Nations conventions and Security Council Resolution 1373 already provide the legal basis for cooperative action. The United States needs, however, to encourage the international community to focus on the implementation of these international conventions and resolutions, as well as the need to strengthen domestic legal regimes. The United States can assist in local enforcement actions by doubling the ATA program to about $250–300 million annually. Such assistance, however, also must be complemented with a serious commitment of economic aid to states and regions that are fertile breeding grounds for terrorists.

The Department of State should reassert its primacy in coordinating and directing the national assistance strategies while retaining a very tight focus on the goal: to crush terrorist organizations by arresting their operatives and denying the organizations any space to assemble, plan, or execute another cataclysmic act of terror.

Finally, the U.S. government must remain focused on the threat. The diplomacy of counterterrorism requires a thorough understanding and engagement at the highest levels of government, patient application of diplomatic and political pressure to sustain the coalition, and the resources—reflecting the importance of these priorities—to succeed.

Notes

1. Afghanistan would still be the preferred gathering place for al-Qaeda. It will remain a sanctuary, but not a sanctuary of impunity. It is unlikely that al-Qaeda will have the same extensive military training facilities—camps, barracks, and so forth—in Afghanistan in the near future.

2. Thomas Ricks and Kamran Khan, "U.S. Urges Pakistan Toward New Attacks," *Washington Post,* 12 May 2002.

3. Bradley Graham, "al-Qaeda, Taliban Leaders Elusive," *Washington Post,* 30 March 2002.

4. "Bin Laden at Afghan Border, Officials Tell Paper," Reuters, 28 August 2002; available at www.myafghan.com.

5. Michael Ware, "Taunts from the Border," *Time,* 20 October 2002. Attempts by the Pakistan government to pursue al-Qaeda in this region also have faced considerable local protest and resistance; see "Pakistani Tribesmen Protest Al Qaeda Hunt," Reuters, 5 September 2002; available at www.myafghan.com.

6. Associated Press, "Official: al Qaeda Still Dangerous," 10 October 2002; available at www.myafghan.com.

7. Reuters, "Bin Laden at Afghan Border."

8. Cathy Newman, "Bin Laden Supporters 'Still Funding al-Qaeda'," *Financial Times,* 8 May 2002.

9. Tony Karon, "How's al Qaeda Doing," *Time,* 3 July 2002.

10. Shaul Shay and Yoram Schweitzer, "The 'Afghan Alumni' Terrorism. Islamic Militants against the Rest of the World," Institute for Counter-Terrorism, 6 November 2000; available at www.ict.org.il.

11. Reyko Huang, "In the Spotlight: Jemaah Islamiah," Terrorism Project, Center for Defense Information, 1 April 2002; available at www.cdi.org.

12. Raymond Bonner, "Southeast Asia Remains Fertile Ground for al Qaeda," *New York Times,* 28 October 2002.

13. Edmund Andrews, "German Officials Find More Terrorist Groups, and Some Disturbing Parallels," *New York Times,* 26 April 2002.

14. Susan Schmidt and Dana Priest, "U.S. Fears Low-Level Al Qaeda Attacks," *Washington Post,* 9 September 2002.

15. Susan Schmidt and Dan Eggen, "Key Suspect in 9/11 Attack Is Apprehended in Pakistan," *Washington Post,* 15 September 2002.

16. S/RES/1373(2001), UN Security Council Resolution, 28 September 2001.

17. This argument on the need to ground counterterrorism in international law was made in the Report of the Policy Working Group on the United Nations and Terrorism.

18. U.S. Department of State, *Patterns of Global Terrorism 1999, Annual Report of the Office of the Coordinator for Counterterrorism,* April 2000.

19. Office of Management and Budget, *Budget of the United States Government. Fiscal Year 2003, State and International Assistance Programs*, September 2002; available at www.whitehouse.gov/omb.

20. See Budget of the U.S. Government Fiscal Year 1999 and 2003, available at GPO Access (wais.access.gpo.gov), pp. 678 and 963–70, respectively.

21. Raymond Bonner, "At Embassy in Pakistan, Home Is Next Objective," *New York Times*, 12 May 2002.

22. Elizabeth Bumiller, "Bush Vows to Aid Other Countries in War on Terror," *New York Times*, 12 March 2002.

23. James Dao, "U.S. Sends More Troops to Philippines in Rebel Fight," *New York Times*, 20 April 2002.

24. Michael Gordon and James Dao, "U.S. Broadens Terror Fight, Readying Troops for Yemen," *New York Times*, 2 March 2002.

25. Bumiller, "Bush Vows to Aid Other Countries in War on Terror."

26. U.S. Department of State, International Information Programs, "Boucher Summarizes International Support for War on Terrorism," 1 March 2002.

27. Office of Management and Budget, *Annual Report to Congress on Combating Terrorism*, August 2001; available at www.whitehouse.gov/omb.

28. See Report of Special Oversight Panel on Terrorism Opening Hearing on Biological, Nuclear and Cyber Terrorism, May 2000.

29. Figures from Council on Foreign Relations, "Terrorism: Q & A"; available at www.terrorismanswers.com.

five

INTELLIGENCE

Paul R. Pillar

The basic problem that terrorism poses for intelligence is as simple as it is chilling. A group of conspirators conceives a plot. Only the few conspirators know of their intentions, although they may get help from others. They mention nothing about their plot to anyone they cannot absolutely trust. They communicate nothing about their plans in a form that can be intercepted. They are careful not to expose to others any materials that would betray their intentions. They do not purchase, procure, or build anything that, on the face of it, is suspicious. They live and move normally and inconspicuously, and any preparations that cannot be done behind closed doors they do as part of those movements. The problem: How do we learn of the plot?

The challenge does not stop there. As with many perpetrators of past terrorist attacks, the conspirators whose plans we need to discover may not have had any prior involvement in terrorism or be members of a previously known terrorist group. The target for intelligence is not just proven terrorists; it is anyone who *might* commit terrorism in the future.

Terrorism is a fundamentally different and more difficult subject than the great majority of other topics the intelligence community is asked to cover. The bull's-eye of this intelligence target—an individual terrorist plot—lacks the size and signatures of most other targets, from nuclear weapons programs to political instability. The need to uncover the activities not only of specified groups or states but also of *potential* terrorists makes intelligence questions about terrorism, not just the answers, more indeterminate than with most other topics. Some of the most important limits to collecting information about terrorism are inherent to the subject and the way terrorists operate. Those limits are permanent and ineradicable.

A painful but true implication is that no matter how much brainpower and resources the United States devotes to counterterrorist intelligence, how much brilliance goes into the relevant intelligence operations, and how aggressively the intelligence community is reorganized or revamped to go after the problem of terrorism, some of what terrorists do will remain, for all practical purposes, unknowable. Some terrorist plots will go undiscovered, and some terrorist attacks, including some major ones, will occur. Intelligence has an enormously important role in learning as much as can be learned about terrorists' activities and in so doing reducing the number of terrorist incidents and lives lost. U.S. intelligence has saved lives from terrorism in the past, and how well it performs its mission will be a major determinant of how many American lives will be lost to, or saved from, terrorism in the years ahead. But even the best intelligence will never be able to save them all.

In this chapter I describe the functions that intelligence performs in counterterrorism, as well as what it should *not* be relied upon to do; the directions in which the U.S. counterterrorist intelligence apparatus has already evolved; and the aspects in which future change and evolution hold the most promise of improving (but only modestly) the results. I conclude with a caution about how some well-intentioned attempts to get U.S. intelligence to do even better on terrorism can be counterproductive. I argue for care and restraint in making changes—particularly in the emotional aftermath of wrenching terrorist attacks, which is when most changes to counterterrorist programs are made—and for realism in expectations about the part intelligence can play in helping to safeguard a nation against terrorism.

Functions of Counterterrorist Intelligence

The counterterrorist role that intelligence most commonly is expected to perform is to discover the details of terrorist plots so that the plots can be rolled up before they are carried out or, as a second-best response, the intended targets can be protected by relocating them, augmenting security, or canceling or rescheduling events. This is the most direct, most satisfying, and—when such incidents are made public—the most spectacularly successful way in which intelligence can help to curb terrorism. Certainly intelligence agencies need to do what they can to increase their odds of collecting this kind of plot-specific intelligence. For the reasons mentioned above, however, intelligence specific to terrorist plots often is unattainable. This function, however satisfying and potentially spectacular, therefore will never be the biggest contribution that intelligence makes to counterterrorism.

That truth is uncomfortable not only for the public but for security managers. Given the costs—monetary and nonmonetary—of security countermeasures and preventive actions such as closing an embassy or canceling a flight, there is an understandable tendency to rely on tactical warning so that protective measures can be bolstered when threats are present but relaxed when they are not. As the panel led by retired Admiral William Crowe that studied the bombings of the U.S. embassies in East Africa in 1998 noted, that tendency is a mistake.[1] It puts too much faith in the likelihood of collecting tactical intelligence on whatever will be the next terrorist plot to materialize. Intelligence agencies must work to dispel that misplaced faith. They have a responsibility not only to report to their consumers what useful information they have but also to instruct them on the limits of the intelligence they are providing, including some sense of what is *not* known. There is no subject on which that responsibility is more important than the warning of terrorist attacks.

The largest contribution that intelligence actually makes to counterterrorism is the collection of information on individual terrorists, terrorist leaders, cells, and groups that is used to disrupt terrorist organizations. The information collected can be quite specific (names, addresses, phone numbers, etc.), even if it does not identify specific plots. Terrorists are highly security conscious about their attack plans, but they do not live and operate in cocoons. They have identities (albeit sometimes multiple ones), they meet, they move, and they communicate. There are many types of collectable information that, though fragmentary and incomplete, can provide clues to the location, activities, and associations of suspected terrorists. With enough such clues, a would-be terrorist can be arrested, deported, interrogated, or even prosecuted. Cells can be broken up and their members left to wonder what each one may be telling to the authorities.

Although every counterterrorist instrument must be used to the fullest, in some respects the terrorist-by-terrorist, cell-by-cell disruption of terrorist infrastructures is the most fruitful. To be sure, this instrument—like all the others—has considerable limitations. The most serious is the uncertainty that a would-be terrorist, especially one who has not been involved in previous attacks, will come on to the intelligence agencies' screens in the first place. The potential payoffs, however, also are considerable. Put up security countermeasures around one potential terrorist target and you have protected that one target from attack (probably attack through one particular method), for as long as you keep the security in place. Disrupt a terrorist cell and you have prevented that cell from attacking any target, at any time, with any method. Because terrorists often commit other illegal acts (such as smuggling or use of false documents), disruption of their organizations can build on the enforcement of national laws by foreign police and security services. There also are beneficial secondary effects. Disruption can sow suspicion and distrust within a terrorist organization far beyond the cell that is disrupted, and materials that are confiscated when a cell is broken up often provide intelligence leading to the disruption of other cells—even cells in other countries. Most of the counterterrorist successes by U.S. intelligence have involved such disruption.

Intelligence makes many different types of analytic contributions to counterterrorism. Even the contributions that can be described as warning or assessment of terrorist threats cover a broad range, from the highly tactical to the broadly strategic (see table 5–1). These contributions, in turn, serve a comparably broad range of ways in which the nation tries to meet the threats. Toward the tactical end is the task of sifting through the snips and shards of information about possible terrorists and suspected terrorist cells, trying to make enough sense of it to distinguish terrorists from nonterrorists, to cause possible disruption of terrorist cells, and to guide the collection of further intelligence that would fill knowledge gaps. At a less tactical level there are a host of analytic questions such as questions concerning the intentions and capabilities of large terrorist organizations or the overall terrorist threat in a given country or region. Intelligence analysis at this level has saved lives; for example, the assessment that the terrorist threat to U.S. forces in Saudi Arabia was high at the time of the bombing at Khobar Towers in 1996 underlay security measures that prevented the truck carrying the huge bomb from penetrating the perimeter of the military compound. Penetration would have produced a death toll far higher than the nineteen servicemen who did die. At the most strategic level, analysis becomes a task of educating the consumer of intelligence on global trends and patterns in international terrorism. The policy decisions informed by this kind of analysis include overarching decisions involving the resources devoted to counterterrorism and how counterterrorism should fit in the larger foreign policy agenda.

Intelligence supports other counterterrorist instruments in many ways that go beyond warning or assessment of terrorist threats. Intelligence about the nature and activities of extremist groups provides the basis, for example, for decisions on designating foreign terrorist organizations (FTOs) under U.S. law. Intelligence makes a similar contribution regarding the activities of state sponsors of terrorism. It supports diplomacy not only by informing senior officials who have to make designation decisions and persuade other governments to cooperate in counterterrorism but also in developing material that can be shared with those governments. When military force is used in a counterterrorist mode, the contribution of intelligence includes the determi-

Table 5-1　Spectrum of Terrorism Warning and Threat Assessment

Types of Threat Information		Plot-Specific	Tactical	Strategic	Grand Strategic	Educational
Specificity of information	Location	Exact address	A few cities	Country or region	Regions	Worldwide
	Time	Exact date	Days or weeks	Weeks or months	Months or years	Years or decades
	Targets	Single named target	Several named targets	Single category of interests (e.g., embassies or military bases)	Several categories of interests	U.S. interests
Possible countermeasures		Roll up the plot; evacuate or relocate the target	Short-term, high-cost security measures; watch for the perpetrators	Raise alert levels; temporary but sustainable security measures	Permanent new physical measures and procedures	Legislation; major national programs

nation of responsibility for terrorist attacks to which the military action is a response, as well as the same sort of support to military targeting that is provided whenever armed forces are used for other purposes. Support to law enforcement includes detailed exchanges of information and following up on leads, not just to determine responsibility for terrorist crimes but to chase down the perpetrators.

Intelligence analysis on terrorism is all-source analysis. That is, it draws on every available source of information—human and technical intelligence sources, as well as what is publicly available—to develop insights about terrorist activity. Much of the analysis parallels analytical work outside government, but the intelligence analyst is the only one who can meld the classified information with the unclassified and guide the efforts of intelligence collectors to attempt to fill in the gaps.

Counterterrorist intelligence analysis includes a couple of other functions that, though valid, are—like the collection of plot-specific tactical intelligence—not as large a part of the job of intelligence as is often supposed. One is the prediction of terrorist tactics and techniques (which is related to the issue of targets). Among the frequent reactions to a terrorist attack is the posing of the question, "Why didn't someone think of that method of hitting us?" The answer usually is that the tactic was indeed considered—but so were dozens of other possible methods that terrorists could use, many of which were equally plausible. Intelligence reporting sometimes reveals that certain groups are interested in a particular method of attack or even developing the capability to use that method. Intelligence analysis must use that reporting in sensitizing security managers and policymakers to the range of terrorist tactics they should be prepared to counter and in explaining why terrorists may be turning more to some tactics than to others. Intelligence agencies have no special advantage, however, in blue-sky speculation about methods terrorists might use in the future. Thinkers outside government do plenty of that kind of speculation. Whether inside or outside government, predicting the specific method to be used in the next major terrorist attack gets back to the basic problem of trying to uncover plot-specific information. (Before the attacks on September 11, 2001, there was much speculation about ways in which terrorists could hit the U.S. homeland. Most of that speculation involved biological, nuclear, or other exotic materials or methods—musing that may yet turn out to be useful in anticipating future attacks but was irrelevant to the hijackings that did occur.)[2] An agency (or individual analyst) that boldly and correctly predicted the method of the next terrorist attack might be applauded after the fact for prescience, but that prediction probably would be nothing more than a lucky guess.

Another function that is prominent in public perceptions of intelligence analysis is that of "connecting the dots" of information about a terrorist plot in the making. This function is the analytical equivalent of the task of collecting plot-specific information. As with that task, intelligence agencies (usually working in concert with law enforcement) must continually search for all possible connections among whatever fragments of information they have. This function is at the heart of the tactical-level analytical work that intelligence agencies do continually, through techniques such as cross-checking of names and other information with previous reporting and tasking intelligence assets to fill in gaps that may involve still other connections. The reality that the agencies face—and often is overlooked in the aftermath of a major terrorist incident, when there is an understandable focus on the bits of information that pertained to that one incident—is that there is never just one set of "dots" but many of them, each of which can be connected in multiple ways. All of them must be vigorously pursued through all of the name-checking, asset-tasking techniques that are available. Successful pursuit usually results in a disruption—which is likely to prevent future, still-unknown terrorist attacks—rather than the rolling up of a plot in progress. There seldom is a basis for pointing to any one set of "dots" as predictive of the next terrorist attack and worthy of more attention than all the other sets.

Intelligence analysis on terrorism illustrates a principle that is applicable to intelligence analysis generally: It is a business not primarily of prediction but of helping the consumers of intelligence deal with an unpredictable world.[3] It involves enlightening the policymaker about the range of threats, the directions threatening developments may take, the relative likelihood of each direction, the indicators suggesting that one direction is being taken rather than others, and the implications for the nation's interests of each of the possibilities. In one sense analysis of counterterrorism is even farther removed from prediction than is analysis of other national security issues because the whole purpose of "predicting" a terrorist event would be to prevent it. Counterterrorist analysts could never get as much satisfaction as their intelligence colleagues covering other topics from seeing their predictions come true. A world in which intelligence never "failed" to foresee a terrorist attack would be a world in which there was no longer any terrorism. One prediction that can be made with confidence is that such a world will never materialize.

Evolution of Counterterrorist Intelligence

Amid the rhetoric about how September 11 and the U.S. response to it marked a sea change from an earlier world, the continuity and history of U.S. efforts against terrorism get overlooked. The intelligence portion of that effort has received close attention for more than a decade and a half. The methods and institutions that perform the counterterrorist intelligence mission today are the product of evolution throughout that period, with many lessons applied and innovations tried.

Americans first became highly concerned about international terrorism in the 1980s, with buildings bombed and hostages taken in Lebanon and a spate of airplane hijackings elsewhere. (Until September 2001, the deadliest terrorist attack against Americans had been the bombing of the Marine barracks in Beirut in 1983.) The report in 1985 of a task force headed by then-Vice President George H. W. Bush led, in part, to creation the following year of the Directorate of Central Intelligence (DCI) Counterterrorist Center (CTC), which pulled together and augmented counterterrorist work that previously had been performed in different parts of the Central Intelligence Agency (CIA) and the intelligence community. The establishment of the CTC was a bureaucratic revolution, cutting across established hierarchies in the CIA to create an integrated element unlike anything that had come before. The novel aspect of the center was to bring operations officers, analysts, reports officers, technical experts, and other specialists into a single organization. It provided one-stop shopping on everything related to terrorism. It maximized synergy by having members of these different disciplines working literally side by side. The CTC became a model for centers later established to work on subjects such as narcotics and counterintelligence.

Subsequent refinements enhanced the synergy as well as the expertise of the CTC. A permanent professional corps of counterterrorist analysts was established in the mid-1990s, for example, replacing an earlier system in which analytical resources had to be borrowed from other offices in CIA. Particular emphasis was placed on developing the multiagency character of the center. More than a dozen agencies—including agencies with intelligence, law enforcement, and regulatory responsibilities—came to have full-time representation in the CTC. Sharing and cross-checking of data became easier when, for example, an officer of the Immigration and Naturalization Service (INS) was just a few desks away from a CIA analyst working on a case that involved someone entering the United States. The critical relationship between intelligence and law enforcement received special emphasis, particularly through cross-assignments of personnel. These cross-assignments included a deputy chief's job in the CTC being reserved for a senior Federal Bureau of Investigation (FBI) officer, with a CIA officer of comparable rank filling a corresponding position at the FBI. Such arrangements proved valuable not only in facilitating the flow of information but in breaking down what had been significant cultural barriers between the intelligence and law enforcement portions of the U.S. counterterrorist apparatus.

The intense commitment and imaginative organizational arrangements embodied in the CTC were applied in an even more concentrated way to special topics such as the threat posed by Osama bin Laden. In the mid-1990s, well before bin Laden became a recognized name in the United States or had been placed under indictment and well before anyone had heard of al-Qaeda, the CTC created a special unit focused solely on bin Laden. Resources were shifted into a coordinated effort to learn everything possible about bin Laden and his activities, to develop additional sources of information about him, and to formulate options for policymakers to deal with the threat he posed. Procedures for communicating between headquarters and the field were streamlined to assure quick responsiveness. The unit became a prototype for dealing in a well-focused way with vexing but high-priority problems.

The concentrated intelligence work on bin Laden provided the depth of understanding that became apparent in the wake of later incidents. This work enabled culpability for the bombings of embassies in 1998 to be determined so swiftly and certainly that the president could order a retaliatory strike in a matter of days. It also enabled CIA Director George Tenet to say with high confidence in the first hour after the attack on September 11, without any claims of responsibility and before any postincident reporting, "This has bin Laden all over it."[4]

The development of the CTC took place within a larger context of increasing priority and focus that the intelligence community devoted to counterterrorism. After sharing in general cuts to national security programs in the first half of the 1990s, the CTC and other counterterrorist-related efforts in the intelligence community were given higher priority in mid-decade after incidents such as the bombing at Khobar Towers raised concerns about terrorism; the priority was raised even further when the embassies in Africa were attacked in 1998. Since at least as far back as the embassy bombings, no subject has received higher priority from the intelligence community than counterterrorism—especially efforts to develop well-placed sources with a chance of obtaining information about plans for future terrorist attacks.

The point of this history is that most of the roads worth trying in counterterrorist intelligence have already been tried. Most of what needed to be reorganized has been reorganized, most of the institutional barriers that needed to come down have been smashed, most of the needed reprioritization has already been done, and most of the fires that needed to be lit under bureaucracies to keep them energized have been burning for some time. The distance the intelligence community has come in improving its counterterrorist efforts is reflected in its considerable successes in the form of terrorist operations preempted, terrorist infrastructures disrupted, and individual terrorists captured and brought to justice. Unfortunately, the intelligence officer's curse of being unable to reveal most of his successes while his failures become public applies in spades to counterterrorism, where the failures are dramatic and traumatic and most of the operations that underlie the successes are especially perishable were they to become known. What the Director of Central Intelligence (DCI) has been able to say publicly about the successes only scratches the surface.[5]

Any posture that smacks of "business as usual," however, will not be tolerated, particularly in the post–September 11 climate. Any answer that sounds like "we were already doing all that could reasonably be done" does not fly before a Congress and a public that want change. There will be continued pressure for new procedures, new organizations, new *something*. Finding things that look new and actually have a chance of improving counterterrorist intelligence will be difficult.

Responding to National Trauma

Significant events that are perceived as intelligence failures invariably are followed by voluminous commentary, as well as statements by congressmen and other quotable figures, on the theme that the U.S. intelligence community has deep flaws and needs overhauling. This phenomenon is especially true of major terrorist incidents. Because of the enormity of the death toll, the aftermath of the attacks on September 11 became the best example. The House Intelligence Committee expressed the prevailing tone in its report accompanying the next intelligence authorization bill by stating that "there is a fundamental need for both a cultural revolution within the intelligence community as well as significant structural changes."[6]

This urge to overhaul is a natural response to the pain of the moment and to the desire to believe that by changing things we can somehow avoid a recurrence of the pain. The unfortunate irony is that these moments when there is the greatest political support for change in some respects are the least favorable times for enacting sound, well-thought-out changes. The sheer emotion and atmosphere of recrimination do not lend themselves to well-reasoned debate. There usually is rush to legislate, with anniversary dates in mind as arbitrary deadlines (true of the omnibus counterterrorist legislation hurriedly passed in 1996 as the one-year anniversary of the Oklahoma City bombing approached and of debate on the homeland security bill in 2002 before the September 11 anniversary). Application of hindsight to a terrorist event that has just taken place distorts the realities that faced intelligence agencies before the event, with a blurring in the public consciousness of what was known before the incident with what was discovered afterward.

The greatest perceptual problem about intelligence is the tendency to focus narrowly on whatever errors were committed relevant to the most recent case and to draw larger conclusions about overall performance without placing those data points in any larger context. An example from the September 11 case is the issue of communication between the U.S. intelligence and law enforcement communities. A couple of well-publicized mistakes (the CIA's tardiness in placing two of the hijackers on a watch list and resistance by FBI headquarters to letting an FBI field office check some names with the CIA) became the basis for a widely accepted belief—repeated unquestioningly by scores of commentators—that "the FBI and CIA don't communicate with each other." The errors were a tiny fraction of what has been, since increased integration in the mid-1990s, a huge daily flow of terrorist-related leads and other information between those two agencies, as well as between the larger law enforcement and intelligence communities. To base conclusions about what needs to be changed on the publicized errors would be akin to a blind man diagnosing the ailments of an elephant based on a wart he is feeling on one of the animal's legs.

Similar narrowness characterized some other aspects of what came to be accepted wisdom about the U.S. intelligence community's performance relative to September 11. The shock of that event made it easy to overlook how similar the intelligence realities of that case had been to earlier ones—*viz.*, an absence of plot-specific tactical intelligence in the face of plotters who kept their plot well hidden, amid good strategic intelligence about the threat a group was posing to U.S. interests. The September 11 hijackers appear to have taken simple but effective steps, as in the prototypical terrorist plot described at the beginning of this chapter, to keep their plans under wraps. They do not appear to have communicated the existence of their plan, let alone the details of it, to anyone beyond a small circle of knowledgeability. Osama bin Laden, in the most revealing of his videotapes, said that even some of the hijackers were unaware of the nature of the operation.[7] Probably only the operation's ringleader, Mohammed Atta; a few of the other pilot/hijackers; and bin Laden and a handful of his lieutenants knew what was going to happen. It is difficult to refute President Bush's contention that the attack was not preventable or the conclusion reportedly reached by members of the Congressional intelligence committees investigating the disaster that there was no single piece of information that, if properly analyzed, could have prevented it.[8]

The strategic intelligence on the terrorist threat that al-Qaeda posed to the United States as September 2001 approached was strong. Director of Central Intelligence George Tenet, in his annual testimony to Congress in February 2001 on worldwide threats to U.S. national security, highlighted the threat from terrorism as "real" and "immediate." He spoke of terrorists as having become more operationally adept, seeking ways to deal with increased security around government and military facilities, and using strategies such as simultaneous attacks to increase the number of people they kill. "Osama bin Laden and his global network of lieutenants and associates," Tenet stated, were "the most immediate and serious threat."[9] These statements were the general warnings in unclassified testimony; as always, the classified intelligence provided to policymakers was more specific. Information collected as the year wore on led the intelligence community to conclude that the threat was becoming even more immediate and serious. Tenet was described as "nearly frantic" during the summer with concern over this threat, and he repeatedly conveyed his warnings to senior administration officials.[10] This was not the face of an intelligence community that failed to recognize a danger. It was a community that recognized the danger clearly, was exploiting every opportunity to collect further information on it, and felt first-hand the frustration of being unable to collect the details of exactly what, when, and where the next attack would be.

Good strategic intelligence with a lack of tactical intelligence has been a recurrent theme in postmortem examinations of major anti-U.S. terrorist incidents. It was a finding of the inquiry led by General Wayne Downing into the bombing of Khobar Towers in 1996.[11] It was a finding of the Crowe panel that examined the bombings of the embassies in Africa in 1998.[12] The theme recurs not because different cohorts of intelligence officers keep making the same mistake and not because of some systemic flaw that the intelligence community stubbornly refuses to correct. It recurs because of the intrinsic difficulty of cracking into the plans of terrorist groups and because of the type of intelligence that earnest and comprehensive efforts to cover terrorism tend to yield.

Proper understanding of past tragedies is important not to determine whose heads should roll or whose professional pride should be wounded but for two more basic reasons having to do with how intelligence efforts against future terrorism ought to be designed and organized. One reason is that fixing something requires a clear understanding of what is—or is not—broken. Change for the sake of change may help a losing baseball team, say, but it is unlikely to save lives from future terrorism.

Another reason is to understand how much of a contribution intelligence can and should make to the overall counterterrorist effort. Getting plot-specific tactical information clearly is an intelligence responsibility; it is hard to imagine any "policy failure" at that level because the obvious response to getting such information is to roll up the plot. At the more general level where most of the available information exists, however, the intelligence community often can only lead the policy horse to water but not force it to drink.

An example is the employment of military force in Afghanistan. The United States used arms in the autumn of 2001 to sweep away al-Qaeda's headquarters, its training camps, and the regime that hosted them because the attack on September 11, like the Japanese attack on Pearl Harbor, so enraged the American public and government that they were willing to assume costs and risks they would have shunned in the absence of such a calamity. Unlike Pearl Harbor (before which there might have been doubt about Japan's intention to make war against the United States), however, September 11 revealed nothing new about the intentions or general capabilities of al-Qaeda. The size and scope of the group's presence in Afghanistan, its relationship with the Taliban, its global reach, and most of all its intention to do the United States deadly harm were the subjects of repeated—and accurate—production by the intelligence community. Military intervention in Afghanistan did not extinguish al-Qaeda, and a preemptive attack there would have been harder to justify internationally than the post–September 11 operation that took place. The intelligence community's performance had very little to do with the United States waiting until after the September 11 disaster to finally clean out the terrorist den that Afghanistan had become.[13]

Organizations, Personnel, and Cultures

The dominant themes in discussions of how to improve U.S. intelligence have been sounded for years. They are heard more frequently following major terrorist attacks. Truly new ideas are scarce. Few of the ideas expressed relate specifically to terrorism. Many of them involve valid principles for a sound intelligence program but do not entail change from what is already being done. Many of them relate less to how the intelligence community actually operates than to lore, passed from commentator to commentator, of how it is presumed to operate. Almost none of them offer a way of cracking the conundrum of penetrating terrorist plots.

How does the intelligence community (or the president, or Congress) respond to entreaties such as to "get more human sources of intelligence on terrorist groups"? There certainly is no substitute for a human source within a group, particularly within the inner circle that does the plotting and planning—which is why the leadership of the intelligence community has placed such high priority on the recruitment of such sources. One has to search hard, however, amid expressions of dissatisfaction with the intelligence community's performance, to find even semispecific ideas about how the community might do things differently.

One subject of potential ideas is the organization and structure of the intelligence community. The decades-old issue of the DCI's control (or lack of it) over the entire community, for example, is receiving renewed attention.[14] That attention is healthy, and the issue is important for other reasons. It is difficult to see, however, how redefinition of the DCI's relationship with intelligence agencies other than the CIA—or other mixing or merging of agencies—would make any discernible difference in the quality of counterterrorist intelligence. The integration already achieved through such mechanisms as the CTC, along with the consensus among all agencies that counterterrorism deserves top priority, makes discussion of, say, where the National Security Agency (NSA) should fit in the government's organization chart seem almost irrelevant.

An organizational change that would make a greater difference for counterterrorism would be to centralize work on the subject even further by merging the counterterrorist functions of the intelligence and law enforcement communities. One proposal would do this by essentially shifting the CTC to the FBI.[15] Although this shift would appeal to the oft-expressed objective of enhancing cooperation between intelligence and law enforcement, it would have the disadvantage of separating the resulting counterterrorist entity from the field elements (necessarily run by the CIA's Directorate of Operations) that collect human intelligence on terrorism. Integration in counterterrorist work is important—which is why so much has been done already—but it already is near the point beyond which further integration would yield little or no improvement. That is the main reason it is important to have a clear understanding of existing cooperation between the intelligence and law enforcement communities.

Another frequent subject of comment is the quality of the intelligence community's personnel. A common refrain is that the community needs to recruit more bright, talented people to work on counterterrorism. "When I was there, we could not get a single person from the Ivy League to join the CIA," complained one retired (and anonymous) official. "To fight terrorism, we need to deal with the dregs of the Earth, and we need very bright Americans who can figure out how to go overseas and do these things."[16] Recruitment into this segment of public service, like most other segments, no doubt has been affected adversely by the relative attractiveness of career opportunities in the private sector (although the Ivy League has been represented at the CIA all along). The end of the economic boom of the 1990s and a surge in interest in intelligence work following September 11 already may be changing the incentives of potential recruits.[17] Quality of personnel matters, of course, and this particular security need is just one of many reasons to maintain strong incentives for talented people to enter and remain in public service. It would be the hubris of the best and the brightest, however, to think that the problem of penetrating terrorist groups is solvable simply by applying enough smarts to the problem.

A related theme centers on the alleged eclipse of a certain type of CIA specialist: the field operations officer, fluent in the language and steeped in the culture of the country in which he works and collecting critical information through wits, daring, intrigue, and local knowledge. This theme—heard disproportionately from former operations officers—includes the complaint that reward structures have evolved to where "a year in some country where it was dangerous to drink the water would get you no farther up the ladder than a year pushing paper in Langley."[18] The type of officer whose deemphasis is lamented is indeed critical to the collection of intelligence on terrorism—which is why that type has not been deemphasized at all for at least the past five years. To the contrary, a major priority of the CIA and the congressional committees that authorize and appropriate its funds has been the recruitment and training of that type of officer—part of a long-term effort to reverse earlier downsizing of the field operations corps.

Valuable though the individual, unilaterally collected nugget of terrorism intelligence may be, the rarity of true nuggets (because of the inherent difficulty of penetrating terrorist groups) means that most intelligence breakthroughs against terrorism will continue to involve the piecing together of nonnugget-like information from a variety of human, technical, and open sources. Critical contributions to such breakthroughs are made by analysts who do the piecing together, reports officers who get information into the hands of those who can exploit it, and managers who ensure that collection resources are deployed where they will complement rather than duplicate other sources of information. The transnational nature of the terrorism that most threatens U.S. interests accentuates the importance of piecing together disparate information collected in widely separated places. Terrorist operations that are funded on one continent, planned on another continent, and carried out on a third by perpetrators of multiple nationalities (as was true of the attacks on September 11) are unlikely to reveal their entire shape to even the most skillful local collection effort. Living where the water is bad, by itself, is apt to yield more stomach ailments than insights about terrorism—insights that are at least as likely to be gleaned in the papers being pushed at Langley.

Another theme of discussions of U.S. intelligence concerns institutional culture. Critics of the CIA in particular repeatedly describe it as "risk averse."[19] This label has become such common currency that it gets repeated matter-of-factly by commentators who have no way of knowing whether it is true—and in the face of the few public indicators of the actual level of risk-taking in the agency (such as the fact that the first U.S. death from hostile fire during Operation Enduring Freedom in Afghanistan was a CIA officer, killed while interrogating detainees for terrorist-related information).

The issue of risk aversion has centered around CIA guidelines established in 1995 that required additional senior-level headquarters approval for recruitment of intelligence sources suspected of having committed human rights abuses or other serious acts of violence. The National Commission on Terrorism recommended rescinding the guidelines, which it charged had inhibited recruitment of sources with potentially valuable information on terrorism.[20] The commission's recommendation appeals to the sense that anything that involves more bureaucracy is bad and anything that lets risk-taking officers in the field get on with the job of fighting terrorism is good. "After all," points out one commentary on the subject, "James Bond never had to fill out paperwork or myriad bureaucratic forms."[21] However, the effect, if any, that the guidelines have had on recruitment of sources of intelligence on terrorism has been greatly overstated. Every proposal that has come to headquarters for approval under the guidelines has been approved, with delays too minimal to affect either the success of the recruitment or the usefulness of any information gathered. Moreover, if risk aversion is a problem, having senior management buy into a potentially controversial recruitment before it is made reduces the risk to the individual officer who does the recruiting.

At least the commission's recommendation had the virtue of being specific. Codifying it, however—as Congress attempted to do in the Intelligence Authorization Act of 2002—is more difficult. (How does one tell the head of an agency *not* to exercise supervision intended to ensure respect for human rights?) The result sounds like a buzzword-laden exhortation rather than a law. The legislation instructed the DCI to replace the 1995 guidelines with "new guidelines that more appropriately weigh and incentivize [*sic*] risks to ensure that qualified intelligence officers can and should swiftly gather intelligence from human sources in such a fashion as to ensure the ability to provide timely information that would allow for indications and warnings of plans and intentions of hostile actions or events, and ensure that such information is shared in a broad and expeditious fashion so that, to the extent possible, actions to protect American lives can be taken."[22] This kind of flourish is of little use as guidance in establishing operational rules and procedures. Nonetheless, the agency has rescinded the 1995 guidelines and has tried to make the human rights considerations underlying them an integral part of the larger headquarters review process that is essential to any human intelligence operation. The process is essential because other information must be applied to direct human collection resources to where they are most needed and likely to be most effective, as well as to assess the credibility and access of agents. It is ironic that much commentary about counterterrorism notes the need to integrate data from different sources but overlooks this aspect of integration in managing the collection of human intelligence.

Reality, Not Romanticism

The image of the Ivy Leaguer who goes where it is dangerous to drink the water and—unencumbered by annoying instructions from headquarters—applies his brilliance and James Bond-like daring to the job of saving America from terrorism appeals to our imaginations but has little to do with the real business of intelligence and counterterrorism. The task ahead for the intelligence community appears more mundane, not only because it lacks the romantic aspect of that image but because it is not all that different from what it has been for some time. Obviously there is room for improvement—as there will be as long as the counterterrorist batting average is not 1.000, which means indefinitely—but even large increases in what U.S. intelligence does, or major changes in how it does it, offer only modest prospects for more reassuring results.[23]

More well-trained operations officers in the field, as well as more analysts and other critical personnel and the monetary and technical resources to go with them, will make a difference, but not in the sense of closing some key and well-defined gap that has kept the United States from going the last mile it needs to go to find out what terrorists are up to. Rather, such increases would marginally heighten the chance of gaining useful information and insights about terrorist activity, which in turn would marginally heighten the chance of forestalling some future terrorist attacks and saving some lives. They would do so by alleviating shortages that—despite the considerable increases in dollars and manpower devoted in recent years to counterterrorism—still limit the ability of several agencies to carry out the sweeping tasks they are now being relied upon to perform. The FBI, for example, simply does not have the manpower to surveil and investigate everyone in the United States who ought to be scrutinized for possible connections to terrorism.[24] Similarly, there would be less risk of slip-ups or slowness at the CIA or NSA in processing, exploiting, and disseminating information if the typical crushing load of information to be processed could be distributed into more manageable proportions to be handled by more hands. Sound management and adroit use of automation are critical but can go only so far. The core of the work to be done—the part that will be the stuff of inquiries after future major terrorist incidents—will still have to be done by skilled people collecting, assessing, and acting on individual pieces of information.

Beyond the question of resources, there are two principal areas in which to look for potential improvements in intelligence about terrorism. Both go beyond what the intelligence community itself can do. The first concerns the acquisition of information from foreign governments. Probably no other intelligence topic depends more on foreign liaison than does terrorism. Certain foreign governments will always be better able than the United States to operate against certain terrorist groups, for reasons of geography, culture, or past contacts. The willingness of those governments to share intelligence depends not only on what the CIA does to cultivate the liaison relationships but also on the overall state of bilateral relations with the United States, and that is a function of broader U.S. foreign policy. Moreover, some of the governments with the most intelligence to share about terrorists are ones that have presented significant problems, including terrorist-related problems, for U.S. policy. To collect intelligence on terrorism, the United States needs to take risks in dealing with regimes—not just individuals—with blood-stained pasts.

The other area for attention involves the integration of intelligence with nonintelligence sources of information. This does not primarily mean the criminal investigations of law enforcement agencies such as the FBI, where integration with intelligence for counterterrorist purposes already is extensive. The greatest potential opportunities for further integration of information involve other types of data about the movements and activities of large numbers of people—especially data on travel and immigration. Encyclopedic mining of such data for intelligence purposes (as distinct from spot inquiries concerning cases already being investigated) has not been done to date for several reasons, most of which involve the needle-in-haystack aspect of any such endeavor and the prospect that it would yield a meager payoff on a very high investment. A host of practical problems, ranging from the use of pseudonyms by terrorists to the reluctance of some owners of data banks to make them available for such scrutiny, reduces the probable yield further.[25] Moreover, some of the key elements of exploiting information would still have to be done by live analysts assessing *sui generis* cases; they could not be programmed into a data-mining algorithm. Despite all these limitations, the change since the September 11 attacks in national priorities and in the thresholds for spending resources for counterterrorism warrants fresh attention to this frontier in the exploitation of potentially useful information.

The converse of mining data on the movements of large numbers of people to extract terrorist-related intelligence also deserves renewed attention—that is, the use of intelligence to restrict the movements of potential terrorists. This is already done with the use of watchlists to guide decisions by consular officers in granting visas and officers of the INS in admitting foreigners at points of entry. Although there have been well-publicized instances of the lists either not being used or being incomplete, the system generally works smoothly and has kept scores of suspected terrorists out of the United States. The best candidate for broadening the use of such procedures would be civil aviation. How was it, for example, that at least a couple of the September 11 hijackers had come to the intelligence community's attention for prior contacts with suspected terrorists and yet were able to buy tickets and board civilian airliners in the United States under their true names? Probably the only way to avoid a recurrence would be a drastic revision of aviation security that in essence would require all air passengers to undergo a background check. This strategy raises issues of privacy that also would apply to some data mining. These issues, along with the question of whether the small payoffs would be worth the high costs and the intrusion, call for public debate and extensive consideration by Congress.

Domestic Intelligence

Tradeoffs between counterterrorism and privacy abound in the collection of intelligence within the United States, which must be a major part of the overall counterterrorist intelligence function. Debates in the United States about homeland security have been slow to address the most important issues of domestic intelligence collection. Discussion of intelligence during congressional consideration of the homeland security bill of 2002 had to do with what kind of intelligence element the new Department of Homeland Security would have and how the department would relate to the FBI and the CIA. This issue need not have been controversial. The department's intelligence arm can perform the same sort of role as the State Department's Bureau of Intelligence and Research—an analytical and coordinating office that works closely with the rest of the intelligence community to meet its own department's intelligence needs.

The biggest departure the United States could take regarding counterterrorist intelligence—one that has not been a subject of congressional debate—would be to create a domestic security service, separate from foreign intelligence agencies such as the CIA and NSA and law enforcement agencies such as the FBI. The United States is atypical in not having an agency comparable to MI-5 in the United Kingdom, the Federal Office for the Protection of the Constitution (BfV) in Germany, or the Public Security Investigation Agency in Japan. Collection of intelligence on foreign terrorists within their respective homelands is a major mission for these and similar agencies in other countries.

Whether to create such an agency in the United States is largely an issue of whether this mission should be left to the FBI. (The CIA would be an inappropriate place for the job, mainly because its mission of collecting foreign intelligence differs in important respects. Recruiting a foreign spy, for example, may involve persuading that person to violate the laws of his own country.) The principal argument against establishment of a new service is that the FBI, although primarily a law enforcement organization, has long had the secondary mission of collecting intelligence on persons or groups posing threats to national security. In the wake of the September 11 attacks, FBI Director Robert Mueller, through reorganization and reallocation of resources, has given increased emphasis to the collection and preemptive use of counterterrorist intelligence. Another consideration is that creation of a new service would mean one more set of organizational lines that information would have to cross—information that, given the relationship between law enforcement and the gathering of information on threats within the United States, needs to flow as freely as possible.

The main argument in favor of establishing a new service is that because the culture and expertise of the FBI center around law enforcement and the assembling of criminal cases for prosecution, the intelligence mission—no matter how much emphasis the bureau's directors place on it—will always be a secondary mission in fact if not in name. And no mission can be performed really well if it is only somebody's secondary mission. The bureau's ethos is so closely centered around law enforcement and criminal prosecutions that it remains uncertain how well-suited it is to an intelligence mission, no matter how many adjustments are made from the top. The training, skills, and promotability of FBI special agents all revolve around the criminal law function. This fact is evident in countless habits and patterns of work, such as a disinclination of FBI agents to document many substantive discussions—such documentation being second nature to an intelligence officer—out of concern about creating a written record that would be discoverable in a trial.

The traditional autonomy of FBI field offices, with the informational disconnects such autonomy can cause, also would argue for creation of a new intelligence service. Director Mueller has attempted to address this issue with creation of a headquarters-based "supersquad" that would direct terrorist investigations that traditionally have been handled by field offices. Yet field-to-headquarters relationships may be one of the aspects of an organization's culture and operating habits that is most resistant to change. And although something like the investigation of a bank robbery usually can be handled fully within the locale of the crime, inquiries into terrorist groups—with their transnational dimensions—cannot.

Another possible reason to create a new domestic intelligence and security agency would be the symbolic value of such a major step, with all of the signals it would send regarding the nation's commitment to the agency's mission and the resources and legal powers necessary for it to do its job properly. It would represent a break with past shortcomings and a sea change in national priorities. A new organization would be unencumbered by the baggage of the CIA and the FBI, including past controversies involving alleged abuses or overstepping of bounds and popular perceptions of past failures.

Regardless of whether the domestic counterterrorist mission is performed by a new service or by a reoriented FBI, many other questions about the mission will be unavoidable topics of controversy and appropriate topics of debate. Besides the ubiquitous matter of resources, there are issues involving legal authorities to monitor activity and conduct searches and seizures. Skepticism that met Attorney General John Ashcroft's widening of the FBI's monitoring powers in May 2002 reflected deep and longstanding American reservations about such authorities.[26] Another question is whether U.S. citizens and noncitizens should be targeted in the same way. The American public might be willing to support more intrusive investigative powers aimed at noncitizens (who probably include most of the terrorist threats). Yet even foreign terrorist groups can enlist—and, to a limited degree, already have used—U.S. citizens.

There also is the problem of where investigative leads come from. It may be somewhat easier to search a haystack in one's own yard than a haystack elsewhere, but it is still a haystack. The criticism of the Terrorism Information and Prevention System (TIPS)—an effort to encourage reporting by individual citizens of suspicious circumstances or behavior that could have terrorist implications—highlighted the biggest barrier to more extensive domestic intelligence collection: Americans don't like to be spied on, by either their government or their fellow citizens. For many Americans, TIPS carried the odor of an East German-style system of friends and family members "ratting" on each other.

Another subject that already has an odor in the United States but cannot be avoided in considering how to focus the search of the haystack is profiling on the basis of religion, race, or ethnicity. The best profiling systems use other indicators that are less controversial and more closely correlated with the behavior one is trying to detect. In trying to narrow the gargantuan task of finding as-yet-unfound threats in a nation of nearly 300 million people, however, an uncomfortable fact is that religion and ethnicity would have some search-narrowing value. Somehow that fact will have to be dealt with in any enhanced domestic intelligence effort.

Above All, Do No Harm

The intensity of pressure on the intelligence community to be seen doing things in new and different ways, coupled with the meager prospects that such change actually will reduce the chance of more major terrorist attacks, means that the challenge for U.S. intelligence will be not only to do the best possible job of collecting and analyzing information about terrorism but to respond to the demand for change in ways that avoid doing more harm than good. One of the most important "risks" for the CIA and the rest of the intelligence community is the political risk of standing up to these short-term pressures to avoid undermining long-term effectiveness.

Since September 11, U.S. intelligence agencies have devoted an even larger proportion of their resources than before to counterterrorism. This reallocation has been the kind of nimble shift that the CIA in particular often—and mistakenly—has been criticized for not being able to do. The shift means pulling analysts and collectors off other important subjects, however. The House Intelligence Committee expressed concern about this shift in its report accompanying the intelligence authorization bill for fiscal year 2003, noting that the "significant and inventive" counterterrorist efforts that the intelligence community had under way were being achieved by shifts of personnel "that create gaps in coverage and understanding in other areas of national security interest."[27] In responding to the inevitable pressures to move more resources to counterterrorism, the intelligence community must be careful not to denude itself in these other areas. The costs of doing so would be felt not only with other U.S. foreign policy interests but, over the long term, with counterterrorism itself. Although understanding political stresses and socioeconomic patterns in foreign lands does not bear the "counterterrorist" label, this work often addresses the conditions that tend to breed terrorists and therefore is important in anticipating future terrorism and supporting U.S. policy efforts to do something about it.

Another hazard involves the rules and restrictions under which the intelligence community operates and how the mood of the moment, in which counterterrorism has become an overriding public priority, has changed those rules. The September 11 attacks appear to have swept aside many old suspicions and concerns about the country's national security agencies. The changes are reflected in such things as the congressional directive regarding recruitment guidelines and the omnibus counterterrorist legislation enacted in October 2001 that, among other things, gives the CIA access to grand jury testimony.[28] The public mood will change again, however. If a couple of years go by with the United States successful enough and fortunate enough to avoid another major terrorist attack, counterterrorism will no longer be an overriding priority. Human rights, privacy, and similar issues will get renewed attention. Then what? What happens to the "incentivized" intelligence officer who takes the risk of making a recruitment that becomes controversial, and how will his agency be viewed after the members of Congress who changed the rules have moved on to other committee assignments? And does a step such as giving intelligence agencies access to grand jury records contain the seeds of future congressional inquiries reminiscent of the Church and Pike committees of the 1970s?[29] The changes may be warranted, and there is no reason to anticipate abuses. Those making the changes should remember, however, that among the most effective weapons the United States has in fighting terrorism is the long-term strength of its intelligence agencies, based in part on their integrity and the trust they have with the American people.

Public confidence in the counterterrorist role of intelligence agencies also is put at risk when that role is misappropriated to serve purposes other than saving lives from terrorism. The very prominence of counterterrorism in the wake of September 11 has increased the temptation to misuse the counterterrorist issue in this way. Supporters of the war against Iraq did so when they exploited the militant post–September 11 mood of the American public to muster support for the war, which they had long favored chiefly for reasons other than counterterrorism.[30] Selling the war involved playing up any link that could be found between Saddam Hussein's regime and terrorism—especially between the regime and al-Qaeda. Proponents of the war used intelligence not to identify threats and inform policymaking but to justify a policy decision that already had been made.

The intelligence community withstood the policy pressures fairly well. Its treatment of Iraq and al-Qaeda did not go beyond detailed description of the minimal and inconclusive "links" between the two—as was evident on a careful reading of the administration's only public statement on Iraq that had a direct intelligence community input: Secretary of State Powell's presentation to the United Nations Security Council in February 2003.[31] Nonetheless, the Iraq episode damaged the intelligence community's ability to play its part in counterterrorism. Servicing the administration's public relations requirements on this issue consumed vast amounts of time and attention on the part of counterterrorist specialists, who thereby were diverted from their main mission of locating and countering actual and impending terrorist threats.

The American public's understanding of the role of state sponsors in international terrorism was badly distorted, in a way it would not have been if intelligence had been used publicly in a more straightforward manner. Most important, as postwar difficulties in Iraq became increasingly apparent and the failure to find weapons of mass destruction caused alleged misuse of intelligence to become a major issue, the integrity of the intelligence community was called into question. This outcome will make public trust harder to win the next time intelligence identifies a major terrorist threat, even if the threat is real and the assessment of it unpoliticized.

Conclusion

The most useful thing that Americans can do about U.S. intelligence assets in the campaign against international terrorism may be to acquire a realistic appreciation for what those assets can and cannot accomplish. It is important to understand the small chance of obtaining critical inside information on the next terrorist plot and the multitude of other ways intelligence contributes to counterterrorism. Such understanding would guide strategy on how much reliance to place on the intelligence community's "first line of defense" against terrorism and how much needs to be done by the other lines. It would help to avoid reinventing wheels that the intelligence community invented some time ago and focus attention on areas—particularly a more comprehensive integration of intelligence with nonintelligence data—where there is at least a modest chance of major new initiatives yielding results. Moreover, clearing away misconceptions would sharpen the focus on important issues—particularly what compromises Americans are willing to make to their privacy and liberties to facilitate the collection of information about possible threats in their own homeland—that still need debate.

Almost all of the functions of, and possible new initiatives in, counterterrorist intelligence discussed in this chapter rest on strong and knowledgeable public support. Such support is critical for resources, of course, in the form of appropriations by Congress. Public acceptance also would be vital to implement the kinds of procedures necessary for an expanded domestic intelligence collection effort to be effective. Although less immediately apparent, the amount of public backing that U.S. officials have when they solicit cooperation from foreign governments also helps to determine how successful such solicitations are.

The upsurge in Americans' support for counterterrorism in the wake of the September 11 attacks provides the principal grounds for optimism about realizing the full potential of what intelligence—despite all of its continuing limitations—can contribute to the larger counterterrorist effort. The markedly increased success since the attacks in freezing of terrorist financial assets, for example, is due not to the intelligence suddenly getting better but to the national strength of commitment that has enabled U.S. officials to pound on the desks of foreign officials and insist that they act on the intelligence that was already available. And Operation Enduring Freedom in Afghanistan was the most forceful possible example of acting on intelligence about the principal source of the principal terrorist threat of the day. To the extent that American interest in counterterrorism can be sustained longer than after previous spikes in such interest, there will be more successful applications of intelligence to the problem of international terrorism, beyond the eternally hoped-for uncovering of details of the next plot.

Notes

The views in this article are the author's and not those of any government agency.

1. *Report of the Accountability Review Boards on the Bombings of the U.S. Embassies in Nairobi, Kenya and Dar es Salaam, Tanzania on August 7, 1998*.

2. Most speculation was exactly that, rather than rigorous analysis. The best analysis of the subject is Richard A. Falkenrath, Robert D. Newman, and Bradley Thayer, *America's Achilles' Heel: Nuclear, Biological, and Chemical Terrorism and Covert Attack* (Cambridge, Mass.: MIT Press, 1998). Related scholarly treatments include Jessica Stern, *The Ultimate Terrorists* (Cambridge, Mass.: Harvard University Press, 1999); Jonathan B. Tucker (ed.), *Toxic Terror: Assessing Terrorist Use of Chemical and Biological Weapons* (Cambridge, Mass.: MIT Press, 2000); and Gavin Cameron, *Nuclear Terrorism: A Threat Assessment for the 21st Century* (London: Macmillan, 1999).

3. Cf. Sherman Kent, *Strategic Intelligence for American World Policy* (Princeton, N.J.: Princeton University Press, 1949), especially chap. 4, and Richard K. Betts, "Warning Dilemmas: Normal Theory vs. Exceptional Theory," *Orbis* 26 (winter 1983): 828–33.

4. Dan Balz and Bob Woodward, "America's Chaotic Road to War," *Washington Post*, 27 January 2002, A11.

5. See testimony by George Tenet, U.S. Senate Select Committee on Intelligence, *Worldwide Threat 2002: Current and Projected National Security Threats to the United States*, 107th Congress, 2d session, 6 February 2002.

6. House Report 107–219, on HR 2883.

7. Karen DeYoung and Walter Pincus, "In Bin Laden's Own Words," *Washington Post*, 14 December 2001, A1.

8. For the president's statement, see his speech on 6 June 2002 proposing creation of a Department of Homeland Security, available at www.whitehouse.gov/news/releases/2002/06/20020606-8.html. On the congressional investigation, see Dana Priest and Juliet Eilperin, "Panel Finds No 'Smoking Gun' in Probe of 9/11 Intelligence Failures," *Washington Post*, 11 July 2002, A1.

9. Statement by DCI George Tenet, U.S. Senate Select Committee on Intelligence, *Worldwide Threat 2001: National Security in a Changing World*, 107th Congress, 1st session, 7 February 2001.

10. Barton Gellman, "A Strategy's Cautious Evolution," *Washington Post*, 20 January 2002, A17.

11. Department of Defense, *Report to the President and Congress on the Protection of U.S. Forces Deployed Abroad* (August 1996), Annex A.

12. *Report of the Accountability Review Boards.*

13. The Bush administration subsequently was reported to have moved to a more general policy of military preemption against possible terrorist threats. Thomas E. Ricks and Vernon Loeb, "Bush Developing Military Policy of Striking First," *Washington Post*, 10 June 2002, A1.

14. See, e.g., *Preparing for the 21st Century: An Appraisal of U.S. Intelligence*, report of the Commission on the Roles and Capabilities of the United States Intelligence Community (Washington, D.C.: U.S. Government Printing Office, 1996), 47–59; and Mark W. Lowenthal, *Intelligence: From Secrets to Policy* (Washington, D.C.: CQ Press, 2000), 24–32, 130–31.

15. Ashton B. Carter, "The Architecture of Government in the Face of Terrorism," *International Security* 26 (winter 2001/02): 18–19; and Ashton B. Carter, John Deutch, and Philip Zelikow, "Catastrophic Terrorism: Tackling the New Danger," *Foreign Affairs* 77 (November–December 1998): 80–94.

16. Quoted in Chuck McCutcheon, "Fixing U.S. Intelligence: A Cultural Revolution," *Congressional Quarterly Weekly*, 6 October 2001, 2307.

17. Eric Schmitt, "Job Seekers Flood Spy Agencies," *New York Times*, 22 October 2001, B7.

18. Thomas Powers, "The Trouble with the CIA," *New York Review of Books*, 17 January 2002, 31.

19. The most formal expression of this view is in *Countering the Changing Threat of International Terrorism*, report of the National Commission on Terrorism (June 2000), 8.

20. Ibid.

21. Frank J. Ciluffo, Ronald A. Marks, and George C. Salmoiraghi, "The Use and Limits of U.S. Intelligence," *Washington Quarterly* 25 (winter 2002): 69.

22. Section 403, Intelligence Authorization Act for fiscal year 2002.

23. On the theme that further changes to the intelligence community are likely to yield only small payoffs, see Richard Betts, "Fixing Intelligence," *Foreign Affairs* 81 (January–February 2002): 43–59.

24. Ronald Kessler, "Double the Size of the FBI," *Washington Post*, 15 June 2002, A23.

25. See the comments of former INS Commissioner Doris Meissner in "On the Fence" (interview), *Foreign Policy* 129 (March–April 2002): 24.

26. Neil A. Lewis, "Ashcroft Permits F.B.I. to Monitor Internet and Public Activities," *New York Times*, 31 May 2002, A18.

27. Quoted in Walter Pincus, "House Votes Billions for Intelligence: Panel Says Anti-Terror Fight Creates 'Gaps' in U.S. Coverage," *Washington Post*, 26 July 2002, A11.

28. USA Patriot Act, P.L. 107–56, Section 203.

29. Cf. Tim Weiner, "The C.I.A. Widens Its Domestic Reach," *New York Times*, 20 January 2002, 4.1.

30. Joseph Cirincione, "Origins of Regime Change in Iraq," *Carnegie Endowment Proliferation Brief* 6, no. 5 (March 19, 2003).

31. The text of Secretary Powell's statement is at www.state.gov/secretary/rm/2003/17300.htm.

six

LAW ENFORCEMENT

Lindsay Clutterbuck

Terrorism today can occur at any time and in any country. It has a long history behind it—dating back to the late years of the nineteenth century and beyond—and although its proponents, perpetrators, and the causes they espoused have changed over the years, terrorism continues to be used by non-state actors as both a strategy and a tactic.[1] Not only is it still with us today, it is growing increasingly lethal. Clearly it cannot be considered as only a recent manifestation, and because it does not appear to be amenable to a solution, it must be moved from being considered as a "problem" into the category of a permanent phenomenon. Consequently, it is inappropriate to think of countering terrorism in terms of a war, with its accepted connotation of the eventual victory of one state over another. Terrorism is not a tangible entity, so it cannot be "defeated" in any realistic sense. The "war on terrorism" is no more a war than is the "war on crime"; hence, its prosecution is not amenable solely to the use of military means.

An act of terrorism is a crime, and the perpetrator of the act is a criminal whom we also designate as a "terrorist." Terrorists may commit criminal acts that also can be committed in other contexts—for example, murder or the possession of weapons and explosives—or they may commit acts that have been made criminal offenses as a specific consequence of their use by terrorists (e.g., fundraising or belonging to a terrorist group). In addition to contravening national laws, terrorist acts may contravene international laws and conventions (e.g., the hijacking of aircraft or the use of chemical and bio-logical weapons). Indeed, since the resurgence of terrorism in the late 1960s, it is this conception of "terror as crime" and not "terror as war" that has pri-marily driven the response to terrorism of the liberal democratic nations.

Terrorism is a phenomenon that is global in its range, constant in its pres-ence, and inevitably involves the commission of crime. Any national or in-ternational mechanism to counter it must be predicated on that understand-ing. Liberal democracies have well-developed legislation, systems, and structures to deal with crime; consequently, the criminal justice system should be at the heart of their counterterrorism efforts.

The threat terrorism poses to society today, however, is such that the re-sponse to it must extend beyond this core to engage the intelligence services, the military, and even the individual citizen. In that way, all the options—from prevention to deterrence, from preemption to disruption, and from in-telligence operations to evidential investigations—can be deployed as ap-propriate. The current challenge is to devise and implement a proactive and dynamic strategy that will achieve this end.

In this chapter I initially focus on the two main conceptual models of counterterrorism: the criminal justice model and the war model. I examine whether these models adequately address the reality of the counterterrorism strategy currently employed by the United Kingdom (UK) in particular and by the European Union (EU) in general. I then describe how the UK counter-terrorism strategy is unequivocally underpinned by the criminal justice sys-tem and how the police, intelligence agencies, and military act together in a cooperative and coordinated way to implement it.

The succeeding section of the chapter has an international perspective. In it I outline how police-to-police cooperation in counterterrorism has evolved among the EU member states since the early 1970s and how this process has accelerated since the events of September 11. As a consequence, the EU as an institution has become increasingly engaged with many aspects of counter-terrorism policy, strategy, and operations. I conclude the chapter by offer-ing some suggestions on how the effectiveness of existing systems and struc-tures can be increased.

As a preliminary step in this process, it is appropriate to examine the basic premise to which liberal democratic states have tried to adhere for the past thirty-five years when terrorism took on the form with which we are most familiar. It may then be possible to determine if an alternative is either possible or desirable.

Terrorism as Crime: Current Theoretical Models

Among the academic community, the search for a widely accepted definition of the phenomenon that is considered today to be "terrorism" has occupied many years. In 1977 Laqueur wrote, "It can be predicted with confidence that disputes about a comprehensive, detailed definition of terrorism will continue for a long time, that they will not result in consensus and that they will make no noticeable contribution to the understanding of terrorism."[2] Laqueur's words have proven to be prophetic. Some clarity has been achieved, but the task has already proved itself to be exceedingly difficult, and complexity is being added continuously by the involvement of new types of actors, driven by new ideation and using new tactics and weaponry to achieve their aims. In addition to the longstanding academic debate about what should or should not be called terrorism, a parallel debate has had to take place among policymakers, legislatures, and counterterrorism practitioners. Two main theoretical models have been offered to delineate the counterterrorism strategies that states can exercise in the suppression of terrorism: the criminal justice and war models.[3]

Terrorism is a phenomenon that affects not only individuals and communities but also the state in its entirety. In his book *Terrorism and the Liberal State*, Paul Wilkinson lays out the central challenge to be met by those responsible for forging the response of the liberal democratic state to the threat from terrorism: "The primary objective of counter-terrorist strategy must be the protection and maintenance of liberal democracy and the rule of law. It cannot be sufficiently stressed that this aim overrides in importance even the aim of eliminating terrorism and political violence as such."[4] Terrorism inevitably involves the commission of violent crimes such as murder, grievous assault, and kidnapping. Consequently the investigation, trial, and punishment of the perpetrators of these offenses, irrespective of the motive behind their commission, are unequivocally a matter for the wider criminal justice system and, in particular, the police.

The second strategy, based on the war model, places greater emphasis on the countering of terrorism by force, which may lead to an overriding or suspension of the democratic principles enshrined in the criminal justice model. As would be expected, the military plays a prominent if not dominant role. Ronald Crelinsten usefully characterizes the differences between the war model and the criminal justice model as those between the "rules of war" and the "rule of law," and this approach can be extended to the "maximal use of force" as opposed to the "minimal use of force."[5]

From the perspective of the counterterrorism practitioner, it can be argued that "terror as crime" and "terror as war" are but two possibilities situated at the opposite ends of a wide continuum of response. There are many alternatives between these two ends of the theoretical spectrum. For example, Ami Pedahzur and Magnus Ranstorp try to account for the significant disparity between the models and the reality of counterterrorism "on the ground."[6] They propose an "expanded criminal justice model" that could act as a conceptual bridge between the other two models. Its goal is "to include all those 'grey' areas that are so commonly practised in the war against terrorism yet are not accounted for in either the 'war' or 'criminal justice' models. . . ."[7] In their purest forms, neither of the two main theoretical models are practical end states; no comprehensive counterterrorist response can be based entirely on the narrow enforcement of the law alone, nor can it rely exclusively on the warfighting capabilities of the military. They also should not be viewed as mutually exclusive alternatives. Between these two positions lies an almost infinite area of policy, strategy, operations, and tactics within which the state in its entirety must maneuver in pursuit of its goal.

The experiences of the UK in counterterrorism and counterinsurgency over the past century, both in the UK itself and abroad, have determined its current holistic approach to counterterrorism. At first sight, the wider relevance of this approach in the world today may not be apparent. A closer examination shows, however, that there are both generic principles and operational imperatives that may be usefully applied in other circumstances.[8] Foremost among them are three strategic concepts, all of which have been developed and further refined in the context of terrorism in Northern Ireland and, since 1972, its impact on the British mainland.

The first of these strategic concepts is the need for sustainability in the response. The people of Northern Ireland have been subjected to terrorist attacks and political violence on an almost daily basis over the past forty years. The death toll has been significant, with 3,601 fatalities between 1969 and 1999.[9] The Irish Republican Army (IRA) detonated the first improvised explosive device (IED) on the British mainland in 1972. Today there is still a real and continuing threat of terrorist attack, not only in connection with Irish republican terrorism but also from international terrorism.[10] Consequently, the UK has had to devise counterterrorism systems and structures that can operate over this timescale and are generic in their applicability, whatever the ultimate source of the terrorist threat.

The second concept is the need for coordination and cooperation (though not necessarily through central control) in devising and implementing counterterrorism policy, strategy, operations, and tactics. Without it, organizational gaps, duplication of effort, and overlapping responsibilities are inevitable. These weaknesses can then be exploited by terrorists.

Finally, there is the need to foster, promulgate, and sustain the concept of individual and community responsibility in the overall counterterrorism effort. Terrorism can have an impact on anybody at any time; consequently, countering it must involve everyone. Every person, whether they are employed directly in counterterrorism, in any other official capacity, or as a member of a community and the wider public, has a responsibility to assist in countering it. An awareness of the threat from terrorism and how it might manifest itself must become embedded throughout society.

In addition to these three central concepts, there are other, more specific issues that underpin the UK counterterrorism strategy that can usefully be examined. For example, the paramount concern of the police at all times is that of public safety. This attitude does not change because the threat to public safety comes from terrorism. The imperative of public safety by no means implies, however, that the police must be the sole instrument in countering terrorism. The rule of law and the principles of criminal justice do not preclude the state from making the widest possible use of any of its policy instruments that can usefully make a contribution. In the UK, it is universally understood that no matter which organization or arm of the state makes a contribution to countering terrorism, it does so in the certain knowledge that it must operate within these principles and by cooperating with other organizations in pursuit of a common goal. Not only does this principle apply to the police; it also applies with equal force to the intelligence services and the military. I examine how this integrated position has evolved in the following section.

Terrorism as Crime: The Evolution of the Criminal Justice Approach

Beginning in the early 1970s, a range of terrorist groups with differing aims began to carry out attacks across Europe: the Red Army Faction (RAF) in Germany, the IRA in the UK, and the Palestine Liberation Organization (PLO) in various countries. As a response to this development, a process commenced of developing legislation aimed against terrorism and operating at both the national and international levels. The process continues today.

The legislation broadly focused on three levels. First, specific crimes that are particularly associated with terrorists have been targeted by specific legislation, both to prevent them from occurring and to subject the perpetrators to increased penalties if they are committed (e.g., the hijacking of commercial aircraft). Second, an increasingly diverse number of activities that terrorists need to engage in if they are to function have been newly criminalized (e.g., engaging in money raising, eliciting support, or openly recruiting). Third, extraordinary investigative powers have been given to the numerous law enforcement and other investigative agencies whose responsibility it is to deal with crime committed by terrorists.

At the national level, the speed and comprehensiveness with which this framework was erected bore a direct correlation to the extent to which a state felt itself to be under threat from terrorist activity. In the UK, for example, it began with the passing into law of the Prevention of Terrorism Act in the immediate aftermath of the IRA bomb attacks on two public houses in Birmingham on November 21, 1974, when 21 people were killed and 162 were injured.[11]

Concerted international cooperation was more problematic, however, because of the complexities of arriving at a generally acceptable definition of "terrorism"; hence, it has moved ahead at a slower pace. Nonetheless, international agreement recently has gained momentum and become more widespread. In 1997 the United Nations (UN) adopted the Convention on the Suppression of Terrorist Bombings, and in 1999 the UN followed up with the Convention for the Suppression of the Financing of Terrorism. Although the practical impact of these resolutions may be limited, their significance lies in the global acceptance of what generally constitutes terrorism and the threat it poses to all nations. In addition, the member states of the EU now have agreed definitions of what constitutes "terrorist offenses" and a "terrorist group."[12]

The net result of this international convergence has been for states to consider terrorism as a crime and to use a constantly expanding web of legislation to underpin their efforts to counter it. Increasingly, legislation is now international in its scope and impact. The successor in the UK to the original Prevention of Terrorism Act is the Terrorism Act 2000, which creates specific offenses relating to the commission, preparation, and instigation of terrorist acts in the UK that are intended to be implemented in countries other than the UK. Similarly, the EU Framework Decision on combating terrorism lays down a legally binding obligation on all EU states to ensure that their national jurisdiction over terrorist offenses is extended across the EU.[13]

In addition to the skeleton provided by this legislative approach, other common themes have emerged. A report to the U.S. Congress, based on a review of how five developed countries have organized their counterterrorism efforts, found a broad consensus in the counterterrorism philosophy of the countries surveyed and in the mechanisms that they used to implement it.[14] In addition to the legislative approach outlined above, they also noted common areas of endeavor involving

> interagency co-ordination bodies to co-ordinate both within and across ministries . . . [clear designation of] who is in charge during a terrorist incident . . . national policies that emphasize prevention of terrorism . . . executive branches [that] provide the primary oversight of organizations involved in combating terrorism [and] funding decisions . . . based on the likelihood

of terrorist activity actually taking place, not the countries overall vulnerability to terrorist attack.[15]

If it is accepted that terrorism—in the terms in which it is increasingly defined by national and international legislation as well as in its practical impact on society—is a crime committed by a certain type of criminal, does this mean that countering it must inevitably and solely be a task for a law enforcement agencies? A strong argument can be advanced that such an approach to "terrorism as crime" would be too narrow in focus and too restricted in effect to have any significant impact. However, a factor that militates strongly in favor of dealing with terrorism predominantly through the mechanism of the criminal justice system is that crime has now become the root system that both anchors and nourishes terrorism.

From an operational perspective, the world of twenty (and certainly twenty-five) years ago contained a clear demarcation between the main motivation of persons who engaged in terrorism and those who committed serious crimes. Criminal activity by terrorists tended to be undertaken as a means to an end, either in the actual commission of terrorist crime or as a source of money to finance terrorist acts and the underground lifestyle of the group. For example, armed bank robberies were a commonly used method by which terrorist groups in many countries obtained cash.

On the other hand, the vast majority of armed bank robberies are committed by criminals who have no political motive for their actions. Their sole aim is the acquisition of personal wealth. In short, terrorism was committed by terrorists to enable them to pursue their overall political objectives, whereas serious crime is committed by criminals who are motivated by their desire to enrich themselves. The difference appeared to be generally clear-cut; hence labels were relatively easy to assign.

Today the demarcation appears to be breaking down, and the unique features of terrorism and serious crime (or, at least, our perceptions of them) have become increasingly unreliable in identifying the motivation of the perpetrators.[16] Theft, extortion, and fraud in all their many varieties have now become regular activities for terrorist groups and involve many groups in many different countries. In Japan, the Aum Shinrikyo cult was involved in fraud.[17] In Colombia, the Revolutionary Armed Forces of Colombia (FARC) are nourished by money raised from the narcotics trade and by kidnapping for ransom. Most recently in the United States (June 2002), two individuals from Hezbollah were convicted in South Carolina of raising money for the group by smuggling tobacco. Even the ideologically hard-line Marxist-Leninist terrorist group known as Revolutionary Organization 17 November (17N), which has been active in Greece since 1975, may have been regularly involved in human trafficking and smuggling.[18]

Of course, it is still possible to distinguish between crime and crime committed in pursuance of terrorism, but it is becoming much more difficult to do so quickly and accurately. This can be illustrated by the problem of financial offenses. In purely criminal terms, the whole concept is to convert money obtained illegally into legitimate money and assets. In terrorist terms the procedure can be reversed: legally held money, as well as the proceeds of crime, frequently are channeled into illegal activities needed to support and carry out terrorism.

The paradox of motive and hence perpetrator is at its most acute in terms of attacks on electronic systems. When an attack occurs, it is important to know as soon as possible who is carrying it out. Is it a hostile foreign power, a criminally motivated hacker, a reckless teenager, or a terrorist? Although in each scenario the internal response by the electronic system under attack will be similar if not identical, the broader political implications and operational response will be very different.

In the case of Northern Ireland, the situation has moved beyond terrorist groups using crime predominantly as a means to fund terrorism. Here groups and individuals formerly involved in terrorism have now transformed themselves into organized crime groups. According to the Northern Ireland Organized Crime Task Force,

> Seventy-eight groups involving some four hundred individuals have been identified as meeting the National Criminal Intelligence Service (NCIS) definition of organized crime. Just over half of the groups identified have current or historical links to republican or loyalist paramilitary organizations.[19]

Central to this organized criminal activity is money laundering, which in turn is fed by illegal profits from fuel and tobacco smuggling, drugs, fraud of all types, and intellectual property theft—counterfeiting items such as electronic games, compact discs (CDs), and designer clothing.[20] Police figures indicate that from this type of activity, each year the Provisional IRA generates $6.5 million to $8 million (£5 million–£8 million), the Real IRA $6.5 million (£5 million), and various Loyalist groups $2.6 million (£2 million).[21]

Recognition of the blurring of the line between crime and terrorism has not occurred solely as a consequence of the activities of terrorist groups becoming more like those of criminal organizations. The converse also has occurred as criminal organizations now use tactics and weaponry that once were the preserve of the terrorist. For example, in France in March 1996 an armored vehicle was attacked and robbed by several men using machine guns, grenades, and a rocket launcher, and in May 2002 three men armed with a rocket launcher robbed an armored vehicle of nearly $2 million.[22]

This process of assimilation of terrorist methodology by a criminal organization was demonstrated most clearly by the Sicilian Mafia during 1992 and 1993. As a result of a concerted effort by the Italian state, the organization's illegal activities were being severely disrupted. The Mafia made a direct effort to intimidate the Italian state from carrying out its investigation by using violence against individual servants of the state, its symbolic heritage, and the general public. Their efforts bore many of the diagnostic features of terrorism.

At the forefront of the activity against the Mafia were two state prosecuting magistrates—Poalo Borsellino and Giovanni Falcone—who thus became particular targets. Borsellino was killed by a bomb placed under his car; Falcone, his wife, and three police officers were killed by a massive Semtex and TNT bomb placed in a culvert running under the road and triggered by a command wire. The assassination of rivals and state officials who opposed them has long been a tactic employed by the Mafia, but the use of it against such prominent symbols of the state was a new development.

When it became apparent to the Mafia that these deaths did not have the desired effect of stopping or alleviating the pressure being exerted on them by the Italian authorities, the following year they changed their tactics. The Sicilian Mafia left a massive car bomb outside the Uffizi Museum in Florence. It detonated without warning on May 27, 1993, killing five people and destroying several priceless works of art. The following month the Mafia placed two more car bombs, which exploded within a few minutes of each other. The first was outside the Museum of Modern Art in Milan, where five people were killed; the second bomb caused extensive damage to the Basilica of Saint John Lateran and the adjacent Bishop's Palace in Rome.

It is instructive to examine why this series of incidents can be viewed as an escalation of criminal violence into terrorism. First, there was a clear intention by the Mafia to coerce and intimidate the Italian government into stopping its investigations into its criminal activities. The Mafia made no claims of responsibility, thus deepening the public fear caused by its actions and increasing the political pressure on the government. Its actions therefore had political aims. Second, the organization used large quantities of explosives, military and commercial, to construct a culvert bomb, under-car booby trap bombs, and car bombs. These techniques have become the recognized stock-in-trade tactics of various terrorist groups throughout the world such as the IRA, Euskadi ta Askatazuna (ETA), and many others. Finally, the Mafia was careless or reckless of the loss of innocent lives. Although academic issue may be taken with whether this was terrorism, in practical terms it was terrorism in its concept, execution, and impact.

Ten years after these events, the prime minister of Serbia, Zoran Djindjic, was assassinated by a sniper in the center of Belgrade on March 10, 2003.

A wave of arrests followed, focusing on a particular organized crime group: the Zemun Clan. There appears to be little doubt that once more, organized crime resorted to terrorism to advance its aims. Whether the employment of terrorist-like violence by organized crime groups or others in pursuit of criminal gains remains the exception or is an ominous but as yet isolated portent for the future remains unclear.[23]

Terrorism as a Facet of Counterinsurgency: An Integrated Response

If we accept that an effective counterterrorism strategy must be underpinned by the guiding principle of the rule of law and implemented through the criminal justice approach, can there be a role within it for the military, and if so, what might that role be? As far as the UK is concerned, it has long been recognized that the military does indeed have a role to play and that this role will vary according to the circumstances. In the long retreat from Empire during the twentieth century, time and again the army in particular has been called upon to deal with situations where terrorism has been unleashed, in places as diverse as Kenya, Malaya, Cyprus, Aden, and Northern Ireland.

For the army, the body of doctrine that defines its role in combating terrorism is contained within the concept of "Operations Other Than War" (OOTW). A particular element of OOTW is counterinsurgency (COIN), and this concept in turn encapsulates terrorism and counterterrorism. The military contribution to an overall counterterrorism strategy is channeled through the three operational objectives of a COIN operation: find the insurgents, fix them into position, and then strike.[24] Frank Kitson, in his seminal book *Low Intensity Operations,* encapsulated the essence of a COIN campaign:

> Although intelligence is of great importance, it does not usually come in the form of information which will immediately enable a policeman or a soldier to put his men into contact with the enemy. . . . The sort of information which intelligence agencies produce has to be developed by a different set of processes to those used by the organizations themselves before it can be used for putting government forces into contact with insurgents. . . . Two separate functions are therefore involved . . . collecting background information and . . . developing it into contact information.[25]

Experience gained initially by the UK military in COIN operations abroad has been broadened and refined since August 1969 with the continuous involvement of the army and other elements of the military in Northern Ireland. In turn this has led to the refinement and formalization of the kind of activities that may become necessary for them to undertake in the civilian environment. The overall heading of "Military Aid to the Civil Authorities" (MACA) encapsulates three separate types of operation: "Military Aid to the Civil Community" (MACC), "Military Aid to the Civil Ministries" (MACM), and "Military Aid to the Civil Power" (MACP).

These operations "are quite distinct from one another in having differing legal bases and political and military implications. One theme, however, is common to them all: that of legitimacy."[26] The concept of legitimacy and the need to anchor military activity firmly within it is of crucial importance not only at a national level but also at the international level. It is reiterated by the member states of the North Atlantic Treaty Organization (NATO) as part of the Strategic Concept of NATO. This strategic concept obligates NATO members to act "in accordance with the principles of the United Nations Charter [and] based on common values of democracy, human rights and the rule of law."[27] The result of this evolutionary process is that the UK government now has at its disposal a legally sound, graduated response to the threat from terrorism, whether in the UK or against UK citizens and interests abroad.

There is no doubt that in the aftermath of September 11 and the consequent reordering of the UK national objectives in connection with international terrorism the military is well aware of its role and the multifaceted approach that it will once more be required to fulfill. On December 10, 2001, the chief of the Defense Staff, Admiral Sir Michael Boyce, outlined the strategic breadth of the task ahead and its overarching principle:

> We will need to act and plan concurrently across the political, diplomatic, economic, military, legal and information spectrum. In doing this we have to wrest the initiative back from the terrorist, we have to negate his advantage in striking at the time and place of his choosing by restricting his space through legislation, military action, surveillance, diplomacy and deterrence. . . . Above all, what we do must be legal, or otherwise we jeopardize our legitimacy. . . .[28]

The essence of how the UK seeks to achieve an integrated counterterrorism strategy is therefore twofold. In the UK itself it is primarily a matter for the police and the intelligence services, supported by the specialist skills and expertise of the military when necessary. Where military assets are employed, they are used in a very tightly defined way, and only to further criminal justice or diplomatic aims.

This philosophy may mean that the military is employed in novel ways or in unprecedented operational scenarios—a fact that was acknowledged in the last update of the analysis that underpinned the policy framework of the

1998 Strategic Defense Review.[29] Since then terrorism has become even more of a global issue. Whether the military is deployed to lawless zones or failed states such as Afghanistan and Iraq or engaged on counterterrorism missions overseas, this trend inevitably will increase.

Only by taking the broadest possible approach to detecting, preventing, countering, and investigating terrorism, however, does it becomes possible to reduce terrorism's impact. Relying on military force as an alternative to the criminal justice approach, rather than as an integrated and specialized part of it, has been characterized as "narrow, counterproductive, and reflective of bureaucratic inflexibility."[30] It may result in a temporary, short-term fix, but in the longer term it will undermine the strategic imperatives of the broader counterterrorism campaign by giving rise to an alienated and resentful population that in turn will produce the next generation of terrorists. Examples of this phenomenon abound throughout history; I refer here only to one. The rapid courts martial and execution in 1916 of fifteen leaders and members of the Irish Volunteers who had just taken part in the Easter Rising against British rule in Ireland created such popular resentment that by 1919 the conditions were right for Michael Collins and the IRA to launch a systematic campaign of terror in which many hundreds of people were killed. By 1922 the last British soldier had left, and the Irish Free State was proclaimed.[31]

An Integrated Counterterrorism Response: A Possible Model

London is the capital of the UK, the seat of government, and a global financial and business center. It has been the scene of numerous terrorist attacks over the past thirty years. The perpetrators have been numerous: the Irish Republican Army (IRA) and its later dissident faction, the Real IRA; international groups linked to conflicts and events in the Middle East and the Indian subcontinent; domestic extremists such as the Angry Brigade; animal extremists; and even "lone actors."

Over many years, a counterterrorism strategy has been developed that encompasses three strands: prevention, investigation, and consequence management. The boundaries between the activities within each strand are not fixed; in places they inevitably overlap or shade gradually into each other. Two main crossover points exist—one preincident, where intelligence-based covert preventive operations meet with evidential investigations, and the second postincident, where evidential investigations meet with consequence management. The result is a complex web of overlapping activity that provides London with a defense in depth that starts beyond the borders of the UK.

The objective of the first strand is the prevention of terrorist activity; hence it has a wide focus. Broadest of all are "antiterrorism" measures, designed to deter and detect. They are likely to include physical structures and systems designed to achieve "target hardening," and increasing reliance is being placed on technological solutions (e.g., closed-circuit television cameras, metal detectors, biometric identification systems). However, the concept of embedding antiterrorism into as wide a field as possible during routine, day-to-day police operations also must not be neglected. For example, internal briefing systems must be put in place to ensure that all police officers and staff, whatever their normal role, are fully aware of the level of terrorist threat and what the current terrorist methodologies and their diagnostic features are. Similarly, they must be instructed in what action they must take should they be called to a potential or actual terrorist incident and, if their suspicions are aroused at any time, to whom they must forward their information.

Also contained within this strand are efforts directed toward resident, diaspora, and migrant communities. The use of a "hearts and minds" campaign as an integral part of a wider counterterrorist campaign was first successfully employed by the UK military in Malaya during the early 1950s. Since then it has become increasingly clear that communities play a key role in containing terrorism, and their support is vital. This support cannot be assumed, however, and vigorous efforts must be made to encourage and cultivate it.

A key element in the prevention of terrorism strand is counterterrorism operations. Here there is a gradation of activity, ranging from purely intelligence-gathering operations—in which the possibility of acquiring evidence is unlikely (although it is never nonexistent)—to those in which the primary objective is to gather evidence to put before a court of law subsequent to the eventual arrest of the suspects. It is here that the complexities lie because it often is necessary to acquire evidence while protecting intelligence assets and operational methodology from unnecessary exposure during court proceedings.

As indicated above, the investigative strand may well become engaged in advance of an actual terrorist incident, or it may become activated as a result of an incident occurring. If the incident involves an explosive device or a shooting, complexity is once more the order of the day as several processes are set in motion: saving lives and dealing with casualties, scene management to maximize the recovery of evidence, utilization of evidence and intelligence to assist in identification of the perpetrators, and any immediate actions that are required to prevent a further occurrence. A similar but modified response will be required if the incident is an aircraft hijacking or a siege or involves a chemical, biological, radiological, or nuclear (CBRN) element; in these cases, there will be heightened involvement and activity within the relevant sections of the military and government.

Two vital but less well known aspects of the investigative strand are worthy of mention. One is the use of forensic methods to obtain evidence of terrorist methodology and link specific individuals to the crime. In addition, the media, in all its forms, provide a mechanism for the police to obtain the assistance of the public (specifically and generally) and to reassure them that all possible investigative and preventive steps are being taken.

The final strand concerns management of the consequences of a terrorist incident. In cases involving CBRN, this will become a major issue in itself and necessarily will involve many aspects of government—health, media handling, and political decision making, to name but a few.

It is instructive to note the general areas where the military forms an integral part of the planning and response to terrorist activity within the borders of the UK, over and above its specific role in support of the police in Northern Ireland. The military contributes to the preventive strand by providing an "on call" explosive ordinance disposal (EOD) capability throughout the UK, both for conventional and CBRN incidents.[32] It also provides a highly trained response to assist the police during sieges and the hijacking of aircraft or vessels. Since September 11, 2001, the role envisaged for the military in counterterrorism has increased dramatically as it is required to "develop a more active role in stop and search missions on land, at sea, or in conducting search and destroy raids on key terrorist facilities . . . acting to destroy terrorist cells with military action and perhaps, in the last instance, acting against those regimes which support, protect, nurture and direct terrorism."[33] This global mission is a far cry from the military's traditional, internal role in counterterrorism.

Finally, in terms of consequence management, the UK government proposed in a discussion paper on June 12, 2002, that a reaction force of 6,000 members of the Territorial Army Volunteer Reserve (TAVR) be designated and trained to support the emergency services within a few hours of an incident occurring.

Clearly the counterterrorism strategy for both London and the UK contains much activity that is in the domain of the police. In addition, it is fully integrated with both the military and the intelligence agencies; thus, their experience and expertise can be drawn upon quickly and easily. In the following section I show how the response to terrorism is coordinated on an international basis and focuses mainly on the systems and structures that exist to facilitate this coordination on a Europe-wide basis.

Evolution of International Police Cooperation in Counterterrorism: A European Perspective

Various structures, formal and informal, now exist to facilitate police-to-police cooperation in the investigation of terrorist offenses and in the exchange of information and intelligence. In terms of an international approach to the problem of transnational crime and criminals, the International Criminal Police Organization (ICPO) has been the main structure since its formation in 1923. INTERPOL, as the organization is more commonly known, is not an investigative body; it acts as a conduit for requests for assistance to be channeled from one member country to another. Its strength is that most countries in the world are members. However, its impact on terrorism and terrorists has been minimal.

Article 3 of the INTERPOL Constitution, drafted in 1956, prohibits it from taking any action in cases of a political, military, religious, or racial character.[34] To enable the organization to become engaged with violent crimes committed by terrorists, INTERPOL adopted in 1984 a resolution that states, "In general, offenses are not considered to be political when they are committed outside the conflict area and when the victims are not connected with the aims or objectives pursued by the offenders."[35] Despite this provision, Article 3 still applies; accordingly, any assistance INTERPOL renders must be "in accordance with Article 3 of the Constitution and as far as national legislations allow."[36]

From a trans-European perspective, a formal international structure to coordinate national responses to terrorism first crystallized in 1975 with the formation of the Trevi Group.[37] This initiative involved regular meetings at the government ministerial level, between senior officials, and for relevant practitioners within three working groups (terrorism, public order, drugs and organized crime). In turn, the Trevi Group had recognized and built upon a loose network of police agencies from countries where terrorism was having the most impact: the UK (the IRA and Middle Eastern groups), Germany (the Red Army Faction, RAF) and Italy (Red Brigades). Representatives of the relevant police units from each of these countries established the Police Working Group on Terrorism (PWGT). Its main objective was to facilitate the exchange of operational information on terrorist activity. The importance of this function was later acknowledged by the Trevi Group with the absorption of the PWGT into the Trevi Group framework.

In 1995 the Trevi Group was superseded by the European Union's "Third Pillar" intergovernmental criminal justice arrangements, but the PWGT continues to this day. Under the auspices of the PWGT, the concept of police Counter Terrorism Liaison Officers (CTLO) was developed. Three countries—the UK, France, and Germany—agreed to exchange officers in the relevant police agencies in each country to improve the speed and flow of intelligence and information. Liaison with the other countries in the PWGT is carried out on an agency-to-agency basis, using a dedicated, secure communications network.

As part of the drive to facilitate the free flow of goods, services, and people throughout the EU, the Schengen Accord was signed in 1985 to allow for the establishment of cross-border police communications systems between France, Germany, The Netherlands, Belgium, Luxembourg, and Spain.[38] Following agreement in the negotiation of the Treaty of Maastricht in 1995, the structure was expanded to include all the members of the EU, although it is not yet fully implemented in the UK or Ireland as a result of a specific derogation by both countries.

The Schengen Information System (SIS) was designed and built to support the concept of a free flow of goods and people. The concept behind the SIS was to strengthen the external borders of the EU as a compensatory measure for the weakening of the internal, national ones. The SIS is predominantly an immigration database, but it also enables the exchange of police operational information on individuals and vehicles that may be involved in transnational criminality within the EU. Therefore it is one more tool that may be utilized to detect terrorists.

The next major step in enhancing police cooperation in the EU—probably the most significant and far-reaching action taken to date—came with the establishment of EUROPOL. Its genesis was long and complex, beginning in 1991 when the idea was first formally proposed by Germany at an EU summit. It finally took on tangible form when it moved into its permanent headquarters building in the Hague on February 16, 1994.[39]

The initial role of EUROPOL was to assist member states to improve their effectiveness in combating drug trafficking and organized crime.[40] It did not encompass terrorism. However, after sustained pressure from Spain in particular, the remit of EUROPOL was expanded to include terrorism from January 1, 1999, and subsequently a small unit was established to explore how best EUROPOL could make a contribution to the existing systems and structures. Eighteen months later, its efforts were given renewed impetus.

European Police Cooperation in the Aftermath of September 11

Article 29 of the Treaty on the European Union sets the EU an objective "to provide its citizens with a high level of safety within an area of freedom, justice, and security." It specifically refers to terrorism as one of the serious forms of crime to be subject to common action by "closer cooperation between police forces, customs authorities and other competent authorities, including Europol."[41] Article 30 deals specifically with police cooperation in criminal matters, including terrorism. The EU has taken two important recent legislative steps that will assist in the process of enhancing police and judicial cooperation.

On June 22, 2002, a "Framework Decision on Combating Terrorism" came into force throughout the EU.[42] Framework decisions are binding on member states and set out exactly what they must achieve. However, the methods and forms by which they do so are left to the national authorities. The framework consists of thirteen articles; it defines what criminal offenses are deemed as terrorist offenses (Article 2) and ensures that all member states have jurisdiction to investigate these offenses (Article 9) and that the penalties for them are appropriate (Article 5). Its provisions came into effect on January 1, 2003.

A second Framework Decision, on the European arrest warrant and surrender procedures between member states, is now in the process of consultation. It is expected to commence on January 4, 2004.[43]

Various other additional measures have been taken to enhance police cooperation and coordination across the EU. Almost immediately after September 11, a Counter Terrorist Task Force (CTTF) was set up with the objective of researching and refining an EU-wide threat assessment in light of the attacks in the United States. Within EUROPOL, the number of staff involved in counterterrorism was increased threefold, and in April 2002 its budget was increased by 45 percent.[44]

Over the past few years, police and intelligence agencies of the Group of Seven (G-7) countries[45] have started to come together with increasing frequency to discuss matters of mutual interest with regard to terrorism and counterterrorism. The meetings tend to fall into two categories—the first involving "practitioners" and the second focused at a more strategic level, attended by "experts." At a full G-7 summit (plus Russia) in July 1996, twenty-five measures on counterterrorism were advocated.[46] With the formal acceptance of Russia as a full partner, thus creating the G-8, the span of its activities will inevitably increase.[47]

Whether the "European" approach to international police cooperation, involving a judicious mix of formal structures and systems supported by informal contacts and liaison, continues to prove its worth in face of the current and potential threat will be of critical importance over the next few years. In addition, it is clear that the military, perhaps coordinated through NATO, is being driven to take on a more "police-like" role, especially outside the traditional area of NATO operations. Therefore there will be a need to integrate this activity into existing and forthcoming national, EU, and NATO structures in an effective and systematic way.

Conclusion

The theoretical constructs of "terror as crime" and "terror as war" are valid and useful concepts. In addition, there is no doubt that it is possible to create a theoretical strategy for countering terrorism that is based exclusively on the tenets that each of them sets forth. In this chapter, however, I have attempted to demonstrate that in practical terms, adopting a rigid "either/or" approach toward countering terrorism is not the best way forward.

The nature of the terrorist threat is continually changing. To combat this threat, the response must be innovative and flexible and engage all the resources that are available. Terrorism is a crime, and therefore the primary mechanism of any liberal democracy in its efforts against it should be its criminal justice system, supported by the military and intelligence services, with all these elements acting in full accordance with the rule of law. A wide spectrum of response is required.

The experience of the UK has led to its current "concept of operations" where policy, strategy, operations, and tactics are firmly anchored in the criminal justice system, and their implementation encompasses virtually all the organs of the state. The intelligence services[48] and the military are the most prominent and specialized of these agencies, but many others also play an active part: Customs, Immigration, and the Emergency Services, to name but a few.

The nature of the threat is continually changing, and the once-prevalent perception that terrorism and serious crime were separate and distinct entities is becoming increasingly tenuous. Not only are terrorists becoming firmly rooted in acquisitive crime in order to pursue their political objectives (with increasing amounts of such crime at a surprisingly low and unsophisticated level), but the gap also is closing from the other end as organized and serious criminals turn to the use of terrorist weapons and tactics to pursue their own criminal enterprises.

Another area of congruence between terrorists and criminals is their transformation from traditional hierarchical groups into network forms of organization. Undoubtedly, this shift increases the difficulties faced by those charged with countering them because "network structures . . . are resistant to disruption, have a high degree of resiliency, and are adaptable to changing environments."[49]

It may be precipitate to infer that counterterrorist organizations, which tend to be both hierarchical and bureaucratic, therefore are bereft of all the advantages possessed by a network form of organization. In counterterrorism terms, the task is to emulate the brain, where each nerve cell has its own specialized function and yet also is connected into a network of other cells. The result of this cooperation and coordination is a fully functioning organism.

The counterterrorism network is composed of many different organizations and agencies, and each of them can be regarded as acting as a node in its own right. In turn they have their own networks, constructed and maintained to undertake specific tasks. All of the nodes are linked by a common purpose: the deterrence, prevention, detection, disruption, and investigation of terrorism. If these linkages, nationally and internationally, are constructed and maintained in a robust and effective way, a "network of networks" can be achieved.

The challenge now is to encourage new points of linkage between nodes, to strengthen existing linkages, and to expand the network to include linkages to any organization that can make a contribution to countering terrorism. Rigid structures that focus only on internal objectives must be replaced by flexible systems targeted on a common goal, and external links between organizations must be forged and sustained at all levels. Above all, the individuals who operate within these organizations must not only be skilled in "the interoperability of the mind,"[50] they also must be able "to see beyond disciplinary boundaries and to challenge bureaucratic barriers [as] in times of flexible threat, flexibility of thought and actions is essential."[51]

Much work already has been done to create such a linked framework at the international level, at the UN, within the EU, by the G-8 nations, and at other relevant fora. The fifteen nations that constitute the EU already have mapped out the immediate future with their Framework Decisions on combating terrorism and the European arrest warrant and extradition procedures. Without initiatives such as these, and the close links forged between practitioners at the operational level, the advantage the terrorist enjoys—determining the time, the place, and the method—cannot begin to be mitigated.

The cornerstone of all of these efforts, national and international, must be the rule of law and its implementation through the criminal justice approach. Only by utilizing the criminal justice system—supported by the intelligence services and, when necessary, the military—can the appropriate balance be struck between countering terrorism and compromising as little as possible the rights, values, and principles that liberal democratic governments exist to preserve.

There is no operational "magic bullet" that can infallibly detect and prevent all acts of terrorism. For such a feat to be even conceivable, all of the measures described in this chapter—along with many more besides—would need to work all the time, every time, and everywhere. Despite the continuing and unrelenting commitment of many nations to trying to achieve such an objective, the words of the IRA—uttered in the aftermath of the unsuccessful attempt in 1984 to assassinate the prime minister of the UK, Margaret Thatcher—must be constantly borne in mind: "Today you were lucky. We have to be lucky once. You have to be lucky all the time."

Notes

The views expressed in this article are those of the author and not necessarily those of the Metropolitan Police.

1. See David Rapoport, "The Four Waves of Modern Terrorism," chapter 2 in this book.

2. Walter Laqueur, *Terrorism* (London: Weidenfeld and Nicolson, 1977), 101.

3. Others also exist, foremost among them the "communication model" of Ronald Crelinsten. See, for example, his "Analysing Terrorism and Counter-Terrorism: A Communication Model," *Terrorism and Political Violence* 14, no. 2 (summer 2002): 77–122. Mordechai Yerushalmi postulates a "control model" in which terrorists and governments alike agree on rules and boundaries to minimize the impact of terrorism on noninvolved parties (even the author concedes that this model may seem "utopian"). See Mordechai Yerushalmi, "A 'Control Code' Model of Terrorism," in *International Terrorism: The Domestic Response,* ed. Richard Ward and Harold Smith (Chicago: Office of International Criminal Justice, University of Illinois, 1987), 77–83, and Yerushalmi citing Denis Szabo and Ronald Crilinsten [*sic*], "International Political Terrorism: A Challenge for Comparative Research," *Terrorism: An International Journal* 1, no. 2: 346.

4. Paul Wilkinson, *Terrorism and the Liberal State* (London: Macmillan, 1986), 125.

5. Ronald Crelinsten, cited by Ami Pedahzur and Magnus Ranstorp, "A Tertiary Model for Countering Terrorism," *Terrorism and Political Violence* 13, no. 2 (summer 2001): 1–26.

6. Ronald Crelinsten and Alex Schmidt, cited by Pedahzur and Ranstorp, "A Tertiary Model for Countering Terrorism," 4.

7. Pedahzur and Ranstorp, "A Tertiary Model for Countering Terrorism,"4.

8. It is accepted that a direct "read over" from the UK to the United States may not be possible because of a host of reasons; among them are legal, cultural, and historical differences. This constraint applies equally, however, to the situation that exists between the UK, the states of the EU, and beyond. It does not negate the principles involved, nor does it preclude dissemination of best practice for others to adopt and adapt as they see fit.

9. For a comprehensive and detailed analysis of the death toll, see Marine-Therese Fay, Mike Morissey, and Marie Smith, *Northern Ireland's Troubles: The Human Costs* (London: Pluto Press, 1987).

10. On March 8 the IRA planted four car bombs in London. Two exploded; two were discovered and defused. One person died of a heart attack, and more than 150 were injured. Between that episode and 1999 there were 582 bomb attacks and 33 shootings carried out on the British mainland by Irish republican terrorist groups. Of these, 365 and 17, respectively, have occurred in London. Royal Ulster Constabulary, *Chief Constable's Annual Report 2000.*

11. The 1974 Act and its subsequent amendments eventually were replaced by the Terrorism Act in 2000. This Act retained and refined the extraordinary investigative powers given to the police and extended them to include investigations into international terrorism committed in the UK and abroad. Certain additional and very specific offenses also were created (e.g., training for terrorist purposes). The U.S.A. Patriot Act is akin to the British legislation but broader in its ramifications. It covers certain areas that are dealt with under separate UK legislation (e.g., detention of suspected UK noncitizens). Financial offenses and retention of communications data are dealt with by the Anti-Terrorism, Crime and Security Act, 2001. All other aspects of surveillance (electronic and nonelectronic) are covered by the Regulation of Investigatory Powers Act, 2000.

12. "Council Framework Decision of 13 June 2002 on Combating Terrorism," *Official Journal of the European Community*, L164/3, June 2002.

13. Ibid., Article 9.

14. "Combating Terrorism: How Five Foreign Countries Are Organized to Combat Terrorism," U.S. General Accounting Office, Report to Congressional Requesters, GAO/NSIAD-00–85, April 2000. The five countries were Canada, France, Germany, Israel, and the United Kingdom.

15. Ibid., 4, 5.

16. For an exploration of the relationship between serious crime and terrorism, see Phil Williams, "Terrorism and Organized Crime: Convergence, Nexus, or Transformation?" in *Hype or Reality? The "New Terrorism" and Mass Casualty Attacks,* ed. Brad Roberts (Alexandria, Va.: Chemical and Biological Arms Control Institute, 2000).

17. Angus Muir, "Terrorism and Weapons of Mass Destruction: The Case of Aum Shinrikyo," *Studies in Conflict and Terrorism* 22, no.1 (January–March 1999): 83.

18. See Tamara Makarenko and Daphne Biliouri, "Is This the End of 17N?" *Jane's Intelligence Review* 14, no. 3 (September 2002): 6–10.

19. *The Threat to Northern Ireland Society from Serious and Organized Crime: Northern Ireland Threat Assessment 2001*, RUC Analysis Centre, Northern Ireland Organized Crime Task Force, 5.

20. Ibid., 6, 16.

21. Police evidence to House of Commons Northern Ireland Select Committee, reported in *The Guardian*, 3 July 2002, 6.

22. *The Guardian*, 9 February 2001, 16; *EmergencyNet News; Daily News Summary*, 31 May 2002, available at www.emergency.com.ennday.htm.

23. See www.guardian.co.uk/international/story/0_3604_913000_00.html and www.guardian.co.uk/international/story/0_3604_913449_00.html.

24. G. Bulloch, "The Application of Military Doctrine to Counterinsurgency (COIN) Operations: A British Perspective," *Studies in Conflict and Terrorism* 19, no. 3 (1996): 247–59.

25. Frank Kitson, *Low Intensity Operations* (London: Faber and Faber, 1971).

26. Ibid., 258.

27. *UK Strategic Defence Review*, Appendix, 65.

28. Admiral Sir Michael Boyce, "UK Strategic Choices Following the Strategic Defense Review and September 11th," speech presented at Royal United Services Institute (RUSI), 10 December 2000.

29. *The Future Strategic Context for Defence*, 7 February 2001, available at www.mod.uk/index.php3page=2449.

30. Audrey Kurth Cronin, "The Diplomacy of Counter Terrorism: Lessons Learned, Ignored and Disputed," in *United States Institute of Peace Special Report* (Washington, D.C.: United States Institute of Peace, January 2002).

31. For more details, see Robert Kee, *The Green Flag* (London: Weidenfeld and Nicolson, 1972), 573.

32. The exception is in London, where the Metropolitan Police Service has its own EOD capability.

33. Boyce, "UK Strategic Choices."

34. Interpol Constitution, Article 3.

35. *Violent Criminality Commonly Referred to as Terrorism,* Interpol Resolution No. 6, Luxembourg General Assembly 1984. Cited in Paul Swallow, "Of Limited Operational Relevance: A European View of Interpol's Crime Fighting Role in the 21st Century," *Transnational Organized Crime* 2, no. 4 (1996): 116.

36. Andres Bossard, "The War Against Terrorism: The Interpol Response," in Ward and Smith, *International Terrorism.*

37. Trevi was "formal" in the sense that it had a structure and all the governments involved acknowledged its existence, but it was not constituted by treaty and hence it should strictly be considered as "informal." See J. C. Alderson and W. A. Tupman, eds., *Policing Europe after 1992: Proceedings of an International Seminar* (Exeter, England: University of Exeter, 1989).

38. For a good resume of the genesis of Trevi, the Schengen Accord, and the Schengen Information System, see John Benyon, Lynne Turnbull, Andrew Willis, Rachel Woodward, and Adrian Beck, *Police Cooperation in Europe: An Investigation* (Leicester, England: Centre for the Study of Public Order, University of Leicester, 1993).

39. Michael Santiago, *Europol and Police Cooperation in Europe* (London: Edwin Mellen Press, 2000).

40. Ibid.

41. *Treaty on the European Union, 1992.*

42. "Combating Terrorism" (see note 14).

43. *Proposal for a Council Framework Decision on the European Arrest Warrant and the Surrender Procedures between Member States*, Council of the European Union, Outcome of Proceedings, 14867/1/01 REV 1, 6/7 December 2001.

44. No official figures have yet been released.

45. The G-7 countries were Canada, France, Germany, Italy, Japan, the UK, and the United States.

46. *Proposal for a Council Framework Decision on Combating Terrorism*, Council of the European Union, Outcome of Proceedings, 1485/1/01 REV 1, 6 December 2001.

47. On May 28, 2002, an agreement was signed to formally create a new NATO-Russia Council. Consequently, Russia will now play a formal part in the NATO planning and consultative process and hence is likely to participate in the formulation of future NATO counterterrorism strategy.

48. The UK has two main intelligence agencies. The Security Service deals with national security and terrorism in the UK. It has no executive powers, and there is no direct U.S. equivalent. The Secret Intelligence Service (SIS) operates abroad and is akin to the U.S. Central Intelligence Agency (CIA). Both services are supported by the Government Communications Headquarters (GCHQ), which is the UK equivalent of the U.S. National Security Agency (NSA).

49. "Global Security Beyond 2000: Executive Summary of the Conference Proceedings," University of Pittsburgh Centre for West European Studies, Pittsburgh, Pennsylvania, 2000.

50. Boyce, "UK Strategic Choices," 7.

51. David Veness, "Terrorism and Counterterrorism: An International Perspective," *Studies in Conflict and Terrorism* 24, no. 5 (2001): 415.

52. *An Phoblacht/Republican News*, October 1984. Contained in press statement released by the IRA.

seven

MILITARY FORCE

Timothy D. Hoyt

The tragic events of September 11, 2001, drove a paradigm shift in the use of military force against terrorism. The formidable military capability of the United States—a devastating force amply demonstrated against al-Qaeda and the Taliban in Afghanistan and in the Persian Gulf in 1991 and 2003—was symbolically unleashed through a proclamation of war on international terrorism. Given the long history of U.S. restraint in authorizing military responses to terrorism, it is worth examining the limits of military power as we enter a new era fighting an elusive adversary.

It is a mistake to assume that the high-technology tools of conventional conflict can be utilized freely and easily in opposition to the forces of transnational terrorism today. Although terrorism is a political act of violence—something like war, if we use Clausewitz's definition—the response to terrorism must be carefully weighed in light of its potential political effect. This represents a serious problem of strategy—the relationship between political ends and available means. The use of military force may prove spectacularly unsuccessful if it is not carefully correlated with political objectives.

Military options in the current war against terrorism fall in a very broad spectrum of potential violence, but that spectrum is not continuous. Terrorist violence is fundamentally tactical: Small numbers of activists with increasing but still limited firepower engage in attacks that resemble ambushes rather than set-piece battles. However, terrorists do not engage in continuous combat, in linear combat, or (in most cases) in sequential attacks—therefore, a wide range of military options deriving from the Western focus on the operational level of war may be inapplicable. Critical concepts such as continuity, pursuit, and the culminating point of victory must be reexamined in a conflict against small, ruthless groups that do not shirk from violating the laws of war but also command the sympathy and potentially the allegiance of important elements of the public and elites in the Islamic world. Military force represents a powerful tool in the war on terrorism. It is, however, a tool that must be used very skillfully and in careful coordination with other tools of policy if the United States is to convert military victories into long-term strategic success.

Changing Rules: Military Operations against Terrorism

This chapter is laid out in three sections. In the first section I briefly discuss traditional restraint in American military responses to terrorism. In the 1983–2000 period, the United States authorized military responses to terrorist acts on only three occasions. This record suggests that policymakers faced strong constraints when they were considering military retaliation. Traditional opposition to a military response to terrorism falls into two categories: arguments about the legal grounding for military response and concern over the possible political effects. In the new international environment, in which the United States has declared "war" against the amorphous forces of international terrorism, military force becomes a more viable retaliatory option.

The *practicality* of military operations against terrorist groups, however, deserves very serious consideration. Although the utility of, and preference for, military force may increase in times of war, there are distinct and profound limitations on its potential application. In the second section, therefore, I discuss the difficulties of combating terrorism with military forces configured for conventional wars.

In the third section I examine options for maximizing the effectiveness of military force in combating terrorism. Applying military force for the achievement of political aims is the realm of strategy. Despite the obvious differences between conventional interstate war and war with a diffuse transnational terrorist group, the development of appropriate strategy for dealing with this new emerging threat remains pertinent, applicable, and indeed critical to success.

The U.S. Military and Terrorism: Constraints in the Late Twentieth Century

The study of the use of military force constitutes an important, but relatively small, part of the existing literature on terrorism. Military force is a blunt instrument—one that carries with it profound political consequences, particularly when state boundaries are violated or innocents slain. As Paul Pillar points out, however, in the past decade military instruments have increased in precision and lethality and may be more useful against terrorists in the future.[1] Precision stand-off weapons combined with highly trained ground forces offer new military options for confronting terrorists. The new and lethal combination of Predator unmanned aerial vehicles (UAVs) armed with Hellfire missiles has demonstrated its effectiveness in both Afghanistan and Yemen, for example. These new capabilities may limit the "footprint" of U.S. or multinational troops deployed abroad, minimizing the inevitable political friction that results from the interaction of foreign troops and local populations.

The use of force against terrorists, either in response or preemptively, has always been difficult and controversial. The United States used military force in response to terrorism on just three occasions in the 1983–2000 period:

- The El Dorado canyon strikes against Libya, in retaliation for the bombing of the La Belle discotheque in 1986[2]
- Cruise missile strikes on Iraq's intelligence agencies in 1993, responding to an assassination attempt on President George H. W. Bush[3]
- Cruise missile strikes launched against facilities in Afghanistan and Sudan, which were believed to be affiliated with Osama bin Laden's al-Qaeda network, in response to the 1998 bombing of two U.S. embassies in Africa.[4]

The U.S. experience, and the literature surrounding it, consider military options from a very distinct and limited perspective.[5] The United States has not experienced widespread terrorism on its own soil at the hand of separatist movements, for example.[6]

Other states have long traditions of using military force against terrorists. This use, however, generally has been directed either at terrorist groups located within their own territories (a form of counterinsurgency, discussed below) or at well-known terrorist sanctuaries in other states. The range of military options in response to terrorism in Northern Ireland, for instance, is considerably greater—and, indeed, represents a *constant*, rather than episodic, factor in counterterrorism operations.[7] Similarly, Israel utilized a variety of responses to deal with terrorist threats from Lebanese territory, ranging from full-fledged conventional war in 1982 to retaliatory strikes in the late 1990s.[8] Any study of U.S. response to terrorist acts in the past twenty years, however, must note the severe constraints on military options.[9]

These constraints fall into two main categories. The first category of objections is legal. Military force must be used according to the principle of proportionality, and many analysts point out "the fear that in using force we too might kill innocents and somehow validate terrorism."[10] This is an ongoing issue in international law, as well as an issue of both domestic and international political concern.[11] For the United States, military force has been used to respond to, rather than preemptively attack, terrorist organizations—until the tragic events of September 11, 2001.[12]

An additional legal concern, particularly for democracies, is the constitutional issues associated with using military forces to support law enforcement or criminal justice efforts. Police are trained very differently from military forces, have greater legitimacy in the eyes of the public, and are less likely to overreact with excessive violence in crisis situations. In extreme circumstances, however, military forces have been ordered to supplement traditional forces of law and order, for example in Northern Ireland.[13] The United States traditionally has limited the role of the military in domestic affairs. These limits may be modified in an era of increased concern over homeland security. In addition, U.S. armed forces are being forced to take on greater constabulary and policing roles in postconflict Afghanistan and Iraq.

A second set of constraints lies in the political realm. Military retaliation for terrorist attacks creates unpredictable political effects in the international system. Terrorists thrive on the impression that they are weak. Retaliatory strikes that use the might of state-funded, high-technology conventional forces reinforce the disparity between terrorists and target states, gaining possible sympathy for the terrorists and frequently resulting in international condemnation for the retaliating states.

From a practical perspective, many states lack control over terrorist groups operating from their territory and may consider the threat of alienating terrorist groups to be more dangerous than the threat of continued retaliation from external powers. In addition, individuals who make key decisions regarding protection and support to terrorists may not be affected by retaliation or may not be under the firm control of national leadership.[14] Military retaliation also may strengthen unfriendly regimes, increase terrorist support abroad, or strengthen hostile factions in neutral or friendly states. Finally, the message behind external retaliation is not always clear; sometimes it can even be the result of intelligence failure or flawed policy.[15]

Military retaliation also is constrained by other political concerns. Violation of international law or norms adversely affects the ability of the responding power to gain international support for its retaliation. Unilateral retaliation risks offending allied, neutral, and hostile powers. During the cold war, retaliation risked escalating the conflict into a potential regional or superpower confrontation, particularly when the target was Palestinian terrorist groups sheltered by Soviet proxies or other Arab states. Military failure can increase the perceived power of and support for terrorist groups in the international system, as well as alienating potential allies. It also is difficult to decisively affect the efforts of terrorist groups through military force—the primary impact of military retaliation is symbolic, demonstrating national determination and will.

The constraints on military action changed fundamentally as a result of the terrorist attacks on the Pentagon and the World Trade Center on September 11, 2001. As we look at the potential use of military force in the twenty-first century, particularly during the "war on terrorism," we must remember that many of these political objections or constraints have been diminished or undermined by the state of war. In theory, the U.S. government now has a much freer hand in the use of its formidable military capability.

Military Limits in the War on Terrorism

President George W. Bush's "declaration of war on terrorism" effectively eliminates many of the previous barriers to U.S. counterterrorist operations, particularly in terms of military responses. By invoking the principle of self-defense, the United States has legitimized its use of force against terrorist groups and the states that support them, although the international community remains divided in its acceptance of the U.S. position.[16] In addition, the savage nature of al-Qaeda's assault and the heroic efforts of the rescue workers drew almost universal support and sympathy from the international community. The remnants of this support remain a powerful legitimizing force for U.S. military action.

By declaring war, even rhetorically, the president also cemented in the public mind the need for a *military* response. As other analysts have noted, the United States appears to have a unique strategic culture that regards war as a last resort rather than, in the words of Carl von Clausewitz, "the continuation of policy by other means."[17] As a result, the United States is most comfortable waging relatively *unlimited wars*—wars in which the objective is the overthrow of a regime, for instance, or the complete conquest of an enemy in order to compel the enemy to submit absolutely.[18] This crusading impulse leads to a policy preference, once war is declared, for using maximum force as quickly as possible, to end the war quickly and return to the preferred state of peace.[19]

The "declaration of war" has changed the range of counterterrorist options, at least with regard to the United States. The United States is creating a new paradigm with increased options for military response, codified in the new National Security Strategy of the United States.[20] This new paradigm includes the following elements:

1. Increased legitimacy for the use of military retaliation
2. Less concern over the proportionality of response
3. Greater willingness to undertake high-risk operations
4. Greater legitimacy for preemptive action
5. Legitimization of regime overthrow as a response.

The new paradigm dismisses many of the previous objections to military retaliation, arguing that the international situation has fundamentally changed since September 11. In some respects this assessment is correct. The United States no longer needs to fear, for example, that an attack on a state supporting terrorism will be construed as destabilizing by a hostile Soviet Union. This new approach by the United States still risks destabilizing the international system, however, particularly in areas of regional conflict. Other states, including Russia and India, may adapt elements of the U.S. paradigm—particularly the emphasis on preemption—to justify strikes on their neighbors.

By proclaiming a war on terrorism, the president has endowed the terrorists with a quasi-legitimacy—they are a recognized force that the United States must fight, but not one that the United States can ever negotiate with.[21] In such circumstances—and given the deaths of Americans and other nationals on September 11—concerns for proportionality and tacit recognition fall by the wayside. The use of overwhelming force against terrorists traditionally has been avoided for fear of causing sympathy for the enemy—the "David and Goliath" syndrome.[22] In the past, military retaliation has focused primarily on sending political messages, rather than crippling the physical capabilities of terrorist organizations.[23] A "declaration of war" significantly increases the potential range of military options.

Similarly, in previous eras tactical and political risk have constrained military responses to terrorism. The tactical risk issue is particularly evident in hostage rescue operations, where terrorists can respond immediately by killing the hostages, whose safety is the military objective. The Munich catastrophe of 1972 led to the creation of special antiterrorist and hostage rescue units and tactics, but the record of their efforts is decidedly mixed.[24] A failed military operation is a massive propaganda asset for the target terrorist group or state, particularly if high military casualties are involved. The failed 1998 strike on bin Laden's terrorist infrastructure, for example, turned a marginal figure into a hero in much of the Islamic world.[25] In wartime, however, the willingness to take such risks increases.

The new paradigm also affects political calculations about the costs of military operations. When the United States attacked state sponsors of ter-

rorism in the past, it targeted facilities or entities associated with the terrorism itself, rather than other national targets. Examples include Iraq's intelligence headquarters, Libyan military targets, and even the now-infamous Su-
danese pharmaceutical factory. To discourage Libyan support for terrorism,
it might have been more effective to cripple Libya's oil industry—but this action would have appeared disproportionate to the international community
and might have undermined the broader coalition the United States hoped
to achieve against Libyan terrorism.

Many of these objections no longer have the same strength. The United
States has effectively declared war on terrorists and the states that support
them, turning active state supporters into legitimate military targets. In many
cases, the United States no longer distinguishes between terrorist and state
entities—as the attack on Afghanistan amply demonstrates. In Operation Enduring Freedom, the United States undertook very risky tactical operations,
including insertion of special forces in a hostile political and geographic environment, and utilized overwhelming force wherever possible—all with the
objective of punishing and then overthrowing the regime that supported al-
Qaeda and the forces of international terrorism. The United States used a similar approach to overthrow Saddam Hussein and the Ba'ath Party in Iraq in
spring 2003. The linkages between al-Qaeda and Iraq remain ill-defined, however, and international support for U.S. military operations was limited.

Given this new paradigm, driven by the single most successful terrorist
attack ever carried out, the overwhelming high-technology military capabilities of the United States have been committed to this conflict. What, then,
are the limits to the use of military force as a response to terrorism in war?
To understand the military limitations, we must delve into military theory—
a subject that has only rarely been applied to the study of terrorism.[26]

Three factors deserve special investigation. The first, and foremost, is
whether terrorism actually can be considered a form of war, rather than ma-
licious criminal behavior. This criterion deals with the *ends* terrorists seek to
achieve. The second factor examines the *means*—how they fight, in military
terms. The third factor examines the operation of terrorist forces in *space
and time* and the limits these methods place on the terrorists as well as the
military forces fighting terrorism. These factors determine the type of war
terrorists actually fight and help define the difficulties modern military organizations face in dealing with this threat.

Is Terrorism a Form of War?

According to Clausewitz, war is simply a continuation of politics by other
means.[27] Clausewitz means that the primordial violence of warfare is channeled in the interests of achieving a political goal. The objective of war is to

impose one's will on the enemy through the use of force—which will result, one hopes, in a favorable political outcome.[28] In theory, at least, all military operations or uses of political violence must be coordinated in pursuit of the political aim.[29]

Does terrorism utilize violence in pursuit of a political aim? Unquestionably. Terrorism, in the words of a leading expert, can be defined as "the deliberate creation and exploitation of fear through violence or the threat of violence in pursuit of political change."[30] Hoffman further explains that

> Terrorism is designed to create power where there is none or to consolidate power where there is very little. Through the publicity generated by their violence, terrorists seek to obtain the leverage, influence and power they otherwise lack to effect political change on either a local or an international scale.[31]

At their most ambitious or extreme, terrorist groups seek to overthrow the established political order and replace it with a new one, derived from their own philosophies.[32] This appears to be the case with al-Qaeda, which seeks a new Islamic caliphate, among other ambitions. In Clausewitzian terms, this objective is relatively *unlimited*, implying the complete overthrow of existing regimes and, therefore, relatively high stakes.[33]

How Do Terrorists Fight?

Again looking at Clausewitz, war requires the imposition of one's will upon one's enemy. This goal can be accomplished in two ways: destruction of enemy military forces and *ability* to resist, or destruction of enemy will and *desire* to resist.[34] The former assumes that destruction of enemy forces in the field will incline your adversary to negotiate or risk suffering even harsher terms.

Targeting enemy will is more difficult and may be partially achieved through losses on the battlefield and other destruction. In the twentieth century, political terrorism has been used as a weapon both in internal struggles and in interstate wars.[35] Terrorists seek to target enemy will through indiscriminate attacks on civilians, to undermine political legitimacy and support over an extended period of time.

Terrorists do not carry out predictable, sequential operations. In many cases, according to Admiral J. C. Wylie, war follows a sequential pattern:

> We consider a war as a series of discrete steps or actions, with each one of this series of actions growing naturally out of, and dependent on, the one that preceded it . . . [I]f at any stage of the war one of these actions had happened differently, then the remainder of the sequence would have had a different pattern.[36]

Terrorists, however, use what Wylie refers to as a *cumulative* approach. In the cumulative approach, the sequence of activity does not matter. No action depends upon the ones that precede or follow it. What is ultimately important is the cumulative effect—the overall impact of a series of individual shocks or attacks.[37]

This distinction is important because, unlike Delbruck's strategy of exhaustion, this concept does not require constant battlefield contact and attrition. Through a long conflict waged with episodic acts of shocking violence, terrorists aim to degrade the legitimacy of existing regimes, undermine the confidence of the body politic, and weaken public will to the point that, rather than facing continued tension, the existing regime surrenders or is replaced. Recognizing that they cannot decisively win through direct military encounter, terrorists seek instead to control the conflict so that it may be waged on their own terms to maximum effectiveness.

> The primary aim of the strategist in the conduct of war is some selected
> degree of control of the enemy for the strategist's own purpose; this is
> achieved by control of the pattern of war; and this control of the pattern of
> war is had by manipulation of the center of gravity of war to the advantage
> of the strategist and the disadvantage of the opponent.[38]

Operations in Time and Space

Terrorists fight wars of the weak. They do not put large, organized forces in the field, except in very unusual circumstances. The attacks of September 11, which involved nineteen terrorists and cost less than $1 million, were highly sophisticated and professional by terrorist standards, involving massive deception and careful coordination. Terrorists therefore have limited military means. Even extraordinary independent groups, such as al-Qaeda, can access funds only on the order of several hundred million dollars—the cost of one major surface ship or a handful of modern jet fighter aircraft. In conventional terms, these resources are simply inadequate for major military operations. Even small developed states with modest military capabilities, such as Hungary, have annual military budgets that are larger than this amount.

Terrorists operate primarily on the technical and tactical levels of combat.[39] Most terrorists are trained primarily in light arms, with only a few technical specialists moving into other tasks such as bomb-making.[40] "Battles," when they occur, are skirmishes or ambushes involving small groups with light weapons—which are quite destructive even in unskilled hands. Terrorists do not attempt to hold ground; they try to melt away into the background as quickly as possible. As a result, in practical terms, they cede control of physical space in order to control *time*. Terrorists can maintain the initiative against their opponents by not being fixed in space, and therefore being difficult to locate and anticipate, and by waging extended, nonsequential campaigns that involve only episodic acts of high publicity and destruction rather than continuing military operations.

The issue of geography or space is crucial to the definition of terrorist groups and to the means by which they are combated. Many terrorist groups are distinctly and permanently linked to particular regions. Groups such as the Provisional Irish Republican Army, Euskadi Ta Askatasuna (ETA—the Basque separatist organization), the Jammu and Kashmir Liberation Front, and Irgun have fought struggles of national liberation, maintained the political support of elements of the local population, and used the geographic object of their campaigns as their base area. As a result, the counterterrorist campaigns against these and other similar groups have strongly resembled classic counterinsurgencies, in which military forces are fielded in support of law enforcement and carry on garrison, patrolling, and other routine duties.

A second set of spatial concerns is the issue of sanctuaries. Many terrorist groups have relied on foreign sanctuaries to carry out cross-border terrorist activities against an adjacent state. Hezbollah, the PLO in the late 1970s and early 1980s in Lebanon, Jaish-e-Muhammad and Lashkar-e-Taiba in Pakistan, and Kurdish and other groups based in both Iraq and Iran constitute examples of terrorists working under geographic sanctuary.

In the 1970s and 1980s, state sponsorship provided sufficient funds for some terrorist organizations to prosper, and the PLO even began fielding quasi-regular forces in brigade-sized formations, armed with obsolescent tanks and artillery. These forces could be mustered and supported only in a sanctuary—Lebanon. Al-Qaeda forces played a similar role in support of the Taliban regime in Afghanistan, acting as the "shock troops" in the war against the Northern Alliance.[41]

Concentration in space, whether in a sanctuary or in "liberated areas" of a territory, leads to significant military vulnerability. It also leads, potentially, to loss of surprise—a crucial advantage of terrorists. Once terrorists are located in large numbers in base camps of various kinds, they become easier to track and easier to strike; moreover, burdened by large amounts of conventional equipment, it becomes relatively more difficult for them to disappear. Reaching this level of mobilization, whereby terrorist organizations field conventional as well as guerrilla units, may seem like an opportunity for a crushing military defeat.[42] As we have seen with the Viet Cong in the 1960s and with al-Qaeda and the Taliban in the twenty-first century, however, the destruction of overt forces of this kind may simply result in their disappearing back into the countryside and cities and the resumption of less conventional terrorist activities.

Current terrorist threats do not necessarily rely heavily on geography, either for sanctuary or for political support. As a result, these groups are less amenable to military retaliation. Because they do not rely on a single state for sanctuary—and, indeed, may be found embedded in friendly states—combating them requires considerable international cooperation. This cooperation takes the form of law enforcement and intelligence coordination, as well as occasional joint military operations. These types of cooperation have heavy political components, which further limits the opportunity for independent military retaliation.

Terrorist forces therefore rarely fix themselves in space—denying easy targeting opportunities for sophisticated conventional forces. They rarely mass in significant numbers—denying the opportunity to use the massed precision strikes that are the hallmark of sophisticated modern militaries. They manipulate time by avoiding sequential operations, creating an environment of unpredictability and instability, and striking at times and places of their own choosing, generally preserving the initiative.

Terrorist operations are aimed at attacking the will of the adversary, rather than depleting or eliminating the adversary's capabilities. Political will is attacked through the deliberate targeting of civilians for maximum shock effect and publicity.[43] The hope, for the terrorist, is that over time states and citizens will become unwilling to bear the burden of episodic but devastating attacks and will succumb to the political desires of the terrorists. Terrorism, in effect, is a war of exhaustion in a nontraditional form—a series of nonsequential attacks aimed at eroding public support for resistance over an extended period of time. Terrorists engage only selectively, in times and places of their own choosing; only on rare occasions do they voluntarily stand their ground and fight conventionally.

This combination of means and ends, along with control of the elements of space and time, poses sharp constraints on and difficulties for military organizations. Modern high-technology militaries focus on the operational level of war, where concentrations of force in space and time allow large enemy forces to be fixed and defeated decisively.[44] Historically, the alternative is a longer, slower war of attrition, with increased casualties on both sides. Traditionally, however, this attrition has been managed through constant contact with enemy forces and steady combat—a difficult task against elusive terrorist groups.

Military forces aim, at least in theory, at an enemy "center of gravity"—an asset that, if destroyed, will cause extraordinary loss of effectiveness in enemy forces.[45] Destroying the center of gravity in some respects is a substitute for physically destroying enemy forces, depriving them of the ability to resist or operate effectively.[46] High-technology militaries frequently target enemy command and control capabilities as a center of gravity—the focus of twentieth-century *blitzkrieg* and late–twentieth-century Air-Land Battle and strategic bombing doctrines.

These traditional military methods are difficult to apply to terrorism. Terrorist organizations do not exist at the operational level. Lacking numbers, they also tend to lack the elaborate hierarchy of organization and logistics required by modern conventional militaries. Because of their limited numbers, as well as their tactical preferences, terrorist groups are difficult to fix in place—they dissolve during or immediately after an attack and prefer to relocate, if possible. Command and control sometimes is highly centralized—as in the Abu Nidal organization—but al-Qaeda is highly decentralized and geographically dispersed.[47] Therefore it is difficult to find, difficult to fix, and difficult to destroy and lacks a military center of gravity.

Thus, most of the tools and expertise developed for fighting military organizations will have limited utility in fighting al-Qaeda and similar groups, unless and until they are fixed in place geographically. Afghanistan represents a case in point—but it may be unique. Al-Qaeda may emerge in force elsewhere, but it is unlikely in the current atmosphere that any state will formally give it sanctuary. More likely, it will establish a less permanent presence in an ungovernable region of a weak or failing state—if, indeed, it chooses to make such a strategic error again.

Certain types of military capability remain extremely useful—special operations forces, for example, with their extremely high degrees of effectiveness in light infantry combat—but are dependent on strategic and tactical intelligence. Strategic bombers, precision-guided weapons, tanks, and aircraft carriers all have limited utility, particularly when terrorists are most likely to be located in extremely rugged or crowded terrain such as the Afghan mountains or the cities and suburbs of Western and Middle Eastern states. According to current U.S. Army doctrine on operations and war fighting, "without operational art, war would be a set of disconnected engagements with relative attrition the only measure of success."[48] This assessment succinctly defines the difficulties of relying exclusively on military force in the war on terrorism because that is exactly the military condition terrorists hope to achieve.

The War on Terrorism: Dilemmas of Strategy

Classical strategic thought, as analyzed by Michael Handel, emphasizes the importance of coherent political direction, meticulous correlation of military means to political ends, and identification of a center of gravity as crucial to the efficient conduct of war.[49] Handel also cautions, however, that although battlefield success should be exploited, each offensive reaches a point at which further operations are counterproductive; that fighting more than one major enemy at a time is unwise; and that short wars are preferable, in general, to longer wars of attrition.[50]

The use of "war" as a paradigm for dealing with al-Qaeda, and with terrorism more generally, provoked immediate criticism.[51] It is indisputable, however, that the United States has entered into a war with al-Qaeda—a conflict that, in the president's own words, may last for many years and in which the use of military force is subject to fewer political constraints than previously. The proclamation of war, the thousands of casualties resulting from the attacks of September 11, and the declaration that the United States is acting in self-defense all help to create a vastly more permissive environment for the use of military implements.[52] Nevertheless, military forces will continue to be limited by both military and political considerations in the ongoing conflict against bin Laden and international terrorism.

There appear to be four different broad situations in which the United States might confront terrorism with conventional military force. These situations are defined, at least in part, by geography; the issues of space and time remain fundamental to the effective application of U.S. and Western military advantages.

The first, and most obvious, new opportunity is the ability to operate against terrorist regimes. The overthrow of the Taliban regime not only caused great discomfort and inconvenience for al-Qaeda, it also rid the region and the international community of a genuine problem.[53] Before September 11, the Taliban had been "handled" by a combination of sanctions, refusal of diplomatic recognition, and covert aid to the Northern Alliance opposition forces.[54] The demonstrated ability and intention of the United States to overthrow terrorist regimes constitutes a significant escalation in the use of military force against terrorism. Because the Taliban was physically fixed and relied on standing forces to combat resistance and secure internal order, it was more easily attacked by conventional forces, and the official sanctuary provided to al-Qaeda could be functionally eliminated. Other governments—or quasi-governments with significant autonomy—might offer similar sanctuary and protection to al-Qaeda in the future; lawless regions of Sudan, Somalia, and Yemen, for example, have been identified as potential sites. In addition, however, President Bush identified the now notorious "Axis of Evil" as possible targets—an issue addressed further below.

A second potential set of targets would be regimes that are not friendly to the U.S., and which allow terrorists to train or operate from their territory. Again, the options for the use of military force have expanded since September 11. After the La Belle discotheque bombing, for example, the United States dramatically limited the Libyan targets it struck in retaliation. After the Lockerbie bombing, the United States and the United Kingdom pursued international condemnation and sanctions instead of a military response. If Colonel Qaddafi were to permit al-Qaeda to stage raids from Libyan territory today, he would risk being treated like the Taliban in Afghanistan—facing, at best, significant military attacks and at worst the overthrow of his regime.[55] These options were considered disproportionate in the past but are now politically permissible—a significant deterrent to those who might seek to aid al-Qaeda's cause.

A third possible situation—and an exceedingly likely one—is the case in which al-Qaeda and other terrorists train in and operate from a country that is friendly to the United States. Military options in these cases are severely constrained by political factors. Related cases include states that support insurgents or terrorists but not al-Qaeda or groups that are directly involved in conflict with the United States. Pakistan is an interesting example of both phenomena, hosting a variety of jihadist and insurgent groups warring against India and simultaneously acting as a (possibly unintended) sanctuary for thousands of al-Qaeda and Taliban refugees. This situation poses great difficulties for the United States, particularly as India accuses Pakistan of infiltrating Kashmiri insurgents and elements of al-Qaeda into Indian-administered areas of Jammu and Kashmir.

A fourth potential opportunity for expanded use of military force is against states that are only tangentially related to al-Qaeda—the focus of the war on terrorism—but are actively engaged in anti-U.S. policies and actions. The "Axis of Evil" falls in this category. No convincing argument has emerged for a North Korean connection to al-Qaeda, and definitive links with Iraq remain inconclusive. Iran reportedly has provided shelter for some al-Qaeda members, but it also has turned others over to authorities in neighboring Persian Gulf states.

The war against Iraq in spring 2003 exhibited the overwhelming power of U.S. conventional forces, reaffirming the successes of Desert Storm (1991) and Operation Enduring Freedom (2001). Iraqi military resistance, despite pessimistic reports in the second week of the war, was sporadic and ineffective. The regular military rarely engaged in combat, the Iraqi Air Force never flew a combat mission, and the Republican Guard was crushed through sophisticated joint operations of U.S. and coalition forces. By the beginning of May 2003, President Bush was confident enough to declare that the fighting in Iraq was over. It remains to be seen, however, whether the military victory against Iraq can be translated into a strategic success in the war on terrorism.

In these operations, as well as any other military operations against al-Qaeda, several key military concepts again must be considered. The first, the principle of *continuity*, refers to the notion that once success has been achieved the victor must pursue the enemy with maximum effort to secure the greatest benefits of military victory.[56] This pursuit is more difficult against terrorist organizations. First, they frequently deny the option of pursuit by not remaining fixed in place—simply vanishing from the playing field, so to speak. Second, when they are fixed in place they may simply dissolve and shift from conventional fighting to insurgency or terrorism. The benefits of pursuit therefore are not as tangible and may lead to considerable frustration.

Another important concept is the *culminating point of victory*: that place where the strength of the attacker is sufficiently weakened and that of the defender sufficiently increased that the offense must finally cease from lack of momentum and resources. This is the point where the defender may initiate a counteroffensive.[57] Because the forces in this case lack physical contact in space, the culminating point of victory in a given campaign may exist in a notional *political* space—that point where local or international opinion shifts sufficiently against the United States that an operation must be ended.

Afghanistan and Iraq provide useful examples here. The United States now pursues wars with the intent of overthrowing repressive, entrenched regimes, preferably with both local and international support. In the case of Afghanistan, the early and decisive operations that removed the Taliban from power had broad international support. As U.S. operations have dragged on—including a series of highly publicized incidents that have killed civilians—international and Afghan opinion has become more negative. Reports suggest that the Taliban's leader, Mullah Omar, has established a formal resistance council to oppose international peacekeeping forces.[58]

The overthrow of the Ba'ath regime in Iraq was accomplished without a formal submission; the Iraqi government simply disappeared. This development left the United States and its allies in a difficult position. Having won the operational side of the war with stunning success, allied forces were abruptly asked to take over and manage a country whose economic infrastructure was gutted from twenty years of war and sanctions and whose political and legal infrastructure was nonexistent. The U.S. commitment to creating a more democratic regime in Iraq effectively precluded the cooptation of former Ba'athists and military leaders to provide an interim regime. The result was chaos and instability—a condition that continues to fester.

U.S. policy must focus much more carefully on the postconflict phase of these (and future) operations. Once the battle is over, there remains a role for military forces in the aftermath. In this context, it may be revealing that the deputy secretary of defense, Paul Wolfowitz, referred specifically to the "battle of Iraq" and "the battle of Afghanistan" in his commencement address at the Naval War College on June 20, 2003.[59] Although looking at Iraq and Afghanistan as battles in a greater war on terrorism is useful, it might be more appropriate to refer to them as "campaigns"—defined by the Department of Defense as "a series of related military operations aimed at accomplishing a strategic or operational objective within a given time and space."[60] The operational objective is the decisive defeat of enemy conventional forces, but the strategic objective is to contribute to eventual success in the war on terrorism.

In each case, U.S. and allied forces have triumphed on the battlefield, destroying or scattering the forces of the adversary. In the context of the broader war on terrorism, however, the United States now faces the problem of establishing institutions that will provide for long-term political stability and both physical and economic security for these countries. These objectives contribute to a larger sequential campaign against the potential support base for al-Qaeda in the Islamic world. At the same time, however, these postconflict missions require significantly different responses from U.S. military forces. U.S. forces will not be able to exercise their operational dominance in constabulary roles and in fact will face the same kinds of challenges posed to the British Army in Northern Ireland or multinational forces in other peacekeeping or nation-building exercises. Failure in these missions could lead to setbacks on three fronts: creation of effective indigenous resistance movements, complicating stabilization efforts; creation of enclaves for al-Qaeda and associate groups, as they aid these local insurgents; and continuing resentment from the Islamic world and the international community as the theoretical benefits of American intervention in both countries fail to emerge. In the context of these campaigns in the war on terrorism, therefore, it could be argued that the culminating point of victory is related to the ability of the United States and its allies to establish stable and secure regimes to replace the Ba'ath Party in Iraq and the Taliban in Afghanistan. This phenomenon will reemerge in subsequent conflicts, if the U.S. objective remains overthrow of an existing regime.

Finally, in the absence of other measures of effectiveness and the unwillingness to accede quietly to a war of attrition waged primarily on al-Qaeda's terms, the United States will seek other centers of gravity. One of these is terrorist leadership—Osama bin Laden and the next level or levels of al-Qaeda's commanders. Another may be technical specialists, including the bomb makers, financial planners, and logistical experts who make terrorist organizations more deadly or efficient.[61] The difficulty with attacking al-Qaeda, in part, is its lack of centralization; it is organized as a network rather than a hierarchy. As a result, it may be relatively resistant to military operations, and financial networks or other novel centers of gravity will be chosen and attacked by nonmilitary organizations in an effort to accelerate resolution of the conflict.[62]

Other options for the use of the military exist, of course. The role of the military in cooperating with other tools of policy—in effect, joint operations with other arms of the U.S. and foreign governments—will be crucial in winning the war on terrorism. This cooperation can take many forms. President Bush has suggested, however, that operations against al-Qaeda leadership have been very successful, announcing that "65 percent of al-Qaeda's leaders and operational managers had been killed or captured" since September 11, 2001.[63]

Military support for law enforcement operations, both at home and over-seas, will be crucial. The military will be asked to participate in maintaining homeland security. More important, however, it also will be asked to cooperate with foreign law enforcement bodies in areas with vastly different legal procedures and sometimes complex social codes, such as Pakistan's North–West Frontier Provinces. U.S. support will be particularly important in allied states where the loyalty or effectiveness of local military organizations might be in question. Obviously, this is an area of great political sensitivity.

Military intelligence assets will be crucial to the war on terrorism. The military intelligence budget represents a significant percentage of overall U.S. intelligence resources. If—as was the case in the 1990s—the emphasis continues to be on providing intelligence to the warfighter, there may be serious conflict over resources. Human intelligence assets, in the U.S. case, are particularly critical as well as particularly vulnerable; military action is likely to cause these sources to dry up, at least temporarily. Utilizing information such sources acquire in cooperation with foreign intelligence and law enforcement agencies puts them at extreme risk. If the military is operating in a region, will it act as an "800-pound gorilla" and monopolize intelligence resources that might be used more effectively elsewhere?[64]

The lessons of this struggle for intelligence in Iraq are not yet clear. Lt. Gen. John Abizaid told the U.S. Senate that the intelligence available for Operation Iraqi Freedom was "the most accurate that I've ever seen on the tactical level, probably the best I've ever seen on the operational level." However, it was also "perplexingly incomplete on the strategic level with regard to weapons of mass destruction."[65] The reported politicization of intelligence on Iraqi weapons of mass destruction, the uncertain nature of reports from human assets in the preconflict period (particularly from Ahmed Chalabi's Iraqi National Congress), and the continuing competition for control of intelligence assets and budgets suggest that the availability and accuracy of intelligence and the disposition and prioritization of intelligence assets remain pressing and unresolved issues in the war on terrorism.

There will be an increasing call on "low-density/high-demand" military capabilities, including special operations forces, unmanned aerial vehicles (some armed with precision-guided weapons), and electronic monitoring equipment of various kinds. Again, competition over limited resources can be expected. Special operations forces also are crucial for training friendly forces in counterterrorism operations—another resource constraint. Special operations forces were crucial to the allied war effort against Iraq, entering the country days before hostilities actually started, seizing key airfields and missile launch facilities in western Iraq, and cooperating with Kurdish rebels to open a northern front near Kirkuk and Mosul. Secretary of Defense Rumsfeld has committed the Department of Defense to a much greater emphasis on special forces in the future, but calls for a rapid increase in their numbers must be balanced against the dangers of reducing current rigorous standards and training.

These considerations highlight a crucial difficulty for the U.S. military, even though military operations have become relatively easier in the new international environment. For the military to have the greatest impact on the war on terrorism, it must cooperate in joint operations with other services—in this case including the State Department, intelligence services, and even economic entities—and in *combined* operations with other states. A proclamation of war has simplified only some aspects of the use of military force. These other aspects are far more politicized and quite open to political interference.

Conclusion

The war on terrorism marks a significant discontinuity in the use of military force, particularly by the United States, as a response to terrorism. A more permissive environment for military retaliation now exists, and the United States is aggressively using this environment. The United States now asserts the right of preemptive self-defense against terrorism, as well as the willingness to engage and overthrow regimes supporting international terrorism.[66] The demonstrated capability of the U.S. military to intervene with crushing effectiveness virtually anywhere on the globe will be useful in the war on terrorism, but it cannot be regarded as a panacea.

The focus of military development in the twentieth century has been the operational level of war and the decisive defeat of the massed armies created by the combination of the forces of nationalism and the industrial revolution. Terrorism undercuts many of these capabilities. Terrorists force combat on the tactical level, in difficult terrain, and without regard for civilian lives—effectively neutralizing modern military advantages of precision firepower, mass and maneuver, and decisive force.

The exception—and an area for significant military use—is the continuing existence of terrorist sanctuaries. Even these sanctuaries are difficult targets, however—as the ongoing military operations in Afghanistan demonstrate. Many sanctuaries are in the territory of friendly or neutral countries, which introduces a significant political dimension to military intervention. Pursuit of al-Qaeda into its Pakistani hideouts represents a significant and continuing problem, for example.

In addition to the operational limitations of using force against terrorism, the U.S. policy of overthrowing regimes creates additional complications for the military. The overwhelming operational capability of the U.S. and allied militaries results in a rapid defeat of enemy conventional forces. The adversary in both Afghanistan and Iraq melted away—leaving a political, social, and economic vacuum in its aftermath. Rebuilding national infrastructure in the absence of established law enforcement and legal systems requires continued military presence—but in a stabilizing rather than warfighting role. This difficult mission is further complicated by the continued existence of remnants of the Taliban and Ba'athists, operating as terrorists and insurgents and potentially providing the core of a greater anti-American resistance. Perversely, quick, decisive military victories appear to lead, in the current environment, to prolonged occupation and constabulary duty—areas in which the operational and technical proficiency of U.S. and allied military forces do not translate as readily into decisive advantage and effectiveness.

A new environment that legitimizes increased use of military force against terrorism undeniably exists, and Western military forces have a wide range of increasingly lethal and precise new capabilities. If these capabilities are used as the only, or even the primary, means of combating al-Qaeda, they will almost certainly fail. In the pursuit of operational dominance, modern Western military organizations have moved increasingly toward the concept of "jointness"—coordination and cooperation among all of the military services to maximize effectiveness—as a solution.

In the war on terrorism, the military will now have to deal with two additional levels of jointness. The first level is dramatically increased interagency cooperation, utilizing *all* the tools of national power to seek out, suppress, and, when possible, eliminate al-Qaeda and organizations like it. The second level is increased cooperation with coalition partners—a much-debated but ultimately inescapable dimension of war with a transnational terrorist organization. The U.S. military may be capable of singlehandedly overthrowing regimes through conventional war, but it requires multinational assistance in other vital areas of the war on terrorism: intelligence collection and sharing, interdiction of financial and personnel traffic, and post-conflict stabilization and nation-building, to name just a few.

The war on terrorism will not be a rapid and decisive conflict, at least in part because the operational level of war simply does not exist for our primary adversary. As we have seen in Afghanistan, the military can now play an enhanced role in the war on terrorism, and that role can be both spectacular and very effective. Decisive operational military victories can contribute to overall success in the war on terrorism, and the changes in U.S. policy since the September 11 attacks have enlarged the role for military force in that war. The conversion of military victory into strategic success, however, will require the military to operate skillfully and effectively in nonoperational—and often noncombat—missions as well. The U.S. military cannot defeat al-Qaeda alone; used skillfully in cooperation with other institutions and with coalitions, however, it can provide capabilities that are crucial to long-term success. In the words of Lawrence Freedman:

> In the end, terrorism is best defeated through isolating militants from their claimed constituency, demonstrating the shameful and counterproductive nature of their methods, and, if possible, addressing the grievances upon which they feed.[67]

Notes

The views expressed in this article are the author's own and do not reflect the policies or judgments of the Department of Defense, the U.S. Navy, or other government organizations.

1. Paul R. Pillar, *Terrorism and U.S. Foreign Policy* (Washington, D.C.: Brookings Institution Press, 2001), 97.

2. A detailed account can be found in Charles G. Cogan, "The Response of the Strong to the Weak: The American Raid on Libya, 1986," *Intelligence and National Security* 6, no. 3 (1991): 608–20.

3. An analysis of the legal ramification of this strike is Dino Kritsiotis, "The Legality of the 1993 U.S. Missile Strike on Iraq and the Right of Self-Defence in International Law," *International and Comparative Law Quarterly* 45, no. 1 (January 1996): 162–77.

4. Michele L. Malvesti, "Explaining the United States' Decision to Strike Back at Terrorists," *Terrorism and Political Violence* 13, no. 2 (summer 2001): 86.

5. Admittedly, limiting the period of study to the post-1983 period also filters out important cases of U.S. military response to terrorism, including counterinsurgency operations against the Viet Cong, the hostage rescue attempt in 1980, and U.S. operations in Lebanon in 1983. The point, however, is that in a period of significant terrorist activity, U.S. military response was sharply constrained at least in part as a result of previous experience.

6. Obviously, the United States has suffered from domestic terrorism; examples include the Weathermen during the Vietnam War and the Oklahoma City bombing.

7. For a brief study of the role of the military against geographically fixed terrorist groups like the Provisional Irish Republican Army, see Paul Wilkinson, *Terrorism Versus Democracy: The Liberal State Response* (London: Frank Cass, 2001), 124–36.

8. On the 1982 Lebanon War, see Ze'ev Schiff and Ehud Ya'ari, *Israel's Lebanon War* (New York: Simon and Schuster, 1984). For a highly critical report of Israeli military operations in 1982, see Emmanuel Wald, *The Wald Report: The Decline of Israeli National Security since 1967* (Boulder, Colo.: Westview Press, 1992). For the impact of coercion against the PLO's terrorist operations, see Victor T. Le Vine and Barbara A. Salert, "Does a Coercive Official Response Deter Terrorism? The Case of the PLO," *Terrorism and Political Violence* 8, no. 1 (spring 1996): 22–49. Regarding Israel's response to terrorism in 1996, see Philip B. Heymann, *Terrorism and America: A Commonsense Strategy for a Democratic Society* (Cambridge, Mass.: MIT Press, 1998), 65–70.

9. An example is Edmund Ions, "Clinton's Conversion," *The World Today* 49, nos. 8–9 (August–September 1993): 162, which suggests that the strike on Iraq was a "defining moment for the United States."

10. David Tucker, *Skirmishes at the Edge of Empire: The United States and International Terrorism* (Westport, Conn.: Praeger, 1997), 93.

11. For a discussion of the difficulties, see Abraham D. Sofaer, "International Law and the Use of Force," *The National Interest* (fall 1988): 53–64. This article examines, among other issues, the U.S. use of the concept of self-defense to justify military strikes against Libya in 1986.

A more recent discussion is Michael Byers, "Unleashing Force," *The World Today* (December 2001): 20–22.

12. Pillar, *Terrorism and U.S. Foreign Policy*, 97. Charles T. Eppright, "'Counterterrorism' and Conventional Military Force: The Relationship between Political Effect and Utility," *Studies in Conflict and Terrorism* 20 (1997): 333–44. The exception to this constraint is the attack on a pharmaceutical factory in Sudan in 1998. The factory was suspected of producing or researching chemical weapons for al-Qaeda.

13. See Paul Wilkinson, "The Role of the Military in Combating Terrorism in a Democratic Society," *Terrorism and Political Violence* 8, no. 3 (autumn 1996): 4–5.

14. Both of these possibilities are worth considering in relation to Pakistan today.

15. Heymann, *Terrorism and America*, 73.

16. The legal ramifications of this argument are beyond the scope of this chapter. The right of self-defense, however, implicitly includes the use of force.

17. Carl von Clausewitz, *On War*, edited and translated by Michael Howard and Peter Paret (Princeton, N.J.: Princeton University Press, 1976), 87. *Politik*, the German word, can be translated as either "policy" or "politics" and probably actually means both domestic and foreign considerations.

18. U.S. conduct of unlimited wars tends toward the Clausewitzian extreme: "War is thus an act of force to compel the enemy to do our will" (*On War*, 75). However, Clausewitz is aware that wars are fought for different reasons and that in many cases the political objective of the war is limited—perhaps a piece of territory or simply the denial of an enemy attack. In these cases, maximum effort may not be necessary, or indeed appropriate—an issue Clausewitz deals with in *On War*, 601–4.

19. Writings on this "American Way of War" include Russell F. Weigley, *The American Way of War* (Bloomington: Indiana University Press, 1973); Carl H. Builder, *The Masks of War: American Military Styles in Strategy and Analysis* (Baltimore: Johns Hopkins University Press and RAND, 1989); and Samuel Huntington, *The Soldier and the State* (Cambridge, Mass.: Belknap Press, 1957). More recent studies include Victor Brooks and Robert Hohwald, *How America Fought Its Wars* (Conshohocken, Pa.: Combined Publishing, 1999); and Michael D. Pearlman, *Warmaking and American Democracy* (Lawrence: University Press of Kansas, 1999). For the most recent comments, including critiques of the Kosovo campaign of 1999, see General Wesley K. Clark, *Waging Modern War* (New York: Public Affairs, 2001); and Eliot A. Cohen, "Kosovo and the New American Way of War," in *War Over Kosovo*, ed. Andrew J. Bacevich and Eliot A. Cohen (New York: Columbia University Press, 2001), 38–62.

20. *The National Security Strategy of the United States of America* (Washington, D.C.: Government Printing Office, September 2002).

21. This remains a major objection by those who feel that the war on terrorism should be defined in other terms.

22. Tucker, *Skirmishes at the Edge of Empire*, 94.

23. Pillar, *Terrorism and U.S. Foreign Policy*, 109.

24. Pillar, *Terrorism and U.S. Foreign Policy*, 98–99. Entebbe (Israel) and Mogadishu (Germany) were highly successful, whereas Egypt's assault on an Egypt Air plane in 1985 and the well-known Iran hostage rescue attempt were disasters.

25. Peter L. Bergen, *Holy War, Inc.: Inside the Secret World of Osama Bin Laden* (New York: The Free Press, 2001), 125.

26. One exception to this statement is Everett L. Wheeler, "Terrorism and Military Theory: An Historical Perspective," *Terrorism and Political Violence* 3, no. 1 (spring 1991): 6–33. A second is Ariel Merari, "Terrorism as a Strategy of Insurgency," *Terrorism and Political Violence* 5, no. 4 (winter 1993): 213–51.

27. Clausewitz, *On War*, 87.

28. Ibid., 75.

29. Ibid., 81.

30. Bruce Hoffman, *Inside Terrorism* (New York: Columbia University Press, 1998), 43.

31. Ibid., 44.

32. Some analysts now identify a strain of terrorism that they specifically refer to as a "war paradigm"—a campaign aimed at overthrowing a regime or system rather than extorting or coercing local political concessions. See the discussion in Ian O. Lesser et al., *Countering the New Terrorism* (Santa Monica, Calif.: RAND, 1999), 68–72, 94–96.

33. Clausewitz distinguishes between wars of *unlimited* and *limited* aims. He defines unlimited aims as subordination of the enemy to your will and limited aims as seizing territory or holding it defensively until circumstances for offensive action become more favorable. The objectives of most wars fall within this spectrum—unlimited wars, for example, may seek to overthrow enemy regimes, and limited wars seek territory, economic concessions, or other objectives. See *On War*, 595–616.

34. Hans Delbruck, a German military historian, derives two types of war from reading Clausewitz—wars of decision or annihilation (*Niederwerfungsstrategie*) and wars of exhaustion or attrition (*Ermattungsstrategie*). The former focuses on the annihilation of military forces through decisive battle, and the second relies on cumulative losses to wear down enemy will. See Hans Delbruck, *The History of the Art of War, Vol. I: Warfare in Antiquity,* translated by Walter J. Renfroe, Jr. (Lincoln: University of Nebraska Press, 1975), 135–43. See also Mao Tse-tung, *Six Essays on Military Affairs* (Beijing: Foreign Languages Press, 1972), 305–11.

35. Stalin, Hitler, Mao, and the Khmer Rouge, among others, have been innovative practitioners of the use of political terror for domestic and international purposes. The whole theory of strategic bombing, as originally stated in the writings of Guilio Douhet, is intended as an attack on enemy political will in an effort to shorten the war and avoid the extended attrition of World War I.

36. Rear Admiral J. C. Wylie, USN, *Military Strategy: A General Theory of Power Control* (New Brunswick, N.J.: Rutgers University Press, 1967), 24.

37. Ibid. Wylie uses psychological warfare, economic warfare, and unrestricted submarine warfare as examples to illustrate this point.

38. Wylie, *Military Strategy*, 91.

39. These are the levels at which individuals, small groups, and relatively unsophisticated equipment matter most. For a discussion of these levels of war, see Edward A. Luttwak, *Strategy: The Logic of War and Peace*, rev. and enlarged ed. (Cambridge, Mass.: Belknap Press, 2001), 93–111.

40. These specialists, however, are particularly important. Experts at bomb-making, in logistics, in finance or forgery, or other skills represent one particularly attractive target within terrorist groups; getting rid of them substantially lowers terrorist capabilities and raises their chances of failure or exposure, at least in the short term.

41. When terrorist groups reach this level of sophisticated military organization and mass, it is worth reexamining Mao's theories of the stages of revolution and the move from political mobilization to guerrilla warfare to conventional combat. See Mao Tse-tung, *Six Essays on Military Affairs*.

42. This might be roughly compared to Mao Tse-tung's third stage of revolutionary warfare, in which revolutionary forces organize in large units, take the strategic offensive, and fight using "mobile warfare" in a near-conventional conflict. See Ian Beckett, *Modern Insurgencies and Counter-Insurgencies: Guerrillas and Their Opponents since 1750* (London: Routledge, 2001), 75.

43. In an interview with John Muller in 1998, Osama bin Laden stated that "[W]e do not differentiate between those dressed in military uniforms and civilians: They are all targets." See Bergen, *Holy War, Inc.*, 105, n. 2.

44. For a discussion of the operational level of war, see Luttwak, *Strategy*, 112–37; and *Operations* FM 3-0 (FM 100-5) (Washington, D.C.: Headquarters, Department of the Army, 14 June 2001).

45. In the words of Clausewitz, a center of gravity is "the hub of all power and movement, on which everything depends. This is the point against which all our energies should be directed"; *On War*, 595–96. This is a tactical concept, more easily and readily applied to the immediate battlefield, where a terrain feature or road junction might be a center of gravity, than to broader strategic efforts. Clausewitz also explicitly refers to *centers* (plural) of gravity, implying that more than one may exist.

46. An alternative concept for the center of gravity is found in the ancient Chinese classic *The Art of War*. This source identifies "what is of supreme importance" in order of preference: first, attacking the enemy's strategy; second, attacking his alliances; third, attacking his army; and finally, attacking cities. Sun Tzu, *The Art of War*, translated and with an introduction by Samuel B. Griffith (Oxford, England: Oxford University Press, 1963), 77–78. Some theorists might argue that by avoiding direct confrontation with superior military strength, terrorists are following Sun Tzu's first preference.

47. Bergen, *Holy War, Inc.*, 116–17.

48. *Operations* FM-3.0 (FM 100–5) (Washington, D.C.: Headquarters, Department of the Army, 14 June 2001), chaps. 2–6.

49. Michael I. Handel, *Masters of War: Classical Strategic Thought*, 3d, rev. and exp. ed. (London: Frank Cass Publishers, 2001), xvii.

50. Ibid., xviii.

51. See Michael Howard, "What's in a Name? How to Fight Terrorism," *Foreign Affairs* 81, no. 1 (January/February 2002): 8–13.

52. Byers, "Unleashing Force," 22.

53. The overthrow of the Taliban, in addition to being a stunning military success, also might be a case of a successful attack on an al-Qaeda center of gravity that caused very significant disruption to that group's assets and operations.

54. These sanctions were spurred, in part, by the apparently unsuccessful U.S. military operation of 1998. The UN imposed sanctions, either in recognition of a new terrorist regime or in hopes of heading off future U.S. independent military retaliation. Tucker, *Skirmishes at the Edge of Empire*, 97–98.

55. Libya currently is not considered an actual or potential sanctuary for al-Qaeda. After September 11, the United States actually received condolences from Col. Qaddafi.

56. This principle is identified in both Sun Tzu—"Keep him under a strain and wear him down"—and in Clausewitz. Once victory "has been won, one must ensure that it touches off a series of calamities which, in accordance with the law of falling bodies, will keep gathering momentum." Sun Tzu, *Art of War*, 68–69; Clausewitz, *On War*, 478, 624–26.

57. Clausewitz, *On War*, 528. On both the principle of continuity and the culminating point, see also Handel, *Masters of War*, 165–93.

58. "Ex-Taliban Leader Picks Resistance Council," *Washington Times*, 25 June 2003; "Taleban [*sic*] Fighters Regroup and Attack Coalition," *London Times*, 25 June 2003.

59. "Commencement Address at the Naval War College," available at www.defenselink.mil/speeches/2003/sp20030620-depsecdef0304.html.

60. DoD Dictionary definition, available at www.dtic.mil/doctrine/jel/doddict/data/c/00834.html.

61. This may lead military forces to a policy of selective assassination—a policy that led to mixed strategic results for Israel and backfired in the United Kingdom during the "shoot-to-kill" controversies of the 1980s. Policies of assassination can have severely negative consequences, particularly if the target list expands to include financiers and other "noncombatants."

62. "What about Al Qaeda's Moneymen?" *Wall Street Journal*, 11 September 2002, discusses some of these issues.

63. "Bush Says Attacks on U.S. Forces Won't Deter Him from the Rebuilding of Iraq," *New York Times*, 2 July 2003.

64. My thanks to Paul Pillar for pointing out this dilemma.

65. "Abizaid Sure Iraq Arms Will Be Found," *Washington Times*, June 26, 2003.

66. "Bush: U.S. Will Strike First at Enemies," *Washington Post*, 2 June 2002. The emerging policy of preemption is justified primarily by the assumed linkage between terrorism and weapons of mass destruction. Although the relative success of counterproliferation strategies remains an issue of debate, the potential saving of thousands of lives provides at least a plausible justification for preemption in some cases. See also "Bush Aides Press Case for Pre-Emptive Strikes," *Washington Times*, 11 September 2002.

67. Lawrence Freedman, "Think Again," *Foreign Policy* (July/August 2003), 18.

eight

THE LAWS OF WAR

Adam Roberts

The laws of war—the parts of international law that are explicitly applicable in armed conflict—have a major bearing on the "war on terror" proclaimed and initiated by the United States following the attacks of September 11, 2001. These laws address a range of critical issues that perennially arise in campaigns against terrorist movements, including discrimination in targeting, protection of civilians, and the status and treatment of prisoners. However, the application of the laws of war in counterterrorist operations has always been particularly problematical. Because of the character of such operations, which are different in important respects from what was originally envisaged in the treaties embodying the laws of war, a key issue in any analysis is not just whether or how the law is applied by the belligerents but also its relevance to the particular circumstances of individual operations. It is not just the conduct of the parties that merits examination but also the adequacy of the law itself. Thus, there is a need to look at the actual events of wars involving a terrorist adversary and at the many ways in which, rightly or wrongly, the law is considered to have a bearing on them.

In this chapter I examine critically certain statements and actions of the U.S. administration, as well as those of the International Committee of the Red Cross (ICRC) and certain other bodies concerned with humanitarian and human rights issues. Although I touch on many ways in which the laws of war impinge on policy, my main focus is on four core questions:

- Are the laws of war, according to their specific terms, formally applicable to counterterrorist military operations?
- In the event that counterterrorist military operations involve situations that are different from those envisaged in the international agreements on the laws of war, should the attempt still be made to apply that body of law to such situations?
- Are captured personnel who are suspected of involvement in terrorist organizations entitled to prisoner-of-war (POW) status? If they are not considered to be POWs, does the law recognize a different status, and what international standards apply to their treatment?
- Is there a case for a revision of the laws of war to take into account the special circumstances of contemporary counterterrorist operations?

The answers to these questions may vary in different circumstances. The U.S.-led war on terror involves action in many countries, with different legal and factual contexts. Much action against terrorism, even if it is presented as part of the war on terror, does not necessarily involve armed conflict of the kind in which the laws of war are formally applicable. The war's most prominent manifestation and the focus of this survey, Operation Enduring Freedom in Afghanistan, did have a phase of international armed conflict, unquestionably bringing the laws of war into play, although other phases and aspects are more debatable with regard to application of the law. Regarding the combat phase of Operation Iraqi Freedom in March–May 2003, there is no dispute that the laws of war were applicable. Although the issue of terrorism was never far beneath the surface in that campaign, there is disagreement about whether—and, if so, to what extent—the campaign is properly regarded as part of the war on terror. Therefore in this chapter I focus on other cases, especially Afghanistan.

The laws of war are not the only body of law that is potentially relevant to the consideration of terrorist and counterterrorist actions. In many cases, acts committed by terrorists would be violations of the laws of war if they were conducted in the course of an international or internal armed conflict. Because they frequently occur in what is widely viewed as peacetime, however, the illegality of such acts has to be established first and foremost by reference to the national laws of states, international treaties on terrorism and related matters,[1] and other relevant parts of international law (including parts of the laws of war) that apply in peacetime as well as wartime—for example, the rules relating to genocide and crimes against humanity and certain rules relating to human rights. All of these legal categories are relevant to consideration of the attacks of September 11. For example, the attacks constitute murder under the domestic law of states; at the same time, they can be regarded as crimes against humanity—a category that encompasses widespread or systematic murder committed against any civilian population.[2]

The Laws of War

The laws of war (also referred to variously as "*jus in bello*" and "international humanitarian law applicable in armed conflict") are embodied and interpreted in a variety of sources: treaties, customary law, judicial decisions, writings of legal specialists, military manuals, and resolutions of international organizations. Although some of the law is immensely detailed, its basic principles are simple: The wounded and sick, POWs, and civilians are to be protected; military targets must be attacked in a manner that keeps civilian casualties and damage to a minimum; humanitarian and peacekeeping personnel must be respected; neutral or nonbelligerent states have certain rights and duties; and the use of certain weapons (including chemical weapons) is prohibited, as are other means and methods of warfare that cause unnecessary suffering. The four 1949 Geneva Conventions—the treaties that form the keystone of the modern laws of war—are concerned largely with the protection of victims of war who have fallen into the hands of an adversary.[3]

Treaties on the laws of war are the products of negotiations between states and reflect their experiences and interests, including those of their armed forces. For centuries these rules—though frequently the subject of controversy—have had an important function in the policies and practices of states engaged in military operations. Given the need for coalition members to harmonize their actions on a range of practical issues, these rules have had particular significance for international coalitions involved in combat. Even in situations in which their formal applicability may be questionable, they have sometimes been accepted as relevant guidelines.

Scope of Application

The laws of war have a scope of application that is not limited to wars between recognized states. They apply in a wide—though not infinitely wide—variety of situations. In the 1949 Geneva Conventions, Common Article 1 specifies that the parties "undertake to respect and to ensure respect for the present Convention in all circumstances."[4] This very general statement does not override the more specific provisions of Common Article 2, which deals directly with the scope of application and specifies that the Conventions "apply to all cases of declared war or of any other armed conflict which may arise between two or more of the High Contracting Parties, even if the state of war is not recognized by one of them"—indicating that the existence or nonexistence of a declaration of war or a formal state of war is not necessary for the application of the Conventions. Common Article 3 contains certain minimum provisions to be applied in the case of armed conflict that is not of an international character, concentrating particularly on treatment of persons who are taking no active part in hostilities. Certain other agreements, especially those concluded since the early 1990s, apply in noninternational as well as international armed conflicts.

The U.S. armed forces have indicated their intention to observe the rules governing international armed conflicts, even in situations that may differ in certain respects from the classical model of an inter-state war. Standing Rules of Engagement issued by the U.S. Joint Chiefs of Staff spell out this principle:

> U.S. forces will comply with the Law of War during military operations involving armed conflict, no matter how the conflict may be characterized under international law, and will comply with its principles and spirit during all other operations.[5]

In certain interstate conflicts, Western armed forces engaging with adversaries showing at best limited respect for ethical and legal restraints have managed to observe basic rules of the laws of war. This was the case in the 1991 Gulf War, in which Iraq mistreated prisoners, despoiled the environment, and had to be warned in brutally clear terms not to engage in chemical or biological attacks and terrorist operations. The U.S.-led Gulf War coalition sought to observe the laws of war not because of any guarantee of reciprocity but because such conduct was important to the maintenance of internal discipline, as well as domestic and international support. Reciprocity with one adversary in one particular conflict is not the only basis for observing the laws of war.

Jus ad bellum and jus in bello

In any use of military force, it is important to distinguish between the legality of resorting to force and the legality of the way in which such force is used. In strict legal terms, the law relating to the right to resort to the use of force (*jus ad bellum*) and the law governing the actual use of force in war (*jus in bello*) are separate. The latter applies to the conduct of international armed conflict irrespective of the right of the belligerents to resort to the use of force.[6]

Despite the lack of a formal connection between *jus ad bellum* and *jus in bello*, there are certain ways in which they interact in practice, especially in a war against terrorists. By observing *jus in bello*, a country may contribute to perceptions of the justice of its cause in three related ways. First, in all military operations, against terrorists or others, the perception that a state or a coalition of states is observing basic international standards may contribute to public support domestically and internationally. Second, if the coalition were to violate *jus in bello* in a major way—for example, by committing atrocities—that action would be likely to advance the cause of the adversary forces, arguably providing them with a justification for their resort to force. Third, in counterterrorist campaigns in particular, a basis for engaging in military operations often is a perception that there is a definite moral distinction between the types of actions engaged in by terrorists and those engaged in by their adversaries. Observance of *jus in bello* can form a part of that moral distinction.

However, the *jus ad bellum* rationale that armed hostilities have been initiated in response to major terrorist acts can raise issues relating to the application of certain *jus in bello* principles. I explore two such issues here: first, whether there is scope for neutrality in relation to a counterterrorist war; second, whether those responsible for terrorist campaigns can be regarded as exclusively responsible for all the death and destruction of an ensuing war.

The right of states to be neutral in an armed conflict is a longstanding principle of the laws of war. Events of the past century, especially the obligations imposed by membership in international organizations, have exposed problems with the traditional idea of strictly impartial neutrality and have led to its modification and even erosion. In many conflicts there have been states that, though not belligerents, have pursued policies favoring one side—for example, joining in sanctions against a state perceived to be an aggressor. The UN Charter provided for the Security Council to require all states to take certain actions against offending states, adding to the erosion of traditional concepts of neutrality, at least in cases in which the Security Council has been able to agree on a common course of action (such as sanctions). The importance of new forms of nonbelligerence, distinct from traditional neutrality, may help to explain the emergence of terms such as "neutral or nonbelligerent powers" in post-1945 treaties on the laws of war.[7] In many episodes in which the use of armed force by a coalition has been combined with the application of general UN sanctions against the adversary state, the scope for traditional neutrality has indeed been limited. The "war on terror" has reinforced this trend.

When fighting terrorism is the basis for resorting to war under the *jus ad bellum,* there sometimes is a tendency for the general indignation caused by terrorist attacks to affect adversely the implementation of *jus in bello.* Because the terrorists started the war, it is sometimes argued, they are responsible for all the subsequent horrors. In early December 2001, discussing civilian casualties, U.S. Secretary of Defense Donald Rumsfeld said, "We did not start this war. So understand, responsibility for every single casualty in this war, whether they're innocent Afghans or innocent Americans, rests at the feet of the al-Qaeda and the Taliban."[8] If such a view implies that the peculiar circumstances involved in the *jus ad bellum* might override certain considerations of *jus in bello* in the war that follows, it has no basis in the law.

Proportionality

Proportionality is a long-established principle that sets out criteria for limiting the use of force. Its main meaning relates to the conduct of ongoing hostilities. As a U.S. Army manual succinctly interprets it, "the loss of life and damage to property incidental to attacks must not be excessive in relation to the concrete and direct military advantage expected to be gained."[9] This meaning of proportionality is an important underlying principle of *jus in bello*, but it often is difficult to apply, especially in counterterrorist operations. It may—but does not necessarily—limit the use of force to the same level or amount of force as that employed by an adversary. It exists alongside the principle of military necessity, which is defined in the U.S. Army manual as one that "justifies those measures not forbidden by international law which are indispensable for securing the complete submission of the enemy as soon as possible."[10] The principle of proportionality is therefore in tension, but not necessarily in conflict, with current U.S. military doctrine that favors the overwhelming use of force to achieve decisive victory quickly at minimum cost in terms of U.S. casualties.[11]

Counterterrorist Military Operations

Counterterrorism has been defined as "offensive military operations designed to prevent, deter and respond to terrorism."[12] Such operations, including those resulting from the events of September 11, may involve interstate armed conflict as principally envisaged in the laws of war. In such cases that body of law applies straightforwardly. Such operations, however, also can involve conflict with other characteristics—a fact that helps to explain why the laws of war often have proved difficult to apply in them. Six factors, all relating to the nature of the opposition, point to potential problems in the application of the laws of war in counterterrorist operations:

- Neither all terrorist activities, nor all counterterrorist military operations—even when they have some international dimension—necessarily constitute armed conflict between states. Terrorist movements themselves generally have a nonstate character. Therefore, military operations between a state and such a movement, even if they involve the state's armed forces acting outside the state's own territory, do not necessarily bring them within the scope of application of the full range of provisions regarding international armed conflict in the 1949 Geneva Conventions and the 1977 Geneva Protocol I.[13]

- Counterterrorist operations may assume the form of actions by a government against forces operating within its own territory or, more rarely, actions by opposition forces against a government perceived to be committing or supporting terrorist acts. In both of these cases, the conflict may have the character of noninternational armed conflict (that is, civil war) more than international war. Fewer laws-of-war rules have been formally applicable to civil as distinct from international war, although the situation is changing in some respects.

- In many cases, the attributes and actions of a terrorist movement may not come within the field of application even of the modest body of rules relating to noninternational armed conflict. Common Article 3 of the 1949 Geneva Conventions is the core of these rules, but it says little about the scope of application. The principal subsequent agreement on noninternational armed conflict, the 1977 Geneva Protocol II, is based on the assumption that there is a conflict between a state's armed forces and organized armed groups that, under responsible command, exercise control over a part of its territory and carry out sustained and concerted military operations. The protocol expressly does not apply to situations of internal disturbance and tension, such as riots, and isolated and sporadic acts of violence.[14]

- Because terrorist forces often have little regard for internationally agreed rules of restraint, the resolve of the counterterrorist forces to observe them also may be weakened, given the low expectation of reciprocity and the tendency of some part of the public under attack to overlook any breaches by their own forces.

- A basic principle of the laws of war is that attacks should be directed against the adversary's military forces rather than against civilians. This principle, which is violated in terrorist attacks specifically directed against civilians, can be difficult to apply in counterterrorist operations because the terrorist movement may not be composed of defined military forces that are clearly distinguished from civilians.

- Some captured personnel who are members of a terrorist organization may not meet the criteria for POW status as set out in 1949

Geneva Convention III. (The question of prisoners is discussed in greater detail below.)

These six factors reflect the same underlying difficulty governments have in applying the laws of war to civil wars—namely, that the opponent tends to be regarded as a criminal, without the right to engage in combat operations. This factor above all explains why, despite the progress of recent decades, many governments are doubtful about, or opposed to, applying the full range of rules applicable in international armed conflict to operations against rebels and terrorists.

For at least twenty-five years the United States has expressed a concern—shared to some degree by certain other states—regarding the whole principle of thinking about terrorists and other irregular forces in a laws-of-war framework. To refer to such a framework, which recognizes rights and duties, might seem to imply a degree of moral acceptance of the right of any particular group to resort to acts of violence, at least against military targets.[15] Successive U.S. administrations have objected to certain revisions to the laws of war on the grounds that they might actually favour guerrilla fighters and terrorists, affording them a status that the United States believes they do not deserve. The strongest expression of this view was a letter of January 29, 1987, explaining why the Reagan administration was not recommending Senate approval of 1977 Geneva Protocol I additional to the 1949 Geneva Conventions. The letter mentioned that granting combatant status to certain irregular forces "would endanger civilians among whom terrorists and other irregulars attempt to conceal themselves." It indicated a concern that the provisions would endanger U.S. soldiers and stated in very general terms that "the Joint Chiefs of Staff have also concluded that a number of the provisions of the protocol are militarily unacceptable." U.S. repudiation of the protocol would be an important move against "the intense efforts of terrorist organizations and their supporters to promote the legitimacy of their aims and practices."[16] Whether all this was based on a fair interpretation of 1977 Protocol I is the subject of impassioned debate that is beyond the scope of this survey. The key point is the U.S. concern—which has not changed fundamentally since 1987—that the laws of war might be misused by some people to give an unwarranted degree of recognition to guerrilla terrorists.

Application of the Law in Previous Operations

Most counterterrorist operations have been largely internal matters, conducted by governments within their own territories. In such circumstances the laws of war may be of limited formal application, but other legal and prudential limits are important. Within functioning states, terrorist campaigns often have been defeated through slow and patient police work (sometimes with military assistance) rather than major military campaigns—for example, the actions against the Red Army Faction in Germany and the Red Brigades in Italy in the 1970s.

History provides other examples as well. Operating within a legal framework was critical to the success of British efforts in Malaya after 1948, according to Sir Robert Thompson, one of the key military figures in that campaign. He distilled five basic principles of counterinsurgency, the second being, "The government must function in accordance with law." He continued:

> There is a very strong temptation in dealing both with terrorism and with
> guerrilla actions for government forces to act outside the law, the excuses
> being that the processes of law are too cumbersome, that the normal safe-
> guards in the law for the individual are not designed for an insurgency and
> that a terrorist deserves to be treated as an outlaw anyway. Not only is this
> morally wrong, but, over a period, it will create more practical difficulties
> for a government than it solves.[17]

Other examples focus on the treatment of terrorists in captivity. In Northern Ireland, the British government—while denying that there was an armed conflict, international or otherwise, and strongly resisting any granting of POW status to detainees and convicted prisoners—came to accept that international standards had to apply to their treatment. The minority report of a UK Commission of Inquiry in 1972 that led to this conclusion is an interesting example of asserting the wider relevance, even in an internal conflict, of certain international legal standards, including those embodied in the four 1949 Geneva Conventions.[18]

In the Vietnam War, U.S. forces classified Viet Cong main force and local force personnel, as well as certain Viet Cong irregulars, as POWs. This choice was made despite the existence of doubts and ambiguities about whether these forces met all the criteria in Article 4 of 1949 Geneva Convention III. Viet Cong irregulars were to be classified as POWs if they were captured while engaging in combat or a belligerent act under arms, "other than an act of terrorism, sabotage, or spying." There was provision for establishing tribunals—in accordance with Article 5 of the Geneva Convention—to determine, in doubtful or contested cases, whether individual detainees were entitled to POW status.[19]

In the Israeli invasion and occupation of southern Lebanon from 1982 to 2000, the Israeli treatment of alleged terrorist detainees also caused controversy. Israel opposed granting them POW status on the grounds that as terrorists they were not entitled to it. The detainees were held in very poor conditions in notorious camps, including al-Khiam (run by the Israeli-created

South Lebanese Army) and al-Ansar (run by the Israel Defence Forces). In a case concerning detainees in Ansar Prison, on which the Israeli Supreme Court issued a judgment on May 11, 1983, the Israeli authorities asserted that the prisoners were "hostile foreigners detained because they belong to the forces of terrorist organizations, or because of their connections or closeness to terrorist organizations." While refusing these prisoners POW status, Israel claimed to observe "humanitarian guidelines" of the 1949 Geneva Convention IV on civilians. [20]

Past evidence suggests that although the application of the law may be particularly difficult in counterterrorist operations, it cannot be neglected. In a counterterrorist war, as in other wars, there can be strong prudential considerations that militate in favor of observing legal standards, which are regarded increasingly as consisting of not only domestic legal standards but also international ones, including those embodied in the laws of war. These considerations in favor of observing the law are important irrespective of whether there is reciprocity in such observance by all the parties to a particular war. It is not realistic to expect, however, that the result of the application of such rules will be a sanitized form of war in which civilian suffering and death are eliminated.

War in Afghanistan

On October 7, 2001, the United States commenced Operation Enduring Freedom in Afghanistan. Numerous issues relating to the laws of war have emerged in the course of this operation. Some, such as the handling of humanitarian relief and refugee issues, are not addressed in this chapter. The main focus here is the applicability of the law generally, the U.S. use of air power, and the treatment of prisoners.

Applicability of the Laws of War to the Armed Conflict

The international community asserted the relevancy of the laws of war to the conflict in Afghanistan long before the initiation of Operation Enduring Freedom. In 1998 the UN Security Council had called on both the Taliban and the Northern Alliance to comply with their obligations under international humanitarian law when it reaffirmed

> that all parties to the conflict are bound to comply with their obligations under international humanitarian law and in particular the Geneva Conventions of 12 August 1949 and that persons who commit or order the commission of grave breaches of the Conventions are individually responsible in respect of such breaches.[21]

The reference to grave breaches would appear to suggest that the Security Council regarded all the rules of the 1949 Geneva Conventions as applicable—not just common Article 3, which deals with civil war. Thus, three years before the United States became directly involved, it joined other powers in regarding the laws of war as applicable to the Afghan conflict.

Like the period of Soviet intervention of 1979–1989—and, indeed, wars in many countries in the period since 1945—the armed conflict in Afghanistan that began October 7, 2001, may be best characterized as "internationalized civil war." This is not a formal legal category but an indication that the rules pertaining to both international and civil wars may be applicable in different aspects and phases of the conflict.[22] During October–December 2001 major aspects of the war were international in character. Following the fall of the Taliban regime and the accession to power of the Afghan Interim Authority on December 22, 2002, the coalition's role essentially was that of aiding a government.

Several of the main laws of war treaties were formally binding on the belligerents in the international armed conflict between the U.S.-led coalition and the Taliban regime in Afghanistan in October–December 2001. The 1907 Hague Convention IV on land warfare applied because of its status as customary law, thereby binding on all states whether or not they were parties to the treaty. In addition, Afghanistan and the main members of the international coalition were parties to the 1925 Geneva Protocol on gas and bacteriological warfare, the 1948 Genocide Convention, and the four 1949 Geneva Conventions.

These treaties provide the basic treaty framework for considering the application of the law in the armed conflict that commenced in October 2001. In addition, rules of customary international law applied. Apart from the provisions of customary law embodied in the foregoing agreements, certain provisions of some later agreements, including 1977 Geneva Protocol I, are accepted as having that status.

With regard to civil-war aspects of the Afghan war, some but not all of the provisions of the aforementioned agreements apply. The 1907 Hague Land War Convention's Article 2 indicates that the convention and its annexed regulations apply only to wars between states. The 1925 Geneva Protocol is not formally applicable to civil wars.[23] The 1948 Genocide Convention is considered to apply to noninternational as well as international armed conflict. In the 1949 Geneva Conventions, Common Article 3 lists certain minimum provisions for humane treatment of individuals taking no active part in hostilities that are to be applied in noninternational armed conflict. However, the UN Security Council's 1998 resolution had called for application of the Geneva Conventions more generally.

Bombing

The development by U.S. and allied forces of techniques of bombing that are more accurate than bombing was in previous eras has improved the prospects that certain air campaigns can be conducted in a manner that is compatible with the long-established laws-of-war principle of discrimination[24] and with the more specific rules about targeting—rules that themselves have changed, not least in 1977 Geneva Protocol I. This is a momentous development in the history of war, yet its effects—especially with regard to operations against terrorists—should not be exaggerated because it cannot guarantee success or no deaths of innocents. Precision-guided weapons generally are better at hitting fixed objects such as buildings than moving objects that can be concealed, such as people and tanks. Civilian deaths will still occur because certain dual-use targets are attacked, because of the close proximity of military targets to civilians, or because of faulty intelligence and human or mechanical errors. In addition, malevolence and callousness can still lead to attacks on the wrong places or people.

Announcing the start of military strikes against Afghanistan on October 7, 2001, President Bush stated: "These carefully targeted actions are designed to disrupt the use of Afghanistan as a terrorist base of operations and to attack the military capability of the Taliban regime."[25] The principle that the bombing of Afghanistan should be discriminate was repeated frequently. On October 21, General Richard B. Myers, chairman of the Joint Chiefs of Staff, said:

> The last thing we want are any civilian casualties. So we plan every military target with great care. We try to match the weapon to the target and the goal is, one, to destroy the target, and two, is to prevent any what we call "collateral damage" or damage to civilian structures or civilian population.[26]

From the start of the campaign in Afghanistan, the United States was particularly sensitive about accusations that it acted indiscriminately. In late October, Rumsfeld accused the Taliban and al-Qaeda leaders of causing and faking civilian damage:

> They are using mosques for command and control, for ammunition storage, and they're not taking journalists in to show that. What they do is when there's a bomb goes down, they grab some children and some women and pretend that the bomb hit the women and the children[27]

What truth there was in all this was and remains difficult to determine.

About 60 percent of the 22,000 U.S. bombs and missiles dropped in Afghanistan were precision guided—the highest percentage in any major bombing campaign. If, as reported, only one in four bombs and missiles dropped by U.S. forces on Afghanistan missed its target or malfunctioned in some way, the 75 percent success rate was higher than that achieved in the 1991 Gulf War and the 1999 Kosovo War.[28]

The bombing aroused much international concern. There were reports of many attacks that caused significant civilian casualties and damage. Accuracy in hitting the intended target area did not by itself necessarily eliminate such problems. An ICRC warehouse in Kabul was hit twice, on October 16 and 26, leading to serious questions about failure to ensure that target lists were properly prepared and, after the first well-publicized disaster, amended.[29] The episode subsequently was investigated by the Pentagon.[30] Some later incidents were even more serious. For example, according to press reports more than 100 villagers may have died in bombings on December 1, 2001, of Kama Ado and neighboring villages in eastern Afghanistan, not far from the cave complex at Tora Bora.[31] On July 1, 2002, during an operation to hunt Taliban leaders, U.S. aircraft attacked four villages around the hamlet of Kakrak. According to reports, this episode followed the firing of guns at two wedding parties and resulted in the deaths of more than 50 people and injuries to more than 100. This incident led to another Pentagon investigation.[32]

It is difficult to arrive at a reliable estimate of the overall number of civilian deaths caused directly by the bombing in Afghanistan. As in the 1991 Gulf and 1999 Kosovo wars, the Pentagon has been reluctant to issue relevant figures. Controversy was caused by an unofficial and questionable estimate of 3,767 as of mid-December 2001.[33] In response to this report, Rumsfeld stated in an interview on January 8, 2002:

> There probably has never in the history of the world been a conflict that has been done as carefully, and with such measure, and care, and with such minimal collateral damage to buildings and infrastructure, and with such small numbers of unintended civilian casualties.[34]

In 2002 several reports that were based on on-site examinations gave a more authoritative, but incomplete, picture. In July the *New York Times* published the results of a review of eleven of the "principal places where Afghans and human rights groups claim that civilians have been killed." It found that at these sites "airstrikes killed as many as 400 civilians." A principal cause was poor intelligence.[35] In September 2002 a San Francisco-based human rights group, Global Exchange, estimated on the basis of a survey conducted in Afghanistan that "at least 824 Afghan civilians were killed between October 7 and January 2002 by the U.S.-led bombing campaign."[36] It is possible that the precise figure for civilian casualties of the bombing in Afghanistan will never be known.

In legal terms, the incidence of civilian deaths per se does not always constitute a violation, absent other factors. Willful killings and intentional attacks against the civilian population as such or against individual civilians not taking part in hostilities clearly are illegal. In addition, the 1977 Geneva Protocol I, Article 57, spells out a positive obligation on the part of commanders to exercise care to spare civilians and civilian objects.

There are strong reasons to believe U.S. statements that civilian deaths in Afghanistan resulting from the U.S. bombing were unintended. Some of the deaths appear to have resulted from errors of various kinds, and some may have been unavoidable "collateral damage." One cause of civilian casualties in October–December 2001 may have been the fact that, in a legacy from the period of Soviet involvement in Afghanistan, many Taliban military assets were located in towns where they were less vulnerable to raids from rural-based guerrillas but where they were, of course, closer to civilians who were at risk of getting hit in bombing attacks. Although much of the bombing was discriminate, questions have been raised about whether all appropriate measures were taken to reduce civilian casualties and damage. Even if much of the civilian death and destruction is not a violation of the law, the resulting adverse public perception risks harming the coalition cause.

The air campaign in Afghanistan confirmed the lesson of earlier campaigns, especially the war over Kosovo in 1999, that there is tension between current U.S. and North Atlantic Treaty Organization (NATO) strategic doctrine and certain international legal provisions on targeting. The 1977 Geneva Protocol I, Article 52(2), opens with the words, "Attacks shall be limited strictly to military objectives." It goes on to indicate the types of objects that might constitute military objectives. This provision presents some difficulties and has been the subject of interpretative declarations by several states.[37] Although the United States is not bound by the Protocol, it has indicated that it accepts this article.[38] Even before the U.S. involvement in Afghanistan, however, several U.S. legal experts had expressed serious concerns about the provision. For example, Major Jeanne Meyer, coeditor of the *Operational Law Handbook*, stated that this article "tries to constrict the use of air power to the specific tactical military effort at hand" and "ignores the reality that a nation's war effort is composed of more than just military components." Although she did not suggest total rejection of the provision, she urged the United States to "resist the pressure to accept restrictive interpretations of Article 52(2)."[39] In general, the United States is anxious to retain some legal justification for attacks on certain targets that may not themselves be purely military but may, for example, constitute key parts of a regime's infrastructure.

Was the U.S. bombing effort in Afghanistan in October–December 2001 undermined by concern over civilian casualties? Its success against the Taliban suggests not. There were reports, however, that the United States had deliberately slowed the pace of the campaign and increased the risk to the people executing it because of legal restraints and moral values. There also were claims that war planners frequently chose not to hit particular targets, even if they were militarily important, and pilots allegedly complained of lost opportunities. Yet the planners could not reveal the reasons for ruling out certain targets because it would give the adversary "a recipe book for not being bombed."

In addition to the direct casualties there also were, inevitably, indirect casualties of the bombing. These indirect casualties appear to fall into two categories. First, the bombing caused thousands of Afghan civilians to flee their homes. Some died in the harsh conditions of flight and displacement. Second, the use of cluster bombs led to immediate and longer-term civilian casualties. Cluster bombs are air-dropped canisters containing numerous separate bomblets that disperse over a given area. The bomblets, which are meant to explode on impact or to self-deactivate after a specific period, can cause particularly severe problems if they fail to do so. There have been objections to their use, principally because they have a tendency—like antipersonnel landmines—to kill people long after the conflict is over.

The UN's Mine Action Programme for Afghanistan (MAPA) estimates that 1,152 cluster bombs were dropped by U.S. forces, leaving up to 14,000 unexploded bomblets as a result.[40] According to the U.S. State Department in July 2002, "the clearance of cluster munitions is being achieved at a rate faster than anticipated. All known cluster munition strike sites have been surveyed where access is possible and are in the process of being cleared."[41] As the law stands, there has been no agreement to outlaw cluster bombs, and although they are not illegal per se their use does raise questions regarding their compatibility with fundamental principles of the laws of war. They are certain to be the subject of further pressures to limit or stop their use or to ensure more effective safeguards against later accidental detonations.

A further issue concerns the use of bombing in the hunt for Taliban and al-Qaeda personnel following the fall of the Taliban regime in early December 2001. In the preceding phase, bombing had been used primarily in support of Northern Alliance frontal operations aimed at capturing the main Taliban-held cities. Once this goal was achieved, a good deal of the bombing was directed against remnant al-Qaeda mountain redoubts. It also was directed against Taliban and al-Qaeda forces and their leaders, but the press reported many incidents in which those killed apparently were neither. The reports drew attention to the difficulty of distinguishing between civilians and these forces. They also raised a question of broader significance in counterterrorist wars: To what extent is bombing an appropriate form of enforcement once a state is, to a greater or lesser degree, under the control of a government that is opposed to the terrorists? At that point, can the focus be transferred to other forms of police and military action that may be less likely than bombing to cause civilian casualties?

Here, the legal argument for greater reliance on the discriminate use of ground force merges into a practical argument that only such means can prevent the escape of the forces being targeted. U.S. civilian and military officials are reported to have concluded that Osama bin Laden had been present at the battle for Tora Bora in December 2001 and that failure to commit ground troops against him in this mountain battle was the gravest error of the war.[42] It does appear that U.S. reliance on bombing and its reluctance to put its own troops in harm's way may have enabled Taliban and al-Qaeda leaders to escape.

Prisoners

Beginning in late November 2001, the status and treatment of prisoners taken in the "war on terror" (most but not all of whom had been captured in Afghanistan) became the subject of major international controversies. These controversies centered on three interrelated issues: first, the extraordinary events relating to prisoners in Afghanistan in late 2001; second, the broader debate about the legal status and treatment of prisoners taken in the war on terror generally, including those in U.S. custody at Guantanamo Bay; and third, possible judicial proceedings against prisoners for precapture offenses.

Prison Disasters in Afghanistan

Initially, international attention focused on one event: the killing of a large number of Taliban and al-Qaeda prisoners who had been taken at Kunduz at around the time of its fall on November 23–24, 2001, and were then involved in the revolt at Qala-e Jhangi Fort near Mazar-e Sharif between November 25 and December 1. The prisoners were killed by Northern Alliance forces under the control of General Rashid Dostum, with assistance from certain UK and U.S. forces. The real cause of the disaster probably was a failure to ensure that there were proper arrangements for receiving and disarming the prisoners before they arrived at the fort.

Other reports about treatment of Taliban and al-Qaeda prisoners, especially at Sebarghan in northern Afghanistan, confirm that the overall approach of the Northern Alliance was defective. By late December there had been numerous reports of prisoners dying in shipping containers and Afghan captors beating their detainees. The ICRC was reported as expressing concern that it had been able to register only 4,000 of the 7,000 prisoners that the United States said it and its Afghan allies had in custody.[43] Long after most of the prisoners had been taken, conditions remained shocking, in violation of all international standards.[44]

In his Pentagon press briefing on November 30, 2001, Rumsfeld indicated—in general terms, not in connection with the prisoner question—that the United States did have influence with the forces with which it operated in Afghanistan:

> We have a relationship with all of those elements on the ground. We have provided them food. We've provided them ammunition. We've provided air support. We've provided winter clothing. We've worked with them closely. We have troops embedded in their forces and have been assisting with overhead targeting and resupply of ammunition. It's a relationship.[45]

Whether the United States and its coalition partners had any influence over Northern Alliance actions in such basic matters as protection of prisoners—and, if so, whether they used it—is open to question.

Legal Status and Treatment of Prisoners Generally

Within the Pentagon it was recognized as early as September 2001 that in the forthcoming military action questions relating to the legal status and treatment of prisoners could be difficult. An unpublished document circulated by the U.S. Air Force's International and Operations Law Division contained the main outlines of an approach that would continue to be influential: Terrorists were to be treated as "unlawful combatants"; it was "very unlikely that a captured terrorist will be legally entitled to POW status under the Geneva Conventions"; however, there was a "practical U.S. interest in application of Law of Armed Conflict principles in the context of reciprocity of treatment of captured personnel." With regard to treatment upon capture,

> if a terrorist is captured, Department of Defense members must at the very least comply with the principles and spirit of the Law of Armed Conflict. . . . A suspected terrorist captured by U.S. military personnel will be given the protections of but not the status of a POW.[46]

Consideration of the legal status and treatment of prisoners taken by the U.S.-led coalition must begin with the distinction that has been drawn between the two main groups: Taliban and al-Qaeda. In principle the Taliban have a connection to a state (Afghanistan), whereas al-Qaeda does not. In certain cases it may not be easy to determine which of these categories an individual belongs in. At Guantanamo there evidently has been a tendency to classify only Afghan prisoners as Taliban. All non-Afghans (some of whom were arrested outside Afghanistan) appear to have been classified as al-Qaeda. It may be doubted, however, whether all foreigners drawn to support an Islamic cause in Afghanistan, Pakistan, or elsewhere who ended up at Guantanamo were necessarily members of al-Qaeda.

Can either of these two groups of combatants be considered lawful? A key factor in determining the lawfulness of a combatant—and therefore the entitlement to participate directly in hostilities—is the affiliation of the combatant to a party to the conflict. Under Article 4 of 1949 Geneva Convention III (the POW Convention), lawful combatants comprise the organized armed forces (including militias and volunteer corps) of a state or otherwise recognized party to a conflict. They also include "members of certain other militias and volunteer corps, including those of organized resistance movements, belonging to a Party to the conflict," provided that they fulfill four conditions: "being commanded by a person responsible for his subordinates," "having a fixed distinctive sign recognizable at a distance," "carrying arms openly," and "conducting their operations in accordance with laws and customs of war." Members of regular armed forces can be lawful combatants even if the regime they serve is not recognized as the lawful government of the state.

I do not address here the question of whether all members of regular armed forces have to meet the four conditions listed specifically with respect to members of militias and resistance movements. Problems and controversies in this regard are not new. With respect to Afghanistan, an argument could be made that some U.S. or coalition personnel failed to meet one of the conditions, such as members of U.S. forces (including Special Forces or forward air controllers) not wearing a uniform or fixed sign and not carrying arms openly. Such possibilities give the United States a potential interest in avoiding restrictive approaches to the granting of POW status and treatment. Civilian contracted personnel, who played a significant part in the U.S. operations, would appear to qualify for POW status provided that they have formal authorization.

All lawful combatants, if captured, are entitled to POW status and all of the rights set forth in the Geneva Convention III. They cannot be punished for the mere fact of having participated directly in hostilities, but they can be tried for violations of the detaining power's law or international law (including the laws of war) that they may have committed.[47]

Questions regarding the status of a variety of detainees who may fail to meet one of the foregoing criteria are not new. In previous wars, POW status seldom was given to persons involved in resistance activities against occupation, or in cases of alleged terrorism. On the other hand, some captured personnel who arguably failed to meet one criterion or another that was applicable at the time were regarded as entitled to POW status.[48]

A procedure for determining who is a lawful combatant, entitled to POW status, is addressed directly in two treaties. The first of these, the 1949 Geneva Convention III, provides in Article 5 that, in cases of doubt, prisoners shall be treated as POWs "until such time as their status has been determined by a competent tribunal." This article does not specify who has to have the doubt, nor the nature of the "competent tribunal." The general principle is clear, however, and is accepted in official U.S. manuals. For example, the U.S. Army manual states unequivocally, "When doubt exists as to whether captured enemy personnel warrant continued PW [prisoner of war] status, Art. 5 Tribunals must be convened."[49]

The second treaty that addressed the procedure for determining who is a lawful combatant is 1977 Geneva Protocol I. Article 45 contains elaborations of 1949 Convention III's provisions on the status of detained persons. It suggests that a detainee has "the right to assert his entitlement to prisoner-of-war status before a judicial tribunal," but it allows for considerable leeway in the procedure by which a tribunal could reach a decision about POW status. The possibilities that the proceedings could take place *after* a trial for an offense and *in camera* in the interest of state security are not excluded. This article recognizes in plain language that not all persons who take part in hostilities are entitled to POW status, but they are entitled to certain fundamental guarantees.

The uncertainties regarding the status and treatment of people who are involved in hostile activities in various ways but fail to meet the criteria for POW status are reflected in muddled terminology. The treaties that implicitly create the category do not offer any satisfactory term to describe such persons. The U.S. Supreme Court in its judgment in the July 1942 case, *Ex Parte Richard Quirin*, used the terms "unlawful combatant" and "unlawful belligerent"—apparently interchangeably—to refer to a person who, "having the status of an enemy belligerent enters or remains, with hostile purpose, upon the territory of the United States in time of war without uniform or other appropriate means of identification."[50] One useful term advanced in the early 1950s by a respected authority as the most appropriate to cover a wide range of combatants who do not meet the POW criteria is "unprivileged belligerents."[51] Current U.S. military manuals use four terms—unprivileged belligerents, detainees, unlawful combatants, and illegal combatants—again apparently interchangeably, to refer to persons who are regarded as not being members of the armed forces of a party to the conflict and not having the right to engage in hostilities against an opposing party.[52] The terminological confusion is not a major problem in itself. The key element of confusion in the debate was the tendency—especially marked in the press in late 2001 and early 2002—to refer to terms such as "unlawful combatants" and "battlefield detainees" as if they were entirely new, were freshly invented by the U.S. government, and were completely outside the existing treaty framework.

The fact that certain detainees may be denied POW status does not mean (as some advocates have argued) that they should be considered civilians, but it also does not mean that they have no legal rights. The provisions of Common Article 3 of the 1949 Geneva Conventions, although they are not specific to this category of person and are formally applicable only in noninternational armed conflict, may be regarded as minimum guarantees to be applied to all detainees. In addition, Article 45 of 1977 Geneva Protocol I addresses the matter much more directly: "Any person who has taken part in hostilities, who is not entitled to prisoner-of-war status and who does not benefit from more favourable treatment . . . shall have the right at all times to the protection of Article 75 of this Protocol." Article 75 elaborates a range of fundamental guarantees that are intended to provide minimum rules of protection for all persons who do not benefit from more favorable treatment under other rules.

Although neither the United States nor Afghanistan is a party to the 1977 Geneva Protocol I, the rules in Articles 45 and 75 are relatively uncontroversial, and it is longstanding U.S. policy that they should be implemented.[53] U.S. officials have repeatedly omitted mention of these articles, however, in connection with the treatment of prisoners held in the "war on terror." The omission appears odd because reference to Article 75 would have been an obvious way of indicating that the treatment of the detainees was still within an international legal framework.[54]

After the status and treatment of prisoners taken in Afghanistan became urgent in November 2001, public statements by U.S. officials were consistent and clear on one point. By referring to these prisoners generally as "battlefield detainees" and "unlawful combatants," the United States signaled its unwillingness to classify al-Qaeda and Taliban prisoners as POWs. However, it was slow to give detailed reasoning and to indicate the principles to be followed in the handling of the detainees. On January 11, 2002, when Rumsfeld was asked whether the ICRC would have any access to the prisoners who had just been taken to the U.S. naval base at Guantanamo Bay in Cuba, he stated:

> I think that we're in the process of sorting through precisely the right way to handle them, and they will be handled in the right way. They will be handled not as prisoners of war, because they're not, but as unlawful combatants. The, as I understand it, technically unlawful combatants do not

have any rights under the Geneva Convention. We have indicated that we do plan to, for the most part, treat them in a manner that is reasonably consistent with the Geneva Conventions, to the extent they are appropriate, and that is exactly what we have been doing.[55]

In succeeding weeks there were numerous expressions of concern in the United States and internationally about the status and treatment of detainees and about the risk that U.S. conduct would lead to a global weakening of the POW regime.[56] There also were intense disagreements within the U.S. administration.[57] The situation was made worse by the Pentagon's inept release on January 19, 2002, of a photograph showing bound and shackled prisoners, heads and eyes covered, kneeling before U.S. soldiers at Guantanamo.

Certain conciliatory gestures were made by the U.S. administration. ICRC officials started interviewing detainees at Guantanamo on January 18, 2002, and were able to establish a permanent presence there. Rumsfeld's suggestion that unlawful combatants have no rights under the Geneva Convention was modified when, on January 22, 2002, he recognized that "under the Geneva Convention, an unlawful combatant is entitled to humane treatment."[58] On February 7, in the first major policy statement on the issue, the White House announced:

- The United States is treating and will continue to treat all of the individuals detained at Guantanamo humanely and, to the extent appropriate and consistent with military necessity, in a manner consistent with the principles of the Third Geneva Convention of 1949.
- The president has determined that the Geneva Convention applies to the Taliban detainees, but not to the al-Qaida detainees.
- Al-Qaida is not a state party to the Geneva Convention; it is a foreign terrorist group. As such, its members are not entitled to POW status.
- Although we never recognized the Taliban as the legitimate Afghan government, Afghanistan is a party to the Convention, and the president has determined that the Taliban are covered by the Convention. Under the terms of the Geneva Convention, however, the Taliban detainees do not qualify as POWs.
- Therefore, neither the Taliban nor al-Qaida detainees are entitled to POW status.
- Even though the detainees are not entitled to POW privileges, they will be provided with many POW privileges as a matter of policy.[59]

The fact sheet contained numerous detailed assurances about the treatment of the detainees at Guantanamo, but it also indicated that they would not receive certain privileges normally afforded to POWs by the Geneva Conventions, including

- access to a canteen to purchase food, soap, and tobacco
- a monthly advance of pay
- the ability to have and consult personal financial accounts
- the ability to receive scientific equipment, musical instruments, or sports outfits.[60]

This U.S. refusal to grant particular privileges was defensible, in the circumstances. A specific indication of this kind can be compatible with an overall approach of respect for a legal regime; it also can contribute to change in that regime. The refusal of these privileges caused no outcry, and parts of the February 7 statement reassured international opinion. The earlier part of the statement was incoherent in certain respects, however. The recognition that the Geneva Convention III did apply to the Taliban, followed by the blanket statement that the Taliban did not qualify as POWs, had the confusing appearance of simultaneous admission and retraction. As for the al-Qaeda detainees, although certain of the stated reasons for not applying the Convention to them are well founded, the particular argument that because al-Qaeda is not a party to the Convention it cannot benefit from it is far from being self-evidently correct. There was a curiously legalistic streak in an approach that put such emphasis on the purported distinction between the Taliban and al-Qaeda detainees yet saw no practical consequences: "No distinction will be made in the good treatment given to the al-Qaida or the Taliban."[61]

A striking feature of the statement is its avoidance of any hint of doubt about status: None of the detainees, even the Taliban detainees, could possibly qualify as POWs. In keeping with this claim, nothing was said about the tribunals provided for in Article 5 of 1949 Geneva Convention III and Articles 45 of 1977 Geneva Protocol I. A further notable omission was the absence of reference to Article 75 of the 1977 agreement. Despite certain merits, the U.S. statement was less technically proficient, and less reassuring, than it could have been. Expressions of international concern regarding the status and treatment of detainees in Guantanamo and elsewhere continued.

In response to the White House statement of February 7, the ICRC press office in Geneva stated the next day that it "stands by its position that people in a situation of international conflict are considered to be prisoners of war unless a competent tribunal decides otherwise."[62] This position overstated the legal requirement—which is not that in all cases prisoners should be considered to be POWs but that *in cases of doubt* prisoners shall be *treated as* POWs. Presumably, there could be many cases in which there is no doubt in the first place. In some statements ICRC press spokesmen went so far as to deny the existence of a legal category of unprivileged or illegal combatant. Given that the category of unprivileged belligerent has a long history, is implicit in the criteria for POW status in 1949 Geneva Convention III, and is more or less explicit in Article 75 of 1977 Geneva Protocol I, the ICRC statements were not well founded. The same basic stance, with the same weaknesses, was taken by Amnesty International in London and Human Rights Watch in New York—both of which asserted, like the ICRC, that all detainees must be presumed to be POWs.[63]

The fundamental U.S. position that many of the detainees taken in Afghanistan should not be accorded the status of POWs—which was defensible in terms of existing law—appears to have been based on three main practical considerations—the first related to conditions of detention of prisoners, the second to their release, and the third to the conduct of judicial proceedings.

With regard to conditions of detention, a main concern was that 1949 Geneva Convention III famously states that POWs are obliged to give only name, rank, date of birth, and number.[64] The United States was anxious to obtain considerably more information from the detainees, although whether a different classification actually improves the prospects of securing accurate information is debatable. The U.S. government also wished to keep the detainees more segregated from each other than the POW regime's provisions would indicate. It probably was a lesser consideration that the United States also was anxious not to recognize such remarkable POW privileges as the right to receive scientific instruments.

With regard to release of prisoners, the Geneva Convention III codifies a practice that normally is pursued after a war—releasing and repatriating POWs. Any such release of all the detainees from the war on terror would pose three problems. First, there may not be a clear end of hostilities: Although the war in Afghanistan may be concluded at a definite date, it may be decades before the "war on terror" can be declared to be over for the United States. Second, unlike POWs in a "normal" inter-state war, some of the prisoners concerned might continue to be extremely dangerous after release given their training, their motivation to commit acts of terrorism, and lack of governmental control over them. Third, their countries of origin might refuse to accept them back, except perhaps as prisoners.

Judicial Proceedings

With regard to judicial proceedings in respect to precapture offenses, from early on in the war the United States reportedly intended to prosecute several al-Qaeda and Taliban leaders, including Osama bin Laden if he were captured. It is not obvious, however, that the point of detaining the prisoners at Guantanamo Bay is to try them. Insofar as the possibility of trials is envisaged, the United States is reluctant to pursue the procedure laid down in Geneva Convention III, which specifies that any sentence of a POW must be "by the same courts according to the same procedure as in the case of members of the armed forces of the Detaining Power."[65] If, following this provision, cases were handled through the normal U.S. military courts, there could be problems, especially regarding the normal U.S. military procedures for appeals.[66] Moreover, if a precapture offense was of a type that would result in a member of the armed forces of the detaining power appearing before a civil court, it is implicit in the terms of the Convention that a POW could appear before a civil court. Such standard procedures, U.S. officials feared, could provide opportunities for al-Qaeda suspects and their lawyers to prolong legal processes and attract publicity. There also was concern that in cases involving defendants with no documents and no willingness to collaborate with any of the procedures, and where evidence might be based largely on intelligence sources, it could be difficult to provide evidence that met high standards of admissibility and equally high standards of proof of direct personal involvement in terrorist activities. Furthermore, al-Qaeda might learn valuable information from evidence in open court—for example, about its vulnerability to intelligence gathering.

Because of such fears about normal judicial procedures, the administration made provision for trial by military commissions. There are numerous precedents for such provision: For example, President Franklin D. Roosevelt's Proclamation of July 2, 1942, was bluntly titled "Denying Certain Enemies Access to the Courts of the United States."[67] President Bush's military order of November 13, 2001, provides for the option of trying certain accused terrorists by military commissions operating under special rules. It applies only to non-U.S. citizens. It specifies that individual terrorists, including members of al-Qaeda, can be detained and tried "for violations of the laws of war and other applicable laws" and that the military commissions would not be bound by "the principles of law and the rules of evidence generally recognized in the trial of criminal cases in the United States district courts." It also contains some extremely brief provisions for humane conditions of detention and provides for the Secretary of Defense to issue detailed regulations on matters such as the conduct of proceedings of the military commissions.[68]

President Bush's military order was the subject of considerable legal and political debate in the United States and elsewhere with regard to its constitutionality, practicability, and advisability. The controversy about the military commissions was part of a larger debate about which particular approach to the prosecution and trial of alleged terrorists should be pursued.[69]

The controversy about the proposed military commissions abated some-what over time. On November 30, 2001, the president's counsel offered several assurances, including that military commissions are one option but not the only option.[70] On March 21, 2002, the Pentagon issued the long-promised detailed regulations concerning the conduct of proceedings of the projected military commissions, the terms of which went some way to meet the expressions of concern regarding President Bush's military order of the previous November.[71] As far as the laws of war are concerned, a key issue (not explicitly addressed in the Pentagon document) is whether the provisions regarding the trial procedure conform with the ten recognized principles of regular judicial procedure outlined in 1977 Geneva Protocol I, Article 75, which relates to persons who are not entitled to POW status. The Pentagon's detailed regulations appear to conform with almost all of these principles—apart, arguably, from the final one, which is that "a convicted person shall be advised on conviction of his judicial and other remedies and of the time-limits within which they may be exercised."[72]

A problem regarding the prisoners held by the United States is the uncertainty regarding whether and when they will be tried and whether they will be held indefinitely or released. More than 600 suspects of many different nationalities are held at Guantanamo Bay. In July 2003 the United States announced that six prisoners would face trial by military commission. Earlier, the United States had indicated that the judicial process might have to wait until after "the war on terror is won," at which distant point the detainees might be tried or released.[73] Their indefinite detention, without any charge or trial, would violate fundamental standards of human rights and would be hard to justify. Yet when the main problem with potential suicide bombers is not what they have done but what they might do in future, trials also are an imperfect solution.

Conclusions

There are ample grounds for questioning whether military operations involving action against terrorists constitute a new or wholly distinct category of war. The coalition operations in Afghanistan, as well as the larger war against terrorism of which they are a part, are not completely unlike earlier wars. Many forms of military action and issues raised since September 11 are similar to those in previous military operations and concern issues already addressed by the laws of war.

Events in Afghanistan have confirmed, however, that there are particular difficulties in applying the laws of war to counterterrorist operations. A war that has as a purpose the pursuit of people deemed to be criminals involves many awkward issues for which the existing laws of war are not a perfect fit. In addition, the use of local forces as proxies (a common feature in counterterrorist wars) risks creating a situation in which major powers are at the mercy of their local agents, whose commitment to the laws of war may be slight. More fundamentally, any war against a grand abstraction—as the "war on terror" undoubtedly is—risks creating a mentality in which adversaries are dehumanized and the cosmic importance of the struggle may be thought to outweigh mundane legal or humanitarian considerations.

Yet treating (or appearing to treat) the law in a cavalier manner risks creating new problems. If a major power is perceived as ignoring certain basic norms, this perception may have a negative effect within a coalition or on enemies. It may involve severe risks to any of its own nationals who may be taken prisoner. It also may affect the conduct of other states in other conflicts. In that wider sense, the principle of reciprocity in the observance of law retains its value.

In particular, the U.S. handling of questions relating to the treatment and status of prisoners has caused widespread concern and criticism. With regard to those under Northern Alliance control, practical arrangements around the time of the rebellion at Mazar-e Sharif as well as subsequently were inadequate. More generally, although many key U.S. positions were defensible— especially that certain prisoners did not qualify for POW status—aspects of U.S. policy and procedures were poorly presented and in some cases did not appear to be fully thought out. The prisoner issue—always sensitive anyway—was especially significant in this war: If the coalition were perceived to have treated prisoners inhumanely or to have regarded their status and treatment as being in international legal limbo, there would be risks of a general weakening of the prisoner regime, with potential serious implications for any coalition personnel taken prisoner in the ongoing war on terrorism. The handling of this issue contributed to the weakening of international solidarity in the war on terror in 2002 and the first half of 2003. The controversies over the prisoner question had special resonance because of other countries' concern that the United States had been moving toward unilateralism generally on a wide range of matters. From this perspective, fairly or unfairly, the U.S. reluctance to accept full application of 1949 Geneva Convention III to those particular prisoners was regarded as one more example of a selective approach to international law.

In the first year of its war on terror, especially in the early handling of prisoner issues in Afghanistan and at Guantanamo Bay, the Bush administration's expression of policies on certain laws-of-war issues was at times hesitant and unskillful. It would be easy to attribute this pattern to the administration's alleged general ideological hostility toward international agreements. Some other explanations may carry more weight, however. The

United States has a record of concern stretching back decades about the ways in which international humanitarian law has been developing, especially with regard to terrorism, as well as with regard to the rules about what is a legitimate target. The Bush administration was right that certain aspects of the law, including aspects of the POW regime, were not appropriate for the treatment of alleged terrorists. Part of the explanation for the administration's failure to handle the particular question of the status of detainees effectively may lie quite simply in the fact that it was proceeding in a reactive manner. In addition, there appears to have been insufficient consultation with the military's own legal specialists.

Whatever the defects of the Bush administration's response, the professionalism of the U.S. armed forces, coupled with the effect of criticism within and beyond the United States, led to policy and practice on the prisoner issues evolving in a generally sensible direction. This evolution has been ad hoc and incomplete. In general, there have been no major public doctrinal statements from the U.S. government on how the laws of war apply to the war on terror—perhaps because application of those laws can indeed be complicated and policymakers do not wish to foreclose options.

This war occasioned a greater degree of tension between the United States on one hand and international humanitarian and human rights bodies on the other than any of the wars of the post–cold war period. The handling of certain laws-of-war issues by the ICRC and various other humanitarian organizations left much to be desired. It was natural that they should be nervous about the U.S. administration's view of international humanitarian law and that they should press for full implementation of that law, especially in relation to prisoners. They were on legally dubious ground, however, in their pressure to regard detainees as entitled to POW status and in their denial that there could be a category of "unlawful belligerents." They missed a major opportunity to point out the relevance of certain provisions of 1977 Protocol I to persons not entitled to POW status. Overall, although the stance of such bodies led to certain useful clarifications of U.S. policy, it also may have had the regrettable effect of reinforcing U.S. concerns (well publicized in debates about the International Criminal Court) about zealous international lawyers standing in unsympathetic judgement on the actions of U.S. forces.

Returning to the four questions set out at the beginning of this chapter, the foregoing account suggests the following responses.

First, according to a strict interpretation of their terms, the main treaties relating to the conduct of international armed conflict are formally and fully applicable to counterterrorist military operations only when those operations have an interstate character. Where counterterrorist operations are simply part of a civil war, the parties must apply, at a minimum, the rules applicable to civil wars. Where operations are simply part of a state's policing, and not part of an armed conflict that would bring the laws of war into play, the laws of war are not formally in force.

Second, in counterterrorist military operations, certain phases and situations may be different from what the main treaties on the laws of war envisaged. They may differ from the provisions for both international and noninternational armed conflict. Recognizing that there are difficulties in applying international rules in the special circumstances of counterterrorist war, the attempt nevertheless can and should be made to apply the law to the maximum extent possible. At the very least, it has considerable value as a blueprint or template. This conclusion is reinforced by decisions of commissions of inquiry, certain resolutions of the UN Security Council, some doctrine and practice of states (including the United States), and considerations of reciprocity and prudence. In the war on terror, although there have been shortcomings in the interpretation and application of existing law by governments and by humanitarian organizations, much of what has been done has been within the framework of the law and has confirmed its relevance.

Third, although the great majority of prisoners taken in war are regarded as qualifying for POW status, in a counterterrorist war—as in other armed conflicts—there are likely to be individuals and even whole classes of prisoner who do not meet the treaty-defined criteria for such status. A procedure outlined in treaty law and in U.S. military manuals is that in case of doubt about their status such people should be accorded the treatment, but not the status, of a POW until a tribunal convened by the captor determines the status to which the individual is entitled. In a struggle involving an organization that plainly does not meet the criteria (especially where, as with al-Qaeda, it is not in any sense a state), however, it may be reasonable to proclaim that captured members cannot be considered for POW status. In cases in which it is determined that certain detainees are not POWs, nonetheless certain fundamental rules are applicable to their treatment, including those outlined in Article 75 of 1977 Geneva Protocol I; there also is a tradition of applying basic norms of the POW regime. Any prisoner, whether classified as a POW or not, can be tried for offenses, including those against international law.

Fourth, there is a case for consideration of further revision of existing law. Suggestions that the existing laws of war are generally out of date in the face of the terrorist challenge are wide of the mark. However imperfect, the law has played—and will continue to play—an important part in influencing the conduct of the war on terror. There has been neither a serious suggestion that the existing legal framework should be abandoned nor substantial proposals for an alternative set of rules. Some modest evolutionary changes in the law can be envisaged, however—for example, regarding conditions of application, classification, and treatment of detainees, the difficult problem of how to respond to suicide bombers, problems of targeting, and possible new rules regarding remnants of war. Application of the law to noninternational armed conflicts is another area in which there has been much development since 1990, and more may be anticipated. Some changes in some of these areas may require a formal negotiating process. Some, however, may be achieved—indeed, may have been achieved—by the practice of states and international bodies, including through explicit and internationally accepted derogations from particular rules that are manifestly inappropriate to the circumstances at hand, as well as through the application of rules in situations significantly different from interstate war.

Notes

Copyright © Adam Roberts, 2002, 2003. This chapter is a revised version of "Counter-Terrorism, Armed Force and the Laws of War," *Survival* 44, no. 1 (spring 2002): 7–32. It incorporates information available up to July 9, 2003. I am grateful for help I received from a large number of people who read drafts, including particularly Dr. Dana Allin, Dr. Kenneth Anderson, Dr. Mary-Jane Fox, Col. Charles Garraway, Richard Guelff, and Commander Steven Haines; participants at the Carr Centre conference on "Humanitarian Issues in Military Targeting," Washington D.C., March 7–8, 2002; and participants at the U.S. Naval War College conference on "International Law and the War on Terrorism," Newport, R.I., June 26–28, 2002. A fuller version appeared in 2003 as volume 79 of the U.S. Naval War College series of *International Law Studies*. Versions of this chapter also have appeared on the website of the Social Science Research Council, New York, www.ssrc.org.

1. For texts of treaties and other international documents on terrorism and useful discussion thereof, see esp. Rosalyn Higgins and Maurice Flory (eds.), *Terrorism and International Law* (London: Routledge, 1997). For more recent treaties and UN resolutions, see the information on terrorism on the UN website, www.un.org.

2. "Crimes against humanity," defined in the Charter and Judgment of the International Military Tribunal at Nuremburg in 1945–46, are more fully defined in Article 7 of the 1998 Rome Statute of the International Criminal Court, which entered into force on July 1, 2002. This statute does not apply retroactively. On May 6, 2002, the United States informed the Depositary that it did not intend to become a party to the treaty and accordingly has no legal obligations arising from its signature.

3. Full titles, texts, and sources of treaties on the laws of war mentioned in this chapter appear in Adam Roberts and Richard Guelff (eds.), *Documents on the Laws of War*, 3d ed. (Oxford: Oxford University Press, 2000); and in Dietrich Schindler and Jiri Toman (eds.), *The Laws of Armed Conflicts: A Collection of Conventions, Resolutions and Other Documents*, 3d ed. (Dordrecht, The Netherlands: Martinus Nijhoff, 1988). Treaty texts also are available at the International Committee of the Red Cross website, www.icrc.org/eng.

4. For an authoritative account of the origins and meanings of Common Article 1, see Frits Kalshoven, "The Undertaking to Respect and Ensure Respect in All Circumstances: From Tiny Seed to Ripening Fruit," in *Yearbook of International Humanitarian Law*, vol. 2, 1999 (The Hague: T. M. C. Asser Press, 2000), 3–61.

5. Chairman of the Joint Chiefs of Staff Instruction, *Standing Rules of Engagement for U.S. Forces*, Ref. CJCSI 3121.01A, 15 January 2000, A-9. Several other U.S. military-doctrinal statements are equally definite that U.S. forces will always apply the law of armed conflict.

6. With regard to the *jus ad bellum* issues raised after September 11, 2001, my own views are in favor of the legality and, indeed, the overall moral justifiability of the U.S.-led military action in Afghanistan.

7. Geneva Convention III Relative to the Treatment of Prisoners of War, Articles 4(B)(2) and 122. See also the references to "neutral and other States not Parties to the conflict" in 1977 Geneva Protocol I Additional to the Geneva Conventions of 12 August 1949, and Relating to the Protection of Victims of International Armed Conflicts, Articles 9, 19, 31, etc.

8. Opening statement at Pentagon news briefing, December 4, 2001; available at U.S. Department of Defense website, www.defenselink.mil/news/Dec2001.

9. U.S. Army, *The Law of Land Warfare*, FM 27–10, Department of the Army Field Manual, Washington D.C., July 1956 (revised July 15, 1976), paragraph 41.

10. U.S. Army, *The Law of Land Warfare*, FM 27–10, paragraph 3. A subsequent official U.S. exposition of the principle states, "Only that degree and kind of force, not otherwise prohibited by the law of armed conflict, required for the partial or complete submission of the enemy with a minimum expenditure of time, life and physical resources may be applied." U.S. Navy, *The Commander's Handbook of the Law of Naval Operations*, NWP 1–14M, Department of the Navy, 1995, paragraph 5.2.

11. I discuss U.S. and NATO strategic doctrine briefly in this chapter in the section on "War in Afghanistan."

12. By contrast, "antiterrorism" has been defined as "defensive measures to reduce the vulnerability of individuals and property to terrorist attacks." Both definitions are from U.S. Army, *Operational Law Handbook (2002)*, International and Operational Law Department, Judge Advocate General's School, U.S. Army, Charlottesville, Va., issued 15 June 2001, ch. 18, p. 3. This annual publication is available at www.jagcnet.army.mil/JAGCNETInternet/Homepages/AC/CLAMO-Public.nsf.

13. In ratifying 1977 Geneva Protocol I in 1998, the United Kingdom made a statement that the term "armed conflict" denotes "a situation which is not constituted by the commission of ordinary crimes including acts of terrorism whether concerted or in isolation."

14. Geneva Protocol II Additional to the Geneva Conventions of 12 August 1949, and Relating to the Protection of Victims of Non-International Armed Conflicts, Article 1.

15. For fuller discussion and evidence that concern about the hazards of coping with terrorism in a laws-of-war framework is not new, see Adam Roberts, *Terrorism and International Order*, Chatham House Special Paper, ed. Lawrence Freedman, Christopher Hill, Adam Roberts, R. J. Vincent, Paul Wilkinson, and Philip Windsor (London: Routledge & Kegan Paul, 1986), esp. 14–15.

16. President Reagan's letter of transmittal of 1977 Geneva Additional Protocol II to U.S. Senate. Treaty Doc. No. 2, 100th Congress, 1st Session, at III (1987), reprinted in *American Journal of International Law* 81, no. 4 (October 1987): 910–12.

17. Robert Thompson, *Defeating Communist Insurgency: Experiences from Malaya and Vietnam* (London: Chatto & Windus, 1966), 52. From 1957 to 1961 the author was successively Deputy Secretary and Secretary for Defence in Malaya. In the course of the Malayan Emergency there were certain derogations from human rights standards, including detentions and compulsory relocations of villages.

18. *Report of the Committee of Privy Counsellors Appointed to Consider Authorized Procedures for the Interrogation of Persons Suspected of Terrorism*, Cmnd. 4901, Her Majesty's Stationery Office, London, 1972, pp. 1–2 and 11–23. The UK government's acceptance of this approach was only a decision, not a complete solution to a matter that continued to be contentious.

19. Two key directives issued by U.S. Military Assistance Command, Vietnam, on the question of eligibility for POW status are Annex A, "Criteria for Classification and Disposition of Detainees," part of Directive 381–46 (December 27, 1967); and Directive 20–5 (March 15, 1968), "Inspections and Investigations: Prisoners of War—Determination of Eligibility." Both

were reprinted in *American Journal of International Law* 62, no. 4 (October 1968): 766–75. The quotation is on p. 767.

20. For details of the case see *Israel Yearbook on Human Rights 1983*, vol. 13, 360–64 (Tel Aviv: Tel Aviv University Faculty of Law, 1984).

21. UN Security Council Resolution 1193 of August 28, 1998, passed unanimously. Identical wording had been used in Security Council Resolution 764 of July 13, 1992, on the war in Bosnia and Herzegovina. This wording did not necessarily mean that the Security Council considered any prisoners taken in these wars to have the full status of prisoners of war, but it implied that they should receive humane treatment in accord with international standards.

22. See esp. Hans-Peter Gasser, "Internationalized Non-International Armed Conflicts: Case Studies of Afghanistan, Kampuchea and Lebanon," *American University Law Review* 33, no. 1 (fall 1983): 145–61.

23. Afghanistan nonetheless is bound by the complete prohibition on possession and use of biological weapons in the 1972 Biological Weapons Convention, which it ratified on March 26, 1975. It is not a party to the 1993 Chemical Weapons Convention, which it signed on January 14, 1993, but has not ratified.

24. The principle of discrimination, which is about the selection of weaponry, methods, and targets, includes the idea that noncombatants and those *hors de combat* should not be deliberately targeted.

25. President Bush, televised address announcing start of military strikes in Afghanistan, October 7, 2001. Text published in *International Herald Tribune* (October 8, 2001), 3. Text also available at www.whitehouse.gov/news/releases/2001/10/20011007-8.html.

26. Richard Myers, interview with *This Week* on ABC TV (October 21, 2001), available at www.defenselink.mil/news/Oct2001/briefings.html.

27. Remarks outside ABC-TV Studio (October 28, 2001), available at www.defenselink. mil/news/Oct2001/briefings.html.

28. These preliminary figures come from interviews in the United States in March 2002 and from Eric Schmitt, "Improved U.S. Accuracy Claimed in Afghan Air War," *New York Times*, 9 April 2002, A-16 (reporting on a detailed Pentagon assessment).

29. Correspondence between ICRC and U.S. Department of Defense, also UK Secretary of State for Defence, November 2001.

30. On March 19, 2002, a CNN report datelined Washington stated that a preliminary Pentagon investigation into the bombings of the ICRC warehouse indicated that numerous clerical errors had led to the mistaken bombings; that the U.S. commander in charge of the air campaign, Lt. Gen. Charles Wald, had "exceeded his authority in ordering the strike" of October 26; and that a key issue was that although the target had been placed on a "No Strike List" at the Pentagon, it was inadvertently left off a separate "No Strike List" maintained by the U.S. Central Command in Tampa, Florida.

31. See, e.g., the early reports by Richard Lloyd Parry and Justin Huggler in *The Independent*, London, 2 December 2001; also available at www.independent.co.uk.

32. Dexter Filkins, "Flaws in U.S. Air War Left Hundreds of Civilians Dead," *New York Times*, 21 July 2002.

33. Marc W. Herold, "A Dossier on Civilian Victims of U.S. Aerial Bombing of Afghanistan: A Comprehensive Accounting," 19 December 2001, available at University of New Hampshire website, http://pubpages.unh.edu/~mwherold/. There are updates on this site. For a strong critique, see the paper by Jeffrey C. Isaac of Indiana University, "Civilian Casualties in Afghanistan: The Limits of Herold's "Comprehensive Accounting," 10 January 2002, available at www. indiana.edu/~iupolsci/doc/doc.htm. In August 2002 Herold stated that "the figure for the October to December period should have been between 2,650 and 2,970 civilian deaths" and that "between 3,125 and 3,620 Afghan civilians were killed between October 7 and July 31." Marc W. Herold, "Counting the Dead," *The Guardian* (London), 8 August 2002, 17.

34. Interview on C-SPAN, 8 January 2002, available at www.defenselink.mil/news/Jan2002/briefings.html.

35. Dexter Filkins, "Flaws in U.S. Air War Left Hundreds of Civilians Dead," *New York Times*, 21 July 2002.

36. *Afghan Portraits of Grief: The Civilian/Innocent Victims of U.S. Bombing in Afghanistan* (San Francisco: Global Exchange, 2002), 3. This short (sixteen-page) report was based on a survey conducted by a five-person team between March and June 2002. It emphasizes that "it was impossible for our survey to be exhaustive and comprehensive" and that the figure of 824 "represents only a portion of civilian casualties" (pp. 3 and 6). It called on the U.S. government to establish an Afghan Victims Fund. Report available at www.globalexchange.org.

37. Geneva Protocol I, Article 52(2). Declarations made by states that have a bearing on their understanding of this article include those by Australia, Belgium, Canada, Germany, Ireland, Italy, the Netherlands, Spain, and the UK. Texts in *Documents on the Laws of War*, 500–11.

38. U.S. Army, *Operational Law Handbook (2002)*, ch. 2, p. 11.

39. Major Jeanne M. Meyer, "Tearing Down the Façade: A Critical Look at the Current Law on Targeting the Will of the Enemy and Air Force Doctrine," *Air Force Law Review* 51 (2001): 166 and 181.

40. Richard Norton-Taylor, "Afghanistan Littered with 14,000 Unexploded Bomblets, Says UN," *The Guardian* (London), 23 March 2002, 18.

41. U.S. Department of State, "Fact Sheet: U.S. Humanitarian Demining Assistance to Afghanistan," Washington D.C., 30 July 2002, available at www.state.gov.

42. Barton Gellman and Thomas E. Ricks, "U.S. Concludes Bin Laden Escaped at Tora Bora Fight," *Washington Post,* 17 April 2002, A1.

43. See, e.g., Carlotta Gall's report from Sebarghan, "Long Journey to Prison Ends in Taliban Deaths: Many Suffocated in Sealed Ship Containers," *International Herald Tribune*, 11 December 2001, 4; and Rory Carroll's report from Kabul, "Afghan Jailers Beat Confessions from Men," *The Guardian* (London), 28 December 2001, 13.

44. Dexter Filkins, "3,000 Forgotten Taliban, Dirty and Dying," *International Herald Tribune,* London, 15 March 2002, 1.

45. Press briefing with General Pace, 30 November 2001, available at www.defenselink.mil/news/Nov2001/briefings.html.

46. International and Operations Law Division—HQ U.S.AF/JAI, *Summary of Legal Issues Relevant to Terrorism Incidents of 11 Sep 01*, Pentagon, Washington D.C., 21 September 2001 [unpublished], 5–6.

47. Geneva Convention III, Articles 99–104. The separate subject of sanctions with respect to offenses against prison camp discipline is covered in Articles 89–98. With regard to judicial proceedings against detainees who do not have POW status, see below.

48. Professor Howard Levie, who has written extensively on the law relating to POWs, suggests that being of a different nationality from that of the army in which one serves would not prevent a combatant from having POW status, but he is more doubtful about spies and saboteurs when they are not operating openly and in uniform. Howard S. Levie, *Prisoners of War in International Armed Conflict,* U.S. Naval War College International Law Studies, vol. 59 (Newport, R.I.: Naval War College Press, 1978), 74–84.

49. U.S. Army, *Operational Law Handbook* (2002), ch. 2, p. 16. See also U.S. Navy, *Commander's Handbook of the Law of Naval Operations,* paragraphs 11.7 and 12.7.1.

50. *U.S. Supreme Court Reports,* book 87, case 317, pp. 4, 5, 14, 16, etc.

51. The classic article on the subject is Richard R. Baxter, "So-called 'Unprivileged Belligerency': Spies, Guerrillas and Saboteurs," in *British Year Book of International Law 1951,* vol. 28 (London: Oxford University Press, 1952), 323–45. Baxter's key conclusion is that this large category of hostile conduct is not per se violative of any positive prohibition of interna-

tional law, but it does expose those engaging in it to trial and punishment by the enemy, for example under the enemy's own laws and regulations. In the years since he wrote this, many terrorist acts have been prohibited in international law, so the category is not necessarily appropriate for those suspected of involvement in terrorism.

52. U.S. Army, *Operational Law Handbook* (2002), ch. 2, pp. 6, 16 and 26; and U.S. Navy, *Commander's Handbook of the Law of Naval Operations,* paragraph 12.7.1.

53. Articles 45 and 75 are among the many articles of the 1977 Geneva Protocol I that the United States regards as "either legally binding as customary international law or acceptable practice though not legally binding." U.S. Army, *Operational Law Handbook* (2002), ch. 2, p. 5.

54. One of the few U.S. publications to note the potential applicability and value of Article 75 was Lee A. Casey, David Rivkin, and Darin R. Bartram, *Detention and Treatment of Combatants in the War on Terrorism* (Washington, D.C.: Federalist Society for Law and Public Policy Studies, 2002). It was published in early 2002, before the White House announcement of February 7. The text also can be found at www.fed-soc.org.

55. News briefing, 11 January 2002, available at www.defenselink.mil/news/Jan2002/briefings.

56. See, e.g., Steven Erlanger, "Europeans Take Aim at U.S. on Detainees," *International Herald Tribune,* 24 January 2002, 1 and 4.

57. See Thom Shanker and Katharine Q. Seelye, "Behind-the-Scenes Clash Led Bush to Reverse Himself on Applying Geneva Conventions," *New York Times,* 22 February 2002.

58. News briefing, 22 January 2002, available at www.defenselink.mil/news/Jan2002/briefings.

59. White House, Office of the Press Secretary, "Fact Sheet: Status of Detainees at Guantanamo," 7 February 2002, 1.

60. Ibid., 2. The privileges cited are outlined in 1949 Geneva Convention III, Articles 28, 60, 64–65, and 72.

61. Statement by White House Press Secretary Ari Fleischer, 7 February 2002, 4.

62. "Bush Decision on Detainees Fails to Satisfy Red Cross," *International Herald Tribune* (London), 9–10 February 2002. See also ICRC, communication to the press 02/11, 9 February 2002, available at www.icrc.org.

63. See, e.g., the article by the executive director of Human Rights Watch, Kenneth Roth, "Bush Policy Endangers American and Allied Troops," *International Herald Tribune* (Paris), 5 March 2002, and various other statements on the Human Rights Watch website, www.hrw.org. Also Amnesty International's long and detailed "Memorandum to U.S. Government on the Rights of People in U.S. Custody in Afghanistan and Guantanamo Bay," 15 April 2002, available at the Amnesty International website, www.amnesty.org.uk.

64. Geneva Convention III, Article 17. Jakob Kellenberger, president of the ICRC, pointed out that there was nothing in humanitarian law to stop a prisoner being questioned but that he could not be forced to answer. "If he does not want to answer, that is his right. Under any system, you cannot do anything to people to make them speak. It is a non-issue." Reuter report from Geneva, "ICRC Rejects Talk of Geneva Conventions Review," 21 March 2002.

65. Geneva Convention III, Article 102. This appears to be the relevant article of the Convention as far as trials for crimes committed before capture are concerned. (The distinct subject of POW discipline issues is addressed in Article 82.) See Jean S. Pictet (ed.), *Commentary on Geneva Convention III* (Geneva: ICRC, 1960), 406 and 470–71. Unfortunately, Pictet fails to consider precapture crimes other than war crimes.

66. The normal appeal procedure for U.S. armed forces personnel is through the appellate court of each service, then through the U.S. Court of Appeals for the Armed Forces, and then on to the Supreme Court.

67. President Franklin D. Roosevelt, Proclamation No. 2561, 2 July 1942, "Denying Certain Enemies Access to the Courts of the United States," *Federal Register* 7 (July 7, 1942), 5,103. On this and other cases of U.S.-established military commissions, see the Congressional Research Service paper, *Terrorism and the Law of War: Trying Terrorists as War Criminals be-*

fore Military Commissions (updated 11 December 2001), order code RL31191 (Washington, D.C.: Congressional Research Service, 2001), 18–26 and 46–48.

68. President George W. Bush, Military Order of 13 November 2001, "Detention, Treatment and Trial of Certain Non-Citizens in the War against Terrorism," Sections 1(e), 1(f), 3, and 4(b) and (c); Federal Register 66, no. 222 (November 16, 2001): 57,833. Text available at the Federal Register website, www.access.gpo.gov/su_docs/aces/aces140.html.

69. For a useful exploration see David Scheffer, *Options for Prosecuting International Terrorists,* special report (Washington, D.C.: U.S. Institute for Peace, 14 November 2001).

70. Statements by president's counsel, Alberto Gonzalez, in address to American Bar Association meeting, 30 November 2001, as cited in *American Society of International Law Newsletter* (November–December 2001), 12.

71. Department of Defense, Military Commission Order No.1, "Procedures for Trials by Military Commissions of Certain Non-United States Citizens in the War Against Terrorism," 21 March 2002, available at www.defenselink.mil/news/Mar2002/d20020321ord.pdf.

72. Geneva Protocol I, Article 75(4)(j). The Pentagon's detailed regulations provide for a post-trial review panel to which the defense can make written submissions, not for a full-blown appeal procedure. A further reservation about the regulations concerns the role of the defense counsel, who would be excluded with the accused from closed sessions; only an "assigned" defense counsel would be present at such sessions, and this assigned counsel would be forbidden to speak with the co-counsel or the accused.

73. Ambassador Prosper speaking in London, 20 September 2002. Owen Boycott, "Guantanamo Britons Still a Threat, says U.S.," *The Guardian* (London), 21 September 2002, 23.

nine

PSYCHOLOGICAL-POLITICAL INSTRUMENTS

Carnes Lord

The war against international terrorism has an important psychological dimension. Indeed, it becomes clearer with each passing day that in such a war military force may turn out to play a far less important role than many people originally thought, given the political and operational limitations on projecting American military power into the Islamic world and the elusive nature of the foe. In the short run, the United States must speak persuasively to foreign governments about mutual interests to enlist their cooperation in vital law enforcement measures and military and intelligence operations. In the longer run, however, whether we are able to achieve anything of enduring benefit will depend to a large extent on our ability to speak persuasively to the people who support or tolerate those governments and above all, of course, the people of the Arab world and the larger community of Islam.

The war on terrorism bears some resemblance to the early years of the cold war, when the ideological dimension of the East-West conflict was especially pronounced and the United States created specialized instruments to wage it. These instruments included the United States Information Agency, Radio Free Europe/Radio Liberty, military special operations and psychological operations forces, covert propaganda and influence capabilities, and, not least, a Psychological Strategy Board in the White House to provide high-level direction and coordination. The religious-ideological commitment of bin Laden-style terrorism constitutes one of its critical strengths, and the United States must devise strategies to counter it, much as it set out during the cold war to counter the ideological appeal of militant Marxism-Leninism.[1]

More precisely, the threat posed by bin Laden and his al-Qaeda movement is a global form of revolutionary guerrilla warfare that bears direct comparison with Communist-inspired revolutionary warfare in Algeria, Malaya, Vietnam, and elsewhere throughout the developing world in the decades following World War II.[2] It employs sophisticated intelligence tradecraft to build clandestine networks of funding and support throughout the world and to penetrate legitimate institutions—particularly educational and religious institutions but also businesses—to spread its message, gain supporters, and prepare operations. Militant Islamist ideology is the glue that holds these networks together, allowing them to operate as relatively autonomous cells but with shared objectives in spite of the ethnic and national diversity of their membership.

The unique challenge the United States and its allies face in the current situation (though it resembles classic counterinsurgency strategy in revolutionary warfare) is the need to isolate militant Islam from the larger "sea" of Islam in which it hides and finds support. The strategy this requires is not merely informational, and it is not properly characterized as psychological. It is political in a broad sense. Recognizing the ill-defined and generally unsatisfactory state of terminology in this too often neglected field, I refer here to the "psychological-political" dimension of the terror war.

The Psychological-Political Instrument

Psychological-political activities may be undertaken by states or nonstate organizations, in peacetime or war. They may be directed at neutral or friendly parties as well as adversaries. The fundamental aim of psychological-political action may be said to be the projection of strategic influence. In a sense, of course, every action of every tool of government policy overseas creates or projects a kind of influence; for that matter, so too does the very character of a state: its ruling regime and institutions, its political leaders and elites, and, not infrequently, its culture. The United States is uniquely influential abroad because of what it is more than what it says—because of its universally recognized commitment to democracy and individual freedom. It also exercises enormous indirect influence through its vital role in the global economy (for example, in the international financial institutions) and the products of its popular culture. In this context, the deliberate projection of strategic influence as a matter of government policy may be able to achieve relatively little, particularly where it runs athwart such massive realities. Nevertheless, it also may be able to leverage them powerfully to advance the nation's interests by reinforcing, reinterpreting, or shaping in various ways foreign perceptions of its character and actions.

Psychological-political action is related to, though distinct bureaucratically from, the public affairs function on one hand and, on the other hand, from military activities (such as port visits) or humanitarian operations undertaken in substantial measure with a view to their psychological or political effect. Psychological-political activities fall under the purview of no single agency of government and in fact tend to cut across departmental jurisdictions. They may be grouped in the following major categories: public diplomacy, information operations, and covert political action.

Public diplomacy is a term that took hold in the United States in the 1970s to describe an array of government programs in the general areas of overseas communication, education and cultural exchange, and overt political action. Until recently, these programs were carried out primarily by the United States Information Agency (USIA) and Radio Free Europe/Radio Liberty (RFE-RL). In 1999, however, USIA was abolished as a separate entity; its function and parts of its organization were absorbed by the State Department under a new Under Secretary for Public Affairs and Public Diplomacy.[3] At the same time, U.S. overseas broadcasting was reorganized under a new, virtually autonomous Broadcasting Board of Governors (BBG) whose membership is drawn mostly from the private sector. In particular, the Voice of America (VOA) was removed from the control of the director of USIA (and the indirect influence of his superior, the Secretary of State) and established as a separate entity reporting only to the BBG. RFE-RL, founded as a "surrogate" broadcasting operation to Soviet-dominated Eastern Europe and the Soviet Union itself,[4] survived the end of the cold war (it continues to broadcast to much of its original audience, at the invitation of their newly democratic governments) but has reoriented itself increasingly to the Middle East. It now operates stations directed toward Iraq, Iran, and (since January 2002) Afghanistan.

The term *political action* covers activities designed to influence political groups and processes abroad. At one time, the Central Intelligence Agency (CIA) took a leading role in this area, but this is much less the case today—especially since the establishment in the 1980s of the National Endowment for Democracy (NED) and its affiliated institutes operated by the Democratic and Republican parties as well as American business and labor organizations. "Nation-building" can be considered a form of political action. The reconstitution of the government of Afghanistan following the fall of the Taliban is a good example of this type of action, and it underlines its strategic importance. Political action in this sense draws not only on military and diplomatic personnel but on resources from government agencies that are not normally involved in foreign affairs.[5]

Within the Defense Department, "information operations" (IO) is a recently coined term of art reflecting the enhanced importance in contemporary military affairs of advanced computer and communications technologies, though with a significantly wider bearing as well. It encompasses electronic warfare, computer network defense/attack, psychological operations (psyop), military deception, and operational security. Whether information operations constitutes a truly integrated discipline, however, may be doubted. Most problematic is the status of psychological operations. Psyop is a longstanding military specialty that currently is embedded in the special operations community; proponency for IO as a whole, on the other hand, rests with the U.S. Strategic Command (since its recent merger with U.S. Space Command, IO's former home). Although there has been some discussion of the potential of Internet-based psyop,[6] the traditional psyop media remain leaflets, loudspeakers, and radio and television broadcasting. The Fourth Psychological Operations Group (POG), based at Fort Bragg, North Carolina, is an active-duty Army unit that is responsible for developing and producing psyop materials and supporting the requirements of joint commanders in the field for communicating with enemy forces or populations. The Air Force also has an important role, both in airdropping psyop leaflets and in radio and TV broadcasting from Commando Solo—a squadron of six specially configured EC-130 aircraft operated by the Pennsylvania Air National Guard.[7]

For the most part, psychological operations (in spite of the overtones of this perhaps unfortunate term) are straightforward, simple, and highly tactical—for example, inducements to surrender or warnings to the civilian population to clear an area that is about to be assaulted. On the other hand, to the extent that they do aim for more strategic effects, they quickly become policy sensitive and tend to attract the attention of high-level civilian officials. Experience has shown that coordination of psyop campaigns can be bureaucratically difficult. It is far from clear whether or how the new IO concept can ameliorate such problems.[8]

In fact, there is a large gray area on the boundary between psyop and public diplomacy that has long complicated the institutional handling of these matters. At the strategic level, much of psyop is hard to distinguish from what might be called defense public diplomacy. This is a function that from time to time has taken on a separate existence in the Office of the Secretary of Defense, most recently during the 1991 Gulf War.[9] Typically, it has involved validation and declassification of intelligence, preparation of talking points and other materials explaining and defending current policies, organization of conferences and briefings, and—not least important—systematic counterpropaganda and counterdisinformation activities. The last of these activities was of considerable importance during the Desert Shield phase of the Gulf War in limiting the damage to the allied cause throughout the Muslim world by Saddam Hussein's hyperactive propaganda machine. Unfortunately, for reasons I discuss later in this chapter defense public diplomacy has never been firmly institutionalized in the Defense Department (or anywhere else in the U.S. government).

We come finally to covert political action. In the past, the CIA has conducted a range of covert operations designed to influence foreign political processes, ranging from the subvention of particular politicians or political parties to the orchestration of coups d'état. The CIA also has had the capability to carry out what are known as black propaganda activities, in the form most significantly of press placements and clandestine radio broadcasting operations in support of a foreign client. It is fair to say that the agency has gotten out of much of this business in recent years. Reportedly, its current propaganda unit has fewer than twenty-five people—only a tenth of its capability a decade or so ago.[10] Meanwhile, the terror war has opened significant new opportunities in this area and created unexpected requirements. The CIA's role in establishing contact and working with the leaders of the Northern Alliance and assorted warlords in Afghanistan in Operation Enduring Freedom is widely known, and it clearly contributed importantly to the quick American victory over the Taliban regime. Also widely reported was the CIA's longstanding interest in fomenting a coup against Iraq's Saddam Hussein.[11] These activities combine elements of political action with secret diplomacy and paramilitary support.

To what extent can the psychological-political instrument stand on its own? There is no simple answer to this classic conundrum, but it is vital not to lose sight of the ultimate dependence of public diplomacy and related disciplines on policy—as well as the inevitable tensions between them. Policymakers frequently regard the way policies are packaged and sold as a tertiary issue of little concern to them, yet policy decisions sometimes cause public relations fiascos that outweigh any gains such decisions otherwise might bring. On the other hand, it is too much for public diplomatists to expect policy to be crafted to suit all of their requirements. There is a certain tendency among public diplomacy practitioners—in the United States, at any rate—to seek to maintain a certain distance from day-to-day government policy to avoid giving the impression to their audiences that they are simple propaganda organs. Obviously, there can be great value for government information organizations in fostering a reputation for accurate and objective reporting—as the British Broadcasting Corporation has done over the years, for example. The credibility of such organizations with their audiences is indisputably a very important asset. Yet there also is a danger that credibility may come to be regarded as an end in itself, providing justification for amplifying or excusing critics of government policy or for refusing to engage in "editorializing" on behalf of it—attitudes that have become increasingly common, particularly at the Voice of America, in recent decades.

The credibility issue certainly highlights a fundamental limitation of all government information programs and raises the question of whether at least some forms of public diplomacy could be carried out more effectively by organizations that are not directly associated with governments. Indeed, at its origins the idea of public diplomacy generally was understood to include such efforts, and many government public diplomacy programs today (youth or artistic exchanges, for example) in reality are simply facilitating devices that support the involvement of private citizens in these endeavors. There undoubtedly is much to be said for people-to-people contacts, particularly where intergovernmental relations are sharply antagonistic. On the other hand, it is necessary to recognize that adversarial populations do not always distinguish clearly between official and nonofficial information sources and that governments are rightly concerned to protect their own capabilities for responsive and authoritative communication.

Psychological-Political Instruments in the Terror War

What are the prospects for success in the psychological-political struggle against Islamic terrorism? What strategy is the United States pursuing, and what are its strengths and vulnerabilities?[12]

There can be little question that the United States has joined the contest from a position of severe disadvantage. Edward S. Walker—until recently assistant secretary of state for the Near East—has said that "public diplomacy . . . has been a critical missing link" in U.S. policy toward the Islamic world.[13] The VOA, for example, reaches barely 2 percent of the radio audience in the Arab countries. Until very recently, the American radio presence has been confined to the shortwave band, which is increasingly out of fashion in comparison with medium wave or television; signal quality leaves much to be desired, given the orientation of American transmitters toward the former Communist world, and programming is too stilted and undifferentiated.[14] Integration of USIA into the State Department seems only to have accelerated the declining prestige of public diplomacy and the resources devoted to it. Few ambassadors spend time cultivating opinion leaders or attempting to address broad audiences in their countries. Language, of course, is a major problem. Few American officials are fluent in Arabic or other languages of the Islamic countries, and analytic expertise in them is thin on the ground in all government agencies.[15]

More fundamental, though, are the attitudes toward the United States that increasingly pervade Islamic opinion, both "street" and elite. America is regarded as the patron and protector of Israel and therefore as implacably opposed to fair treatment for the Palestinian people. Although this factor easily can be overrated, it certainly is real and reinforces the perception that an all-powerful America is bent on dominating the Arab Middle East and destroying Islam. Contributing to this perception is the expanded American military presence in Saudi Arabia and the Persian Gulf since the 1991 Gulf War and, more recently, in Afghanistan and Iraq; American (and British) military operations against Saddam Hussein, as well as the Iraq sanctions regime; and, at another level, the negative impact in the region of American popular culture. After the September 2001 terror attacks, bin Laden-style fundamentalism enjoyed a tremendous boost in prestige for its bold challenge to American power in the name of Islam.

This overall picture has led several knowledgeable observers to a position of deep pessimism regarding the ability of the United States to affect contemporary Arab opinion. As Fouad Ajami has put it, "It's hopeless. We will not get a hearing. I think we are deeply alienated from these societies, in the extreme. . . . Our sins are very evident . . . our good deeds are never really taken in, never factored in." In an extended analysis of Qatar-based Al Jazeera—the most popular TV station in the Arab world (its estimated listenership is 35 million people)—Ajami underlines its fundamental hostility to the United States in spite of a veneer of Western-style objective journalism; others have argued that it is a waste of time for American officials to appear there.[16] A widely publicized Gallup poll taken in the Islamic world during December 2001 and January 2002 indicated, among other things, that only 18 percent of those polled believe that the September 11 attacks were carried out by Arabs, that only 9 percent think American military action in Afghanistan is morally justified, and that only 12 percent say the West respects Arab or Islamic values.[17] In any event it is clear that although most Arabs and Muslims do not subscribe to the worldview or terrorist program of Osama bin Laden, there is a well of sympathy in the region for bin Laden's crude anti-Western message—as well as a powerful romantic appeal to his call for jihad.

Nevertheless, it would be a serious mistake simply to write off the West's assets in this contest. In the first place, there is some reason to believe that the impact of the events of September 11 has not been altogether favorable for Islamic fundamentalism. The overthrow of the Taliban regime in Afghanistan, the destruction of key al-Qaeda cadres and infrastructure, and the display of American military reach and competence so graphically demonstrated in the conquest of Iraq clearly have caused at least some people in the Islamic world to think again about the wisdom or morality of bin Ladenism.[18] In Egypt, some Islamist radicals apparently have begun to question the use of violence to advance their cause.[19] Pro-Western, liberal elites in places such as Kuwait (where a movement to impose *shari'a*—Islamic law—was abruptly halted in reaction to them) have been helped.[20] In Iran, popular opinion continues to build against the clerical regime of the Islamic Republic and in favor of America and the West—which helps explain the initial cooperative attitude of the Iranian government toward the U.S. action against the Taliban.[21] In Pakistan, in spite of the apparently entrenched fundamentalist elements there as well as widespread sympathy for the Taliban throughout the tribal areas of the Northwest Frontier, there has been surprisingly little resistance to President Musharraf's U.S.-inspired crackdown on Islamist schools and organizations and some evidence of a backlash against the fundamentalists on the part of ordinary Pakistanis.[22]

Since the events of September 11, the Bush administration has undertaken several measures to strengthen the U.S. government's capabilities for psychological-political conflict. In the immediate aftermath of the attacks, it moved at once to appoint a new director of the VOA, which had generated widespread criticism for its coverage of the Taliban and Islamic terrorism generally. Working in tandem with the British government, the White House also established coalition media centers in Washington, London, and Islamabad to counter more quickly and effectively Taliban and al-Qaeda propaganda,[23] and it began to reach out to audiences throughout the Arab world by offering interviews with senior American officials to Al Jazeera. The State Department—under a newly appointed Under Secretary for Public Affairs and Public Diplomacy recruited from the advertising world, Charlotte Beers—launched an ambitious effort to market the American "brand" of social and political order to the Muslim world and to demonstrate American benevolence toward Islam as a religion.[24] The Defense Department, in a worthy though ill-fated initiative, created a new and generously funded "Office of Strategic Influence" tasked with developing an overarching strategy and programs designed to counter the appeal of radical Islamism. On the ground in (and in the air over) Afghanistan, U.S. psyop troops quickly geared up for a major leaflet and broadcasting campaign intended to facilitate military operations there and begin winning Afghan "hearts and minds."[25] A Radio Free Afghanistan service was started up by RFE-RL in January 2002. Initial steps (notably, the purchase of a 600-kilowatt AM transmitter) also were taken to create an ambitious Arabic-language "Middle East Radio Network" that is intended eventually to improve dramatically American access to radio audiences—particularly young audiences—throughout the Arab world. Known in the region as Radio Sawa ("together" in Arabic), this network went on the air in March 2002; it broadcasts a mix of news, opinion pieces, music, and other features in five Arabic dialects to audiences in Egypt, Sudan, Yemen, Jordan, the Palestinian territories, Iraq, and the Persian Gulf.[26] Finally, U.S. Central Command used psyop extensively as an integral part of its military campaign against Saddam Hussein's Iraq.[27]

If one turns to the actual performance of the United States to date, however, the picture is discouraging. Conceptual and structural problems of very long standing continue to bedevil the American effort. These problems are visible particularly in the VOA's stumbles in the immediate aftermath of September 11 and the fratricide within the Pentagon over the newly created (and now defunct) Office of Strategic Influence. Perhaps most worrisome of all, however, is the failure of the U.S. government as a whole to develop and articulate an overall strategy to shape these various initiatives.

On September 25, 2001, VOA's Pashto service managed to obtain an interview with the Taliban leader, Mullah Mohammed Omar, to comment on President Bush's speech to the nation about the terrorist attacks. The service taped the interview without policy clearance and, when State Department and National Security Council officials got wind of the matter and protested, aired parts of it anyway. In the interview, Omar was of course unapologetic, saying among other things that "America has created the evil that is attacking it." Nor was this an exceptional performance. The day after the attacks on the twin towers, a VOA reporter in London filed a story quoting remarks critical of the United States by Yasir al Serri, identified only as "a leader of Egypt's largest Islamist group, the Gama'a Islamiyya, which has worked to overthrow the Egyptian government." This interview was said to provide "balance" to an interview with a Muslim cleric who had warned against accusing any Islamists or Arab groups of the crime until the full truth was known—apparently an insufficiently radical posture for VOA. What the reporter did not note was that the Gama'a Islamiyya itself is a terrorist organization that has murdered scores of foreign tourists, as well as Egyptian security officials, and is affiliated with al-Qaeda. When called on the story, VOA's news director acknowledged that al Serri had been improperly identified but maintained that interviews with terrorists would continue to be "part of our balanced, accurate, objective and comprehensive reporting, providing our listeners with both sides of the story."[28]

When VOA was created in 1942, its stated mission was to report the truth about the world war in which the United States was then engaged. This mission remains worthy. What it demands, however, is simply straightforward reporting of the news; it has little to do with the recent VOA practice of airing the opinions of persons who wish this country ill in a misguided attempt to "balance"—in effect—sense with nonsense.[29] Something more also is necessary, however. At least in wartime, government broadcasting has to be in the business of actively shaping the attitudes and behavior of enemies and allies alike. At a minimum, this requires selectivity and emphasis in the editing of news that may differ in significant ways from the approach of a commercial news organization. (Note that even commercial news organizations have modified longstanding habits in their coverage of the aftermath of September 11.)[30] It also should require a willingness to convey official statements in a positive spirit and to provide other commentary that presents the policies of the nation favorably.

Although VOA's new director, Robert Reilly, took immediate steps to prevent repetition of these egregious blunders, fundamental changes in the outlook of VOA should not be expected anytime soon. The attitudes on display are deeply rooted in the organization's journalistically oriented culture,[31] as well as in the new governing arrangements put in place after the dissolution of USIA. The Broadcasting Board of Governors is representative of the broadcasting industry more than it is of the U.S. government. In the Omar flap the board reportedly was divided and unable to agree on the proper course and therefore did nothing. It also is necessary to recognize that similar constraints operate with respect to the BBG's other principal broadcasting asset, RFE/RL—in spite of a popular perception of the mission of these services as old-style "propaganda." Radio Free Iran, in particular, has come under attack for embracing too uncritically the so-called moderate wing of Iran's clerical regime.[32]

Reilly's abrupt resignation as VOA director at the end of August 2002 was the culmination of a lengthy struggle with the BBG, reflecting differing visions of the future direction of all U.S. overseas broadcasting. The board looks to a commercial broadcasting model, with particular emphasis on attracting young listeners through popular music and other nonsubstantive programming, whereas Reilly represented a more traditional emphasis on substantive programming (that is, hard news and features with political content) that directly or indirectly supports national policy. The BBG vision not only accepts but promotes a blurring of the traditional identities of VOA and the surrogate radios (already apparent in Radio Sawa), if not their eventual complete privatization, and seems increasingly disinclined to accept direction or oversight of any kind from any component of the U.S. government. The fact that neither the White House nor the Congress seems concerned over (or even fully aware of) this situation is itself a commentary on the low estate of public diplomacy in the policy world of contemporary Washington.

The flap over the Defense Department's Office of Strategic Influence (OSI) points to another—and related—fault line within the bureaucracies responsible for wartime information: the perennial tension between the mission of informing the domestic audience and the mission of managing dissemination of information abroad to serve the strategic goals of a war. The OSI was created by Under Secretary of Defense for Policy Douglas Feith shortly after the September 11 attacks to develop a strategic approach and supporting programs to counter the appeal of radical Islamism within the Muslim world. Its director was Brigadier General Simon P. Worden, a highly respected Air Force officer and expert in information operations in the military sense of the term. As the title of the office suggested—and was meant to suggest—the scope of its activities exceeded public diplomacy as traditionally defined and involved a significant psychological operations and political action component, suggesting that the OSI was interested in reviving the full gamut of psychological-political activities historically practiced within the U.S. government. Not surprisingly, in due course an article appeared in the *New York Times* claiming that the Pentagon was considering providing false information—"disinformation"—to the press as part of its influence campaign.[33] More surprising was that these vague allegations were not promptly quashed by the Pentagon. It soon became apparent that the reason was that they had been leaked to the newspaper, almost certainly by officials in the Pentagon's office of public affairs.[34]

The ensuing media firestorm seems to have caught the Pentagon leadership unprepared. In any event, after repeated denials that anyone in the Defense Department was planning to lie to the press, Secretary Rumsfeld threw in the towel and announced on February 26, 2002, that the OSI could no longer function effectively and was being shut down. A subsequent internal review by the Pentagon's general counsel turned up no proposals using the word "disinformation" (except in the context of countering enemy disinformation) or advocating lying to the press. Instead, according to a variety of published accounts, the OSI was concentrating its efforts on matters such as countering Iranian propaganda against the new Karzai regime in Afghanistan, on reaching the Iraqi people more effectively,[35] and perhaps most notably on weakening the hold of the Islamists on Pakistan's *madrassas* and opening these critical purveyors of terrorist philosophy to Western influence through, among other things, underwriting the purchase of computers and Internet connections. Reportedly, Pakistani President Musharraf was enthusiastic about this program and supported it fully.[36] The OSI's projects seem to have encompassed traditional battlefield psyop but also activities geared to influencing opinion in third countries in the Middle East, Asia, and Western Europe, including campaigns involving foreign media and the Internet. Some small proportion of these activities apparently were intended to be covert.[37]

Policy Lessons

The OSI fiasco reflected not just a bureaucratic turf fight, though it surely was that. It reflected disagreement over the fundamental approach the U.S. government should take to waging information warfare. In contrast to the more strategic and political approach favored by the Pentagon, the State Department and the White House supported a more tactical, media-oriented, and public relations-style effort—as exemplified by the Coalition Information Center initiative. These two approaches are not necessarily in conflict. Indeed, both arguably are necessary to address the problem effectively. The latter approach now dominates the field. The interagency structures intended to coordinate between public affairs, public diplomacy, and military psyop remain in place, but their vital signs are weak.[38] Yet there have been some encouraging developments. The White House has moved to transform the Coalition Information Center into a permanent and fully staffed Office of Global Communications, headed by a counselor to the president; its purpose is not to supplant the activities of other agencies but to add "thematic and strategic value."[39] At the same time, the State Department has acknowledged that a central aspect of a long-term public diplomacy strategy in the Muslim world must involve "supporting the education of the young."[40] And Congress has been very favorable toward significant increases in spending on public diplomacy programs of various kinds.

A central problem with the tactical and media-oriented approach is that the United States has such limited access to media in the Islamic world, as well as such low credibility, that it seems unlikely to have any great impact there (though it would be a mistake to underestimate the potential receptivity of audiences in Iran in particular).[41] Yet its greater weakness is simply its failure to come to grips with the ideological nature of the war on which we have embarked. The key challenge is not to sell the product of American democracy or society to Islamic consumers. Still less is it to convince the Muslim world that the United States does not hate Islam (though it surely is useful to emphasize the reality of religious tolerance in America).[42] The primary challenge is to undermine and ultimately destroy the appeal of radical Islamism and marginalize its terror-minded supporters. This task, however, requires a willingness to engage the Islamic world over an extended period of time—and to do so not merely at the level of information but ideologically and politically.

What are the requirements of such a strategy? Clearly, the United States has to be prepared to challenge the claim of bin Laden and other Islamic extremists to speak for the larger Islamic community. This requires that it not shy away from addressing substantive religious issues, which the U.S. government for obvious reasons has found difficult in the past and has attempted to avoid in its official language identifying the enemy in this war as "terrorism" generically rather than Islamic terrorism. In fact, of course, it is *only* Islamic terrorism that constitutes a serious threat to the United States, and in that sense at least we are indeed at war with Islamism.[43] Recognizing—as we should—that the United States is in a weak position to instruct Muslims in the nature of their faith, nonetheless it is essential for this country and its Western allies to develop a clear picture of the character and essential sources of Islamic terrorism and to be prepared to speak about these things in a serious and nonpolemical way. In some measure, this means being prepared to engage in theological dispute not only with bin Laden but with the nonterrorist conservative Islamic world from which he emerged.[44] In terms of particular nations, it means above all Egypt, Pakistan, and Saudi Arabia. It also means Muslim communities in Africa, Asia, Europe, and the United States itself that have come increasingly under militant Islamist (or, more broadly, Saudi) influence. Ironically, then, and unlike during the cold war, friends rather than adversaries are likely to constitute the primary front of the ideological struggle—in many ways, a more delicate and daunting problem. For many purposes, we clearly will be better served by surrogate spokesmen from the Islamic world—political and religious leaders, academics, journalists, and the like—than by American government officials, for the aforementioned credibility reasons.[45] Of course, mobilizing such spokesmen may be easier said than done.

The question of whether or to what extent "democracy" should be promoted in the Arab or Islamic world as part of our public campaign against terrorism is complicated and cannot be addressed adequately here. Suffice to say that the United States should neither push a "one size fits all" model of democratic governance on its Muslim interlocutors nor ignore democratic aspirations where they exist and can support U.S. policy goals. There seems to be little to be gained, however, by making American-style democracy the center of gravity of our public diplomacy efforts rather than militant Islamism, given the ambivalence with which many people in the Muslim world view the individualism and hedonism they see as inseparable from American political freedoms. This is not to say that we should make no effort to present American society and politics in a favorable light to Muslim audiences or attempt to counter the gross misconceptions and slander against this country pervading the Arab media. Counterdisinformation activities are an essential aspect of any effective public diplomacy or psyop engagement. By itself, however, this effort will not win the war.

Finally, something should be said about the importance of public diplomacy efforts in the non-Muslim world. Throughout the cold war and especially during its endgame in the 1980s, Western Europe was a key battleground for American and Soviet propaganda warriors. Today the Europeans and other key U.S. allies such as Japan have publicly expressed solidarity and support for the global antiterror campaign launched by the Bush administration and have provided important material and moral (including public diplomacy) assistance.[46] At the same time, there are clear differences of interest and perception that have complicated American relations with these allies and with other important countries as the campaign has developed. Notably, these differences have involved matters such as how to deal with the Israeli-Palestinian conflict and whether or how the United States should take action to overthrow the regime of Saddam Hussein. More general European concerns about U.S. "unilateralism" have combined with these disagreements to create levels of distrust and mutual incomprehension that are worrisome and potentially dangerous, particularly if the terror war or our military engagement with Iraq is protracted or takes some bad turns.[47] Traditional diplomacy certainly can help to contain these problems, but public diplomacy also has an important role to play. The United States surely can do better than it has to date in explaining the logic behind its policies and actions to the public and (perhaps especially) to disgruntled political elites in Europe, as well as in countering the crude misconceptions of America that too often are allowed to stand unchallenged in their media. This is partly a matter of clarifying the policy issue of the North Atlantic Treaty Organization's (NATO) role in support of U.S. efforts in the terror war; but it also involves the tone and style of American official commentary on our allies' sometimes exasperating behavior and our own unilateralist prerogatives.

Conclusions

Over the longer run, decisive victory in the war on terrorism will not be possible without the destruction of militant Islamism, or at least the dismantling of its key institutions and other sources of political strength. Any strategy designed to achieve this objective must have multiple dimensions and be global in scope. Such a strategy would seem to have three key parts. The first is informational: a war of ideas geared essentially to making the argument that Islamism is a travesty of Islam itself—reactionary, fascistic, immoral, and uncivilized and a recipe for disaster for the Islamic world as a whole. The second is political-legal: a concerted campaign by governments in the Islamic world and elsewhere (particularly in Europe) to crack down on public advocacy of extreme Islamism and organizations espousing it; this task includes, in particular, better policing of government-controlled media organs in key allied countries such as Egypt and Saudi Arabia. The third is political-institutional: suppression of the Pakistani theological schools (*madrassas*) that have evolved over the years into training and indoctrination centers for al-Qaeda and the Taliban, the purging of Islamist elements from public universities, and the creation where necessary (but notably in Pakistan) of new state-controlled educational institutions that are free of Islamist domination if not influence. I use the terms "suppression" and "purge" deliberately to underline the gravity of this task and the resolution the West and its Muslim allies will need to see it through.

None of this is meant to suggest that U.S. psychological-political strategy should be conceived in wholly ideological terms. Particularly in dealing with the conspiracy-minded and generally very poorly educated and poorly informed populations of the Middle East, more primitive dimensions of feeling must be tapped: fear of loss, hopes of gain, awe at manifestations of unimaginable military power and technological prowess. It is important to reassure innocent populations, as we are doing now in Afghanistan and Iraq, that we intend them no harm and have no interest in remaining on their territory longer than absolutely necessary. It is equally essential to leave no question about our resolve or capacity for violence against terrorists and the regimes that shelter them.

Notes

1. For an overview see Carnes Lord and Frank R. Barnett (eds.), *Political Warfare and Psychological Operations: Rethinking the U.S. Approach* (Washington, D.C.: National Defense University Press, 1989); Carnes Lord, "Public Diplomacy: Past and Future," *Orbis* 42 (winter 1998): 49–72.

2. See Michael Vlahos, *Terrorism's Mask: Insurgency Within Islam* (Laurel, Md.: Johns Hopkins University Applied Physics Laboratory, 2002).

3. For a recent discussion from the State Department perspective, see Christopher Ross, "Public Diplomacy Comes of Age," *The Washington Quarterly* 25 (spring 2002): 75–83.

4. See, notably, Arch Puddington, *Broadcasting Freedom: The Cold War Triumph of Radio Free Europe and Radio Liberty* (Lexington: University Press of Kentucky, 2000).

5. See Kurt M. Campbell and Michéle A. Flournoy, *To Prevail: An American Strategy for the Campaign Against Terrorism* (Washington, D.C.: CSIS Press, 2001), ch. 13.

6. Angela Marie Lungu, "WAR.com: The Internet and Psychological Operations," *Joint Force Quarterly* 28 (spring/summer 2001): 13–17. The media-intensive Kosovo war was the first to involve significant official and nonofficial Internet activity.

7. For a thorough analysis of this relatively antiquated system, see *Report of the Defense Science Board Task Force on the Creation and Dissemination of All Forms of Information in Support of Psychological Operations (PSYOP) in Time of Military Conflict* (Washington, D.C.: Department of Defense, May 2000).

8. For some recent history see Col. Jeffrey B. Jones, "Psychological Operations in Desert Shield, Desert Storm, and Urban Freedom," *Special Warfare* 7 (July 1994): 22–29.

9. J. Michael Waller, "Winning Page from Reagan Playbook," *Insight Magazine*, 20 August 2001.

10. J. Michael Waller, "Losing a Battle for Hearts and Minds," *Insight Magazine*, 22 April 2002.

11. Early in 2002 President Bush apparently signed a new covert action "finding" authorizing American agents to kill Saddam Hussein under certain circumstances as part of such an effort. See Bob Woodward, "President Broadens Anti-Hussein Order," *Washington Post*, 16 June 2002.

12. The discussion that follows has benefited substantially from the research (including extensive interviewing in Washington in early 2002) of CDR Timothy J. Dourey, USN. This assistance is greatly appreciated.

13. Quoted in Robert G. Kaiser, "U.S. Message Lost Overseas," *Washington Post*, 15 October 2001.

14. Listeners complain about "condescending, irrelevant, and/or outdated programming," as well as about the use of classical Arabic and pure Persian as opposed to country and regional dialects and colloquialisms. Increasingly sophisticated print media in some countries also have made inroads into radio listenership. See Haleh Vaziri, "Significant Trends Facing International

Broadcasters in the Middle East and North Africa in 2000," unpublished paper (Washington, D.C.: Intermedia Survey Institute, 2000).

15. See especially Anthony J. Blinken, "Winning the War of Ideas," *The Washington Quarterly* 25 (spring 2002): 101–14; Campbell and Flournoy, *To Prevail*, ch. 11.

16. Fouad Ajami, "What the Muslim World Is Watching," *New York Times Sunday Magazine*, 18 November 2001. Note also the comments of former U.S. ambassador to Israel Samuel Lewis, in Francine Kiefer and Ann Scott Tyson, "In War of Words, U.S. Lags Behind," *Christian Science Monitor*, 17 October 2001.

17. Andrea Stone, "In Poll, Islamic World Says Arabs Not Involved in 9/11," *USA Today*, 27 February 2002. Although questions have been raised about some aspects of this poll, it remains fair to say that the level of psychological "denial" concerning terrorism in general remains astonishingly high even among relatively educated and pro-Western Arabs.

18. Ben Barber, "Taliban's Defeat, TV Images Boost Support for War," *Washington Times*, 30 November 2001.

19. Howard Schneider, "Egyptian Radicals Veering Away from Violence," *Washington Post*, 12 May 2002.

20. Yaroslav Trofimov, "As a Taliban Regime Falls Inside Afghanistan, So Do Islamic Convictions Outside Its Borders," *Wall Street Journal*, 31 December 2001.

21. In response to this situation (more specifically, the demonstrated weakness of the Khatami government since that time), President Bush has shifted the focus of the United States' Iran policy from diplomacy to public diplomacy. See Glenn Kessler, "U.S. Changes Policy on Iranian Reform," *Washington Post*, 23 July 2002.

22. Yvonne Abraham, "Pakistan Set to Try Again to Curb Schools Run by Clerics," *Boston Globe*, 29 November 2001; Doug Struck, "Religious Radicals Facing Backlash in Pakistan," *Washington Post*, 28 January 2002.

23. Karen DeYoung, "U.S., Britain Step Up War for Public Opinion," *Washington Post*, 1 November 2001.

24. Peter Carlson, "The U.S.A. Account," *Washington Post*, 31 December 2001.

25. See, for example, Bradley Graham, "U.S. Beams Its Message to Afghans," *Washington Post*, 19 October 2001; Greg Jaffe, "Elite Army Psychological Unit Aims a Propaganda Campaign at Afghans," *Wall Street Journal*, 8 November 2001; Philip Smucker, "The U.S. Army's Men in Black . . . Turbans," *Christian Science Monitor*, 30 May 2002.

26. This initiative of a member of the Broadcasting Board of Governors actually predated September 11. See David Rogers, "U.S. Takes Steps to Set Up a Radio Network in Effort to Close Gap with Young Arabs," *Wall Street Journal*, 27 November 2001; Joyce Howard Price, "U.S. to Go On Air in Arabic," *Washington Times*, 25 April 2002.

27. According to Defense Department sources, "any attack would be preceded by covert programs to win the sympathy of some Iraqi military commanders. A war information campaign would make it clear to Iraqi forces that the U.S. intention is to dispose of Saddam, not to rule Iraq." Rowan Scarborough, "Inside Help Against Iraq Weighed," *Washington Times*, 10 June 2002. See further Walter Pincus, "U.S. Plans Appeal to Iraqi Officers," *Washington Post*, 30 September 2002.

28. Quoted in William Safire, "Equal Time for Hitler?" *New York Times*, 20 September 2001. See further Ellen Nakashima, "Broadcast with Afghan Leader Halted," *Washington Post*, 23 September 2001; William Safire, "State Out of Step," *New York Times*, 1 July 2002.

29. Robert Reilly, the new VOA director, put the matter perfectly in an internal memo circulated within hours of taking office: "We are in a war of ideas. We are on one side in that war. The other side presents the United States as the source of all evil in the world and contends, therefore, that it must be destroyed. One of the many differences that characterize our side in the war of ideas is that we are not afraid to tell the truth. Telling the truth requires a great deal more than simply recounting the positions of the various sides in a dispute. It requires an act

of discernment as to the veracity of the contending claims." Cited in Kenneth R. Timmerman, "The Other Air War," *Wall Street Journal*, 9 November 2001.

30. Howard Kurtz, "CNN Chief Orders 'Balance' in War News," *Washington Post*, 31 October 2001; Bill Carter, "CNN, Amid Criticism in Israel, Adopts Terror Report Policy," *New York Times*, 21 June 2002.

31. See Carnes Lord, "In Defense of Public Diplomacy," *Commentary* 77 (April 1984): 42–50. During the 1991 Gulf War, to cite another egregious case, VOA's "balanced" treatment of Saddam Hussein in its Arabic-language service was perceived as so damaging to the coalition that it prompted telephone calls to then-President George H. W. Bush from the leaders of Egypt and Saudi Arabia.

32. Timmerman, "The Other Air War."

33. James Dao and Eric Schmitt, "A Nation Challenged: Hearts and Minds; Pentagon Readies Efforts to Sway Sentiment Abroad," *New York Times*, 19 February 2002.

34. See especially Franklin Foer, "Flacks Americana," *The New Republic*, 20 May 2002.

35. See Michael Gordon, "Radio Transmitter to Oppose Hussein Wins U.S. Backing," *New York Times*, 28 February 2002.

36. See especially Rowan Scarborough, "Rumsfeld Expresses Doubt on New Propaganda Office," *Washington Times*, 25 February 2002; "Rumsfeld Shuts Down Office Criticized for Propaganda Role," *Washington Times*, 27 February 2002; Waller, "Losing a Battle for Hearts and Minds."

37. Eric Schmitt and James Dao, "A 'Damaged' Information Office Is Declared Closed by Rumsfeld," *New York Times*, 27 February 2002. Thomas E. Ricks, "Rumsfeld Kills Pentagon Propaganda Unit," *Washington Post*, 27 February 2002, quotes an unnamed military officer as saying that the new office was involved mainly in "defense marketing" (i.e., defense public diplomacy) and that only 5 percent of its planned work would have involved covert operations. It is important to note that press placements, even those done covertly, are *not* the same as "disinformation"; they may involve stories that are totally "objective" by commercial media standards. In any event, all of these efforts clearly were directed at the foreign press, not the domestic press.

38. On the chronic problem of interagency coordination in this area, see *Report of the Defense Science Board Task Force on Managed Information Dissemination* (Washington, D.C.: Department of Defense, October 2001).

39. Karen DeYoung, "Bush to Create Formal Office to Shape U.S. Image Abroad," *Washington Post*, 30 July 2002.

40. Statement by Charlotte Beers, U.S. Senate Committee on Foreign Relations, *America's Global Dialogue: Sharing American Values and the Way Ahead for Public Diplomacy*, 107th Congress, 2d session, 11 June 2002.

41. The Radio Sawa approach seems especially misguided as applied to Iran, where young people are heavily exposed to Western popular music already but are curious about and quite favorably inclined toward the United States.

42. It is equally effective to remind Muslims of the tolerant character of traditional Islam, as distinct from contemporary Islamism. What must be avoided is to patronize and pander to Muslims. On the missteps of the Beers approach in this regard see particularly Stephen F. Hayes, "Uncle Sam's Makeover," *The Weekly Standard*, 3 June 2002.

43. Andrew Sullivan, "This *Is* a Religious War," *New York Times Sunday Magazine*, 7 October 2001. See also Daniel Pipes, "Aim the War on Terror at Militant Islam," *Los Angeles Times*, 6 January 2002.

44. Some progress is being made in this respect. Muslim scholars recently met with U.S. officials to discuss ways to dissociate the term *jihad* from terrorist activity: Larry Witham, "Muslims See Wordplay as Swordplay in Terrorism War," *Washington Times*, 24 July 2002.

45. David D. Perlmutter and Mustafa Saied, "How to Win the War of Words," *USA Today*,

18 December 2001, make a good case for the centrality of American Muslims in any such effort and provide a cogent statement of key themes.

46. To the latter category belongs invaluable British assistance in the weeks after September 11 in making the public case for a linkage between the terror attacks and Osama bin Laden, as well as more recently in supporting the hard line of the Bush administration toward Iraq.

47. See, for example, Charles Moore, "Our Friends in Europe," *Wall Street Journal*, 8 March 2002.

ten

FOREIGN AID

Patrick M. Cronin

The catastrophic events of September 11, 2001, highlighted the need for intense focus in U.S. foreign aid policies, which far too often had been omnivorous in promises but anorexic in results. In trying to do everything nearly everywhere, American foreign aid had become slave to the conceit that everything was equally important—the classic recipe for losing focus. Several other specific factors also accounted for the problem. First, American foreign assistance remained an incoherent mix of earmarks from Congress and initiatives from the White House. Since the passage of the Foreign Assistance Act of 1961, Congress has added new program earmarks to the development agenda each year (and very few of those initiatives are ever terminated by their supporters). Second, until September 11, 2001, no urgent need to establish clearer priorities had emerged. After the cold war's end, the 1990s saw a steady addition of self-evidently worthy issues—coping with globalization, the AIDS pandemic, gender discrimination, democracy advocacy, and dealing with the information revolution. Each became an important development theme in the post–cold war era, but none compelled a systematic refocusing of existing foreign assistance policy. Most ironically, during the relative prosperity of the 1990s American aid declined in the absence of a dominant foreign policy objective related to the developing world. The unwillingness to set priorities was pervasive, and in the absence of sufficient resources the results were often disappointing.

Focus with respect to September 11 implies concentrating on key geographic areas, countries, and communities in the Islamic world. Yet most aid increases have been directed toward doing more in sub-Saharan Africa, where global challenges such as environmental degradation and infectious diseases are acute national problems. With the exceptions of the al-Qaeda camps in Sudan and the embassy bombings in Kenya and Tanzania, development assistance rather than counterterrorism has remained the primary focus of American engagement in Africa. That is not to say that various humanitarian crises related to the region's conflicts are not serious security concerns, given the risk of state failure in West Africa and the Great Lakes region. Nor does this imply that increased foreign aid to combat terrorist financing in Africa is trivial. In the absence of significant increases in overall aid, however, the U.S. government must make painful and calculated choices.

There are obvious dangers in focusing on the Middle East and South Asia as epicenters of terrorist activity, training, and support when in fact, like many other enterprises, terrorism has gone global. Admittedly there is no more unique a link between terrorism and Islam than there is between terrorism and any other major religious faith: Christianity, Hinduism, Buddhism, and Judaism all have had connections to radical terrorist groups. The hard reality, however, is that the U.S. State Department's list of terrorist organizations currently draws attention to mostly Muslim countries that harbor and aid such groups.

Although strongly condemning the attacks on September 11, most Arab and Muslim governments do not feel that they bear any special responsibility in the war against terrorism.[1] In fact, many people among the general public of those countries perceive the war against terrorism as political cover for a more ambitious U.S. political agenda. For some, the war to oust Saddam Hussein confirmed this perception. Moreover, one Egyptian scholar explains that to the broad public, "the U.S. definition of terrorism does not distinguish between those launching a just armed struggle against the illegal occupation of their land and those using force against elected, legitimate governments."[2] Thus, the perceived double standard in American policy in response to Israeli actions in the West Bank and Gaza Strip acts as political immunization for many Arab and Muslim communities that remain skeptical about the motives of the U.S.-led "war on terrorism." Partly in response to this critical perception in Arab countries—as well as to harness long-term economic policies in support of civil society, economic opportunities, and education—Secretary of State Colin Powell announced a new Middle East Partnership Initiative in December 2002.[3]

Focus means deciding where to invest serious time, money, and effort to achieve the best results and, concomitantly, what to shut down and stop doing to avoid wasting money. In other words, after September 11 new priorities emerged, forcing policymakers—who could no longer pretend that all tasks were equally important—to make a basic choice. Thus, there was a new locus of activity: front-line states, largely in the Muslim world, especially programs tailored to the most critical areas—from rebuilding Afghanistan at one extreme to more narrow niche educational programs in neighboring Pakistan at the other.

Foreign aid is now regarded as an integral part of U.S. national security strategy: The Bush administration introduced it formally into its national security strategy in September 2002, and there is growing public support for increasing assistance levels.[4] Yet most people ignore the absence of a causal link between poverty and terrorism when they profess their newfound support for increased foreign aid. Moreover, little or no distinction is made publicly between development assistance programs that have poverty alleviation as their primary objective and foreign assistance funding that often serves to garner political support from important regional allies. Policymakers spend their time privately reconciling the economic and political aims of foreign aid in an effort to avoid too many tradeoffs.

From a strategic perspective, if foreign aid is to play its part against terrorism it must ensure that there are islands of stability in the developing world and that the roster of failing states does not grow any longer. This task requires addressing failing states with critical humanitarian assistance that also can contain state failure, if not also point to a path of successful development. It also requires making sure that the poor countries of the developing world that want to help themselves receive sufficient development assistance, delivered in a manner most likely to produce sustainable results. Countries that are committed to good governance—political freedom, market reforms, and investing in their own people—need and deserve help in mobilizing resources to address the acute economic problems afflicting their people. To do so, foreign aid first must be reconceptualized to address longstanding development goals in an effective and sustainable manner. Only then will it be able to meet the foreign policy expectations of the American public. A quiet revolution in development assistance continues to unfold, driven by the urgent need to address the growing gap between the industrialized and developing worlds that stems from a global economy. In this context, aid effectiveness is characterized primarily as catalyzing institutional development and policy changes that ultimately will promote and sustain economic growth. The history of foreign aid has shown that economic growth remains the most effective route out of poverty; this reality has not changed in any degree after September 11.

The notion that foreign aid can be an effective tool against terrorism is closely tied to cautions about the "strategic significance" of global inequalities in income levels and economic growth that were made before the events of September 11. Jeffrey Sachs counsels that "as a general proposition, economic failure abroad raises the risk of state failure as well" and warns that "when foreign states malfunction, in the sense that they fail to provide basic public goods for their populations, their societies are likely to experience steeply escalating problems that spill over to the rest of the world, including the United States."[5] The contagion effects associated with nation-state failure (e.g., international criminality, drug trafficking, refugee movements, mass famine, infectious disease, and terrorism) are well documented but not exclusive to failing states. Although failed states are at the nexus of development and security policy, focus should be placed on assisting Arab and Muslim countries that are at risk of developing—or, indeed, may have contracted—one or more of the symptoms of state failure. Such countries present the greater test to decision makers in terms of wielding foreign assistance as an effective instrument of American foreign policy. In this chapter I address two critical questions that are directly related to this challenge:

- What has the role of foreign aid been to date?
- What are the main ways in which foreign aid can help in the war on terrorism?

These questions, of course, are not the only ones, and they are sufficiently broad to encompass many other questions that also deserve attention. They are a starting point, however, for a more informed discussion about how the centrality of fighting terrorism is transforming U.S. foreign assistance policies and practices (as well as addressing which practices should not be changed). There are no easy answers in development; nor are there easy answers in the war on terrorism. The basis for constructive solutions begins, however, with a broad understanding of what we have asked foreign aid to do as an instrument of policy over the past five or more decades.

Foreign Aid as a Policy Instrument

Evolution of U.S. Foreign Aid

Long before grants for project assistance became the mainstay of U.S. foreign aid, the United States sought to use economic instruments of power to shape foreign relations. In the aftermath of World War I, for instance, the United States was an integral actor in determining the reparations to be paid by Weimar Germany. Major policy initiatives such as the Dawes Plan in 1924 were intended to allow good business practices to help prevent a reversion to conflict by reorganizing the bankrupt German Reichsbank under Allied supervision. An international conference adopted the plan, and the U.S. guaranteed a $110 million loan. The fact that even such large economic initiatives did not succeed in averting a radical political takeover and a subsequent world war should be a stark reminder of some of the limits of economic aid.

The field of economic development and the contemporary practice of foreign assistance grew out of the end of World War II. Clearly, the pecuniary and punitive treatment of Weimar Germany was hotly debated, and the growing awareness even before war's end of the likely competition with Soviet power was accelerating the need to fill the vacuum left by combat and a reduction of British influence. In May 1946 a communist-led civil war broke out in war-torn Greece. In February 1947 Truman administration officials were first becoming aware of the fact that the British no longer had the resources to provide aid in Europe, most notably Greece and Turkey. On June 5, 1947, the Truman administration called for massive foreign assistance to aid Greece and Turkey and to preserve them as democracies.

Underlying the new aid programs were the beliefs that economic, technical, and military assistance could be effective instruments in preserving and bolstering democracies that were threatened by communist takeovers; that the United States should be committed to a long-term policy of promoting its basic values of political and economic freedom; and that, given the altered balance of power, only the United States could lead this effort on behalf of free peoples.[6] In early 1948 Congress enacted legislation creating the Economic Recovery Administration, and between 1948 and 1952 the Marshall Plan spent nearly $17 billion (roughly $100 billion in current terms) in seventeen countries—most of which were not nearly as poor as parts of the developing world are today. There was a European focus to the effort, which sought to rebuild economies and conditioned aid on acceptance of the Bretton Woods economic system, although Congress soon also agreed to provide economic aid to "the area around China," which was in the throes of a communist revolution. Thus, Burma, French Indochina, Thailand, the Philippines, and, by 1949, Korea were added to the list of countries that were eligible to receive U.S. foreign assistance monies.

The U.S. foreign assistance strategy led by President Truman and his secretary of state, George Marshall, was an attempt to use economic, technical, and military assistance to reinvigorate a devastated Europe that was under pressure from the Soviet Union. An integral element of the Marshall Plan was that the nature of the assistance fully allowed for local ownership and, perhaps more important, local political will and leadership. Rather than having the United States imposing a plan from Washington, development was "demand driven": Strategic investments were examined from the ground up (albeit working with governments), and everyone within any country seemed to understand how the money could help reconstruction aimed at economic growth. Countries that were more deeply committed to strong leadership were given more funds; thus, Britain, Germany, and France received more assistance than other countries. Finally, the assistance was tied to overall economic and political reform in that the condition for accepting money was to comply with the Bretton Woods economic rules of the road.

With these best practices in aid effectiveness built in, the Marshall Plan represented the first of three major waves in U.S. foreign assistance policy. By 1960 support from the American public was waning, in part because of the publication in 1958 of the novel *The Ugly American*, by William J. Lederer and Eugene Burdick.[7] The novel, which was about the arrogance and incompetence of American foreign and military assistance programs in Southeast Asia, made foreign assistance an issue in the 1960 presidential campaign. The second attempt, led by President John F. Kennedy, to give strategic direction to foreign aid was in 1961, concomitant with the creation of the U.S. Agency for International Development (USAID). At the center of Kennedy's thinking was the need to use economic instruments strategically because, as he had written four years earlier in *Foreign Affairs*, the United States "cannot scatter its assistance on each parched patch of misery and need." Instead, first as a senator and then as president, Kennedy argued for economic reform and a strong commitment to sound policies as a precondition for receiving U.S. foreign aid. As the 1960 Democratic platform put it, "We shall establish priorities for foreign aid which will channel it to those countries abroad which, by their own willingness to help themselves, show themselves most capable of using it effectively."

The foreign policy priorities of the United States continued to change, and by the end of the 1960s—notwithstanding successful individual programs in some countries—the overarching policy in Washington turned away from economic growth. Meanwhile, as American engagement in Vietnam deepened, military instruments of power were gaining greater currency: Between 1968 and 1973, total military assistance doubled, while USAID assistance remained roughly constant. Foreign aid increasingly was a gift to countries that were willing to back U.S. policies, whether that meant resisting pressures from the Soviet Union and China or providing the United States with political or military support. In the early 1970s functional accounts were created—which had the perverse effect of siphoning off funds from a strategic country plan—and multilateral mechanisms for delivery were increasing, thereby further diluting a reform agenda.

The aftermath of the Vietnam War and the new power of Western European countries—now fully recovered from World War II—turned the development debate away from good governance, reform, and economic growth and toward poverty alleviation, provision of basic needs, and numerical targets of development aid needed from wealthy donors. If only wealthy countries provided 0.7 percent of their gross domestic product (GDP), the argument went, poverty would be greatly reduced. The question of how to sustain such development, especially in areas bereft of good governance, was less clear. A huge increase in U.S. aid expenditures focused on budget support to Israel and a vast mixed aid program to Egypt as part of a program to reward those countries for reaching the Camp David peace agreement.

In the 1980s the Reagan administration attempted to return to an economic growth approach to foreign aid, but by then there were too many vested interests, and a breakdown in consensus led to a myriad of activities and approaches rather than the required hard choices. The potential of economic tools thereby was weakened. What the Reagan administration did accomplish, however, was a marked increase in aid to Latin America, which was at a turning point in its economic and political institutions and policies. The greatest decade of foreign assistance to Latin America from the United States—at least in terms of appropriations—was the 1980s, to an even greater extent than the Alliance for Progress, which focused on Latin America in the 1960s. The fact that trade and investment in the region today are high priorities was made possible in part by these earlier investments.

The 1990s saw significant global progress in development, but the reason behind the gains had more to do with economic growth in China and India—the two most populous developing countries—rather than the effects of foreign aid. Meanwhile, the amount of USAID assistance, in constant dollars, remained basically the same overall; even this statistic, however, masks the fact that USAID lost 1,800 trained foreign service officers—leaving only 1,200 and reducing the ranks of specialists in development economics, agriculture, education, and engineering. Moreover, USAID accelerated the trend toward working through U.S. nongovernmental organizations (NGOs) rather than governments in the developing world, thereby further diminishing the state-level impact of aid and defining success as the lowest possible project level.

The Marshall Plan remains the high point of the American experience in foreign aid. Fifty years later, President George W. Bush and his policy advisors face the dual challenge of returning to successful development practices and increasing the means available to do so more effectively. Much of the Bush administration's policy formulation has been driven by the lessons learned from aid effectiveness literature and best practices gleaned from the history of aid performance. Before attempting to compare current efforts to those of the past, however, we need to bear in mind one major trend of the past decade—globalization. In the twentieth century, about three-fifths of U.S. assistance to the developing world emanated from the public sector. Today the opposite is true: Three-fifths of the money flowing to the developing world comes from the private sector, trade and investment, and remittances.

For policymakers today, no event captured the complexity of globalization better than the ten-day World Summit on Sustainable Development (WSSD) in August 2002. More than 60,000 people arrived in Johannesburg, South Africa, to participate in a ten-year review of the action plan adopted by 172 countries a decade earlier at the United Nations Conference on Environment and Development (UNCED) in Rio de Janeiro. The organizing theme of the WSSD was to measure global progress with respect to sustainable development.

Two years earlier at the Millennium Summit in New York, the UN General Assembly reaffirmed its support for the Millennium Development Goals. Although this was not the first attempt by wealthy countries to establish specific benchmarks for helping the developing world, the goals aim to achieve measurable improvements in the lives of poor people and set a deadline of 2015 for meeting specific numerical targets for improving human development (ranging from halving extreme poverty to achieving universal primary education). The legacies of the UN meetings in New York and Johannesburg, we should hope, will be the realization that current policies are incapable of confronting the development gap we face today. If anything, the development community must ensure that past definitions of success—big international summits replete with major donor commitments, greater NGO involvement, and new action plans—do not limit what can be achieved on the ground.

By and large, a decade of public campaigns to raise awareness of development issues has been successful. Yet most stakeholders would agree that past performance has shown that increased levels of foreign assistance will not ensure positive or sustainable development outcomes. Today's global development agenda is expected to address a wider range of policy concerns than in previous decades (e.g., HIV/AIDS, water scarcity, corruption, human trafficking), and the international development community also is expected to demonstrate tangible results with a newfound sense of urgency. From the perspective of the development community, the war on terrorism becomes another urgent and important priority in this complex agenda. The stark reality is that future success is likely to rest on two pillars: pursuing policy innovations with partner governments and applying the best practices on the ground. Without them, a third wave in foreign aid is doomed to failure.

Foreign Aid Objectives

At the beginning of the twenty-first century there was roughly $55 billion in official development assistance (ODA) flowing from governments worldwide.[8] The United States provides more than $11 billion in total ODA. The Millennium Challenge Account (MCA) would increase the amount to roughly $16 billion by 2005, of which $5 billion would go directly to countries that are highly committed to sound growth policies. (A separate new initiative, the Emergency Fund for HIV/AIDS, could push U.S. ODA to more than $20 million a year by 2008.) The remainder would go to a variety of other political needs, such as counternarcotics or peacekeeping, as well as additional food and disaster assistance monies. Development aid ordinarily focuses on underdeveloped nations—the seventy or so nations with an average per capita income of less than $2 per day (most of these countries are in sub-Saharan Africa)—as well as some of the forty low-middle income countries with an average per capita income of about $4 per day. Development aid also is provided to wealthier countries such as India, however, where many people still live in poverty despite a higher overall income. It also includes political aid to recipients such as Israel, Northern Ireland, Russia, and Turkey. In essence, there are four fundamental uses of foreign assistance. The multiplicity of roles—not to mention the complex funding accounts; the division of labor across the State Department, USAID, and nearly fifty departments, agencies, and offices; and an active legislative role—serve only to obfuscate aid decisions and performance measurements.

The first role of development assistance is to promote economic growth in countries committed to political and economic freedom and willing to invest in their people; these "good performers" represent the most promising environment for effective development. This is the challenge laid out in the proposed $5 billion-a-year MCA. In outlining his vision for an independent Millennium Challenge Corporation, President Bush remarked that "greater contributions from developed nations must be linked to greater responsibility from developing nations." The second role of development assistance is to help countries that are poor performers in the areas of political and economic freedom and social development and thus will need specific assistance in those areas to have a better chance of becoming eligible for MCA-related assistance.

The third role of development assistance is to support creation or restoration of stability in fragile, failing, or failed states. Humanitarian crises, whether caused by man or nature, remain an important variable in the development equation. From the Balkans to Colombia to Angola and Afghanistan, foreign aid is being used to quell violence and produce a foundation of stability and governance that can lead, in turn, to successful development.

A fourth role is to support security or political objectives—such as compensation for assisting a military effort or a global or transnational goal as broad as preventing climate change or the spread of the HIV/AIDS pandemic—that often are unrelated to the first two goals. At present, the largest single gain in existing accounts for "Development Assistance" and "Child Survival and Health" is the prevention, treatment, and support of persons with or at risk of acquiring HIV/AIDS. Notwithstanding the multifaceted impact of AIDS on a nation's economy, these programs are only tangentially related to improving governance or building institutions because so much of this assistance has to be provided outside of health ministries.

These roles are not simply a theoretical structure; they have a deep and abiding basis in resource debates. That is, the MCA account will focus on the "best performers" in the developing world—countries that are most committed to sound political, social, and economic policies. The second role roughly corresponds to the $3 billion Development Assistance and Child Survival and Health accounts. The third goal is addressed specifically by an account for International Disaster Assistance, as well as the Office of Transition Initiatives and accounts that provide food (Public Law 480 Title II)—the trio of which receive more than $1.2 billion. The fifth and final goal can best be aligned with Economic Support Funds, which total more than $2 billion. Where reality and theory deviate, however, is in the fact that all of these accounts are used for multiple purposes, further blurring the purposes of foreign aid.

There remains, however, a mismatch between the objectives for which the United States hopes to use foreign aid and the means available for such assistance. Indeed, as a percentage of U.S. GDP, spending for foreign assistance has dropped from 0.5 percent to 0.1 percent.[9] The needs of the developing world—even the Islamic world alone—greatly surpass available donor aid. The Marshall Plan pumped the equivalent of nearly $100 billion into seventeen countries over three or four years—significantly more money than even the largest missions, such as in Egypt or Indonesia, receive today. The sum was large enough to be used for major investments; there was local ownership of the projects; and the recipient governments committed to broad economic reforms and support for political pluralism. After World War II, economic aid was a large component of the initial effort to meet U.S. foreign policy objectives, but the Korean War and the militarization of U.S. efforts to contain the Soviet Union changed those ratios to what they are now. If the United States is willing to adapt aid programs to address the sources of terrorism, or at least to promote moderate institutions that can serve as bulwarks against terrorism and its supporters, we will have to devote the necessary resources and focus on specific areas and ends.

Foreign Aid Goals Related to the War on Terrorism

Terrorism fueled by religious extremism often masks large, simmering pools of frustration and anger. Grassroots frustration and anger are particularly common in Muslim communities across much of the world, and a broad sweep of public opinion in the Muslim world shows that much of this anger is directed toward Western nations—particularly the United States.[10] Thus, we now face the dual challenge of waging a broader war against terrorism while attempting to contain Muslim anger with the West.

There are certain prerequisites if aid is to have an impact on a country's economic growth and development, regardless of whether the country is Islamic. To begin with, there must be a semblance of peace before good governance is possible. Even assuming a foundation of a modicum of peace, however, leaders must be committed to reform and freedom. These commitments must translate to policies that promote democratic reforms, transparency in financing and banking, and crackdowns on corruption. There must be an equally strong commitment to increasing economic opportunities, whether that is reflected in strengthening the country's credit rating or removing obstacles to starting a business. The challenge will be in creating development programs that have built in the right incentives to achieve such changes. Finally, foreign aid—whether provided to support economic growth or other foreign policy aims—should be treated as a conscious strategic investment. Too often, foreign aid programs are simply set in motion and kept alive by the inertia of bureaucracies and self-interested implementing partners. Policymakers have erred by focusing on singular tasks without considering alternative uses for public money and by forgetting that foreign aid accounts for a relatively small part of the budget compared to other expenditures. Development aid totaled about $54 billion in 2000; this amount was only one-third as much as foreign direct investment in developing countries ($167 billion). The United States, for example, contributed $11 billion in official development assistance in 2001. American private capital investment in developing countries averaged roughly $12 billion a year over the past three years. Given this discrepancy in scale, aid effectiveness has to come primarily through catalyzing institutional development and strategic policy changes that promote economic growth.

Although the United Nations Development Program's (UNDP) *Arab Human Development Report 2002* addresses only a portion of the Islamic world, it identifies several major problems confronting many Muslim countries today.[11] The UNDP report argues that these nations face three distinctive deficits compared to the rest of the world: a *freedom deficit* measured in terms of both political and economic governance; a *human capabilities/knowledge deficit* resulting from the tendency to tolerate a low quality of education, particularly high illiteracy rates among women; and a *women's empowerment deficit* deriving from the tendency for Muslim nations to deny women the opportunity to participate broadly in the workforce or in policymaking. These deficits, which plague many non-Arab Muslim countries as well, may partially explain widespread anger and frustration in these countries.

The quest for economic growth also presents significant challenges for the region. The World Economic Forum's *Arab World Competitiveness Report 2002–2003* found that the most telling economic fact of the Arab world today was that whereas rates of investment in the region have long been among the highest in the developing world, growth rates are among the lowest.[12] Despite a declining foreign direct investment (FDI) trendline, the prospects for growth can improve in several countries if they sustain reforms in three critical areas: public institutions, physical infrastructure, and human resource development. Another area that is ripe for improvement is trade performance; export diversification has remained low because Persian Gulf country exports are limited mostly to hydrocarbon products. Measured by their export share in GDP, the non–fuel-exporting Arab countries are still fairly closed economies. In Egypt, for example, the exports-to-GDP ratio has remained below 20 percent, and its export growth rate continues to fall short of GDP growth rate.

The challenge in the Arab world—as well as for the non-Arab Muslim nations of Africa and South and East Asia—will be in radically increasing economic opportunities available to the disadvantaged masses of their populations. To effectively address the broader context from which terrorism arises and the internal forces that allow terrorism to go unchecked, however, assistance programs also must address the problems especially of young males in high-risk communities. This effort will require aid donors to identify institutions and leaders that are most effectively investing in the accumulation of productive social capital at the community, provincial, or national level to address the three deficits in a particular country. At times, these leaders may belong to religious groups or organizations that might oppose legal or other conditions imposed by Western providers of aid.

Foreign Aid Triage

Foreign aid programs that are designed to counter terrorism use a variety of direct and indirect approaches. In general, however, foreign aid cannot cripple terrorists in the short or medium term. Rather, aid works over time to strengthen general order, moderate institutions, and influential community and national leaders as bulwarks against extremism and indiscriminate violence. Therefore what is needed is *foreign aid triage*, whereby donors begin to assign degrees of urgency to determine the order of treatment for at-risk nations.

A primary purpose of aid is to help provide peace and security, without which economic development, human security, education, and health cannot flourish. Creation or restoration of civil order, or peace, often is a prerequisite for development and frequently is discussed in the aftermath of violence, whether it involves genocide in Rwanda or the Balkans or civil war and military intervention in Afghanistan or Iraq. If states with few effective institutions are breeding grounds for terrorist training or recruiting, foreign aid may be able to create conditions for eventual order and prosperity.

A second use of aid—particularly with the goal of thwarting terrorism in mind—is to build durable and moderate institutions that can maintain order and deliver basic justice, economic opportunity, and social services. For example, the World Bank and other donors have learned the hard lesson that project lending in poor policy environments typically has much lower returns than in countries with good policies. They also understand that loan conditionality does not alter the policies of recipient countries that are not already committed to change for their own reasons. Therefore, foreign aid should help to enhance a country's ability to invest in its own human capital, form civil society structures, and improve transparency and accountability.

A third use of aid is nurturing people—whether they are leaders who are open to Western thinking and freedom or community figures such as teachers, administrators, and doctors. Building human capital allows individuals and their communities to contribute to national economic, social, and political policymaking. This approach, in turn, strengthens civil society structures that provide critical support for durable and moderate institutions. The public also is likely to develop a healthy appetite for transparency and accountability, which in turn can help prevent poor and ineffective policies from taking hold in a country.

Although humanitarian aid and financial transfers can be fairly quick, capacity building (as opposed to simply having outsiders do the work) necessarily takes time. Moreover, these are mostly indirect ways to counter terrorism, which can be a lethally specific and narrow threat. So if foreign aid cannot help thwart terrorism, why invest billions of dollars in aid in the name of countering terrorism? The answer is twofold: First, these programs can indeed undermine support for terrorism and strengthen partners around the world who are willing to work with us to fight terrorism. Second, these programs must be regarded as part of a comprehensive strategy to thwart terrorism—the battle against which offers no silver bullets or nostrums for quick success. In other words, we must set realistic, specific counterterrorism goals and pursue them in carefully selected countries and areas to have a decent prospect of improving the target environment.

Policy Lessons

At least five major policy lessons can be derived from past development that are directly applicable to the current war on terrorism.

Winning the Peace, Not Just the War

Winning wars is not enough. We must help cement the peace and then play a leading role with the international community in "draining the swamps," dealing with refugees, providing security, and then setting the countries involved on a path of good governance and economic growth.

Although Iraq is the immediate object of attention, the enduring needs in Afghanistan following the removal of the Taliban government in 2001 provide a salient test case for focused "nation-building." In the case of Afghanistan, razor-sharp generalizations on the op-ed pages—that the Bush administration has been better at destroying than rebuilding—tilted the public's perception without elaboration during the first nine months of the mission. Have other donors done more? Does development occur in the absence of a stable political environment? The answer to these two questions is a simple no, but the overall development equation is more complex and the tendency toward reductionism in the face of multiple challenges is still great.

In January 2002 major donor governments met in Tokyo to assemble $235 million in immediate assistance for Afghanistan and then pledged roughly $5 billion in aid over the next five years. But assistance of any kind—whether it is for peacekeeping or road-building—is difficult to collect and administer at the international level, given the woeful state of donor coordination and accountability.

The sole exception is in the area of humanitarian relief in the wake of natural or human-generated disasters. For example, during the first few months of relief work in Afghanistan unprecedented amounts of food were delivered in record time by the UN World Food Program (WFP) with funding and support provided by USAID. More than 9 million men, women, and children were fed with wheat, oil, and lentils delivered from the United States, which continues to play a leading role in meeting urgent needs for food, water, shelter, and medicine in Afghanistan. The long-term development challenges are formidable, however; approximately 26.8 million people still live in absolute poverty, and virtually all of the country's institutions have been destroyed. Literacy is at only 36 percent, and the unemployment rate at an estimated 50 percent; agriculture remains the way of life for 80 percent of the people.[13]

For USAID, rehabilitating the agriculture sector, education, and health-care systems are urgent humanitarian priorities. To enhance the country's security and political stability, Economic Support Funds (ESF) coordinated through the Department of State are used to fund the demobilization of former combatants, peacekeeping operations (PKO), and the training and equipping of Afghanistan's new national army.

The difficulties arise when donor priorities do not match completely with those of the recipient government. Consider, for example, the challenge of finding $150 million required to rebuild the major highway artery between the country's two largest cities, Kabul and Kandahar. No one doubts that this road is a major priority in terms of reuniting—both literally and figuratively—a still fragmented Afghanistan (only 20 percent of Afghan roads are paved). Yet there are legitimate competing priorities that continue to hold the attention of donors, despite the entreaties of the government in Kabul. In summer 2002, the Asian Development Bank was willing to loan $150 million for this road project, and the Japanese government was ready to step in with a $50 million project grant. The Afghan government, however, expected the road project to be financed entirely by grant aid, given its dire financial situation and its expectation that the pledges made in Tokyo would be fulfilled. After the Afghans refused the loan offer, they learned that the terms of the Japanese aid stipulated that their funds could be used only to improve secondary roads, not major highways. Meanwhile, the U.S. Congress was considering a new bill pledging an additional $1 billion-plus that did not include significant funding for roads, and the European Union continued to debate whether to provide $60 million or $80 million to overhaul the road connecting Kabul to Jalalabad, which was being used by thousands of returning refugees.

Faced with mounting media criticism over this issue, the American, Japanese, and Saudi Arabian governments held private meetings in September 2002 during the UN General Assembly that led to an agreement by the three nations to fund the $150 million highway. The Kabul–Kandahar project was not the only infrastructure project plagued by unrealistic project expectations, slow bureaucracies, and trickling aid flows. This coordination problem also is pervasive in the United Nations, which typically has multiple agencies (including UNHCR, UNDP, UNICEF, and UNWFP) working in a postconflict environment. At the end of the day, it was the commitment by President Bush that helped ensure the essential completion of the highway—which has enormous political importance in Pushtan areas—by the end of 2003.

The larger issue, however, is that the donor community forgot an important lesson from historical experience: A country that has true ownership makes a project succeed. A second lesson is that the vast majority of aid projects are successful only when aid funds are flowing. In a postconflict situation, assistance levels increase sharply only to fall dramatically once the contingency passes and humanitarian relief agencies have fulfilled their missions. A significant gap in assistance then emerges, pending the arrival of long-term development aid organizations. In terms of both humanitarian relief and development aid, it is important initially to assess whether projects on the ground are designed to be sustainable once donor funding comes to an end.

Building a major highway in Afghanistan is a complex, costly, and time-consuming task, made all the more challenging in the ashes of three decades of war. But will rebuilding Afghanistan prove to be more challenging than what Douglas MacArthur encountered with war-torn Japan? That appears to be the case. No single individual or institution in Afghanistan today can exercise the authority or marshal the resources that the "American Caesar" in Tokyo could. One of the paradoxes of nation-building in this century is that multiple donors and massive funding do not guarantee swifter results or improve aid effectiveness in a country—particularly given the persistent misalignment of priorities, strategies, and resources among donors. The challenges in Afghanistan, moreover, were a harbinger of things to come in Iraq—notwithstanding the asymmetries between the two countries and the two military operations.

Democracy and Governance in the Muslim World

Democracy and governance in the Muslim world can no longer be neglected. Yet the United States cannot impose democracy, and advances in good governance will take time and take root in different ways. If Francis Fukuyama was right about the end of History being the victory of liberal democracy,[14] the salient question for Muslim countries is this: What will be the pace and profile of their inevitable transformations? The reasons Muslims have emigrated to the United States over the past three decades offer insight into why such a transformation has not manifested itself so easily in the Islamic world. Daniel Pipes and Khalid Durán, in their article "Faces of Islam," argue that Muslim countries, which are disproportionately dominated by dictators, have driven off some of the most talented and wealthy people from the Middle East, South Asia, and beyond.[15] Some of the reasons Muslims cite for immigrating to the United States include ethnic persecution, religious persecution, Islamism, anti-Islamism, and war.

Another major reason they cite is education. By the 1990s American colleges and universities attracted more than a half-million foreign students, many of whom chose to remain in the United States. Female students were particularly inclined to stay because of the independence, self-sufficiency, and opportunities for assertiveness that life in America offered to them. The question remains unanswered whether foreign aid is the appropriate vehicle to introduce the social and political incentives needed in a country to stem this brain drain. A related question is whether economic growth is at the root of this problem. Judging by the tightening of immigration regulations in the Western world, the conventional wisdom is that there are far more economic migrants leaving the Muslim world than there are asylum seekers. In fact, 51 percent of Arab youths want to emigrate, particularly to European countries.[16] This desire is driven mostly by the fact that these youths do not believe that their countries can create jobs for them in the future.[17] If demography is indeed destiny, we need to carefully analyze the policy implications of a Muslim population that is significantly younger than the global average. In the Arab world, 39 percent of the population is younger than fifteen years of age, and annual population growth rates in most Arab countries exceed their economic growth rates.[18]

The growing population pressure in Muslim countries requires reexamination in the context of foreign aid and terrorism, if only because so much attention has focused—perhaps without empirical evidence to support it—on "draining the swamp" filled with economic despair and social inequity from which terrorists emerge. This debate misses the essential point that "terrorists" comprise two distinct groups: leaders and foot soldiers. Terrorist leaders tend to be older, educated (e.g., Osama bin Laden and Mohammed Atta), and sometimes from the political elite.[19] They frequently rely, however, on disenfranchised and often desperately poor communities for safe harbor—as in Afghanistan and Pakistan—or look mostly to the young to do the "dirty work," as in the case of suicide bombers.[20] Efforts to bring social, economic, and political opportunities to young, poor, and disenfranchised masses might help deny terrorists safe harbor and new recruits, but longer-term aid programs will do little to frustrate the immediate aims of terrorist leaders.

The Weak Link between Poverty and Terrorism

The 2002 National Security Strategy builds the case that development is central to preserving peace around the world.[21] As President Bush noted, "The events of September 11th, 2001, taught us that *weak states,* like Afghanistan, can pose as great a danger to national interests as strong states. Poverty does not make poor people into terrorists or murderers. Yet poverty, weak institutions, and corruption can make weak states vulnerable to terrorist networks and drug cartels within their borders."[22] If failing (or failed) states are looming threats to American security, foreign aid is far too important to be left simply to development economists and diplomats.

It is important, however, that we temper expectations about whether a reduction in poverty or an increase in education in the developing world will somehow reduce the risk of terrorism in this country. Economists Alan Krueger and Jitka Maleckova have published a study focusing on the Middle East that found the link between poverty, education, and terrorism to be "indirect, complicated and probably quite weak."[23] They concluded that terrorism was "more accurately viewed as a response to political conditions and longstanding feelings (either perceived or real) of indignity and frustration that have little to do with economics."[24] An important point to bear in mind, however, is that their research did not address the particular problem of nation-state failure and its relationship to poverty and terrorism. Foreign aid must be more effective in addressing the economic needs of Muslim and Arab nations simply because most are on the wrong development trajectory.

National security planners will find development policy options limited by a single immutable fact: The rate at which poverty is reduced in a country is directly related to the rate of its economic growth. Achieving sustained growth in a globalized economy is fraught with unforeseen risks. In many Muslim countries the security situation has had a significant impact on economic activity, particularly tourism. Major terrorist bombings such as the one in Bali, Indonesia, can devastate a national economy overnight—at least temporarily. On the first day of trading after the attack, the Jakarta stock market plunged 10 percent, and several regional currencies slid sharply against the dollar. The resulting sharp spike in unemployment can lead to political instability by exposing historical social fault-lines and creating ethnic and religious polarization within communities. Integration of security policy into foreign aid strategy remains a priority, given the political volatility associated with the economic instability of many Muslim countries.

Education: A Critical Driver of Moderate Institutions

Basic and higher education, as well as jobs training, can be useful in building stable, moderate educational alternatives to more radical religious schools, especially the most fanatical *madrassas*. An alarming number of education systems in the Muslim world have utterly failed to support their countries' economic development. By failing to align their education systems to the evolving needs of the global economy, many of these countries risk being left behind in terms of their competitiveness. The UN *Arab Human Development Report* concluded, "A mismatch between educational output on the one hand and labor-market and development needs on the other could lead to Arab countries' isolation from global knowledge, information, and technology at a time when accelerated acquisition of knowledge and formation of human skills are becoming prerequisites for progress."[25] Not surprisingly, after a decade of declining education aid budgets, education funding remains a high priority for the U.S. government. USAID invested $357 million in education in 2002—25 percent more than in 2001—and is strengthening education in more than twenty-five countries. The Peace Corps devotes more than $80 million a year to basic education in more than fifty countries.

In *The Elusive Quest for Growth*, William Easterly cites various studies that show a lack of association between increased spending on schooling and GDP growth (the most glaring example was the trickle of growth that followed an education explosion in Africa in the 1960–1970s).[26] Other studies have held that investment in human capital is as important as investment in physical capital, but the links between education and technology and a country's economic competitiveness are still not fully understood. It also is clear that although education is no panacea, the emphasis should not be exclusively on economic growth. The main drivers of development outcomes are developing country institutions and the policies and public investments that they generate. A country's education system creates the knowledge and skills base from which the institutions and policies ultimately will emerge—or collapse.

Easterly also warns that incentives for economic growth will disappear when policymakers cater to multiple interest groups.[27] These interest groups often polarize a country, and the polarization eventually manifests itself in two ugly forms: class warfare and ethnic violence. In the war against terrorism, education assistance will be an important strategic investment in stemming class warfare and ethnic violence. By improving the literacy and knowledge of all social and ethnic groups, foreign aid for education can help remove the historical inequalities that are deeply embedded in a country's political and economic system.

Education for girls is a particularly useful and cost-effective approach. At the primary and secondary level, however, girls in the Muslim world continue to be enrolled at rates well below those of boys.

The most egregious proponent of gender inequity in education by far was the Taliban regime in Afghanistan. Under Taliban rule, women in Afghanistan were denied the opportunity to engage in political, economic, or social life. Girls above the age of eight could not go to school; there was a brutally enforced restrictive dress code; and women were forbidden to venture outside their homes without a male relative. Under Taliban rule, 92 percent of the country's girls did not attend school, and 70 percent of the teachers were forced to resign simply because they were women. The Taliban's interpretation of Islam and its treatment of women were radical departures from that of the vast majority of Muslims. The imperative to fulfill the basic education rights of girls must be stressed more strongly to many other Muslim countries, however. The benefits of educating girls in terms of improving public health, reducing infant mortality, and fighting illiteracy are widely documented and have led to important best practices in the development community.

The World Economic Forum's *Arab World Competitiveness Report* frames the challenge as follows: "Although the nations of the Arab world vary in terms of available resources and differ in many of the specific economic and social challenges that they face, all must begin in earnest to redefine the learning objectives they will pursue, and thoughtfully consider how education can be better organized to assure the development of a sustainable capacity to compete in a changing and evolving global economy."[28] Tellingly, all Arab constitutions and laws affirm the equal right of women to education; the problem is that of families ensuring this right for their daughters and government officials enforcing the laws of compulsory education.

On the Ground

In terms of aid effectiveness, there is no substitute for being on the ground; donors must be immersed in the culture and language of a country and networked with the local leaders who ultimately must make key policy decisions. USAID's comparative advantage comes from its extensive in-country experience, strong field presence, and having earned the trust of host country officials and other development partners. If future development efforts are about preventing new nations from being added to the roster of failing and failed states, those three elements must be preserved in policymaking.

Robert Rotberg offers a model definition for nation-state failure: "Nation-states fail because they no longer deliver positive political goods to their people. Their governments lose legitimacy and, in the eyes and hearts of a growing plurality of its citizens, the nation-state itself becomes illegitimate."[29] Officials and institutions in these countries have completely failed to deliver political goods such as national security, public safety, economic opportunity, education programs, health services, and the rule of law. Afghanistan, Angola, Burundi, the Democratic Republic of Congo, Liberia, Sierra Leone, Somalia, and Sudan represent failed or collapsed states of the past ten years, and many more have been on the brink.[30] In all of these cases, the state failure was caused by human actions; each resulted from policy decisions and leadership failures rather than from natural disasters, geography, or pestilence. Resulting vacuums in power and authority attract criminal and terrorist networks that have demonstrated time and again their global reach. Once inside, these groups hide behind the professed sovereignty of the failed states, and their extraction becomes a diplomatic and military challenge. Prevention clearly is better than cure; once military operations cease, the arduous task of nation-building begins. We cannot expect, however, to strengthen weak states remotely from Washington, D.C. We must recognize that failed states put development professionals at considerable risk, but realistic prevention efforts require people on the ground "focusing on existing conditions and working to rebuild and reconstruct viable institutions."[31]

Conclusions

Foreign aid and economic tools of power can be used as a carrot (incentive) or as a stick (sanction). Both are legitimate uses to support foreign policy, although sanctions have received far more attention. The utility of sanctions has been severely hampered, however. A comprehensive discussion of sanctions is beyond the scope of this chapter; suffice to say that sanctions work far better when they are focused, when there are few alternative sources of the money being withheld, and when the sanctions are enforced rigorously.

With regard to development effectiveness, the U.S. government is taking a greater leadership role in major international forums by challenging development orthodoxy, promoting best practices, and increasing future aid commitments. These efforts are at the center of a quiet revolution that is shaping the future of development assistance. Yet if one were to summarize U.S. foreign assistance ends and means over the past five decades and then consider how to adapt them to the war on terrorism, one might begin by making the following generalizations.

First, when economic instruments of power have been well funded and strategically focused, they often have delivered specific results—whether on European recovery, the development of the Asian Tiger economies, or specific development policy objectives.

Second, because of U.S. global demands, the independence and internationalization of development policies, and the accretion of years of Washington politics that have prevented a more strategic or agile foreign aid bureaucracy from evolving, the United States has used economic instruments of power relatively poorly, and those instruments have atrophied for the most of the past three decades or more. Meanwhile, reliance on military instruments of power—reflected in relative spending on defense as opposed to international affairs and foreign assistance—has grown.

Third, the Bush administration is on the cusp of ushering in a renewal of foreign aid—a renewal that will require bipartisan support, to be sure, but has the potential to refocus aid to deliver on successful development and contribute in meaningful ways to the war on terrorism. The White House has successfully transformed the international debate away from merely how much aid was being spent and increasingly toward the effectiveness of aid. Recipients of development assistance must now demonstrate a strong commitment to good governance if they expect to receive future aid. The debate has also moved from an outmoded reliance on public-sector money toward harnessing resources from the private sector, domestic savings, foundations, and nongovernmental organizations.

There remains the difficult question of whether foreign assistance should be distinct and separate from development assistance if we intend to design a foreign assistance strategy that is commensurate with national security interests. We now know that effective development assistance will require donors to make the difficult decision to disengage from countries where economic performance is deteriorating because of poor governance, lack of commitment to reform, or failure to invest in their own people—all of which create a hostile development environment. We also know that in many instances foreign aid will be the favored inducement to gain the support of critical developing countries in the war against terrorism. What happens, however, when some of those same countries willfully mismanage their economies and repress basic freedoms at home? Will policymakers abandon best development practices and subordinate the freedom of others to secure the safety of this country? These are some of the tough questions that lie ahead.

Notes

1. See Mustafa Al Sayyid, "Mixed Message: The Arab and Muslim Response to 'Terrorism,'" *The Washington Quarterly* (spring 2002), 177.

2. Ibid., 188.

3. "The U.S.-Middle East Partnership Initiative: Building Hope for the Years Ahead," remarks by Secretary of State Colin L. Powell to the Heritage Foundation, December 12, 2002; available at www.state.gov.

4. See part seven of *The National Security Strategy of the United States*, September 2002, available at www.whitehouse.gov.

5. Jeffrey D. Sachs, "The Strategic Significance of Global Inequality," *The Washington Quarterly* (summer 2001), 187.

6. For a succinct discussion of the administration's challenges at the time, see Robert J. Donovan, *Conflict and Crisis: The Presidency of Harry S Truman, 1945–1948*, (New York: W. W. Norton, 1977), 275–91.

7. See the latest edition: Eugene Burdick and William J. Lederer, *The Ugly American* (New York: W. W. Norton, 1999).

8. This ODA figure excludes almost all military assistance and aid to middle-income recipients such as Israel, Russia, and Northern Ireland.

9. Net foreign aid spending rose from $6 billion to $17 billion between 1960 and 2000 (excluding military assistance). However, the ODA totals were $3 billion to $11 billion, respectively, discounting foreign aid to nations other than the low- and low-middle income countries. Asian aid was high early in that period but dropped significantly after the Vietnam war; aid to the Near East was modest before the 1973 Mideast war and oil shocks but increased significantly after the Camp David Accord; Eurasian aid is a relatively new, mostly post–cold war phenomenon.

10. See, for example, Sarah El Deeb, "A Rare Public Opinion Poll Shows Arabs Dislike America But Not Democracy," *Associated Press*, 30 October 2002; "Poll: Muslims Call U.S. 'Ruthless, Arrogant,'" 26 February 2002, available at www.cnn.com/2002/US/02/26/gallup.muslims/; and V. K. Malhotra, "Consequences of War: Arabs' Anti-American Sentiment Rising as Iraq War Looms," 28 November 2002, available at http://abcnews.go.com/sections/wnt/DailyNews/roadtowar_arabs021127.html.

11. United Nations Development Program (UNDP), *Arab Human Development Report 2002*, available at www.undp.org/rbas/ahdr/.

12. World Economic Forum, *The Arab World Competitiveness Report 2002–2003* (New York: Oxford University Press, 2003).

13. U.S. Central Intelligence Agency, *The World Factbook 2002: Afghanistan*, available at www.cia.gov/cia/publications/factbook/geos/af.html.

14. See Francis Fukuyama, *The End of History and the Last Man* (New York: Free Press, 1992).

15. Daniel Pipes and Khalid Durán, "Faces of Islam," *Policy Review* no. 114 (August/September 2002), 49–60; available at www.meforum.org/article/pipes/441.

16. UNDP, *Arab Human Development Report 2002*, 30.

17. Ibid.

18. Ibid., 37.

19. Rex A. Hudson, *Who Becomes a Terrorist and Why: The 1999 Government Report on Profiling Terrorists* (Guilford, Conn.: Lyons Press, 1999), 75–77.

20. See, for example, Hudson, *Who Becomes a Terrorist and Why*, 183; Ariel Merari, "The Readiness to Kill and Die: Suicidal Terrorism in the Middle East," in *Origins of Terrorism: Psychologies, Ideologies, Theologies, States of Mind*, ed. Walter Reich (Washington, D.C.: Woodrow Wilson Center Press, 1990); and Ehud Sprinzak, "Rational Fanatics," *Foreign Policy* 120 (September/October 2000): 66–73.

21. *The National Security Strategy of the United States of America* (Washington, D.C.: The White House, September 2002), available at www.whitehouse.gov/nsc/nss.html.

22. Ibid.

23. Alan Krueger and Jitka Maleckova, "Education, Poverty, Political Violence and Terrorism: Is There a Causal Connection?" unpublished paper, May 2002, 1.

24. Ibid.

25. UNDP, *Arab Human Development Report 2002*, 51.

26. William Easterly, *The Elusive Quest for Growth* (Cambridge, Mass.: MIT Press, 2002), 71–84.

27. Ibid., 262.

28. World Economic Forum, *Arab World Competitiveness Report 2002–2003*, 222.

29. Robert I. Rotberg, "The New Nature of Nation-State Failure," *The Washington Quarterly*, (summer 2002), 85.

30. Ibid., 90.

31. Ray Takeyh and Nikolas Gvosdev, "Do Terrorist Networks Need a Home?" *The Washington Quarterly* (summer 2002), 105.

eleven

HOMELAND SECURITY

Daniel Gouré

Even before September 11, 2001, the U.S. government and the national security community realized that the nation was increasingly vulnerable to terrorist attack and that existing policies, institutions, and capabilities to counter such attacks were woefully inadequate. The Commission on U.S. National Security in the Twenty-First Century (the Hart-Rudman Commission) issued a widely publicized warning that "the combination of unconventional weapons proliferation with the persistence of international terrorism will end the relative invulnerability of the U.S. homeland to catastrophic attack. A direct attack against American citizens *on American soil* is likely over the next quarter-century."[1] Studies by the Gilmore and Bremmer commissions as well as the Center for Strategic and International Studies not only provided similar warnings but also, like the final report of the Hart-Rudman Commission, proposed sweeping reforms in U.S. security strategy, defense policy, and homeland security practices to address the emerging terrorist threat to the U.S. homeland.[2] After September 11, a wealth of quick analyses were published proposing a wide range of organizational changes, procedural improvements, and funding increases for programs and activities related to homeland security.[3]

The most common recommendation made by the various studies and analyses was the need for a national strategy for counterterrorism, or homeland defense.[4] In its second report, *Towards a National Strategy for Com-*

bating Terrorism—published before September 11—the Gilmore Commission emphasized the need for a national strategy that would "express preparedness goals in terms of an 'end state'" toward which the program should strive. The idea of an "end-state" was critical, in the opinion of the commission, for three reasons. First, it would guide resource allocations. Second, it would serve as the basis for establishing accountability. Third, it would help establish priorities.[5] As the commission noted in its first report, there is a danger of simply overcompensating for previous years of neglect without an understanding of what can realistically be achieved or how best to spend relatively scarce resources.[6]

Whereas the overwhelming majority of studies, both pre– and post–September 11, called for a national strategy that integrates different aspects of homeland security and the various levels of government, virtually none provided what could be deemed a credible strategic vision. Ironically, the Bush administration's National Strategy for Homeland Security failed to remedy this situation. It provided a statement of objectives and a series of mission areas related to those objectives. As the Strategy itself pointed out, this approach is primarily a means of aligning budget resources with tasks to be performed. It acknowledged that there is no mathematical formula to establish the appropriate balance between measures sufficient to reduce the nation's vulnerability to terrorism and unacceptable limitations on personal liberties. It suggested that the judgment regarding how much is enough must be left in the hands of the country's political leaders.[7] As the document itself acknowledged, instead of a strategy it proposed a process to support a form of national mobilization.[8] For reasons discussed in detail below, there is relatively little strategy in the Strategy.

The policy community and the Bush administration have taken as an article of faith the idea that it is possible to craft a strategy for homeland security. Yet to date the construction of a homeland security strategy has proven frustratingly elusive. This is not because of lack of attention to the topic. Instead, I argue in this chapter, it is the nature of the subject. An examination of the factors and issues involved in defining and implementing a program to provide protection of the U.S. homeland against terrorist attack demonstrates the difficulties involved in formulating a strategy. Indeed, the question that must be addressed is whether it will be possible for the United States to devise a strategy for homeland security.

Strategy and Homeland Security: Basic Premises and Issues

Strategy is about relating ends and means. The ways ends and means are related is through a strategic plan. Plans must have measures of effectiveness

(MOEs)—ways of assessing progress toward objectives. There also must b
methods for altering the distribution and application of resources or the ap
plication of means as the plan unfolds.[9] Strategy is about choices. As one
treatise on strategy notes, "A strategy sets priorities and focuses available resources—money, time, political capital, and military power—on the main effort."[10] Inherent in the definition of strategy is the assumption that it is an active process that seeks to control the environment, rather than reacting to
it. Thus, according to another work on strategy, "Strategy is all about how
leadership will use the power available to the state to exercise control over
sets of circumstances and geographic locations to achieve objectives that support state interest. Thus, the first premise of a theory of strategy is that
strategy is proactive and anticipatory."[11]

A good strategy has certain basic elements. The first is clear, definable, and
attainable objectives or goals. Defining appropriate goals for a homeland security strategy is a particularly challenging undertaking. Dr. Ruth David, the
president of the ANSER Corporation, describes this challenge as follows:

> One of the most difficult questions has to do with defining success. What is
> the goal of the homeland security mission? Are we defending America—the
> nation—or protecting every individual American from every conceivable
> terrorist threat? This question is not part of the national security agenda,
> but it is at the core of the homeland security debate. If we set the bar too
> high we face unaffordable resource requirements—a black hole of spend-
> ing—and untenable loss of personal freedom. If we set it too low, American
> citizens may lose confidence in their government's ability to protect the na-
> tion from terrorism. If we fail to answer the question we have no context
> for decision making—no way to prioritize investments—and no way to
> measure progress.[12]

A good strategy must understand the factors to be addressed in achieving the desired goal. Typically, in national security planning the circumstances involve an adversary or threat against which a state is contesting for
an objective or goal. An appreciation of the circumstances or context of the
conflict or competition—including the motivation, behavior, strategy, and
goals of the adversary—also is required. There may be proximate or inter-
mediate goals, such as the defeat of hostile military forces, as a prerequisite
for attainment of the ultimate objective, whether that entails occupation of
the adversary's territory, regime change, or some other end.

A good strategy rests on a theory of conflict or warfare. During the cold
war it was containment, backed by deterrence, supported by escalation control, and, at the bottom of the structure, continental-scale warfighting. There
were particular theories related to different types of warfighting, such as nu-

clear war at sea, land combat, and different levels of conflict. Theories of conflict can be offensive-oriented or defensive-oriented as well.

A good strategy also must have established and tested means by which to apply resources to the attainment of desired objectives or goals. These means generally are referred to as operational concepts. The manner in which resources are applied is the essence of strategic planning. A traditional strategic plan will lay out the employment of different elements of military power. A military plan will detail the ways in which military force will be employed, the timing and sequencing of their employment, the targets of their actions, and the ways in which different military force elements are required to interact.

A good strategy must strive to be efficient. Not only must ends be related to means; they also must be appropriate and relevant to the objective. Strategists speak of the need for a balance between the objectives, the methods employed to pursue the objectives, and the resources available.[13] Strategy must avoid means that demand resources in excess of those available. Conversely, merely because resources are available, they need not be employed. Strategy also must eschew overexpenditure of resources.

The exception to the foregoing is a strategy of deterrence. Although there are infinite nuances to the concept of deterrence, in the main it is a strategy that seeks to maintain peace through minimum expenditure of resources prior to hostilities, based on the threat of a disproportionate, even excessive, expenditure of resources (such as weapons) once hostilities begin.[14] Because deterrence models seek to condition an adversary's behavior a priori, there is a natural tendency to maximize the deterrent threat. The relevance of deterrence as a strategy to the problem of homeland security is much debated in the strategic community, without consensus to date.[15]

Finally, strategy also is about working within limits. The limits may be a function of the methods being employed (economic, diplomatic, or military) or the resources available (in the case of military methods of pursuing strategy these limits would be air, land, and sea power). Politics must dominate in the development of a national security strategy or any of its subvariants—the National Military Strategy and the National Homeland Security Strategy. This feature of strategy is particularly important in a discussion of homeland security, not least because of the interplay between the requirements of living and those of surviving. It is not a great exaggeration to say that absolute homeland security would require absolute control over the lives and activities of all Americans. Any strategy that seeks to preserve the American way of life by restricting the freedoms of Americans must face an inherent contradiction.

In addition, there is the problem of the limits of strategy itself. Although any national administration can bring great power to bear on the problem of making the homeland more secure, the very magnitude and scope of that power imposes limits on the ability of government to act. The challenges posed by the span of control limit the ability of decision makers to marshal and direct power toward stated objectives. There also is the potential problem of misapplication of strategy. A strategy employed successfully in one context, against one opponent, may be inappropriate or inadequate in another context or against another opponent. The example often cited by historians and strategists is the German blitzkrieg strategy, which was appropriate for the relatively short distances involved in warfare in western Europe but inadequate to the challenges of the expanses of European Russia.

Well before September 11, the first Gilmore Commission report criticized the U.S. government for failing to develop a "comprehensive, fully coordinated national strategy."[16] Bruce Hoffman of the RAND Corporation emphasized the importance of a comprehensive strategy in testimony before Congress on the subject of counterterrorism:

> The articulation and development of such a strategy is not simply an intellectual exercise, but must be the foundation of any effective counter terrorism policy. Failure to do so, for example, has often undermined the counterterrorism efforts of other democratic nations; producing frustratingly ephemeral, if not sometimes, nugatory effects and, in some cases, proving counterproductive in actually reducing the threat. This was among the key findings of a 1992 RAND study that examined, through the use of selected historical case studies in Britain, West Germany, and Italy, the fundamental requirements of an effective counterterrorism policy.[17]

The development of a comprehensive and effective strategy for homeland security must be understood as one of the most complex and daunting tasks ever to confront government. Yet it is absolutely necessary if the United States is to successfully address the challenge of twenty-first-century terrorism. The U.S. government has not been notably successful in previous efforts to develop such a comprehensive strategy to address the war on poverty and the war on drugs. Any formulation of a homeland security strategy must adequately address three key elements of a homeland security strategy:[18]

1. What should be the goals of a homeland security strategy? (ends)
2. What is attainable, and how can progress toward the goals (ends) be determined? (means and MOEs)
3. What can be done in light of shortfalls between ends and means? (limits)

It is important to remember, however, that in the end, although a good strategy must possesses a variety of specific characteristics, there is always the element of chance—what Clausewitz called "friction"—that will confound any strategy. The elements of good strategy discussed above do not constitute a scientifically based methodology. One of the pioneers of modern strategic theory, Bernard Brodie, opined on the subject of strategy that "inasmuch as the [latter] term suggests something comprehensive, coherent and on a level of high-policy decision, we are still far from having found out how to do it scientifically." Instead, Brodie asserted, strategy is part art and part science.[19]

Homeland Security Models: Identifying Ends

The one universal among all the public and private analyses, assessments, and proposals on homeland security has been the call for a comprehensive national strategy to combat terrorism. The meaning of the expression "comprehensive strategy" warrants examination, however. Does a comprehensive strategy mean addressing all threats to the homeland, whether from terrorists or rogue states?[20] Or, as other analyses suggest, should the comprehensiveness of a strategy be judged according to how it organizes a hierarchy of response measures?[21]

The term "comprehensive" most often is employed to reflect the idea that the proposed strategy should address all types of threats to the homeland—or, at the very least, all threats by terrorists. According to the National Strategy, homeland security is "a concerted national effort to prevent terrorist attack, reduce American vulnerability to terrorism, and minimize the damage and recovery from attacks that do occur."[22] Other sources have put forward more expansive definitions of the scope of homeland security—including, for example, threats ranging from ballistic missiles to those to be addressed by a homeland security strategy.[23] Secretary of Defense Donald Rumsfeld appeared to conflate the objectives of a counterterrorism strategy with the broader national security goal of enhanced homeland defense. He stated that "our central objective in the Global War on Terrorism is to stop another 9/11—or worse, a chemical, biological, or even nuclear 9/11—before it happens. Whether that threat comes from a terrorist regime or a terrorist network is beside the point. The objective must be to prevent such attacks if humanly possible."[24] The challenge of identifying the ends of a homeland security strategy is rendered even more difficult by the absence of agreement on the bounds or limits of the subject.

Those who assert the need for a comprehensive strategy do so on the basis of a set of assumptions—some implicit and most untested. The most central of these premises is that the United States faces an unprecedented new threat in scope and scale from so-called rogue states and international and domestic terrorism.[25] Although some analyses and reports suggest that the likelihood of the worst-case threats—those involving weapons of mass destruction (WMD)—is low, they acknowledge that because the consequences of such attacks would be so catastrophic, such threats must be addressed as a priority, inevitably driving both the ends of strategy and overall resource requirements.[26]

The second basic assumption is that if some preparation is good, more is better. "Comprehensive," in this sense, focuses on the employment of all available means to address the threat. This view appears to be driven, in part, by the expansive definition of the threat against the homeland—particularly that engendered by the prospect of a WMD attack. It also appears to be driven by the notion that a layered defense is better than a less comprehensive "point defense" that is designed to protect specific targets or address particular threats. This view was expressed most directly by the Gilmore Commission:

> It is axiomatic that, the better we prepare, through a broad spectrum of antiterrorist and counterterrorist activities, the more likely we are to reach the ideal situation—the deterrence, prevention or interdiction of any terrorist event before it occurs. Given the nature of the potential threats, it is likely that no amount of preparation will cover all possible threat scenarios, and that adequate measures must be undertaken to respond to an event should it occur, in a way that will—first and foremost—minimize human casualties, and that will also mitigate damage to property and to the environment.[27]

Even if the scope of a homeland security strategy were restricted to non-military challenges—that is, terrorism—the issue of achievable ends remains open. The theoretical goal of any homeland security strategy is to prevent terrorist attacks on any domestic target, public or private, as well as to minimize any damage from such attacks. It is evident from any reasonable assessment of the problem that the traditional way of thinking about strategic objectives in war—destruction of the enemy army, occupation of his territory, imposition of peace terms—do not apply in this case. There is one strand of analysis that takes issue with the analogy between counterterrorism and war. The latter has a set of clearly definable parameters and some historically well-validated end-states. The former does not. Thus, there must be an appreciation of the differences in what might constitute the goals or ends of a strategy between traditional modes of conflict and protection of the homeland from terrorist attack.[28]

The theory of war also makes distinction between different levels of hostilities, ranging from small-scale or unconventional conflicts through theater-wide conventional conflict and even nuclear war. Each of these hostility levels poses a different danger to national security and requires different strategic responses. In some instances, the level of danger does not rise above nuisance level and can, in effect, be ignored.

The same problem applies in the effort to build a strategy to cope with attacks on the homeland. A good strategy should distinguish between the dangers posed by different kinds of terrorist attacks. Because resources are finite, a homeland security strategy should start by identifying the most likely and dangerous threats to the nation. Nominally, such an assessment will depend on the kind of attacks terrorists can undertake, the amount of damage they can achieve, and the likelihood of such attacks. As several experts have observed, however, the standard risk calculus is skewed by the prospect of a terrorist attack involving WMD.[29] It was the possibility of such an event and its implications for homeland security that drove the Gilmore Commission's efforts. Yet many observers question not merely the probability of such an attack but its feasibility.[30] How can decision makers prioritize investments and responses when there is no agreement regarding who the adversary is or how he might threaten the homeland?

Clearly there is a lack of clarity, specificity, and definition with respect to the threats that a homeland security strategy must address. Ironically, the first Gilmore Commission report warned of such a possibility.[31] What is lacking is a rigorous threat definition and the kind of risk assessment methodology that would allow for prioritization of threats. Anthony Cordesman described the problem of threat assessment with respect to biological warfare, but in a manner that easily can be generalized to apply to all modes of attack:

> The most important single message that anyone can communicate in regard to biological weapons is that we face a very uncertain mix of existing threats, politics, commercial development and technology that will change constantly as far into the future as we will look. The issue is not what we know, but how little we know and how little we can predict.[32]

According to Bruce Hoffman, "a critical prerequisite in framing such an integrated national strategy is the tasking of a comprehensive net assessment on the terrorist threat, both foreign and domestic, as it exists today and is likely to evolve in the future."[33] Hoffman and several other sources cite the absence of such threat assessments as a major failing of homeland security planning before and after September 11.

A bolder proposition put forward by some analyses is to employ threat assessments as the first stage in the development of risk-assessment models.[34] A risk-assessment methodology can support a homeland security strategy that prioritizes responses to threats, including investments of resources on the basis of both the likelihood of an event and the consequences should one occur.[35] Equally important, such an approach guards against the danger of basing strategy on worst-case scenarios or equal attention to all threats— both of which are options that would bankrupt the national treasury and not necessarily enhance security.[36]

Identification of an adversary or threats is only one aspect of a good strategy and the first in a sequence of steps that supports the formulation of strategic objectives or ends. Another is a theory of conflict. Most theories of conflict pertaining to homeland security/counterterrorism follow a common logical division of the problem into three components: deterrence, prevention, and consequence management.[37] Deterrence in this context is different than during the cold war. Rather than basing deterrence on the threat to impose costs on the opponent, in the context of homeland defense the focus is on denying terrorists their objectives. Deterrence is based on the terrorists' perception of the robustness of preventive measures designed to detect and respond to threats prior to an incident or to protect/harden potential targets against attacks. Prevention involves the panoply of measures, from intelligence through preemption to crisis response. Consequence management generally is regarded as a necessary final element in any homeland security strategy but not one that influences either the likelihood or the character of an attack.

What really distinguishes one theory from another is whether the perspective is—to use Phillip Heyman's term—forward looking or backward looking.[38] Both perspectives can seek to achieve deterrence, albeit by entirely different mechanisms. Both also can pursue preventive measures—the former by actions against the terrorist, the latter by actions to harden targets that are subject to attack. The focus of the former would be the foreign perpetrator; the focus of the latter would be the American citizen.[39]

A forward-looking theory would seek mainly to strike at the sources and/or causes of terrorism. In general, it would strive to take the conflict to the adversary—hunting down terrorist organizations, preempting their attacks.[40] In its ultimate form, it might even seek to address the alleged root causes of terrorism through social, economic, and political programs.[41] A forward-looking strategy may be particularly suited to the problem of WMD-based threats.[42]

A backward-looking strategy would focus on addressing actual attacks through a combination of measures intended to punish the attacker, limit the scope of an attack, and, perhaps most fundamentally, address the consequences of an incident. Often this approach is associated with the concept of terrorism as crime and hence a law enforcement issue. A backward-looking strategy also could stem from the realization that no combination of deterrence, preemption, preventive measures, and hardening of targets is likely to eliminate the threat. The consequence of being wrong even once when the threat is of catastrophic terrorism is too great to rely primarily on a forward-looking strategy.

There are notable historical cases of both types of models being employed. The most noteworthy cases involve Israel and the Intifada/suicide bombings and the British versus the Irish Republican Army (IRA) conflict in Northern Ireland. Israel initially employed a backward strategy, regarding the Intifada and the terrorist actions as conducted by a small minority of Palestinians. The Israeli strategy shifted to being forward-reaching as the government increasingly came to regard the conflict as a war between two peoples and states. The Israeli objective has become to anticipate and prevent terrorist attacks by destroying the terrorist leadership and infrastructure.[43] The British, by contrast, began with a forward strategy that treated the IRA as a military problem. They shifted to a backward strategy in the mid-1980s in part in recognition of the factionalism that was splitting the IRA. The British took a very liberal view, however, of what constituted justifiable actions.[44]

The problem of defining objectives or end-states for the U.S. homeland security strategy is rendered more difficult by the unsuitability of existing models. The historical cases were more limited with regard to the scale and scope of the threat. They did not involve the possible use of WMD. Moreover, the lessons that do seem relevant suggest that the most effective strategy is one that is not only forward looking but preemptive in character. Among the more enduring lessons are the need to destroy the mid-level leadership of terrorist organizations, the importance of disrupting financial networks, and the use of counterintelligence to degrade terrorist reconnaissance activities.[45]

The Bush Administration's Approach

Responding to demands from all quarters, the Bush administration formulated the first National Strategy for Homeland Security. It is far-reaching and extremely complex. The threat it proposes to counter is any premeditated and unlawful act that is dangerous to human life or public welfare and is intended to intimidate or coerce the public or government. The National Strategy for Homeland Security states that it is a plan for mobilizing the entire nation for what is termed "a concerted national effort." It is driven by a belief in a sharing of responsibilities among all branches of government and political jurisdictions.[46]

The National Strategy proposes three strategic objectives. The first is to prevent terrorist attacks within the United States. This goal is to be achieved through a combination of deterrence, detection, and preventive—even preemptive—actions both in the United States and abroad. The second strategic objective is systematically and comprehensively to reduce America's vulnerability to terrorism. By virtue of the scope of the proposed objective, this is termed a "strategic effort." The focus of this second objective is on the protection of what is termed critical infrastructure. The third strategic objective is to minimize the damage and recovery time in the event of a terrorist incident.[47] The National Strategy states that these objectives have been arrayed in priority order—meaning that preventing threats is more important than reducing national vulnerability, and both are more important than reducing the consequences of an attack.

The National Strategy also proposes six mission areas: intelligence and warning, border and transportation security, domestic counterterrorism, protecting critical infrastructure and key assets, defending against catastrophic terrorism, and emergency preparedness and response. These mission areas are aligned with the three objectives. In theory it is possible to prioritize mission areas—in part by determining their relationship to attaining each of the strategic objectives—although the National Strategy does not explicitly rank order the missions.

The National Strategy alternatively describes itself as a strategy, a plan, a foundation, and an agenda. It includes a welter of objectives, missions, initiatives, priorities, and foci. It is an approach to addressing a range of terrorist threats, a bureaucratic blueprint, a spending plan, and a political statement.

Is it a strategy, however? There are critics who think that it is not.[48] The United States is in a pell-mell rush to devise mechanisms and institutions with which to address the perceived threat to the homeland. There are numerous means, in search of a multiplicity of ends. It can be argued that the current National Strategy does not adequately define the threats to homeland security or provide a risk assessment that would rank order threats, except to assert that the most dangerous threat is catastrophic terrorism involving WMD. As a result, any alternative strategy could be equally valid. Indeed, it can be argued that strategy that seeks to address virtually all aspects of homeland security equally—in policy terms if not yet in budgetary terms—is likely to be the least cost-effective of all.

It is ironic that the major studies on homeland security conducted before and after September 11 provide almost no assistance in identifying objectives or end-states for strategy. Instead, they tend to provide operational, procedural, and bureaucratic proposals for the management of homeland security resources and programs in lieu of strategic objectives.[49] The National Strategy, in contrast, does directly grapple with the issue of objectives. Unfortunately, the goals offered by the National Strategy are vague and even contradictory. The first goal—prevention of terrorist attacks—in the estimation of all observers and experts is unattainable. Although the *National Strategy* refers to the connection between itself and the National Strategy for Combating Terrorism, there is no indication of how the latter influences the goals or functional characteristics of the former. Nor are the objectives of the National Strategy tied to those in the National Security Strategy. The National Security Strategy notes that the United States cannot wait until attack materializes—implying that severe threats may be met with preemptive action. What is left unclear is the extent to which preemption as a goal of the National Security Strategy addresses the requirement in the National Homeland Security Strategy for prevention.

The goal of reducing vulnerability to terrorist attack is at one level straightforward and based on common sense. It is a consistent theme of all studies and analyses. At the very least, however, the goal is incorrectly stated. The goal is not simply reduced vulnerability, according to some notional scale from absolute vulnerability to invulnerability. Properly stated, the goal is to attain the maximum degree of protection with the minimum disruption to the American way of life. The National Strategy acknowledges that this goal is a balance between security from attack and maintenance of the American way of life, for which there is no formula; hence it requires reliance on government officials for definition.[50] As a result, it is not a meaningful goal because it is subject to continuous revision that is based, at least in part but possibly fully, on the political judgments of government officials.

Finally, the third goal of the National Strategy, to minimize damage and recovery, also is consistent with the broad range of prior and subsequent studies and analyses. Here, however, the difficulty is framing goals in terms that are actionable and measurable. For example, the effort required to minimize damage and facilitate recovery from a nuclear attack in an urban environment is likely to be beyond the peacetime resource investment the United States is willing to make for such a lower probability/higher consequence event. For higher-probability/lower-consequence events, it is not clear what strategic purpose is served by a national goal of mitigating its damage. In other words, terrorist events that are most likely to occur generally will not rise to a level of destructiveness that requires a strategic response. Those that do rise to such a level will be so catastrophic in their effect that there is little that prior planning can do to limit the ensuing damage.

At best, then, homeland security must be a subset of a broader grand strategy to reduce or eliminate the threat. The National Strategy for Homeland Security must reflect the limits of offensive operations and mitigate inadequacies in the National Strategy to Combat Terrorism. There can never be strategic goals for homeland security. Anthony Cordesman, among others, takes a very pessimistic view of the ability to clearly define goals for homeland security strategy:

> Victory cannot be defined in terms of eradicating terrorism or eliminating risk. This war must be defined in much more limited terms. It will consist of reducing the threat of terrorism to acceptable levels—levels that allow us to go on with our lives in spite of the fact that new attacks are possible and that we may well see further and more serious tragedies.[51]

Defining Effective Approaches to Securing the Homeland: Means and MOEs

In its discussion of means with which to implement a strategy for homeland security, the second Gilmore report emphasized the relationship between ends and means. "Setting priorities is essential to any strategy, but priorities require clear, results-oriented objectives. With some meaningful sense of objectives, it will be possible to develop coherent priorities and an appropriate set of policy prescriptions."[52] The report went on to acknowledge that its recommendations for programs and activities had been formulated in the absence of a strategy.

The second Gilmore report is not an exception to the general trend of placing means and methods ahead of strategy. Prior to the issuance of the National Strategy, government studies and private analyses regarding the needs of homeland security typically provided long lists of measures that need to be taken to enhance homeland security. The second Gilmore report provided twenty-two pages of detailed action recommendations. A report by the Heritage Foundation's Homeland Security Task Force that sought to identify actions to be taken by the federal government to address new security requirements created by September 11, based on a review of existing studies, proposed twenty-five priority key steps.[53]

The National Strategy identified no fewer than eighty initiatives—some programmatic, others organizational, procedural, or legal. Forty-three of these initiatives support the six mission areas that, in turn, sustain the National Strategy's three defined strategic objectives.[54] The other thirty-seven sustain the four foundations of homeland security that "cut across all of the mission areas, across all levels of government, and across all sectors of society."[55] In addition, the Bush administration identified four priority areas for investment in fiscal year 2003, based on an internal cost-benefit assessment, and suggested nine additional priority areas for investment in fiscal year 2004.[56] Writing about the U.S. domestic preparedness program even before September 11, counterterrorism expert Richard Falkenrath remarked on the radical nature of the new approach, which sought to reduce the vulnerability of American society as a whole. In a comment that was even more applicable after the publication of the National Strategy, Falkenrath declared that "this effort bears a superficial resemblance to the U.S. civil defense programs of the 1950s and 1960s, but its scale and complexity were unmatched."[57]

In the absence of clear strategic objectives and a theory of conflict, it is virtually impossible to sensibly rationalize and coordinate the different initiatives and investment priorities. In fact, two of the four investment priorities identified for fiscal year 2003 focus not on the National Strategy's first priority—prevention of terrorist attacks—but on protective and responsive measures.[58] Although these areas arguably could be those with the greatest disparity between current levels of effectiveness and desired operating capabilities, without a coherent strategy and assessment methodology it is impossible to make such a judgment about their priority status or assess the importance of the proposed investments to the three national objectives.

An alternative approach was offered by the Brookings Institution's two homeland security reports, *Protecting the American Homeland: A Preliminary Assessment* and *Assessing the Department of Homeland Security*. These studies argued for a more focused strategy than that proposed by the Bush administration or many other major commissions and analyses. The Brookings strategy defined two goals: first, securing the nation's borders and transportation networks and second, protecting critical infrastructure.[59] Intensified collection, analysis, and dissemination of intelligence would be required to support these two strategic goals. Four of the six mission areas identified in the National Strategy would not be included as elements of a national strategy as defined by the Brookings studies. For example, both Brookings studies suggest that although additional investment should be made to protect against WMD attacks, this area should not be a part of a homeland security strategy.[60] There remains disagreement in the national security and counterterrorism communities regarding how to address catastrophic terrorism.[61]

Means

The operational foci for homeland security can be aggregated into three basic groupings: barrier creation and transportation security; intrusion detection and response; and consequence management. Intelligence cuts across these three areas and is a major supporting component of the first two. Intelligence is not a separate functional area in itself, its own means of pursuing strategic goals.

Barrier creation and transportation focuses on protecting U.S. borders and securing the means of access to the U.S. homeland. To usefully contribute to securing the homeland, barrier systems must provide a reasonable capability to control movement across the barrier and to detect and interdict efforts by terrorists to penetrate it. A successful barrier system must be able to control, detect, and interdict while imposing only a minimal cost in terms of time and dollars on the movement of goods, people, or, in the case of cybersecurity, information. Transportation security focuses on preventing terrorist access to or control over major transportation systems—specifically, air, sea, and land means of movement.

The elements of a barrier system have been well identified by the National Strategy and the numerous homeland security studies. It includes an identification and tracking system for people seeking to enter and exit the country. It also includes a system and appropriate technologies for monitoring cargo and transportation systems, particularly to detect WMD. Finally, it includes means to secure the various modes of transportation against interference, sabotage, or hijacking.

It is important to point out that the structures to implement a program of barrier creation and management already are in place. The National Strategy and various studies cited in this chapter generally are content to maintain pre-September 11 mechanisms, including the operation of the Immigration and Naturalization Service (INS), Border Patrol, Customs Service, Animal and Plant Inspection Service, visa program of the Department of State, and Coast Guard.[62] Although homeland security planning is placing heavy reliance on improvements in intelligence and surveillance technologies, both the means and organizations by which the country has secured its borders and transportation networks for decades, even centuries, are the ones being relied on to implement the strategy of barrier creation. It is somewhat ironic—and troubling—that the means used with little effect in the war on drugs, albeit with some significant increases in manpower and resources, are the same as those being directed at the more difficult and elusive threat of terrorist penetration of U.S. borders. According to David Carr,

> Counterterrorism is the ultimate zero tolerance affair. Yet the same federal assets deployed in the war on drugs—the Coast Guard, U.S. Customs, the INS, the Border Patrol, the CIA, the FBI and the DEA—are the first and last lines of defense in this new war.[63]

It is by no means certain that an effective barrier system can be created—certainly not without imposing absolutely unacceptable costs to the national and global economies. About 7 million people, 200,000 ships, 5.7 million cargo containers, and 100 million cars and trucks enter the United States every year.[64] Thirteen thousand commercial aircraft land or depart from 450 major airports; the number of private aircraft flights is believed to be as much as ten times that number. A reliable visa program has been discussed for many years, but action toward such a system has been painfully slow.

The sheer magnitude of the problem of monitoring these flows, inspecting or certifying the cargoes and vehicles, and tracking people across the border is likely to defy any reasonable effort to create an effective barrier. There are no technological solutions on the horizon that will provide effective remote monitoring of vehicles, aircraft, and cargo containers. Inspecting each container and vehicle is logistically and operationally impossible. There are simply too many ways of entering the country or moving contraband, including lethal items, into the country.[65] The odds of detection and interdiction are extremely long, which is unsatisfactory when the strategy must demand near-zero tolerance, as Carr notes. It is barely possible to provide enhanced security for U.S. airlines and airports, at great cost in manpower and budgets. Ultimately, effective barrier controls and transportation security are not likely to be significant means for securing the homeland.

If it is not going to be possible to erect a solid barrier to entry, might it be possible to detect terrorists in the country and locate and neutralize them? The National Strategy's term for this methodology is domestic counterterrorism.[66] It encompasses expanded intelligence collection by the FBI, the CIA, the Treasury Department, and other government agencies; sharing of information between agencies and departments and across all levels of government; and enhanced capabilities of local law enforcement. Homeland security studies have argued that the ability to detect and neutralize terrorist threats can be improved substantially simply be empowering law enforcement agencies at all levels with more and better information.[67]

Beyond greater intelligence sharing, more responsive communications, and improvements in the management of large databases such as INS files, there is little in the way of active measures that can be taken to employ domestic law enforcement as a major tool in the pursuit of a homeland security strategy. More "aggressive" pursuit of possible terrorist suspects and greater surveillance of the American public would bring homeland security efforts dangerously close to threatening fundamental civil liberties.

More significant, perhaps, is the fact that by its nature law enforcement is backward looking, reactive in character. As a result, it cannot hope to be a highly effective instrument to prevent terrorist attacks. Even with much improved intelligence, domestic law enforcement will produce a failure rate that is simply too high to provide adequate security. The experience of the past several decades with efforts to detect and respond to organized crime and narcotics smuggling activities suggests that too many criminals slip through the detection system. The failure rate experienced by law enforcement agencies in counternarcotics activities suggests that intrusion, detection, and neutralization cannot be a central means for the conduct of a homeland security strategy.

The third "basket" of means for providing homeland security falls under the broad umbrella of consequence management. Included in this grouping are three mission areas identified by the National Strategy: protection of critical infrastructure and key assets, defense against catastrophic terrorism, and emergency preparedness and response.[68] Some observers believe that improved consequence management can not only reduce the impact of terrorist attacks but also enhance deterrence to the extent that such measures frustrate the objective of such attacks. Critical infrastructure and key asset protection involves securing from attack a range of industries and government facilities that provide critical functions or services—such as power, water, food, and communications/cyber space—or are inherently dangerous and could be a source of catastrophic terrorism (such as chemical processing facilities and nuclear power plants). In essence, this asset protection would be a form of preemptive consequence management. Defense against catastrophic terrorism involves a combination of preventive activities to detect WMD in transit or prior to use and responsive measures to reduce the impact of WMD use through early detection and, in the case of biological attacks, prophylaxis. The final category, emergency preparedness and response, is intended to enhance damage mitigation and speed recovery in the event of an attack, whatever form it might take.

There is no question that there are measures that can be taken to tighten security for critical infrastructure, to improve detection possibilities against WMD, and even to enhance responses to a wide range of terrorist attacks. Many proposed measures, such as creation of a nationwide health status monitoring system or providing rescue equipment to first responders, would serve other national interests beyond that of consequence management. To serve as a major means or tool in a strategic plan to secure the homeland, however, consequence management must deny access to—or effects on—a significant portion of the homeland targeted by terrorists. It is possible that extremely rapid and thorough damage mitigation, including medical prophylaxis in the event of a bioterror attack, could provide similar utility.

Two conditions militate against consequence management as an effective means of combating terrorism, however. The first is the sheer impossibility of providing adequate protection for the range of targets that terrorists might choose to strike. It is difficult even to find authoritative figures for the number of critical facilities and key assets, much less assessments of their vulnerabilities. There are more than 100 nuclear power plants, 300 oil refineries, 450 major airports, 10,000 highway and railroad bridges, and tens of thousands of miles of electronic power lines and natural gas pipelines in the United States. There are hundreds, perhaps thousands, of industrial facilities, most in private hands, that make or use dangerous substances. There are no major publicly available analyses of these various critical industries or of the relative importance of the individual elements within each system.[69] As a result, it is hard to understand how a program of protecting critical infrastructure could be formulated or implemented to serve the ends of a homeland security strategy. A RAND report focusing on cybersecurity observed:

> There is no simple "silver bullet" for enhancing U.S. or global critical information infrastructure protection, or even more broadly, information infra-

structure-based critical infrastructure such as electric power. It is still quite unclear how vulnerable key sectors are, how widespread the effects of a major strategic attack might be, and how effective various responses to that attack—such as work-arounds and reconstitution—might be.[70]

Every assessment of the requirements for infrastructure protection and consequence management has emphasized the need to rely on the resources and manpower of local governments and the private sector.[71] One reason for this approach is that much of the critical infrastructure is privately owned, and security for those facilities, to date, has been a corporate responsibility. In addition, initial responders inevitably will be drawn from the thousands of fire, sheriff, and police departments around the country.

This may be an impossible task to impose on local or even state governments. Many fire and police departments are relatively small and have little time or resources to devote to the additional tasks and training required of them to be effective first responders. Several analysts have suggested that it will be difficult to get these governments to invest the necessary time and resources to prepare for what they view as a low-probability event.[72]

The second condition is the scale of effects involved with the most feared terrorist threat: the use of WMD, specifically biological or nuclear weapons. Simply put, a major biological or nuclear incident is all but certain to overwhelm any effort to reduce physical or human vulnerability to such attacks or their consequences. The "Dark Winter" exercise that simulated a smallpox attack on the United States demonstrated the rapidity with which the situation could exceed the ability of state and national leaders to manage the crisis.[73] The problem would be even greater in the event of a biological attack on U.S. agriculture.[74] Although a single nuclear detonation, even in a major city, would not destroy the country, it is hard to imagine how such an incident would not overwhelm local damage limitation and remediation capabilities.[75] Without adequate training and resources, it may not be possible to elicit desired actions by first responders that could mitigate damage.[76]

Some analysts have argued that the threat of catastrophic terrorism, and the use of WMD in particular, has invalidated traditional and even current approaches to homeland security. These studies argue for a radical transformation not only of homeland security organizations and operations but also of the structure of the federal government and even the legal rights and responsibilities of federal, state, and local governments.[77]

Perhaps most distressing is the lack of useful MOEs by which to assess the applicability of proposed homeland security means to the stated goals. In testimony before Congress, U.S. Comptroller General David Walker noted the absence of MOEs for homeland security programs.

The Congress has long recognized the need to objectively assess the results of federal programs. For the nation's homeland security programs, however, we have not yet seen the development of appropriate performance measures or results-oriented outcomes.[78]

Conclusions

Most experts believe that not all terrorism can be prevented. Regrettably, there is no way to "win the war" or to make the homeland 100 percent secure. Defining where the limits might be can determine how effective a strategy can be. Existing studies and analyses have defined what is likely to be the limit of effectiveness in a variety of areas. The overall conclusion is that an effective homeland security strategy is not possible—at least, not without literally placing the nation on a wartime footing. It is virtually impossible to establish adequate monitoring and controls over U.S. borders or the traffic that crosses those borders on a daily basis. Although better intelligence collection and information sharing can improve domestic policing, this area of homeland security is fundamentally constrained by legal and practical considerations. Finally, efforts to protect critical target sets and provide for damage limitation could be effective as long as terrorists choose to attack only a restricted subset of the available target sets and refrain from using weapons or means that could cause catastrophic damage.

The threat of WMD use poses an insurmountable challenge to any homeland security strategy. The ease with which such weapons can be transported and deployed suggests that preincident programs for their detection and neutralization are not likely to be very successful. Use of such weapons also is likely to overwhelm damage mitigation and recovery measures.

These conclusions lead to a third, more important implication for homeland security. The threat posed by WMD to the U.S. homeland requires an entirely different strategy than that suggested by the Bush administration and the aforementioned highly respected studies. The WMD threat must drive strategy. There is some hope that in the future advances in technology will allow the detection of even a relatively limited amount of nuclear material at a distance, thereby providing a basis for a barrier creation system. Such technologies, however, will not be able to detect biological agents. Moreover, the possibility for "engineering" of biological agents is so great that it would challenge the effectiveness of any program of damage limitation and remediation.

The only strategy that is likely to be effective in securing the homeland is one that emphasizes offensive action and even preemption. This response must be broad-based. It must involve a political strategy to win friends, cow enemies, and delegitimize terror as an instrument of policy or a means of warfare. Terrorist practitioners must be anathematized like slavers were a century and a half ago. Finally, terrorists must be hunted down and destroyed by the most lethal covert operations since World War II.

For the most part, defensive measures such as those proposed by the National Strategy for Homeland Security are likely to consume vast amounts of resources for little if any additional security. Investments in intelligence collection, analysis, and distribution may provide some utility in the homeland context, even if the focus of intelligence collection is on support of offensive actions. In the context of an aggressive offensive counterterrorist campaign, the combination of modest improvements in current homeland security programs that are designed to close obvious gaps and enhance day-to-day performance could provide a relatively high degree of security, at least from WMD threats. In blunt terms, the magnitude of the resource investments already made or proposed for homeland security will be wasted.

Notes

1. U.S. Commission on National Security Strategy/21st Century, *New World Coming: American Security in the 21st Century* (Arlington Va.: U.S. Commission on National Security Strategy, 1999), 141 [hereafter U.S. Commission].

2. Advisory Panel to Assess Domestic Response Capabilities for Terrorism Involving Weapons of Mass Destruction (Gilmore Commission), First Annual Report, *I. Assessing the Threat* (Washington, D.C.: U.S. Government Printing Office, December 15, 1999) [hereafter *Gilmore I*]; Advisory Panel to Assess Domestic Response Capabilities for Terrorism Involving Weapons of Mass Destruction, Second Annual Report, *II. Towards a National Strategy for Combating Terrorism* (Washington, D.C.: U.S. Government Printing Office, December 15, 2000) [hereafter *Gilmore II*]; National Commission on Terrorism, *Countering the Changing Threat of International Terrorism* (Washington, D.C.: U.S. Government Printing Office, June 2000); Joseph Collins and Michael Horowitz, *Homeland Security: A Strategic Approach* (Washington, D.C.: Center for Strategic and International Studies, December 2000).

3. See Kurt Campbell and Michelle Flournoy, *To Prevail* (Washington, D.C.: Center for Strategic and International Studies, November 2001).

4. Michael Vatis, "Combating Terrorism: A Compendium of Recent Counterterrorism Recommendations from Authoritative Commissions and Subject Matter Experts," Institute for Security Technology Studies, Dartmouth College, September 16, 2001, 12.

5. *Gilmore II,* 4–6.

6. *Gilmore I,* 35–36.

7. *National Homeland Security Strategy (NHSS),* viii.

8. Ibid., 4.

9. Daniel Moran, "Strategic Theory and the History of War," in *Strategy in the Contemporary World,* ed. John Baylis and James Wirtz (London: Oxford University Press, 2002), ch. 1.

10. Barry Posen, "The Struggle against Terrorism: Grand Strategy, Strategy and Tactics," *International Security* 26, no. 3 (winter 2001/2002): 42.

11. H. Richard Yarger, "Towards a Theory of Strategy: Art Lykke and the Army War College Strategy Model," 1997, 2; available at www.carlisle.army.mil/authors/stratpap.pdf.

12. Dr. Ruth David, "Homeland Security: In Pursuit of the Asymmetric Advantage" (paper presented to Committee on National Security Systems annual conference, April 2002), 2–3.

13. Yarger, "Towards a Theory of Strategy," 2.

14. George Questor, "American Deterrence Theory and Homeland Defense," *Journal of Homeland Security* (ANSER Corporation), October 2001.

15. See the discussion on the nature of deterrence in the conference report on the ANSER Institute for Homeland Security's Homeland Security conference 2001, 2–3, at www.homelandsecurity.com.

16. *Gilmore I,* 56.

17. See testimony by Bruce Hoffman, U.S. House of Representatives Committee on Government Reform, Subcommittee on National Security, Veterans Affairs, and International Relations, *Combatting Terrorism: In Search of a National Strategy,* 107th Cong., 1st sess., 27 March 2001.

18. It is noteworthy that these elements were explicitly identified as the basis for a strategy by the second Gilmore Commission report. See *Gilmore II,* iii–v.

19. Bernard Brodie, "Strategy as an Art and a Science," *Naval War College Review* (winter 1998), 1; reprinted from the same journal, February 1958. One must remember that the scope of Brodie's assessment dealt with a new but readily definable problem: the strategic relationship between the great powers—in particular, the balance of power between the Soviet Union and Western democracies.

20. Collins and Horowitz, *Homeland Security,* 2–3.

21. David, "Homeland Security," and Ivo Daalder et al., *Assessing the Department of Homeland Security* (Washington, D.C.: Brookings Institution Press, 2002), iii.

22. *National Strategy for Homeland Security,* 2.

23. Collins and Horowitz, *Homeland Security,* 2–10; Randall Larsen and Ruth David, "Homeland Defense: State of the Union," *Strategic Review* (spring 2001), 12–18; "Homeland Security: New Challenges for an Old Responsibility," *Journal of Homeland Security* (ANSER Corporation), 10 October 2002; Michael O'Hanlon, "Action Plan for Defending the Homeland," *Baltimore Sun,* 30 September 2001.

24. Secretary of Defense Donald Rumsfeld, "USA Ready on Several Fronts," *USA Today,* 22 October 2002.

25. *Quadrennial Defense Review Report,* U.S. Department of Defense, 30 September 2001, 7–10; *National Security Strategy of the United States* (Washington, D.C.: U.S. Government Printing Office, September 2002), 5–6; *Gilmore I,* 7–11.

26. *Gilmore I,* vii; Anthony Cordesman, *The Lasting Challenge: A Strategy for Counterterrorism and Asymmetric Warfare* (Washington, D.C.: Center for Strategic and International Studies, 2001); Lauren DeVose, "A National Strategy Against Terrorism Using Weapons of Mass Destruction," unpublished paper, Lawrence Livermore Laboratory, July 2002, available at www.llnl.gov/str/Imbro.html. Congressman Christopher Shays, "Combating Terrorism: In Search of Strategy, Priorities and Leadership," speech before National Governors Association, Washington, D.C., 10 July 2001, 2.

27. *Gilmore I,* 52.

28. Bruce Hoffman, "Forward: Twenty-First Century Terrorism," in *The Terrorism Threat and U.S. Government Response: Operational and Organizational Factors,* ed. James Smith and William Thomas (Colorado Springs, Colo.: U.S. Air Force Institute for National Security Studies, U.S. Air Force Academy, 2001), xix–xx.

29. Frank Cilluffo, Sharon Cardash, and Gordon Lederman, *Combating Chemical, Biological, Radiological and Nuclear Terrorism: A Comprehensive Strategy* (Washington, D.C.: Center for Strategic and International Studies, 2000). On the debate in the United States re-

garding the threat of WMD attack see Richard A. Falkenrath, "Problems of Preparedness: U.S. Readiness for a Domestic Terrorist Attack," *International Security* 25, no. 4 (spring 2001): 149–53.

30. Ehud Sprinzak, "The Great Superterrorism Scare," *Foreign Policy* 68 (fall 1998): 110–24; Gary Ackerman and Laura Snyder, "Would They If They Could?" *Bulletin of the Atomic Scientist* (May/June 2002): 1; J. Fred Singer, "Nuclear Terrorism: Facts and Fantasies," *Washington Times,* 5 April 2002; Michael Barkun, "Defending Against the Apocalypse: The Limits of Homeland Security," available at webdev.maxwell.syr.edu/campbell/Governance_Symposium/barkun.pdf.

31. *Gilmore I,* 35.

32. Anthony Cordesman, *Biological Warfare and the "Buffy Paradigm"* (Washington, D.C.: Center for Strategic and International Studies, 2001), 1.

33. Hoffman, "Twenty-First Century Terrorism," 3. See also Bruce Hoffman, "Re-Thinking Terrorism in Light of the War on Terrorism," testimony before U.S. House of Representatives Permanent Select Committee on Intelligence, Subcommittee on Terrorism and Homeland Security, *Defining Terrorism and Responding to the Terrorist Threat,* 107th Cong., 1st sess., 26 September 2001.

34. *Gilmore I,* 52–54; John Hamre, *Meeting the Challenges of Establishing a New Department of Homeland Security: A CSIS White Paper* (Washington, D.C.: Center for Strategic and International Studies, 2002), 6–7.

35. Raymond Decker, "Homeland Security: Key Elements of a Risk Management Approach," testimony before U.S. House of Representatives Committee on Government Reform Subcommittee on National Security, Veterans Affairs and International Relations, *Combating Terrorism: Assessing the Threat of a Biological Weapons Attack,* 107th Cong., 1st sess., 12 October 2001.

36. *Gilmore I,* 35–36. Also Henry Hinton, "Combating Terrorism: Observations on Biological Terrorism and Public Health Initiatives," GAO/T-NSIAD-99–112, 16 March 1999, 4–5. Cordesman, *"Buffy Paradigm,"* 3.

37. Philip Heyman, *Terrorism and America: A Commonsense Strategy for a Democratic Society* (Cambridge, Mass.: MIT Press, 2001), x–xii. Other sources suggest additional categories, but these categories are readily subsumed under the three proposed by Heyman. See David, "Homeland Security," 3–8; Smith and Thomas, *The Terrorism Threat and U.S. Government Response,* part II.

38. Philip Heyman, "Dealing with Terrorism: An Overview," *International Security* 26, no. 3, (winter 2001/02): 26–27.

39. Ashton Carter and William Perry, "The Architecture of Government in the Face of Terrorism," *International Security* 26, no. 3 (winter 2001/2002): 7–8 .

40. David Tucker, "Combating International Terrorism," in Smith and Thomas, eds., *The Terrorism Threat and U.S. Government Response,* 129–54; Posen, "The Struggle Against Terrorism."

41. Roger Housen, "A Temple of Antiterrorism Strategy," unpublished paper, National Defense University, National War College, spring 2002.

42. Brad Roberts, "NBC-Armed Rogues: Is There a Moral Case for Preemption?" in *Close Calls: Intervention, Terrorism, Missile Defense and 'Just War' Today,* ed. Elliot Abrams (Washington, D.C.: Ethics and Public Policy Center, 1998). Michael Barkun, "Defending Against the Apocalypse," 3–4.

43. Martin Van Creveld, *The Sword and the Olive* (New York: Public Affairs, 2002), 335–52.

44. Tony Geraghty, *The Irish War: The Hidden Conflict between the IRA and British Intelligence* (Baltimore: Johns Hopkins University Press, 2002); Ian Lessing, "Countering the New Terrorism: Implications for Strategy," in Ian Lessing et al., *Countering the New Terrorism,* MR-989-AF (Santa Monica, Calif.: RAND Corporation, 1999), 115–17.

45. Bruce Hoffman and Jennifer Taw, *A Strategic Framework for Countering Terrorism and Insurgency*, N-3506–DOS (Santa Monica, Calif.: RAND Corporation, 1992); Bruce Hoffman and Kim Cragin, "Proven Strategies vs. Terror," *New York Daily News*, 12 September 2002.

46. *NHSS*, 1.

47. Ibid., 2–3.

48. Cordesman, *The Lasting Challenge*.

49. Vatis, "Combating Terrorism," 12–14.

50. *NHHS*, 2.

51. Cordesman, *"Buffy Paradigm,"* 4.

52. *Gilmore II*, 6.

53. Heritage Foundation Homeland Security Task Force, *Defending the American Homeland* (Washington, D.C.: Heritage Foundation, 2002).

54. *NHSS*, 15–46.

55. Ibid., x.

56. Ibid., 67–68.

57. Falkenrath, "Problems of Preparedness," 147–48.

58. The four categories are support for first responders, defense against biological attack, securing America's borders, and using twenty-first-century technology to secure the homeland.

59. Michael O'Hanlon et al., *Protecting the American Homeland: A Preliminary Assessment* (Washington, D.C.: Brookings Institution Press, 2002); Daalder et al., *Assessing the Department of Homeland Security,* 53–56.

60. O'Hanlon et al., *Protecting the American Homeland,* and Daalder et al., *Assessing the Department of Homeland Security,* 21–24.

61. Against a strategic focus on catastrophic terrorism see Falkenrath, "Problems of Preparedness." In favor of a strategic focus on catastrophic terrorism see Ashton Carter, "The Architecture of Governance in the Face of Terrorism," *International Security* 26, no. 3 (winter 2001/2002): p. 5–23.

62. *NHSS, op. cit.*

63. David Carr, "The Futility of Homeland Defense," *The Atlantic Monthly*, January 2002, 54.

64. Stephen Flynn, "America the Vulnerable," *Foreign Affairs* 81, no. 1 (January–February 2002).

65. Heyman, *Terrorism and America,* 92–93.

66. *NHSS*, 28.

67. Richard Best, *Intelligence and Law Enforcement: Countering Transnational Threats to the U.S.*, CRS report RL30252 (Washington, D.C.: Congressional Research Service, 3 December 2001); Heritage Foundation, *Defending the American Homeland*, 53–73.

68. Heritage Foundation, *Defending the American Homeland*, 29–45.

69. On this point see "Guarding the Homefront," *Jane's Defense Week*, 11 September 2002, 18–19.

70. Roger Molander, "Protecting the Information Infrastructure: A National and International Perspective," Federal News Service, 26 July 2000, cited in Collins and Horowitz, *Homeland Security,* 36.

71. Arnaud de Borchgrave et al., *Cyber Threats and Information Security: Meeting the 21st Century Challenge* (Washington, D.C.: Center for Strategic and International Studies, 2001), ch. 5; *Gilmore II,* ch. 3; Collins and Horowitz, *Homeland Security,* 7; Hamre, *Meeting the Challenges,* 16–17; Heritage Foundation, *Defending the American Homeland,* 22–24.

72. Robert Knous, "The Federal Role in Protection and Response," in *The New Terror,* ed. Sidney Drell et al. (Stanford, Calif.: Hoover Institute Press, 1999), 358–59; Heymann, *Terrorism and Democracy*, xiii–xv.

73. *Dark Winter* (Washington, D.C.: Center for Strategic and International Studies, 2000).

74. Cordesman, *"Buffy Paradigm,"* 23–26.

75. Cilluffo, Cardash, and Lederman, *Combating Chemical, Biological, Radiological and Nuclear Terrorism.*

76. Cordesman, *"Buffy Paradigm,"* 25–30.

77. Ariel Levite, "Toward a National Defense Strategy," in Drell et al., *The New Terror,* 360–374; Carter, "Architecture of Governance," 22–23.

78. David Walker, testimony before U.S. Senate Committee on Governmental Affairs, *Homeland Security: Responsibility and Accountability for Achieving National Goals,* 107th Cong., 2d sess., 1 April 2002.

TOWARD AN EFFECTIVE GRAND STRATEGY

Audrey Kurth Cronin

The international terrorist threat to United States and allied interests demonstrated itself dramatically on September 11, 2001, but the formulation of an effective grand strategy to respond remains to be fashioned. This book argues that fundamental changes are occurring in the evolution of international terrorism that have serious implications for global security, yet they are not being met with the best multifaceted, balanced, strategic policy. The changes have been occurring for some time: The tragic events of September 11 were symptoms of a long-term trend that is leaving current, traditional bureaucratic state structures behind. Crafting a grand strategy against a nonstate threat such as terrorism is challenging; the alternative to consciously integrating the resources of the United States and the western powers into a coherent approach, however, is to continue to employ policy instruments in an unbalanced, often contradictory, and even counterproductive manner. If there has been a revolution in military affairs, it has been ushered in not by American military preponderance but by a stealthy, diffuse, nonstate coalition. Tactics, it would seem, threaten to trump technology. There is a longstanding grand strategy in place in the United States—an approach that continues the pre–September 11 emphasis on unilateral action, military instruments, and state targeting. The existing approach will not be successful, however, against a nonstate phenomenon that killed more than 3,000 innocent people on American soil and threatens to kill many more, at home and abroad.

The contributors to this book have analyzed the nature of the threat of twenty-first-century terrorism and have proposed a range of instruments to use in response. What does all of this mean for the policymaker? How can the approaches proposed here be coordinated into a coherent whole? The United States and its allies cannot simply do more of *everything*—that's not a strategy, it's a laundry list. Choices must be made.

The purpose of this concluding essay is to highlight some of the themes of the preceding chapters, draw them together, and create a new synthesis that strives toward the outline of a more effective, balanced grand strategy against international terrorism. To do so, I first review the evolving nature of the terrorist threat, then summarize the major changes in the international system that are relevant to that threat, and finally offer the most promising guidelines for building an agile, long-term, effective grand strategy to respond. In other words, drawing on the lessons of the other chapters in this book, I try to answer the following questions: What is the threat? What is the international context? And what should the United States and its allies do?

What Is the Threat? Terrorism, Terrorists, and al-Qaeda

The first step in formulating any effective strategy is to decide who or what the enemy is. One of the fundamental problems of labeling the current campaign a "war on terrorism" is that it implies that the United States and its allies can fight the tactic in all its forms, throughout the world. All terrorism is wrong and must be condemned; it is a heinous tactic that gathers strength through its shock value. Sometimes, however, that despicable tactic is used on behalf of causes that are not necessarily unjust themselves—the end of apartheid in South Africa, the establishment of a Jewish state, and the creation of an independent homeland come to mind. By making the *tactic* the enemy, the United States and its allies have committed two serious mistakes: First, they have established a strategic aim so ambitious that it cannot be achieved, and second, they have set themselves up to be entrapped in local grievances that are infused with political and moral ambiguity.

Strategy is all about matching means to ends. Means are limited, and not all terrorism is equally threatening to U.S. and allied interests. Choices inevitably are made, making the policy look almost unavoidably hypocritical. Fighting all terrorism as a phenomenon under the guise of the United Nations is one thing; establishing such a goal as national policy is another. Moreover, in launching a war on terrorism, the United States and its allies have run the risk of appearing to underwrite the status quo in areas of the world where the threat of nonstate terrorism may be less serious than the injustices being perpetuated by a given state.

A world without terrorism would be a wonderful place indeed, but it is not realistic. As David Rapoport demonstrates (chapter 2), the scourge of terrorism has been with humankind throughout the modern era and for many centuries before.[1] One is reminded of the Kellogg-Briand Pact: The agonizing pain of huge losses in World War I led to a determination on the part of the European powers to outlaw war. Unfortunately, that noble aim played a role in the coming of World War II—an even more horrible cataclysm in terms of numbers of casualties (especially civilian) than the first. It is folly to believe that terrorism can be eliminated completely, and in our effort to do so we run the risk of increasing the incentives for disparate terrorist groups to join together against a common enemy. Divide and conquer is a time-honored approach: There is great advantage in distinguishing among different terrorist groups and targeting our responses specifically toward the behavior and vulnerabilities of each group. The act of terrorism is always bad, but successfully eliminating the capacity or willingness to engage in it may differ from group to group. As Martha Crenshaw observes (chapter 3), grand strategy cannot mean applying the same approach equally to every situation and every group. A selective, variegated approach is necessary.

It is possible to distinguish between different types of terrorism in the current campaign. The goal for the United States and its allies should be to fight what Rapoport terms "Fourth Wave terrorism"—that is, terrorism that was ignited by the Iranian revolution in 1979, continued through the resistance to the Soviet invasion of Afghanistan, and clearly is connected with al-Qaeda and its associates today. This type of terrorism directly targets the United States and its allies, seeks weapons of mass destruction, controls large amounts of resources, and must be rigorously fought. It is a subset of terrorist activity throughout the world today, which includes a large assortment of ethnonationalist/separatist, left-wing, and right-wing organizations. Of course, the activities of most of those groups also are despicable and must be condemned; however, to the extent that they are not clearly connected to al-Qaeda they are not as directly threatening to the West, to the United States, and even to the current state system. Planning a strategy means making choices about where to target one's resources. Al-Qaeda and associated groups in the fourth wave attacked the U.S. homeland, represent the most dangerous continuing threat, and should be very specifically targeted in return.

The current threat has its roots in the Afghan jihad against the Soviet Union and is a newly threatening globalized form of terrorism. As Rapoport and Sheehan (chapter 4) point out, unlike its predecessors al-Qaeda draws its recruits from a large number of national bases and trains individuals, not organized units. Thousands of *mujahideen* from Algeria, Egypt, Pakistan, Yemen, Saudi Arabia, and other countries trained together in Afghanistan, initially against the Soviet presence in that country and later against the

United States' presence in the region. The result is an international movement—sometimes referred to as the "international jihad"—very directly targeted against the United States and its allies. This group has nonnegotiable aims—another thing that distinguishes it from some contemporaneous terrorist organizations, especially many ethnonationalist/separatist groups. One of the foundational beliefs of al-Qaeda is that the same zeal that drove the Soviet Union out of Afghanistan ultimately led directly to the USSR's disintegration as a state and that attacks on the United States eventually will produce the same outcome. From the American perspective this aim is hardly negotiable. Al-Qaeda seeks to create relationships with other local radical Islamic organizations and has proven quite successful at cynically aligning itself with local causes to gain allies, especially since September 11. To the extent that they adopt al-Qaeda's radical agenda, these other groups must be targeted as well.

The U.S.-led campaign in Afghanistan eliminated the al-Qaeda training camps and their active pipeline of new fighters; the threat has not been eliminated, however, with thousands of trained members now dispersed within the region and to some degree throughout the world. The West now faces a more diffuse enemy, in some cases implanted within our own communities—giving the concepts of "state-sponsored terrorism" and "harboring terrorists" a whole new twist. There are more semi-autonomous cells now, with the capacity to act on their own accord. To date the attacks have been smaller than those of September 11 (although the killing of 200 people, mostly young tourists, in Bali was tragically extensive), but the pattern of attacks, past and present, provides no ground for reassurance about the future. Al-Qaeda may be weakened, but it is too early to predict the outcome of this transitional period. The November 2002 attacks in Kenya demonstrated a capacity for simultaneous attacks, and the May 2003 attacks in Saudi Arabia may have involved a succession leadership for al-Qaeda. Both are unusual and lethal characteristics in the history of international terrorism.[2]

This is not a state-centric threat. Nevertheless, as Martha Crenshaw points out, the United States continues to rely on state-focused means to structure its counterattack. For example, although Saddam Hussein's Iraq was an extremely dangerous state with a despicable regime, it was not the *predominant* source of the current terrorist threat. Al-Qaeda may have operated on Iraqi soil, but the network by no means relied on Iraq to have deadly effectiveness. Weapons of mass destruction are available through black market channels that are unrelated to the Iraqi regime. Indeed, for an organization with the resources of al-Qaeda state sponsorship is unnecessary, particularly for chemical and biological weapons. With the United States occupying the territory of Iraq, from the perspective of fourth-wave terrorists there has been an increase in disaffected potential recruits and a dramatic expansion of vulnerable American targets in the region. Although the military campaign went impressively well, the new Iraq is a state rife with divisions requiring a considerable amount of postconflict stabilizing. There were other good reasons to invade Hussein's Iraq, but from the perspective of counterterrorism it is now a perfect environment for al-Qaeda and associated groups to exploit.

The question is not whether states such as Hussein's Iraq are dangerous (of course they are), but compared to what? How well developed are our tools to meet nonstate threats? What are the costs, as well as the benefits, of targeting states that do not control the current wave of terrorism that threatens the United States and the Western powers? There is an important choice being made that the proliferation of weapons of mass destruction into the hands of rogue states is a more immediate and serious threat than the threat of international terrorism. That assessment may be correct, especially when one considers the potentially catastrophic effects of some types of rogue state-executed WMD attacks. Yet absent a more compelling case for why such new proliferators should risk their survival to become nuclear brokers for Osama bin Laden, it has nothing to do with the events of September 11 except in terms of the political capital available to go to war and the rapidly growing incentives for states such as Iran and North Korea to broaden their current ties with nonstate terrorist groups. From the perspective of fourth-wave international terrorism, that is an extremely dangerous prospect. Terrorism and counterterrorism are interactive phenomena: Like any sophisticated enemy, the so-called international jihad adapts its approaches and methods to what the United States does.

The tools to meet the terrorist threat are vastly underdeveloped and uncoordinated, and they are not being advanced in the focus on using traditional military force against Iraq and other states. At the risk of repeating an old saw, as Mark Twain quipped, when all you have is a hammer, everything around you looks like a nail. We need a wider array of tools tailored specifically to directly attacking the most immediate and uncontrollable threat: al-Qaeda and its associated groups.

What Is the Context? How the International System Has Evolved

The changing terrorist threat is a reflection in part of the far more important tectonic changes that have been occurring in the international system since the late twentieth century. Three developments are particularly notable and are described throughout this book: the increasing influence of antisecular ideologies, the decreasing leverage of the traditional tools of the state relative to other factors, and the growth in conditions leading to state failure.

First, the role of concepts or ideologies in spawning terrorist "waves" is amply described by David Rapoport. The role of ideas is extremely important in understanding the evolution of international terrorism. According to Rapoport, the first wave was inspired by democratic reform, the second by national self-determination, and the third by a belief that existing systems were not sufficiently democratic. What he terms the fourth wave—which should be of greatest concern to the United States and the Western powers—is inspired by an antisecular ideology, specifically radical fundamentalist Islamic concepts. The unifying theme of this wave is the desire to return to (or establish) a truly pure Islamic entity (perhaps a caliphate) in which the prevailing concept of the separation of state and religion is eliminated and even considered evil.

This concept of government is an important development, not because the Muslim world is the enemy of the West but for two other reasons: First, some of the ideas that inspire this terrorism—especially its reference to an earlier, more desirable era of Islam—are attractive to a large number of religious adherents at a spiritual and cultural level. Second, it is a vision that is inconsonant with the current international state system. Although the previous "waves" clearly were not in the interests of particular states or governments and were horribly tragic for the victims involved, they were compatible in the abstract with the elemental characteristics of the Westphalian state. The fourth wave is a fundamental challenge to the organization of the system itself as a community of postenlightenment secular states. That development is important and sobering.

At some level the role of ideas has always been stronger than traditional state power. That usually is an advantage when we are speaking of attractive concepts such as democracy, but not if the fundamental nature of the secular modern state itself is considered evil. Under these circumstances, Carnes Lord's challenge—to undermine and ultimately destroy the appeal of radical Islam though psychopolitical measures (chapter 9)—is both extremely important and extremely difficult. The United States is accustomed to thinking in Manichean terms about democratic and nondemocratic states. This is a paradigm shift, however, in many respects going back to a much earlier era in human history; the dichotomy is between theocratic and secular structures. The United States is engaged in extensive cultural mirror-imaging: We are failing to realize the degree to which we project our own debates and perspectives on our enemies. This is not the cold war; it is not only a fight between democratic and undemocratic states.

Second, the relative power and deliberate leverage of the state within the current international system has been reduced in comparison to that of other, nonsovereign entities. This observation is hardly news. The economic and political effects of globalization are much ballyhooed, but in the realm of security they are both understudied and understated. This is especially the case with respect to international terrorism.[3] For example, as Patrick Cronin observes (chapter 10), whereas during the twentieth century most U.S. assistance to the developing world emanated from the public sector, today the private sector controls more than three-fifths of the money flowing to the developing world. Trade flows are an important means of influence—not just because they dwarf official development assistance but also because they reach countries in the Muslim world that receive little aid. From the perspective of traditional state governments, that influence is largely haphazard and untargeted.

This issue is not just economic; traditional alternatives to the use of force such as economic sanctions are more difficult than ever because the state controls them less and less, and their effects often are at odds with counterterrorism. For example, economic sanctions against North Korea do not necessarily decrease the incentives for Kim Jong Il's government to cooperate with international terrorist groups that control significant financial resources. Economic tools often work against security interests with regard to terrorism, yet there is little effort to rectify and integrate the two.

The much-vaunted international information revolution also has had important effects on terrorist tactics, but not for the reasons usually cited. The threat of cyberterrorism has proven to be mostly economic in its effects—dreaded scenarios such as a terrorist group taking over the air traffic control system or hacking into sensitive defense systems have not happened. Instead, terrorists have used the Internet very effectively in the same way that many legal international actors use it: as a convenient means to communicate virtually anonymously, recruit members, collect money, transcend state controls, and coordinate operations. The globalization of international terrorism is a serious challenge to the power of the state, and it is just another symptom of the broad changes that have been occurring in the international system for decades.

Third, these changes that undermine the traditional power of the state have come not only from above (the international sphere) but also from below (the substate level). The dissolution of many states into warring ethnic entities has been well documented in the last decade of the twentieth century, and that violence continues. So-called failed states and states with "no-man's lands" provide a perfect environment for terrorist groups, offering the protections of sovereignty (typically accorded to even the most dysfunctional state) combined with the freedom of movement and operation on the uncontrolled territory of an ungoverned polity. As Lindsay Clutterbuck points out (chapter 6), it is increasingly difficult to separate terrorism and criminal behavior because crimes such as theft, fraud, drug smuggling, money laundering, and financial offenses become commonplace among interconnected and self-perpetuating terrorist networks. Moreover, extraction of terrorist groups and criminal networks is difficult under these circumstances because they can hide behind state sovereignty even when, in practical terms, the terrorist group is not under the control of the state. From the perspective of a terrorist group, it is the best of both worlds. The traditional policy of holding states accountable for actions undertaken from their territories becomes almost meaningless when the state in question may have no credible ability to govern itself.

Even highly functional states are challenged by the nature of twenty-first-century terrorism. The inflexible bureaucracy of the postindustrialized state is poorly suited for the subtleties of counterterrorism. In the United States financial earmarks, political constraints, entitlement programs, bureaucratic inertia, and numerous other factors conspire to limit agility in policymaking. These democratic instruments are superior to any alternative, of course; they make it difficult, however, to structure effective counterterrorist responses, especially over time. The traditional security strategies of modern states—such as deterrence, punishment, and preemption—are made difficult by the fact that they require the enemy to be visible and destroyable. As Tim Hoyt points out (chapter 7), terrorists avoid being fixed in time and space, rarely mass in significant numbers, and by definition strive to maintain the initiative through the element of surprise. They do not exist at the operational level of war, but that is the level at which most military organizations are focused, he writes. Terrorist organizations, according to Hoyt, "often lack a military center of gravity." Again, that makes it very difficult for the traditional tools of postindustrial states to target them.

What Should the U.S. and Its Allies Do? Creating an Effective Grand Strategy

An effective grand strategy looks beyond the war to the peace; clearly this foresight is essential with regard to prosecuting a "war against terrorism." The contributors to this book have discussed a range of policy instruments that all sound worthy and convincing in their importance to the campaign against international terrorism. Grand strategy, however, is not just about doing more of everything; that is both unrealistic and self-defeating because it would lead to a depletion of all of the means of the state to no logical end. It would be foolish to fight terrorism by squandering the precious assets that we aim to protect. Grand strategy is about choices: choosing an attainable end, placing it above other competing and almost as important ends, and making choices among policy options to get there. For example, is the end to fight against state proliferation of weapons of mass destruction? Is the end reducing the international terrorist threat to the United States and its allies? These questions are related (especially over the long term), but they are not the same—unless one assumes that all proliferators lack disincentives to trade or sell their weapons of mass destruction. Even without a "smoking gun," the threat from weapons of mass destruction proliferation is sufficient to warrant a genuine debate about how to pursue both counterterrorism and counterproliferation goals within realistic means. The current attempt to pretend that the two are coterminous is astrategic, self-deceptive, and self-defeating.

If the primary target of U.S. and allied efforts is international terrorism—which this book argues that it should be—then there are three overarching things that the United States must do: first, integrate counterterrorism tools both within and between states; second, network counterterrorism tools at all levels; and third, balance the tools of counterterrorism more effectively.

Integrate

First, many of the contributors to this book press the need to integrate the tools of counterterrorism more effectively. As Michael Sheehan argues (chapter 4), diplomacy is the cornerstone of a comprehensive, long-term, international counterterrorism strategy. It is a vehicle for maintaining the focus of the United States and its allies on the threat of international terrorism and for leveraging the resources of partners who are more capable of analyzing and tracking the actions of local groups. A truly integrated approach is multifaceted and combines legal, financial, economic, law enforcement, intelligence, and other measures, Sheehan writes. Terrorism ultimately is a political act; it must be met with an integrated political response. Even a very effective political strategy will not eliminate all terrorist attacks. The history of counterterrorism demonstrates, however, that uneven or unidimensional responses to terrorist groups—such as using only law enforcement techniques or only military force—virtually always fail in the long run. Instead, the military and political strategies must be two sides of the same coin—such as military action to oust a regime supporting terrorism followed by sufficient and long-term development. The United States has grossly underinvested in our political strategies abroad, preferring to rely more heavily on military and economic means to exert influence. As the contributors to this book demonstrate, this approach is extremely unwise in counterterrorism.

In the United States, integration of counterterrorism tools is at an extremely primitive state. There is tremendous overlap in the functions of different agencies; as Sheehan points out, the Central Intelligence Agency (CIA), the Federal Bureau of Investigation (FBI), and the Department of Defense all have large "foreign aid" budgets—much larger than that of the State Department. Often these agencies work at odds with one another in counterterrorism; for example, the CIA's desire to have local cooperation in pursuing intelligence leads can be at odds with the military's interest in establishing a base of operations despite local opposition. There is no consistent, effective mechanism to consider these clashes in advance and to determine the broader national interest, especially as it relates to counterterrorism. In other circumstances, agencies allow information to fall between the cracks, with one agency failing to communicate effectively with another: The failure of the FBI and the CIA, despite extensive cooperation, to communicate effectively and track two of the terrorists that flew a plane into the World Trade Center is a frequently cited example.[4]

The theme of integration appears repeatedly in this book. In the area of intelligence, integration is central to successful counterterrorism. As Paul Pillar argues (chapter 5), counterterrorism arguably is the area of intelligence that is most dependent on foreign cooperation for success. Although technological means can be useful, it is very difficult to track terrorists without local information about their movements, cohorts, habits, contacts, even appearance. Yet international cooperation is beyond the capabilities of individual intelligence agencies, except with respect to limited arrangements or specific cases. There must be more effective state mechanisms for working with foreign governments in counterterrorism, exchanging information, and using local sources for insight into local terrorist recruiting and operations. "Fourth-wave terrorism" is a global problem that arises from local sources; no single state or agency within the state can fight it successfully.[5] For instance, the extraordinary amount and detail of information required to track suspicious individuals across borders or to vet religious charities on the ground in remote areas requires an integrated international intelligence effort like none before it.

Likewise, integration within the U.S. bureaucracy is urgently needed. The Joint House and Senate Intelligence committees' inquiry into September 11 concluded that the concept of "jointness" must be instilled throughout the intelligence community, through activities such as a joint career specialty; joint education; and joint exercises between U.S. agencies such as the CIA, the FBI, and the National Security Agency (NSA). The final recommendations of the joint inquiry also called for a Director of National Intelligence (to be a cabinet-level position), as well as a National Intelligence Officer for Terrorism, to serve on the National Intelligence Council. These recommendations are perfect examples of the kind of integration that is essential specifically for increasing the effectiveness of U.S. intelligence, as well as U.S. national strategy against terrorism more generally.[6] The use of military force is another area in need of integration; as Tim Hoyt writes (chapter 7), the Department of Defense must learn to operate jointly not just between the services but with other agencies to succeed in counterterrorism.

At the moment there is no effective mechanism for specifically considering the counterterrorism aspects of specific national policies. Counterterrorism may be overruled as a goal in any given instance; naturally it will not be—and should not be—the top priority in all cases.[7] Without better integration of information and instruments, however, crafting a logical national strategy against terrorism is impossible. The United States is operating in an ad hoc manner, and this approach will never chip away at international terrorism.

Integration is important not only among existing bureaucratic agencies but also among tasks related to counterterrorism. Psychopolitical instruments are a perfect example. As Carnes Lord argues, psychopolitical instruments fall under the purview of several different agencies, including the State Department, the Defense Department, the intelligence agencies, and arguably many others. The traditional postindustrial bureaucratic state is being completely outmaneuvered in this area. It is not just a matter of "tweaking" the message; it is a matter of understanding the fundamental cultural, historical, and political origins of the powerful antipathy that has built toward the United States and developing a focused strategy to change it. The United States does not even have a critical mass of linguists who speak the local languages, much less appreciate the nuances of the culture.

Another area of lack of integration is the foreign aid mission: As Patrick Cronin points out, the integration of security policy into foreign strategy is sorely needed to bring coherence to the American approach to the Arab region—an area that is politically volatile and economically unstable. A piecemeal approach to foreign aid has resulted in disappointing results and arguably is a factor in the dismal American image in the Arab world. How can we effectively target foreign aid when the level of security and instability in the regions where we send aid is so low that we cannot even begin to see results? The situation in Afghanistan is exemplary of this dilemma: Even as we prepared for war in Iraq, Afghanistan was far from stable, with anti-U.S. forces marshalling their strength to drive U.S. forces away from isolated bases in the east and south. The international community's efforts to follow the successful use of force with the successful provision of aid and long-term stability to Afghanistan are a long way from being achieved.[8] At the time this book went to press, the postconflict situation in Iraq was similarly worrisome.

Network

Just as fourth-wave organizations have become more agile, decentralized, and locally empowered—especially after the routing of al-Qaeda's training operation in Afghanistan—so must the U.S. and allied response to this international terrorism become more diffuse. In the 1990s we heard a great deal about the so-called revolution in military affairs: The argument was that our technological capabilities would result in the ability to wage war in a networked, agile formation where sensors, nanotechnology, and stand-off weapons would replace traditional set-piece battles with armies against armies. These concepts coincided with concurrent fashions in management theory—particularly the emphasis on flatter organizations, networked information operations, and individual empowerment. That vision was the legacy of the last years of the twentieth century, and Osama bin Laden is a product of that era. What has evolved in the world of international terrorism is an odd perversion of these concepts.

Al-Qaeda and its associated groups have been weakened by the campaign in Afghanistan; to the extent that they have power, however, it is through their networked links among themselves as well as with other like-minded organizations and individuals. The "international jihad" has evolved into a combination of traditional hierarchical organizations (the professional cadre of trained al-Qaeda members), franchise operations (including indigenous groups such as Laskar Jihad and Jema'ah Islamia in Southeast Asia), grant-giving agencies (providing logistical or financial backing for specific operations), and hastily trained individual walk-ins (e.g., Richard Colvin Reid, the erstwhile shoe-bomber, and Ahmed Ressam, who tried to bomb Los Angeles International Airport in 1999). Some groups dissolve and reconstitute under new names, leaving clunky mechanisms such as the U.S. formal designation as a Foreign Terrorist Organization long behind them. This type of multifaceted operation cannot be fought with traditional hierarchical, bureaucratic organizations alone.

If there ever were a challenge that lays bare the weaknesses and inflexibility of the industrial-era governmental bureaucracy, it is terrorism. Al-Qaeda draws its agility and power from the management concepts and practical tools of the age of globalization; the United States cannot fight al-Qaeda with tactics that date to the cold war.[9] Networking our response and developing a multifaceted, agile organization means developing structures that are less hierarchical and more functionally oriented. We need more agile connections among agencies. Those who are involved in counterterrorism should communicate directly, across agencies, blurring the turf of bureaucracies and depending to a larger extent on the training and expertise of individuals.

This need for agility means that our counterterrorism training must be vastly improved. Counterterrorism experts now are trained within the context of their own agency's mission. (The United States cannot even decide on a common definition of terrorism; each agency casts its own bias on the wording.) The network is only as strong as the individual INS or customs official who detects a threat at the border or on a container ship. How knowledgeable is that person? How well can he or she communicate with others who need to be informed? How much of a deterrent can he or she truly pose? Dan Gouré's arguments about the futility of a strategy for homeland security (chapter 11) are relevant here: Abstract goals for homeland security are meaningful only as a subset of a broader grand strategy that is based on networking counterterrorism capabilities at home and abroad and maximizing their individual effectiveness. There will never be an end to terrorist attacks; however, having a smarter, better connected, more interactive federal, state, and local workforce, using the technologies of the globalized era, and avoiding the dinosaur attitudes of the industrialized, bureaucratic state is the only way that the United States can make consistent, steady progress toward reducing the threat over time. In a sense, it is the ultimate devolution back to the individual and away from the nineteenth-century bureaucratized state.

Balance

Finally an effective grand strategy against international terrorism balances competing goals and requirements in many different dimensions, including balancing policy instruments against each other, balancing values against each other, and balancing positive and negative forms of power. This deliberate equilibrium arguably is the most important characteristic.

Balancing competing policy instruments means, among other things, being conscious of the point of diminishing returns and contradictions between policy instruments like those described in this book. The most obvious imbalance in U.S. policy today is the overemphasis on the use of conventional military force relative to other instruments of counterterrorism. Military force was crucial in the months following September 11 and has continued to be an important element of counterterrorism, particularly in maintaining (or pursuing) stability and security in postwar Afghanistan. Whatever the arguments regarding counterproliferation, however, the assertion that a conventional military invasion of Iraq has been directly beneficial in the campaign against international terrorism has been difficult to follow. Among other things, it has siphoned off resources from counterterrorist operations against al-Qaeda and its offshoots, drawn away special operations forces, and undermined some efforts at allied cooperation even as it has provided a fresh point for anti-Americanism and a plethora of new U.S. targets in the region. Psychopolitical instruments, for example, have been seriously hurt by overreliance on the use of military force in the region. The contributors to this book have argued repeatedly for more balance among the instruments they have examined here, and an effective grand strategy must take into account the relationships among all of them.

The concept of balance also refers to the balance between values such as civil liberties and the empowering of law enforcement agencies at home, as well as the balance between rigorous counterterrorism and international law abroad. Failing to consider the impact on civil liberties of aggressive counterterrorist measures such as the U.S.A. Patriot Act, for example, risks under-mining the civil society that a grand strategy is designed to protect. Careful attention must be paid to the balance between protection of the physical well-being of U.S. citizens and protection of their rights. In the international arena, Adam Roberts argues (chapter 8) that major powers ignore basic norms in the international community only at their peril because such be-havior can have a negative effect on coalition partners, enemies, and even their own citizens. Ignoring such fundamental norms also potentially un-dermines the legitimacy of the actions of the state and advances the politi-cal causes of fourth-wave terrorist organizations. Both outcomes are ex-amples of the pursuit of means at the expense of the ends.

Balance also relates to the relationship between instruments of positive power and instruments of negative power. Terrorists consciously attempt to deploy both: By using horrible, negative events to shock, they aim to draw attention to a "positive" aim—or, at least, an aim that is intended to seem positive or attractive to some audience (on earth or, arguably, in heaven). Yet terrorism is a fundamentally political phenomenon. Over time, terrorist groups have no power if they have no message, no political goal, no vision of an alternative future (on earth or in the hereafter). In fighting terrorism, the United States must use both positive and negative means as well—for ex-ample, providing aid, engaging in reconstruction of broken societies, and pre-senting an image of a universal commitment to democracy and individual free-dom, on one hand, while demonstrating awesome military power, capturing or killing terrorist leaders, and destroying safe havens for terrorist activity, on the other. So-called positive power is aimed not at the terrorists themselves but at the real source of their power: the active or passive communities of support from which they draw resources and potential recruits. The key is to balance negative power, which often is critical in the short run, and pos-itive power, which is essential to counterterrorism success in the long term.

This position is not naiveté or liberalism but pragmatism. As Dan Gouré writes (chapter 11), a truly preemptive strategic approach must not only re-spond to terrorist attacks that already have occurred by tracking down the perpetrators but also strike at the sources of terrorism—which is where this book begins. At all times in the development of an effective grand strategy aimed at long-term success against international terrorism, the crucial con-cept is balance among the instruments of policy, the developmental stages of terrorist activity being targeted, and the means and ends being pursued.

The United States, the most powerful actor in the world today, is being threatened by an enemy that plays effectively on its vulnerabilities. The only way to achieve success in this campaign against international terrorism is to begin by recognizing the weaknesses of the current approach and engaging in vigorous debates akin to those of the early cold war years. The United

States and its allies must recognize that the world has changed, that the threat of international terrorism has evolved, and that they are facing a nonstate enemy that requires a fundamental rethinking of American grand strategy.

Notes

1. Also see David Rapoport, "Fear and Trembling: Terror in Three Religious Traditions," *American Political Science Review* 78, no. 3 (1984): 658–77.

2. See Audrey Kurth Cronin, *Al Qaeda after the Iraq Conflict,* CRS Report for Congress, RL21529, 23 May 2003.

3. See also Audrey Kurth Cronin, "Behind the Curve: Globalization and International Terrorism," *International Security* 27, no. 3 (winter 2002/2003): 30–58.

4. Bill Gertz, "Investigator Says FBI, CIA Mishandled Leads on Attacks," *Washington Times,* 25 September 2002 (accessed at http://asp.washtimes.com on 10 February 2003); and "Report: FBI, CIA Need Overhaul: 'Real Gaps in Performance,' Says Lawmaker," CNN report (accessed at www.cnn.com/2002/US/07/17/attacks.intelligence/ on 10 February 2003).

5. Final Report of Congressional Joint Inquiry Into 9/11, "Recommendations: December 10, 2002" (accessed at www.fas.org/irp/congress/2002_rpt/recommendations.html on 10 February 2003).

6. Ibid.

7. Paul Pillar argues this point in his book *Terrorism and U.S. Foreign Policy* (Washington, D.C.: Brookings Institution Press, 2001).

8. Part of the successful integration of foreign aid into the national security strategy will entail differentiating among different kinds of developing countries: beleaguered states and stateless zones where terrorists operate with relative impunity; pivotal transition countries—some of which find themselves close to the United States since September 11, such as Pakistan or the central Asian republics; cooperative Muslim states threatened by Islamic extremists (such as Egypt and Jordan); and Muslim countries with modernizing forces (such as Turkey, Indonesia, or Iran). All could use a strategy in which aid is more effectively integrated.

9. On globalization and international terrorism, see Cronin, "Behind the Curve." For insight into Osama bin Laden's organization and leadership style, see Peter L. Bergen, *Holy War, Inc.* (New York: Free Press, 2002); and "Interviews: Terrorism's CEO," *The Atlantic* Online, 9 January 2002 (accessed at www.theatlantic.com/unbound/interviews/int2002-01-09.htm on 10 February 2003).

contributors

Lindsay Clutterbuck is a detective chief inspector in the Specialist Operations Department of the Metropolitan Police, London. He has been involved in counterterrorism since 1982 and has undertaken roles in the fields of policy and strategy, operations, analysis, and liaison. He holds a bachelor of science degree and a master's degree in Police and Criminal Justice Studies. In 2002 he was awarded a doctorate by the University of Portsmouth for his thesis on the origin and evolution of British police counterterrorism strategy and operations during the nineteenth century.

Martha Crenshaw is the Colin and Nancy Campbell Professor of Global Issues and Democratic Thought and professor of government at Wesleyan University. She also is the author of *Revolutionary Terrorism: The FLN in Algeria, 1954–1962* (Hoover Institution, 1978) and editor of *Terrorism, Legitimacy and Power* (Wesleyan University Press, 1983) and *Terrorism in Context* (Pennsylvania State University Press, 1995).

Audrey Kurth Cronin is Specialist in Terrorism for the Congressional Research Service at the Library of Congress. Formerly she was a research fellow in the Center for Peace and Security Studies and a visiting associate professor of security studies, Edmund A. Walsh School of Foreign Service, Georgetown University. She was a Marshall Scholar at St. Antony's College, Oxford, and postdoctoral fellow in European Society and Western Security at Harvard University. She is the author of *Great Power Politics and the Struggle over Austria* (Cornell University Press, 1986), as well as a forthcoming manuscript and many articles on terrorism and related subjects.

Patrick Cronin is the assistant administrator for policy and program coordination of the U.S. Agency for International Development and director of the Millennium Challenge Account Task Force. Before his confirmation by the U.S. Senate as assistant administrator, he was the director of research and studies at the U.S. Institute of Peace, an independent federal agency created by Congress to develop knowledge for managing international conflict. Cronin is a specialist in both Asian affairs and global U.S. security policy. Prior to the Institute of Peace, he was at the National Defense University's Institute for National Strategic Studies. As deputy director and director of research at the institute, he directed advanced research efforts by more than twenty senior analysts in support of the secretary of defense, the chairman of the Joint Chiefs of Staff, and other senior Defense Department officials. He directed long-range strategic studies, as well as the institute's Asian-Pacific research program. He is the coeditor (with Robert J. Art) of *The United States and Coercive Diplomacy* (U.S. Institute of Peace, 2003) and (with Michael J. Green) of *The U.S.–Japan Alliance: Past, Present, and Future* (Council on Foreign Relations Press, 1999).

Daniel Gouré is a vice president with the Lexington Institute, a nonprofit public policy research organization. At Lexington he specializes in issues of advanced military technology, homeland security, and international security affairs. Prior to holding his current position, he was deputy director of the International Security Program at the Center for Strategic and International Studies, where he was responsible for analyses of U.S. national security policy, the future of conflict and warfare, the information revolution, counterproliferation, and defense industrial management. He directed analyses of emerging security issues, with a special emphasis on U.S. military capabilities in the next century. In addition, Gouré spent two years in the U.S. government as director of the Office of Strategic Competitiveness in the Office of the Secretary of Defense.

Timothy D. Hoyt is an associate professor in the Strategy and Policy Department at the U.S. Naval War College in Newport, R.I. He was research fellow for Georgetown University's Center for Peace and Security Studies and visiting assistant professor in the Security Studies Program until 2002. Hoyt has written and consulted on a variety of subjects, including the diffusion of military technologies and practices, the proliferation of conventional and unconventional weapons, regional security in the Middle East and South Asia, the evolution of strategy and arms production in the developing world, and the use of terrorism in independence struggles.

Carnes Lord is a professor of strategy in the Strategic Research Department, Center for Naval Warfare Studies, U.S. Naval War College. He was director of international communications and information policy on the National Security Council staff (1981–83), assistant for national security affairs to the vice president (1989–91), and distinguished fellow at the National Defense University (1991–93). Lord also has taught political science, most recently at the Fletcher School of Law and Diplomacy at Tufts University. He is the author of *The Presidency and the Management of National Security* (Free Press, 1988).

Paul Pillar was appointed national intelligence officer for the Near East and South Asia in October 2000 upon his return to the intelligence community from the Brookings Institution, where he had been a Federal Executive Fellow. He joined the Central Intelligence Agency (CIA) in 1977 and served in a variety of analytical and managerial positions, including chief of analytic units covering portions of the Near East, the Persian Gulf, and South Asia. He previously served in the National Intelligence Council as one of the original members of its Analytic Group. He was executive assistant to the CIA's deputy director for intelligence and executive assistant to Director of Central Intelligence (DCI) William Webster. He headed the Assessments and Information Group of the DCI Counterterrorist Center and from 1997 to 1999 was deputy chief of the center. He is the author of *Negotiating Peace* (Princeton University Press, 1983) and *Terrorism and U.S. Foreign Policy* (Brookings Institution Press, 2001).

David C. Rapoport is an emeritus professor of political science at the University of California, Los Angeles (UCLA). He is a political theorist who became interested in terrorism in the 1960s. He founded the Center for the Study of Religion at UCLA in 1995. He is the founding editor and current editor of the *Journal of Terrorism and Political Violence,* a highly regarded academic journal in the field of terrorism studies. He developed an American course on terrorism in 1970, and his book *Assassination and Terrorism* (Canadian Broadcasting Corp., 1971) was the first contemporary volume on the subject. He has published three other books on terrorism-related subjects, the most recent a coedited volume (with Leonard Weinberg), *The Democratic Experience and Political Violence* (Frank Cass, 2001), and he has written thirteen articles on religion and violence.

Sir Adam Roberts is the Montague Burton Professor of International Relations at Oxford University and a fellow at Balliol College. He is an internationally recognized expert on the laws of war and has been writing on terrorism and related issues since the 1970s. He has published dozens of books and articles, including *Documents on the Laws of War* (Oxford University Press, 2000), which he coedited with Richard Guelff.

Michael A. Sheehan was appointed deputy commissioner, counterterrorism, for the New York City police department in June 2003. Previously Sheehan served as Assistant Secretary General, Department of Peacekeeping Operations, at the United Nations (2001–2003). He was ambassador-at-large for counterterrorism at the U.S. Department of State from 1998 to 2000. Sheehan is a retired lieutenant colonel of the U.S. Army Special Forces. He served in Panama as a special forces detachment commander (in a counterterrorism unit), as a company commander in the demilitarized zone in Korea, and as a counterinsurgency advisor in El Salvador. While on active duty, Sheehan served at the White House on the National Security Council staff under presidents George H. W. Bush (1989–1992) and Clinton (1995–1997). He is a graduate of the U.S. Military Academy at West Point and has masters' degrees from the Georgetown University School of Foreign Service and the U.S. Army Command and General Staff College.

index

Abizaid, John, 178
Abkhazia (Georgia), 102
Abu Nidal, 59, 173
Abu Sayyaf, 4, 101
Achille Lauro (ship), 60
Action Directe (France), 56
al-Adel, Saif, 100
Afghanistan: and Clinton administration,
  82, 84; collapse of al-Qaeda in, 64, 65,
  73n77; education in, 256; foreign aid
  in, 251–53; and Geneva Protocols/
  Conventions, 195–96, 206, 216n23;
  Kabul-Kandahar highway project,
  252–53; and al-Qaeda, 99–100, 101,
  113n1; Soviet invasion of, 61, 62; and
  state-sponsored terrorism, 32–33,
  44n40, 171, 174. *See also* Afghanistan,
  U.S.-led war in (2001); al-Qaeda;
  Taliban
Afghanistan, U.S.-led war in (2001), 195–
  208; battle for Tora Bora, 198, 201;
  bombing and air power in, 197–201;
  CIA covert action in, 84, 224; and civilian casualties, 197–200, 216nn30, 33;
  and collapse of al-Qaeda, 64, 65,
  73n77; and conventional military force,
  110, 126, 168, 175–77; counterterrorism strategies and objectives of, 82, 84,
  87–88; and culminating point of victory, 176–77; and foreign aid, 251–53,
  295; and intelligence, 126, 138; as internationalized civil war, 196; and laws
  of war, 187, 195–208, 215n6; and postwar instability, 88; prison disasters,
  201–2; prisoners and, 201–3, 205–10,

211–12; psychological-political instru-
  ments in, 227
African embassy bombings (1998): coun-
  terterrorism focus after, 123; Crowe
  panel on, 117, 125; U.S. strikes in response to, 28, 63, 81–82, 99, 164
Ajami, Fouad, 226
Alexander II, Czar, 51
Alexander I of Yugoslavia, 55, 71n39
Algeria, 53–54, 55, 62, 63, 64, 71n40
Alliance for Progress, 244
American Weather Underground, 56
Amnesty International, 208
Anarchist wave of international terrorism
  ("first wave"), 47–49, 50–52; and creation of doctrine, 50–52; and dynamite
  bombs, 51, 70n25; efforts to eliminate,
  52; factors facilitating, 49; hope and
  revolutionary efforts of, 51, 70n27; and
  international assassinations, 51–52, 57,
  70n31; and terrorism as strategy, 51,
  70n26; and terrorist diaspora, 51–52;
  and third wave terrorism, 56–58;
  women in, 70n25
Angry Brigade, 151
Animal and Plant Inspection Service, 275
ANSER Corporation, 263
anticolonial wave of international terrorism ("second wave"), 47–50, 52–56;
  duration of, 48; emergence of, 52–53;
  and international diaspora groups, 55;
  new terrorist tactics of, 54–56, 71n40;
  self-descriptions and new language of,
  54; and supranational organizations,
  55–56; women in, 56

305

Anti-Terrorism, Crime and Security Act (2001), 159n11
Anti-Terrorism Assistance (ATA) program (State Department), 106, 108, 112
ANZUS (Australia, New Zealand, and U.S. Treaty states), 107
Arab Human Development Report 2002 (UNDP), 248, 255
Arab world: economic growth challenges for, 249; education in, 256; foreign aid and war on terrorism, 239, 249; and perceptions of terrorism, 239; al-Qaeda religious terrorism and Arab anger, 63–64, 73n72; and state-supported terrorism, 33–34; and Voice of America audience, 225, 234n14. *See also* Muslim world
Arab World Competitiveness Report 2002–2003 (World Economic Forum), 249, 256
Arafat, Yasser, 59
Armed Islamic Group, 101
Armenian nationalist groups, 51–52
Arnold, Terrell E., 78–79
Art, Robert J., 77
Ashcroft, John, 134
Asian Development Bank, 252
assassinations, 51–52, 54, 57–58, 70n31, 164
Assassins (terrorist group), 69nn6, 7
Assessing the Department of Homeland Security (Brookings Institution), 274
Atta, Mohammed, 125
Aum Shinrikyo, 32, 61, 67, 81, 146
Australia, New Zealand, and U.S. Treaty states (ANZUS), 107
"Axis of Evil," 174, 175
Azerbaijan, 62

Bali bombing (October 2002), 100, 101, 255, 288
Balkans, 51, 52, 54, 71n39
Basque ETA, 57, 148, 171
Baxter, Richard R., 217n51
Beers, Charlotte, 227
Begin, Menachem, 53, 54, 70n27, 71n35
Beirut, Marine barracks bombing in (1983), 41nn2, 10
Benjamin, Daniel, 73n81
Bergen, Peter, 43n28, 63, 65
Bibawi, Nabil Luka, 41n10
Binalshibh, Ramzi, 102

bin Laden, Osama: Bush administration campaign against, 84; Clinton administration efforts against, 82, 84; and early counterterrorist intelligence, 82, 122; at large, 99; leadership and personality characteristics, 26–27; lionization and sympathy for, 28, 43n28, 63, 167, 226; and September 11 hijackers, 125; and women's roles, 49, 70n16; and worldwide Sunni groups, 64. *See also* African embassy bombings (1998); al-Qaeda
Black September, 57, 91n21
Border Patrol, U.S., 275
Borsellino, Poalo, 148
Bosnia, 62
Boyce, Michael, 150
Bremmer commission, 261
Bretton Woods economic system, 242–43
British Broadcasting Corporation (BBC), 224
British Special Branch, 68n4
Broadcasting Board of Governors (BBG), 222, 229
Brodie, Bernard, 267, 281n19
Brookings Institution, 274
Burdick, Eugene, 243
Burma, 53
Bush, George H. W., 80–81, 121, 164
Bush, George W.: and "Axis of Evil," 174; declaration of war on terrorism, 46, 68n1, 166–68, 174; and end of Iraq war (May 2003), 175; on operations against al-Qaeda, 177–78; on al-Qaeda prisoners, 209–10; on terrorists as fanatics, 41n10; and U.S-led war in Afghanistan, 197; on weak/failing states and terrorism, 254
Bush administration: early counterterrorism and security by, 82, 92n28; and declaration of war on terrorism, 46, 68n1, 84–85, 166–68, 174; foreign aid and development issues, 240, 244, 246, 252, 254; infrastructure projects in postwar Afghanistan, 252; and organization of international coalition, 84; and seizure of "unlawful combatants," 84. *See also* National Security Strategy (2002); National Strategy for Homeland Security (NSHS)

Carr, David, 275–76
Carter, Ashton B., 77, 83, 91n11, 92n34

"catastrophic terrorism," 77, 83, 91n11
Caucasus and central Asia, 101, 102, 107–8
CBRN incidents, 152, 153. *See also* weapons of mass destruction (WMD)
Celmer, Marc, 79
Center for Anti-Terrorism and Security Training (CAST), 106
Center for Strategic and International Studies, 261
Central Intelligence Agency (CIA): in Afghanistan, 84, 224; counterterrorism assistance programs of, 84, 106, 121–22; covert action role, 82, 84, 224; and CTC, 121–22; and FBI, 124, 294; and grand jury testimony, 136; institutional intelligence culture and, 129–30; and integration of counterterrorism tools, 293–94; and psychological-political instruments, 222, 224; risk-taking guidelines and risk aversion, 129–30; before September 11, 82, 124. *See also* intelligence and counterterrorism
Ceylon, 53
Chalabi, Ahmed, 178
Chamberlain, Wendy, 107
Chechnya, 62, 101, 102
Christian terrorism, 36, 61
"The Clash of Civilizations" (Huntington), 35
Clausewitz, Carl von, 162, 166, 168–69, 182n18, 183n33, 184nn45, 56
Clinton administration, 80–82, 84
Clutterbuck, Lindsay, 8–9, 291. *See also* law enforcement and counterterrorism
Coalition Information Center initiative, 230–31
Coast Guard, U.S., 275
cold war, 58–59, 80–81, 220–21, 238–39
Colombia, 57
Commando Solo (Air Force psyop), 223
Commission on U.S. National Security in the Twenty-First Century (Hart-Rudman Commission), 261
Congressional Panel on Terrorism, 109
Continuity IRA, 48
Cordesman, Anthony, 268, 272
counterinsurgency operations (COIN), 149–50
Counter Terrorism Committee (CTC) (United Nations), 104

Counter Terrorism Liaison Officers (CTLO) (European Union), 154
Counterterrorist Center (CTC), 121–23, 127
Counter Terrorist Task Force (CTTF) (European Union), 156
Crelinsten, Ronald, 142, 159n3
Crenshaw, Martha, 6, 37, 39, 287, 288. *See also* grand strategies of counterterrorism
"crimes against humanity," 187–88, 214n2. *See also* laws of war and counterterrorism
Cronin, Audrey Kurth. *See* grand strategies of counterterrorism; sources of contemporary terrorism
Cronin, Patrick M., 12–13, 290–91, 295. *See also* foreign aid and counterterrorism
Crowe, William, 117
Crowe panel on African embassy bombings, 117, 125
Cuba: early terrorist training in, 58; Guantanamo Bay, 84, 203, 205–7, 209–10
Customs Service, 275
cyberterrorism, 277–78, 291
Cyprus, 53–54, 55

David, Ruth, 263
Dawes Plan (1924), 241–42
Delbruck, Hans, 170, 183n34
Department of Defense (DoD): defense public diplomacy role of, 223–24, 229–30, 293; defining war on terrorism, 176; and "information operations" (IO), 223; and Office of Strategic Influence (OSI), 227, 229–30, 236n37; and psychological-political instruments, 223–24, 229–31; and special operations forces, 108, 178–79; and State Department, 230–31
Department of Homeland Security, 68n4, 132
Development Assistance and Child Survival and Health accounts, 247
diplomacy and counterterrorism, 7, 97–114, 293; assistance programs, 106–9, 112; ATA program and, 106, 108, 112; coalition and roles of key partners in, 97–98, 105; coordinating efforts at regional levels, 107–9, 112;

diplomacy and counterterrorism (*cont.*)
and credibility issue, 224–25; defense
public diplomacy and psyop, 223–24,
229–30; defining diplomacy, 98; and
democratic transition, 112; ensuring
proper use of security apparatus,
108–9; in Europe, 232–33; and FTO
designations, 105; funding/budget for,
106–7, 108, 111–12; international laws
and resolutions, 104–5, 112; and law
enforcement, 104, 106–7, 108, 112;
and local terrorist organizations, 103;
and military training assistance, 107,
108; and Pakistan-U.S. relationship,
110–12; and political will, 98, 103,
106; providing alternatives to violence,
110–11; providing financial resources,
108, 112; and psychological-political
instruments, 222, 223–25, 229–32;
public diplomacy, 222, 223–25,
229–32; and al-Qaeda threat, 97–98,
99–103, 109; sanctions and use of
force, 109–10; and State Department,
106–7, 108, 111, 112–13; state-sponsored terrorism and noncooperating
states, 109–10; and UN Conventions on
Terrorism, 104, 112; and UN Security
Council, 104, 112; and zero-tolerance
policies, 103, 104–5, 111, 112
Directorate of Central Intelligence (DCI),
121, 123, 127, 129–30. *See also* Counterterrorist Center (CTC)
Djindjic, Zoran, 148–49
Dostum, Rashid, 201
Downing, Wayne, 125
Dror, Yehezkel, 79–80, 91n22
Durán, Khalid, 253

Easterly, William, 255–56
Economic Recovery Administration, 242
Economic Support Funds (ESF), 247, 251
education: in Arab world, 256; and for-
eign aid, 253, 255–56; and gender in-
equities, 256; immigration for, 253;
madrassas, 25, 110–11, 230, 233, 255
Egypt, 53, 62, 63, 64, 226, 232
El Dorado canyon strikes in Libya
(1986), 164
El Shifa pharmaceutical plant strikes in
Sudan (1998), 28
The Elusive Quest for Growth (Easterly),
255–56

Emergency Fund for HIV/AIDS, 246
Ethiopia, 53
Ethniki Organosis Kyprion Agoniston
(EOKA), 53–54, 55
Europe: diplomacy in, 232–33; law enforce-
ment and counterterrorism, 145, 154–56,
158; al-Qaeda network and, 100, 101.
See also names of individual countries
European Union, 145, 154–56, 158, 252
European Union Framework Decisions,
145, 155–56, 158
EUROPOL, 60, 155, 156
Euskadi ta Askatazuna (ETA), 57,
148, 171
Ex Parte Richard Quirin (U.S. Supreme
Court) (1942), 204
Export Administration Act of 1979, 31

"Faces of Islam" (Pipes and Durán), 253
failed states: Bush on, 254; defining, 241,
257; and foreign aid, 240–41, 246, 247,
254, 257; and link between poverty and
terrorism, 240, 254; and reconstruction
of al-Qaeda, 173; and sources of terrorism, 33, 291
Falcone, Giovanni, 148
Falkenrath, Richard, 78, 273
Federal Bureau of Investigation (FBI): and
CIA, 124, 294; counterterrorism assistance programs of, 106, 293; and creation of domestic security service/
agency, 133–34; and CTC, 122, 127;
and first wave terrorism, 68n4; manpower requirements, 130–31. *See also*
intelligence and counterterrorism
Feith, Douglas, 229
Ferdinand, Archduke Franz, 52
Ferghana Valley, 101
Figner, Vera, 70n19, 72n56
Finance Action Task Force, 104
first wave terrorism. *See* Anarchist wave
of international terrorism ("first wave")
Foreign Affairs, 35, 92n28, 243
foreign aid, evolution of, 241–45;
post–World War I, 241–42; and Marshall Plan, 242–43, 244, 247; Kennedy
administration, 243; creation of USAID,
243; the sixties, 243–44; Vietnam War
and military assistance, 243; poverty alleviation, 243–44; late sixties and early
seventies, 243–44; late eighties and Reagan administration, 244; aid to Latin

America, 244; economic growth approach, 244; the nineties, 244; post–cold war era, 238–39; African development assistance, 239; NGOs, 244; globalization, 244–45; and challenges for Bush administration, 244, 258–59
foreign aid, general objectives of, 245–47; development assistance, 246–47; economic growth, 246, 247; MCAs, 245–46, 247; and mismatch between objectives and means, 247, 259n9; official development assistance, 245–46, 259n9; security or political objectives, 246–47, 295; stability in weak/failing states, 246, 247
foreign aid and counterterrorism, 12–14, 238–60; before September 11, 238–39; adapting aid, 258–59; addressing weak and failing states, 240–41, 254; and Afghanistan after U.S.-led war, 251–53; and building of durable institutions, 250; coordinating donor-recipient priorities, 251–53; economic failure and state failure, 240–41; and education, 253, 255–56; and foreign aid triage, 249–50; and globalization, 244–45, 290–91; humanitarian relief, 212, 251, 252; and integrated approach, 251–53, 295, 299n8; military aid, 243, 258; and Muslim immigration to U.S., 253–54; and Muslim world, 239, 247–50, 253–54, 255–56; and national security strategy, 240–41; and nation-state failure, 257; and necessity of being on the ground, 257; necessity of focusing on terrorist centers, 239–40; and new policy concerns, 245; nurturing and strengthening of civil society, 250; policy lessons derived from past developments, 250–57; providing peace and security, 249–50; question of link between poverty and terrorism, 240, 254–55; and sanctions/incentives, 257–58, 291; strategically-focused economic aid, 243, 248, 258; and sustainability of long-term donor funding, 252–53; and winning the peace, 251–53
Foreign Assistance Act (1961), 31, 238
Fourth Psychological Operations Group (POG), 223
fourth wave terrorism. *See* religious wave of international terrorism ("fourth wave")

France, 56, 60, 154
Freedman, Lawrence, 181
French Revolution, 49–50, 51, 70n17
Friedman, Thomas L., 41n10
Front de Liberation Nationale, Algeria (FLN), 54, 71n40
FTOs (Foreign Terrorist Organizations), 105, 118, 296
Fukuyama, Francis, 253

Gama'a Islamiyya (Islamist group), 228
Gandhi, Rajiv, 72n67
Geneva Conventions (1949), 188–89; Common Article 1, 188; Common Article 2, 188–89; Common Article 3, 189, 192, 196, 205; Common Article 5, 194; Geneva Convention III, 192–93, 194, 203–8, 211; Geneva Convention IV, 195; on civil wars, 192, 196; on international armed conflict, 192; on prisoners, 192–93, 194, 203–8, 211; and U.S.-led war in Afghanistan, 196, 203–8, 211. *See also* laws of war and counterterrorism
Geneva Convention III, 192–93, 194, 203–8, 211
Geneva Convention IV, 195
Geneva Protocol (1925), 196
Geneva Protocol I (1977): Article 45, 204, 205, 207; Article 57, 199; Article 75, 205, 207, 208, 210, 213; on civilians and targeting, 199; on international armed conflict, 192, 193, 196, 197; on prisoners, 204–8, 210, 212, 213; U.S. concerns about, 193, 199, 205; U.S. war on terror and, 199, 205, 207
Geneva Protocol II (1977), 192
Genocide Convention (1948), 196
Georgia, 101, 102, 107
German Revolutionary Cells, 59
Germany: al-Qaeda network in, 101; anarchist groups, 58–59; counterterrorism strategies of, 154, 194; and Red Army Faction, 36, 56, 57–58, 144, 154, 194; Weimar, 241–42
Ghana, 53
Gilmore commission, 261–62, 265, 267, 268, 273
Global Exchange (human rights group), 198
globalization, 38–39, 244–45, 290–91
Gouré, Daniel, 14–15, 296–97, 298. *See also* homeland security

grand strategies of counterterrorism, 6,
74–93, 285–99; and assessments of individual threats, 78–79, 117–18, 287;
and balance, 297–99; and changes that
undermine state power, 290–92; and
counterterrorism networks, 295–97;
creating an effective grand strategy,
292–99; defining and determining the
threat, 286–89; defining grand strategy,
75–76, 91n8; defining policy, 75–76;
and domestic political obstacles, 79–80;
and flexibility, 89, 157, 287, 296; and
integration of tools, 149–53, 157,
293–95; and international support, 90;
linking strategies and policy goals, 89,
286; and measurement of success, 90;
and nonstate actors, 90, 288–89; before
September 11, 76–82; after September
11, 74–75, 82–89; tensions between approaches, 79; and terrorism studies,
78–80. *See also* grand strategy before
September 11; grand strategy after September 11
grand strategy after September 11, 74–75,
82–89; aggressive offensive strategy, 86;
and calls for policy reorientation and alternative strategies, 82–83; critical eval-
uation of, 87–89; debate over, 74–75,
82–83; and declaration of war on terrorism, 84–85; and domestic political
process, 82–83; goal of terrorist threat
elimination, 86; and government response to terrorism, 83–86; and international coalition, 84, 97–98; and Iraq,
85–86, 88–89, 90; possible consequences of, 87–89; postwar occupation
of Iraq, 88–89; and preemption, 85, 86,
88, 93n43; and prospect of continued
terrorism, 88–89; public diplomacy and
"war of ideas," 85; and regime replacement, 85–86; and reliance on old thinking, 90; and "terrorism of global
reach," 87–88; and unilateral actions,
85, 86; and "unlawful combatants," 84;
and war metaphor, 84; and WMD issue,
86, 288–89. *See also* National Security
Strategy (2002)
grand strategy before September 11,
76–82; Clinton administration, 80–81,
84; cold war worldview/framework,
80–81; debate over, 76–77, 91n8; early
responses to terrorism abroad, 81–82,

84; first Bush administration, 80–81; as
inappropriate/impossible, 78–80; and
multidisciplinarity, 78; as multilateral
general approach, 78–80, 81; and neglect of strategy/geopolitical contexts,
77–78; preventive defense and "catastrophic terrorism," 77, 91n11; Reagan
administration, 81; second Bush administration, 82, 92n28; and terrorism
studies, 77–80; and WMD terrorism,
76, 77, 78, 81
Greece, 53, 55, 109
Grivas, Georges, 49
Group of Seven (G-7) countries, 156
Guantanamo Bay, 84, 203, 205–7, 209–10
Guerilla War (Grivas), 49
Gulf War (1991), 59–60, 175, 189,
223–24, 236n31

Hague Land War Convention (1907), 196
Hamas, 72n65
Handel, Michael, 173
Harkat-ul-Mujahiddin (HUM), 105
Hart-Rudman Commission, 261
Heritage Foundation's Homeland Security
Task Force, 273
Heyman, Phillip, 269
Hezbollah, 146, 171
hijackings and New Left terrorism, 57
HIV/AIDS prevention and foreign aid,
246–47
Hobbes, Thomas, 70n27
Hoffman, Bruce, 169, 265, 268
homeland security, 14–15, 261–84; and
appreciation of context, 263; barrier
creation and transportation security,
274–76; basic premises and strategies,
262–67; Brookings Institution approach, 274; and civil liberties, 276,
297–98; and consequence management,
269, 274, 276–79; critical infrastructure
and key asset protection, 276–78; defining effective approaches, 265, 273–74,
296–97; deterrence strategies, 264, 269;
efficiency and resource-use, 263, 264;
emergency preparedness and response,
277; "end-state" goals, 262; forward-
and backward-looking strategies,
269–70; and Gilmore Commission,
261–62, 265, 267, 268, 273; goals/ends
of, 262, 265, 266–74; intelligence role
in, 274, 276; intrusion detection and re-

sponse, 274, 276; and law enforcement, 276; and lessons from prior models, 270; limits to, 264–65, 277–79; means and MOEs, 262–63, 264, 265, 273–79; and minimization of damage and recovery, 270–72; mission areas, 271, 273, 274; necessity of different strategic responses, 267–68; and new terrorist organizations, 29; and NSHS, 262, 270–74; offensive action and preemption, 279–80; prevention component/goal, 269, 270–71, 273–74; recognition of vulnerability before September 11, 261, 265; recommendations after September 11, 261–62, 273; and risk-assessment methodology, 268; and theory of conflict, 263–64, 269–70; vulnerability-reduction goal, 270–71, 272; and WMDs, 266–67, 268, 277, 278, 279–80. *See also* National Strategy for Homeland Security (NSHS)

House Intelligence Committee, 123–24, 135
Hoyt, Timothy D., 9–10, 292, 294. *See also* military force and counterterrorism
Human Rights Watch, 208
Huntington, Samuel, 35
Hussein, King, 57
Hussein, Saddam, 60, 85–86, 168, 224, 234n11

immigration: intelligence data on, 131–32; Muslim, 253–54
Immigration and Naturalization Service (INS), 122, 132, 275
India, 53
Indonesia, 2, 62
intelligence and counterterrorism, 7–8, 115–39; and counterterrorist analysis, 115–21, 135–37; and creation of domestic security service, 133–34; and criminal justice system, 157, 158; and CTC, 121–23; difficulty of, 115–16; and Directorate of Central Intelligence, 121, 123, 127, 129–30; and domestic intelligence collection issues, 132–35, 274, 276; evolution of, 121–23; and field operations corps, 128–29; and foreign governments, 131, 294; and FTO designations, 118; functions of, 116–21; and integration of counterterrorism tools, 293–94; intrusion detection and response, 274, 276; in Iraq, 178–79;

and law enforcement, 119, 121–22, 127; and military force, 118–19, 178–79; and military intelligence budget, 178; and new terrorist organizations, 29; and nonintelligence sources, 131–32; perceptual problems regarding, 123–25; personnel and intelligence community, 126–30; and plot-specific intelligence, 116–18, 119–20, 125–26; political risks of, 135–37; potential changes in, 127, 131–32, 137–38; and prediction, 119–21; and profiling systems, 134–35; and public perceptions/mood, 123–24, 135–36, 137–38; realistic appreciation of role of, 130–32, 137; and recruitment issues, 127–28; resource needs, 130–31; and restricted movements of potential terrorists, 132; and risk-aversion issue, 129–30; risked misuse of, 136–37; before September 11, 122–23, 125–26; and September 11 attacks, 123–26; spectrum of warnings and threat assessment, 119; and state sponsors of terrorism, 118; tactical and strategic analyses, 118–19, 125–26; and travel/immigration data, 131–32. *See also* Central Intelligence Agency (CIA); Federal Bureau of Investigation (FBI)

Intelligence Authorization Act (2002), 129
International Committee of the Red Cross (ICRC): and prison disasters in Afghanistan, 201–2; and status of U.S. prisoners, 205–6, 207–8, 212, 218n64
"International Convention for the Suppression of Terrorist Bombing" (1997), 60
International Criminal Court, Rome Statute (1998), 214n2
International Criminal Police Organization (ICPO), 154
International Disaster Assistance, 247
International Military Tribunal at Nuremberg (1945–46), 214n2
international terrorism, four waves of, 5–6, 36, 46–73, 289–90; defining the wave phenomena, 47–50; first wave (Anarchist wave), 47–49, 50–52; second wave (anticolonial wave), 47–50, 52–56; third wave (New Left), 47, 48, 56–61; fourth wave (religious wave), 47, 49, 50, 61–67, 287–89, 290; American role in, 63–64; American targets, 58, 63–64; and assassinations, 51–52,

international terrorism (*cont.*)
54, 57–58, 70n31; and bank robberies,
71n50; and Christian terrorism, 36, 61;
cold war domestic and foreign goals,
58–59; communication and technology
in, 48–49, 65; comparing first and third
waves, 56–58; democratic ideas in, 65;
difference between waves and organizations, 48; doctrine and culture in, 49,
65; durations/time spans of waves, 48,
63, 64–65, 66; early diasporas of terrorist activity, 51–52, 55; early international
efforts to eliminate, 52; emergence of
waves and factors contributing to, 48–49,
65; and guerrilla-like actions, 54–55,
71n40; and hijackings, 57; hope and revolutionary efforts in, 51, 70n27; international bonds and cooperation between
groups, 58, 63, 72n69; and Iranian revolution, 61–62; and Iraq war of 2003,
67–68; and Islam, 61–65, 66–67, 73n72;
and Israeli-Palestinian conflict, 67; and
Kashmir, 66–67; kidnappings and hostage
crises, 57; and new self-descriptions/
language, 54, 60; and post–September
11 international coalition, 64, 66; and
al-Qaeda, 63–65, 66, 287–88; "revolution" and, 49–50; and state-sponsored
terrorism, 59–60; and suicide bombings,
62–63, 67, 72n67; and United Nations,
55–56, 60–61; and Vietnam War, 56;
and women, 49, 56–57, 62–63, 70nn16,
25. *See also* organizations, terrorist
INTERPOL, 104, 154
Intifada, 269–70
Iran: and Abadan cinema attack (1978),
41n2; and fourth stage Islamic terrorism, 61–62; and Iranian revolution, 31,
61–62; psychological-political operations in, 226–27, 229, 231, 236n41;
and al-Qaeda, 100, 102, 175; and state-
sponsored terrorism, 31
Iran–Contra affair, 79
Iranian revolution (1979), 31, 61–62
Iraq: and Bush assassination attempt, 164;
and first Gulf War, 59–60, 175, 189,
223–24, 236n31; and al-Qaeda, 168,
175; Shiite terror movements in, 62
Iraq, U.S. war against (2003): and alienation of coalition, 88; Bush's declaration of end of, 175; conventional military force in, 297; and culminating

point of victory, 176–77; justifications
for, 67–68, 85–86, 90, 136–37; and key
military concepts, 176–79; and laws of
war, 187; and military intelligence,
178–79; and misuse of intelligence,
136–37; and postwar occupation, 86,
88–89, 176–77, 288–89, 295; and preemption doctrine, 67–68, 86, 88, 90;
psyops in, 227, 235n27, 297; and
regime replacement goal, 85–86, 168
Irgun, 53, 54, 55, 171
Irish Republican Army (IRA), 37; and anticolonial wave, 55; assassinations by,
57, 158; British counterterrorism
against, 143, 144, 154, 270; early, 48,
53, 69n10, 71n33; offshoots of, 48; and
terrorist acts on British mainland, 143,
151, 159n10; terrorist tactics of, 57,
148. *See also* Northern Ireland
Isamuddin, Riudan, 101
Islam and religious wave of terrorism,
61–67, 73n72, 287–88, 290. *See also*
Muslim world; al-Qaeda; religious wave
of international terrorism ("fourth
wave"); Taliban
Islamic Movement of Uzbekistan (IMU),
101
Israel: counterterrorism and strategies of
conflict, 269–70; foreign aid to, 244;
fourth wave terrorism in, 61, 67; invasion of Lebanon, 60, 62, 194–95; laws
of war and POW issues for, 194–95;
and military response to terrorism,
164–65; and al-Qaeda network, 101; and
second wave terrorism, 53–54; and
U.S. grand strategy, 89. *See also* Palestine Liberation Organization (PLO)
Italy: counterterrorism strategies, 154,
194; and Red Brigades, 56, 57, 154,
194; and Sicilian Mafia, 148; terrorist
assassinations and kidnappings in, 57,
70n31; and Trevi Group, 154
Iyad, Abu, 59

Jaish-e-Muhammad (terrorist group),
171
Jammu (disputed region), 171, 175
Japanese anarchists, 52, 70n30
Japanese Red Army, 56
Al Jazeera, 226, 227
Jemaah Islamiyah (JI), 101, 296
Jordan, 57, 59

jus ad bellum, 189–91. *See also* laws of
 war and counterterrorism
jus in bello, 188, 189–91. *See also* laws of
 war and counterterrorism
Justice Department, U.S., 105

Kaplan, Robert, 16n5
Karzai, Hamid, 110
Kashmir, 62, 66–67, 111, 175. *See also*
 Pakistan
Kashmir Liberation Front, 171
Kellenberger, Jakob, 218n64
Kellogg-Briand Pact, 287
Kennedy, John F., 243
Kenya. *See* African embassy bombings
 (1998)
Khobar Towers bombing (1996), 118, 123
Kissinger, Henry, 91n21
Kitson, Frank, 149
Korea, 53
Kosovo campaign (1999), 199
Kropotkin, Peter, 49, 50
Krueger, Alan, 254
Ku Klux Klan (KKK), 47, 49, 68n4
Kurdish terrorist groups, 171
Kurdistan Workers' Party, 99
Kuwait, 2, 62, 226
Kyrgyzstan, 62, 107

La Belle discotheque bombing (1986),
 164, 174
Laqueur, Walter, 142
Lashkar-e-Taiba (terrorist group), 171, 296
law enforcement and counterterrorism,
 8–9, 140–61; characteristics of effective
 networks, 157–58; and civil liberties,
 297–98; consensus on, 145–46; and
 consequence management, 153; conventions and agreements on, 145, 153–55,
 159n11; criminal activities of terrorist
 groups, 146–49, 157, 291–92; criminal
 justice model, 140–43, 144–49,
 157–58; current academic models and,
 140–43, 156–57, 159n3; diplomacy and
 assistance programs, 104, 106–7, 112;
 and domestic intrusion detection and
 response, 274, 276; European perspective, 143–44, 145, 147–56, 157; and
 forensic methods, 152–53; integrated
 counterterrorism response, 151–53,
 157; intelligence and, 119, 121–22,
 127, 157, 158, 274, 276; international
cooperation in, 153–56, 158; and investigation, 152–53; and legislation,
 144–46, 159n11; and legitimacy concept, 150; and the media, 153; military
 role in, 143–44, 149–53, 157, 158, 165;
 and organized crime, 147–49; and police concern for public safety, 144; and
 prevention, 151–52; and sense of indi-
 vidual/community responsibility, 143–
 44, 152; and State Department, 106–7,
 112; and sustainability in response, 143;
 and UK's approach, 143–44, 149–53,
 157; war model, 140, 141, 142–43
laws of war and counterterrorism, 10–11,
 186–219; bombing and air power, 197–
 201; civilian casualty issues, 197–200,
 216nn30, 33; and civilian/military targets, 192; counterterrorist military operations, 186–87, 191–212; and crimes
 against humanity, 187–88, 214n2;
 defining, 188–91; factors in application
 of laws, 191–93, 195, 210–12; Geneva
 Conventions and Protocols, 188–89,
 192–97, 199, 202–9, 212, 213; internationalized civil wars, 192, 196, 199;
 interstate conflicts, 212–13; *jus ad bellum*, 189–91; *jus in bello*, 188, 189–91;
 peacetime-wartime differences, 187–88;
 and prior counterterrorist operations,
 193–95, 210; and proportionality, 191,
 215n10; and revision of existing laws,
 187, 213–14; and scope of applications,
 188–89, 192; and state/nonstate issues,
 191–92; and terrorists' regard for
 rules/treaties, 192; U.S. concern about
 laws-of-war framework, 193, 211–12;
 and U.S.-led war in Afghanistan, 187,
 195–208, 211–12. *See also* prisoners
 and laws of war
Layne, Christopher, 76
League of Nations, 53, 55
Lebanon: fourth wave religious terrorism
 in, 62, 63; Israeli invasion of, 60, 62,
 194–95; laws of war and POW issues,
 194–95; Marine barracks bombing in,
 41nn2, 10; and PLO sanctuary, 63, 64,
 171; Shiite terror movements in, 62
Lederer, William J., 243
left-wing terrorist organizations, 36–37.
 See also Anarchist wave of international
 terrorism ("first wave"); international
 terrorism, four waves of

Lehi, 54

Lesser, Ian, 77–78, 91n12

Levie, Howard, 217n48

Libya: and anticolonial terrorism, 53; and al-Qaeda, 184n55; and third wave terrorism, 60; U.S. strikes against, 60, 164, 168, 174–75

Livingstone, Neil C., 78–79

Lockerbie bombing (1988), 60, 174

Lord, Carnes, 11, 290, 295. *See also* psychological-political instruments and counterterrorism

Low Intensity Operations (Kitson), 149

madrassas, 25, 110–11, 230, 233, 255

Major, John, 57, 72n52

Maleckova, Jitka, 254

Manchuria, 53

Mao Tse-tung, 183nn41, 42

Marighella, Carlos, 49

Marshall, George, 242

Marshall Plan, 242–43, 244, 247

MCA (Millennium Challenge Account), 245–47

McKinley, William, 46

Meyer, Jeanne, 199

Middle East. *See* Arab world; Muslim world

Middle East Partnership Initiative (December 2002), 239

"Military Aid to the Civil Authorities" (MACA), 150

military force and counterterrorism, 8, 9–10, 162–85; in campaigns against al-Qaeda, 176–77; in campaigns against Iraq, 176–79; and classic strategic thought on war, 173–74; and constitutional issues, 165; and conventional force, 163, 166–73, 174–75, 179, 297; and cooperation between military and other services, 107, 179, 180–81, 294; and culminating point of victory, 176–77; and cumulative approach, 169–70; and declaration of war on terrorism, 166–68, 174; and dilemmas of strategy, 163, 173–79; diplomacy and U.S. assistance programs, 107; and geography/space, 170–73; and law enforcement, 143–44, 149–53, 157, 158, 165; legal objections to, 165; limitations of, 163, 164, 165–73, 179, 181n5; local control/regional issues, 171; and

the means of terrorism, 169–70, 183nn34, 35; and military intelligence, 173, 178–79; military theory and key military concepts, 163, 168–74, 175–79; new precision weapons and options, 164; and new terrorist organizations, 29, 170–73, 292; political objections to, 165–66; and preemption, 179, 185n66; and principle of continuity, 175–76, 184n56; and principle of proportionality, 165, 167; reassessing options in war against terrorism, 162–63, 172–81; and regime overthrow, 174, 179–80; and special operations forces, 173, 178–79; targeting enemy center of gravity, 172, 184n45, 292; targeting enemy resistance, 169, 183n35; and terrorism's ends, 168–69, 183n32; and terrorist operations in time and space, 170–73; and terrorist sanctuaries, 171, 179; and terrorists' levels of combat, 170–71; and terrorists' military resources, 170, 177, 183n40; and UK counterterrorism, 149–51; and unlimited war, 166, 182n18

Military Studies in the Jihad Against the Tyrants (bin Laden), 49, 69n15

Millennium Challenge Account (MCA), 245–47

Millennium Challenge Corporation, 245–46

Millennium Summit (New York, 2000), 245

Miller, Steven, 83

Mine Action Programme for Afghanistan (MAPA), 200

Mini-Manual of the Urban Guerrilla (Marighella), 49

Moro, Aldo, 57

Morocco, 2, 53, 62

Moro Islamic Liberation Front (MILF), 101

Moro National Liberation Front (MNLF), 101

Mountbatten, Lord, 57

Mozorov, Nicholas, 49

Mueller, Robert, 133–34

Munich Olympics attacks (1972), 58, 167

Musharraf, Pervez, 227, 230

Muslim world: Arab world, 33–34, 63–64, 73n72, 225, 234n14, 239, 249, 256; democracy and governance in, 232, 253–54; economic growth and de-

velopment in, 248, 249, 255; and education, 253, 255–56; and foreign aid, 239, 247–50, 253–54, 255–56; and immigration to U.S., 253–54; and psychological-political instruments, 225–27, 230–32, 235n17, 236nn41, 42; and religious wave of terrorism, 61–65, 66–67, 73n72; state-supported terrorism and American policy in, 33–34; UNDP report on deficits in, 248; and view of America, 63–64, 73n72, 239, 247–48; and VOA, 225, 234n14. *See also* al-Qaeda; Taliban
Myers, Richard B., 197

National Commission on Terrorism, 129
National Endowment for Democracy (NED), 222
National Intelligence Council, 294
National Military Strategy, 264
National Security Agency (NSA), 127, 294
National Security Council (NSC), 82, 108, 228
National Security Strategy (2002), 85–86, 167; aggressive offensive strategy of, 86, 167; and global military presence, 85, 167; goal of elimination of terrorist threat, 86; goal of reducing vulnerability, 272; and high-risk operations, 167; and National Strategy for Homeland Security, 271–72; as predating war on terrorism, 85; and preemptive actions, 85, 86, 167, 271–72; and proportionality, 167; and regime replacement in Iraq, 85–86, 167; and unilateral actions, 85, 86; use of public diplomacy and "war of ideas," 85; on weak/failing states, 254; and WMD issue, 85, 86
National Strategy for Combating Terrorism, 86, 271, 272
National Strategy for Homeland Security (NSHS): on barrier system and transportation security, 275–76; as "comprehensive," 266; on consequence management, 276–77; criticisms of, 262, 271–74; domestic counterterrorism and intelligence collection, 276; eighty initiatives for, 273; formation of, 270; means and MOEs for, 273–74, 275–77; minimizing damage and recovery time, 270–71, 272; and National Security Strategy, 271–72; prevention goal,

270–71, 273–74; and problematic strategic vision, 262, 271–74; and reducing vulnerability to terrorism, 270–71, 272; six mission areas, 271, 273, 274; three strategic objectives, 270–72, 273–74
Nechaev, Sergei, 49, 50, 67
Neglected Duty (Faraj), 69n15
New Left and third wave of international terrorism, 47, 48, 56–61; American targets of, 58; and Anarchist terrorism, 56–58; and assassinations of, 57–58; and bank robberies, 71n50; conflicts between domestic and foreign elements, 58–59; ebbing of, 60; and hijackings, 57; international bonds and cooperation, 58; kidnappings and hostage crises, 57; radicalism and nationalism in, 56; and state-sponsored organizations, 59–60; and UN role, 60–61; and Vietnam War, 56; women in, 56–57
New York Times, 101, 198, 230
Nicaragua, 57
Nigeria, 53
"no-concessions" principle, 79, 91n21
nongovernmental organizations (NGOs), 244, 245
North Africa, 101
North African Front, 101
North Atlantic Treaty Organization (NATO): and coordination in counterterrorism, 107, 150, 156, 161n47, 233; and laws of war, 199; Strategic Concept of, 150; and U.S. war against Iraq, 88
Northern Ireland: British counterterrorism in, 143–44, 149–50, 164–65, 270; counterinsurgency operations in, 149–50; criminal offenses by terrorists in, 147; and laws of war, 194; and second wave terrorism, 48, 53, 55, 71nn33, 43. *See also* Irish Republican Army (IRA); United Kingdom
Northern Ireland Organized Crime Task Force, 147
North Korea, 175, 291

Office of Global Communications, 231
Office of Strategic Influence (OSI), 227, 229–30, 236n37
Office of Transition Initiatives, 247
official development assistance (ODA), 245–46, 259n9

Okhrana (Russia), 68n4

Oklahoma City bombing (1995), 81, 124

Omar, Mullah, 87, 176, 228

OPEC ministers, kidnapping of (1975), 58

Operation Alamo Sweep, 99

Operation Anaconda, 2, 99

Operation Desert Storm (1991), 175. *See also* Gulf War (1991)

Operation Enduring Freedom. *See* Afghanistan, U.S.-led war in (2001)

Operation Iraqi Freedom. *See* Iraq, U.S. war against (2003)

Organization of American States (OAS), 107

organizations, terrorist: decentralized structures, 28–30, 32–33, 65, 73n81, 99, 100, 296; group dynamics and beliefs, 19, 27–30, 39–40. *See also names of individual organizations*

Oslo Accords, 59

Pakistan: and army intelligence service (ISI), 111; and backlash against fundamentalism, 227; and fourth wave terrorism, 66–67; *madrassas* of, 110–11, 230, 233; and national police (IB), 111; and psychological-political war on terrorism, 230, 232, 233; and al-Qaeda, 64–65, 87, 99, 110–11, 175; and second wave terrorism, 53; as state that not fully supports counterterrorism, 109; as state that supports terrorism, 175; and Taliban, 82, 84, 111; U.S.-Pakistan relationship and diplomacy, 110–12

Palestine Liberation Organization (PLO), 36–37; in contrast to al-Qaeda, 64; and foreign sanctuary, 171; founding of, 48; and fourth wave terrorism, 48, 59, 62–63, 64–65; international character of, 59, 63, 144; in Lebanon, 63, 64, 171; and suicide bombers, 62–63; and third wave terrorism, 48, 56, 58–59, 60–61, 71n50; in Tunisia, 59, 64–65; UN recognition of, 60–61

Palestinian groups and al-Qaeda network, 101

Pankisi Gorge (Georgia), 101, 102, 107

Peace Corps, 255

Pearl Harbor attack on (1941), 126

Pedahzur, Ami, 143

Perry, William J., 77, 91n11

Philippines, 53, 62, 101, 107

Pillar, Paul R., 7–8, 78, 81, 164, 294. *See also* intelligence and counterterrorism

Pipes, Daniel, 253

Police Working Group on Terrorism (PWGT), 154

Polish nationalist groups, 51

Popular Front for the Liberation of Palestine (PFLP), 59

Posen, Barry, 82, 83

poverty and terrorism, 25, 240, 254–55

Powell, Colin, 84, 136, 239

Prevention of Terrorism Act (UK), 145, 159n11

prisoners and laws of war, 201–10, 211–12; Geneva Conventions and Protocols, 192–93, 194, 203–8, 210–13; at Guantanamo Bay, 203, 205–7, 209–10; and judicial proceedings, 208–10, 219n72; legal status and treatment, 202–8, 211–12, 217nn48, 51; POW issues, 187, 192–95, 202–8, 213, 217n48; al-Qaeda and Taliban prisoners differentiated, 202–3, 206, 207; and Red Cross, 205–6, 207–8, 212, 218n64; and trials, 204, 209–10, 219n72; the U.S.-led war in Afghanistan, 84, 201–3, 205–10, 211–12

Prodhoun, Peter, 49

profiling: and domestic intelligence collection, 134–35; psychological, 24–25

proportionality, 165, 167, 191, 215n10

Protecting the American Homeland: A Preliminary Assessment (Brookings Institution), 274

The Protocols of Zion, 68n4

Provisional IRA, 147, 171

psychological-political instruments and counterterrorism, 11–12, 220–37, 290; and Bush administration since September 11, 227–30; and components of a successful strategy, 233–34; covert political action, 222, 224, 230, 236n37; credibility issues, 224–25; defense public diplomacy and psyop, 223–24, 229–30; defining the instrument/activities, 221–25; disagreements over fundamental U.S. approach, 230–31; early cold war instruments of, 220; and information operations (IO), 222, 223–24; and integrated approach, 295; and the media, 231, 236nn41, 42; and Office of

Strategic Influence (OSI), 229–30, 236n37; policy lessons for, 230–33; and projection of strategic influence, 221–22; and propaganda, 227; and psyop, 223–24, 229–30; and public diplomacy, 222, 223–25, 229–33; and religious/theological issues, 231–32; tensions in policy decisions and public relations, 224, 229–30; understanding character and sources of terrorism, 231–32; and U.S.-led war in Afghanistan, 227; and U.S.-Muslim world relations, 225–27, 230–32, 235n17; and U.S war against Iraq, 227, 235n27, 297; and VOA mission issues, 228–29
Psychological Strategy Board, 220
psychology and terrorism, 23–27; and fanaticism, 23, 41n10; and leaders' characteristics, 26–27; and personality disorders, 23, 41n10; and policy prescriptions, 23; and psychological pathology, 23; and psychological profiles, 24–25. *See also* psychological-political instruments and counterterrorism

Qaddafi, Muammar, 109, 174, 184n55
al-Qaeda: in Afghanistan, 99–100, 101, 113n1; and African embassy bombings, 28, 63, 81–82, 99, 164; attack objectives, 63–64, 73n72, 169, 288; bombing against, 200–201; characterized as fanatics, 41n10; clandestine activities of, 100; and Clinton administration, 82, 84; collapse of, 64, 65, 73n77; and decentralized structure, 32–33, 65, 73n81, 87, 99, 100, 287–88, 296; and desire for Islamic state, 64, 73n72, 169; and diplomacy, 97–98, 102–3; effect of Taliban's overthrow on, 174, 184n53; emergence of, 89; and fourth wave religious terrorism, 63–65, 66, 287–88; "gone to ground," 99–100; and group organizational processes, 28–29; and intelligence before September 11, 125–26; membership/size of, 63; network and proxy groups, 100–101, 102, 288, 296; and nonstate-supported terrorism, 32–33, 87; and PLO, 64; and postwar situation, 87, 176–77; and prison disasters, 201–2; as prisoners, 202–3, 206–10; and psychological study of leaders/recruits, 24–25, 26–27; recon-

struction of, 64–65, 66, 87, 100, 102, 173; sanctions against, 109; small-scale operations/attacks since September 11, 100, 288; and state-sponsorship, 44n40, 73n77, 171, 174, 288; training operations, 64, 102, 287–88; and U.S.-led war in Afghanistan, 64–65, 84, 99–100, 200–203, 206–10; view of America, 63, 73n72

Radio Free Afghanistan, 227
Radio Free Europe/Radio Liberty (RFE-RL), 220, 222, 227, 229
Radio Free Iran, 229
Radio Sawa, 227, 229, 236n41
RAND Corporation, 265, 277–78
Ranstorp, Magnus, 143
Rapoport, David, 5–6, 36, 287, 289–90. *See also* international terrorism, four waves of
Reagan, Ronald, 41n10
Reagan administration, 81, 193, 244
Real IRA, 48, 147, 151
Red Army Faction (RAF) (Germany), 36, 56, 57–58, 144, 154, 194
Red Brigades (Italy), 56, 57, 154, 194
Regulation of Investigatory Powers Act (2000), 159n11
Reilly, Robert, 229, 235n29
religious wave of international terrorism ("fourth wave"), 21, 61–67, 287–89, 290; and attacks on American soil, 63–64, 287; and changing American role, 63–64, 288–89; and Christian terrorism, 61; distinctive international features, 63; expected duration and persistence of, 47, 63, 66; and international coalition after September 11, 64, 66; and Iranian revolution, 61–62; and Islam, 61–67, 73n72, 287–88, 290; and Israeli-Palestinian conflict, 67; and Kashmir, 66–67; local organizations' roles in, 67, 294; and new Islamic century, 62; recognizing threat of, 287–88; and relationship between terrorism and ideology, 36–37, 290; and relationships between groups, 63, 72n69; and sacred texts, 50; sleeper cells and new tactics of, 65; and suicide bombings, 62–63, 67, 72n67; and U.S. war in Iraq, 67–68, 288–89; and views of America, 63–64, 73n72; and women, 49, 62, 70n16

Revolutionary Armed Forces of Colombia (FARC), 146
Revolutionary Catechism (Nechaev), 49
Revolutionary Organization 17 November (17N), 146
Rice, Condoleezza, 85, 92n28
right-wing terrorism. *See* religious wave of international terrorism ("fourth wave")
risk: CIA guidelines for, 129–30; counterterrorism and high-risk operations, 167; homeland security and risk-assessment methodology, 268; and risk aversion, 129–30
Roberts, Adam, 10–11, 298. *See also* laws of war and counterterrorism
Rome Statute, International Criminal Court (1998), 214n2
Roosevelt, Franklin D., 209
Roosevelt, Theodore, 46, 52, 68n4
Rosecrance, Richard, 91n8
Rotberg, Robert, 257
Rumsfeld, Donald: on homeland security, 266; and Office of Strategic Influence, 230; and special operations forces in Iraq, 178–79; on U.S.-led war in Afghanistan, 190–91, 197, 198, 202, 205–6
Russian anarchists, 49, 50–52
Russian Federation (Islamic militants), 101

Saadi, Yaacev, 71n40
Sachs, Jeffrey, 241
Sadat, Anwar, 72n65
Salafist Group for Preaching Call and Combat, 101
sanctions: and diplomacy, 109–10; and foreign aid, 257–58, 291; and al-Qaeda, 109; against Taliban, 174, 184n54
Sandinistas, 57
Saudi Arabia, 2, 62, 63–64, 232
Schengen Accord (1985), 154–55
Schengen Information System (SIS), 155
2nd of June (German anarchist body), 58–59
second wave terrorism. *See* anticolonial wave of international terrorism ("second wave")
Sendero Luminoso (The Shining Path), 36, 58, 99
al Serri, Yasir, 228
Sheehan, Michael A., 7, 287, 293. *See also* diplomacy and counterterrorism

Shiite terrorism, 62
The Shining Path (*Sendero Luminoso*), 36, 58, 99
Sicilian Mafia, 148
Sikhs, 61
Simon, Jeffrey D., 79
Simon, Steven, 73n81
Somalia, 63
sources of contemporary terrorism, 5, 19–45; and analyst biases, 20, 21–22; Crenshaw's thesis on globalized civil war, 37, 45n49; and failed states, 33, 291; and four analytical frameworks/levels, 19–20; globalization, 38–39, 290–91; group/organizational level dynamics, 19, 27–30, 39–40; Huntington's thesis on clash of civilizations, 35–37; individual behavior level, 19, 23–27, 39; international level, 19, 35–39, 40; multidisciplinary approach to, 19–20, 39–40; new terrorist organizations, 28–30; and policy implications, 25–30, 36–40; political motivations, 36–37; and psychology, 23–27, 41n10; and regime behavior, 31, 34–35; and relationship between terrorism and democracy, 33–35; and relationship between terrorism and ideology, 35–37; and state-supported terrorism, 19, 30–35, 40; studies on, 20–22, 23–27, 31, 34–37; and transnational terrorism, 32–33
southeast Asia, 101, 107–8
Spain, 56, 57
Sprinzak, Ehud, 72n67
Sri Lanka, 49, 61, 62, 67, 72n67, 105
Standing Rules of Engagement (U.S. Joint Chiefs of Staff), 189
State Department, U.S.: and Afghanistan campaign, 200; and Anti-Terrorism Assistance (ATA), 106, 108, 112; and counterterrorism assistance programs, 106–7, 108, 111, 112–13; and counterterrorism policy after September 11, 85; and Defense Department, 230–31; and FTO process, 105; homeland security and visa program of, 275; and law enforcement assistance programs, 106–7, 108, 112; list of state sponsors of terrorism, 32–33, 44n41, 93n47, 109, 111, 239; and psychological-political instru-

ments, 25, 222, 227, 230–31; and public diplomacy, 222, 225, 227; and Under
Secretary for Public Affairs and Public
Diplomacy, 222, 227; and U.S. foreign
aid role, 246, 251; and VOA, 228
state-sponsored terrorism, 30–35; diplomacy and reconsideration of, 109–10;
and failed states, 33; history of, 31–32;
policy prescriptions and, 30–31, 40;
and al-Qaeda, 44n40, 73n77, 171, 174,
288; and regime behavior, 31, 34–35;
and relationship between terrorism and
democracy, 33–35; State Department
list of, 32–33, 44n41, 93n47, 109, 111,
239; and transnational terrorism,
32–33; and U.S. foreign policy, 31–32
Stein, Arthur, 91n8
Stepniak, Serge, 49, 51
Stern Gang, 54
Sudan, 28, 102, 164
Sunni terrorism, 62
Sun Tzu, 184nn46, 56
Syria, 59, 62, 102

Tajikistan, 62
Taliban: Bush administration campaign
against, 84, 87; Clinton administration
responses to, 82, 84; early sanctions
against, 174, 184n54; education under,
256; and international humanitarian
law, 195–96; overthrow of, 174,
184n53; as prisoners, 201–3, 206, 207;
and state-sponsored terrorism, 44n40,
73n77, 171, 174; the U.S.-led war in
Afghanistan, 176, 200–203, 206, 207.
See also al-Qaeda
Tamil Tigers (Liberation Tigers of Tamil
Elam), 37, 61, 62, 72n67, 73n83, 105
Tanzania. *See* African embassy bombings
(1998)
al Tawhid, 101
Tenet, George, 122, 125
terrorism: defining, 3–6, 296; introduction
of term, 50, 70n17; and nonstate actors, 3–4; political nature of, 3–4, 16n4,
298; and targeting of innocents, 4; and
unpredictability/random violence, 4,
16n5. *See also* international terrorism,
four waves of; sources of contemporary
terrorism; terrorism studies
Terrorism Act 2000 (UK), 145, 159n11

Terrorism and the Liberal State (Wilkinson), 142
Terrorism Information and Prevention
Program (TIPS), 134
terrorism studies: and criminal justice
model, 140–43; and law enforcement
models, 140–43, 156–57, 159n3; and
multidisciplinarity, 19–20, 39–40, 78;
before September 11, 77–80; on sources
of contemporary terrorism, 20–22,
23–27, 31, 34–37; and war model, 140,
141, 142–43; and WMD terrorism, 78.
See also sources of contemporary
terrorism
Terrorist Army Volunteer Reserve
(TAVR), 153
Terrorist Brigade (1905), 52
Thatcher, Margaret, 57, 158
third wave terrorism. *See* New Left and
third wave of international terrorism
Thompson, Robert, 194
Thugs (terrorist group), 69nn6, 7
Time magazine, 100
Tokyo subway gas attack (1995), 32, 61,
81. *See also* Aum Shinrikyo
*Towards a National Strategy for Combat-
ing Terrorism* (Gilmore Commission),
261–62
Treaty of Maastricht (1995), 155
Trevi Group, 60, 154, 160n37
Truman, Harry S., 242–43
Tucker, David, 81
Tunisia, 53, 59, 62, 64–65
Tupac Amaru (terrorist group), 58
Turkey, 55, 56, 60

The Ugly American (Lederer and Burdick), 243
United Kingdom: and American FTO
process, 105; counterterrorism strategies, 149–53, 154, 157; integration of
law enforcement and counterterrorism,
143–44, 149–53, 157; intelligence agencies, 157, 161n48; investigative counterterrorism, 152–53; military role in
counterterrorism, 149–51; and "Operations Other Than War" (OOTW), 149;
and prevention of terrorism, 151–52;
al-Qaeda cells in, 100; and Trevi
Group, 154. *See also* Irish Republican
Army (IRA); Northern Ireland

United Nations: and foreign aid, 245,
  251, 252; and fourth wave terrorism,
  64, 66; and international coalition after
  September 11, 64, 66; and laws of war,
  190, 195–96; Resolution 1373, 104,
  112; and second wave terrorism, 55–56;
  Security Council, 104, 112, 136, 190,
  195–96; and third wave terrorism,
  60–61
United Nations Conference on Environment and Development (UNCED)
  (1992), 245
United Nations Convention for the Suppression of Financing of Terrorism
  (1999), 145
United Nations Convention on Suppres-
  sion of Terrorist Bombings (1997), 145
United Nations Conventions on Terror-
  ism, 104, 112, 145
United Nations Development Program
  (UNDP), 248, 255
United Nations Security Council, 104,
  112, 136, 190, 195–96
United States Information Agency (USIA),
  220, 222, 225
UN's Mine Action Programme for
  Afghanistan (MAPA), 200
U.S. Agency for International Develop-
  ment (USAID), 243, 244, 251, 255, 257
U.S. Strategic Command, 223
U.S.A. Patriot Act, 159n11, 298
USS *Cole*, terrorist strike on (2000),
  63, 81
Uzbekistan, 62, 107

Versailles Treaty, 52–53
Vietnam War, 56, 194, 243–44
Voice of America (VOA): Arab audience,
  225, 234n14; commercial/journalistic
  model of, 222, 229; criticism of, 227,
  228–29, 236n31; original mission and
  current mission, 228–29, 235n29

Walid, Mahfouzm Ould, 100
Walker, David, 278–79
Walker, Edward S., 225
Walt, Stephen, 74, 82–83

Wardlaw, Grant, 79
Washington Post, 100
waves of terrorism. *See* international terrorism, four waves of
weapons of mass destruction (WMD):
  barrier system and transportation security issues, 275; and CBRN incidents,
  152, 153; and Clinton administration
  concerns, 81; and consequence management, 278; and grand strategies before
  September 11, 76, 77, 78, 81; and
  grand strategy after September 11, 85,
  86, 288–89; and homeland security,
  266–67, 268, 275, 277, 278, 279–80;
  and prevention, 86, 277; and U.S. war
  against Iraq, 86
Weber, Max, 65
Weimar Germany, 241–42
Wilkinson, Paul, 142
Wolfowitz, Paul, 176
women: and education, 256; and empowerment deficit in Muslim world, 248;
  roles in modern international terrorism,
  49, 56–57, 62–63, 70nn16, 25
Worden, Simon P., 229
World Bank, 250
World Economic Forum, 249, 256
World Food Program (WFP) (United Na-
  tions), 251
World Summit on Sustainable Develop-
  ment (Johannesburg, 2002), 245
World Trade Center bombing (1993),
  81, 82
World War I, 52, 241–42, 287
World War II, 53, 242, 247, 287
Wylie, J. C., 169–70

Yemen, 63, 102, 107
Yerushalmi, Mordechai, 159n3

al-Zahwahri, Ayman, 99
Zarqawi, Musaab, 101
Zasulich, Vera, 50–51
Al Zawahiri, 65
Zealots (terrorist group), 69n7
Zemun Clan, 149